D0442661

WHO'S WHO
IN
GREEK AND ROMAN
MYTHOLOGY

WHO'S WHO
IN
GREEK AND ROMAN MYTHOLOGY

DAVID KRAVITZ

Illustrations by Lynne S. Mayo

 Clarkson N. Potter, Inc./Publisher NEW YORK

DISTRIBUTED BY CROWN PUBLISHERS, INC.

Text copyright ©1975 by David P. Kravitz

Illustrations copyright ©1976 by Lynne S. Mayo

All rights reserved. No part of this publication may be reproduced, stored in a retrieval system, or transmitted, in any form or by any means, electronic, mechanical, photocopying, recording, or otherwise, without the prior written permission of the publisher. Inquiries should be addressed to Clarkson N. Potter, Inc., One Park Avenue, New York, N.Y. 10016.

First American edition. Originally published (without illustrations) as *The Dictionary of Greek and Roman Mythology* by New English Library, London, England, in 1975. This edition is published by arrangement with New English Library.

Printed in the United States of America

Library of Congress Cataloging in Publication Data

Kravitz, David, 1939-
    Who's who in Greek and Roman mythology.

    Published in 1975 by New English Library, London, under title: The dictionary of Greek & Roman mythology.
    1. Mythology—Dictionaries. I. Title.
BL715.K7   1976   292'.003   76-29730
ISBN 0-517-52746-4
ISBN 0-517-52747-2 pbk.

Third Printing, June, 1978

Note from the Publisher

We believe that this dictionary, with its detailed coverage of an enormous subject, is going to be of immense value to all those who require reference to mythology. This covers not only the student of classics, but the student of the arts in general, those interested in language and all those who daily or weekly enjoy crossword puzzles which were, incidentally, the original source of inspiration for the compiler, David Kravitz.

Complex family relationships provide much of the charm of Greek mythology. This dictionary acknowledges this fully, building up each entry around the family relationships of the subject and, when appropriate, adding details of particular interest. We do not know of another dictionary of similar size which so emphasises and clarifies the intra-family relationships as this one does. For that alone it would be invaluable, but in detail too we think it stands apart.

Mythology is a subject which is based not on fact but on sources which frequently differ. Whenever major authorities describe a situation or relationship quite differently, all versions have been given.

The references and entries have been checked in detail by Mr D. A. Hartnett of the School of Hellenic and Roman Studies at the University of Birmingham, and to him special thanks are due.

For

MARIAN, LAURA AND NICOLA

A

ABANTES A tribe of Thracian origin. Inhabitants of Abae in Phocis. Moved on to Euboea. Kings were Abas, Chalcodon and Elephenor.

ABAS King of Argos. Son of Lynceus and Hypermnestra, daughter of Danaus. Married Ocaleia. Father of twin sons, Acrisius and Proetus, Chalcodon and an illegitimate son, Lyrcus. Founder of Abae in Phocis and conqueror of Euboea. Killer of Lynceus and Megapenthes. He owned a shield, formerly owned by Danaus, his grandfather, which frightened away rebels on sight. At his death he was buried in the same tomb as his parents.

ABAS Son of Melampus and Lysippe. Brother of Mantius and Antiphates. Father of Coeranus and Lysimache, the wife of Talaus.

ABAS (1) Son of Ixion and Nephele. A Centaur and a skilled hunter. (2) A Greek soldier killed in the Trojan War by Aeneas. (3) Trojan companion of Aeneas from Troy to Italy, where he died. (4) Father of Canethus. (5) Possibly the son of Celeus and Metaneira. Brother of Demophon and Triptolemus. (6) Mountain in Syria where the Euphrates rises. (7) Another companion of Aeneas. Killed in storm that led Aeneas to Carthage. (8) A Latin chief who assisted Aeneas.

ABDERA City of Thrace, founded by Heracles. Situated opposite the island of Thasus, at the mouth of the river Nestus (Mesta).

ABDERUS Heracles' armour bearer. Son of Hermes. Born in Opus in Locris. Eponym of Abdera. He was torn to pieces by the mares of Diomedes.

ABSYRTUS King of Colchis (also called Apsyrtus or Phaethon). Son of Aeetes. His mother is variously stated to have been Eidyia or Asterodia or Hecate or Neaera or Ipsia. Grandson of Helios and a nephew of Phaethon, son of Clymene and Helios. Brother of Chalciope and Medea.

Leader of the Colchian pursuit of the Argonauts. Killed either by Medea, who tore him to pieces and threw him into the sea after she and Jason stole the Golden Fleece; or by Jason himself, after Medea lured him to a meeting.

ABYDOS City of Asia Minor, opposite Sestos, by the side of the Hellespont; home of Leander. Inhabitants allied with Troy during the Trojan War.

ACACALLIS (Acalle) Daughter of Minos and Pasiphae. Sister of Androgeus, Ariadne, Catreus, Deucalion, Euryale, Glaucus, Lycastus, Phaedra and Xenodice. Mother of Amphithemis, Miletus and possibly Garamas by Apollo. Mother of Cydon by Hermes or possibly Tegeates. Exiled from Crete to Libya by her father.

ACADEME (Academia) A grove near Athens where Plato used to teach.

ACALLE *See* Acacallis.

ACAMAS Joint king of Melos. Son of Theseus by his second wife, Phaedra. Brother of Demophoon and half-brother of Melanippus and Hippolytus.

Accompanied Diomedes to Troy to demand the return of Helen by threatening war. There he fell in love with Laodice, daughter of Priam. Either he or, much less likely, Demophoon was the father of her son, Munitus. Accompanied Elephenor to the Trojan War. Was in the Wooden Horse, and he and Demophoon rescued their grandmother, Aethra, from Helen. After the war he returned home via Thrace where he was detained by his love for Phyllis whom he later deserted. Arriving in Cyprus, he was killed by his own sword as he fell from his horse.

ACAMAS Son of Antenor and Theano.

Brother of Agenor, Archelous, Glaucus, Helicaon, Polydamas, Laodamas, Polybus, Demoleon, Iphidamas, Coon, Laocoon, Lycaon and Crino; half-brother of Pedaeus. Shared the leadership of the Dardanian forces in the Trojan War with Aeneas and Archelous. Killed by Meriones.

ACAMAS A Thracian captain killed in the Trojan War by Greater Ajax.

ACANTHA A nymph loved by Apollo who turned her into the acanthus flower.

ACARNAN Son of Alcmaeon by his second wife, Callirrhoe. Brother of Amphoterus. Acarnan and his brother were changed by Zeus into adult men in a single day in order that they could avenge their father's murder. They killed first the sons of Phegeus and, later, Phegeus and his wife.

ACARNANIA Received its name from Acarnan. Greek coastal area of the Ionian Sea, opposite the Island of Leucas. Settled in by Acarnan and Amphoterus.

ACASTUS King of Iolcus. Only son of Pelias and Anaxibia or Phylomache. Brother of Alcestis, Hippothoe, Pelopia and Pisidice. Married Hippolyte, daughter of Cretheus, though some call his wife Astydameia. Father of Laodameia, Sterope, Sthenele and unnamed sons. An Argonaut. Present on the Calydonian Boar Hunt. Killed, possibly by Peleus.

ACCA LARENTIA (Laurentia) Heracles (Hercules) challenged Ancus Martius, the king of Rome and temple guardian, to a game of dice, the loser to provide a meal and a girl, Acca Larentia, nurse to Romulus. Heracles won, but the servant imprisoned the girl. She married Carutius and by him became the mother of twelve sons, the Fratres Arvales. At his death he left her his very large estate; after her death she was buried in the Velabrum and was worshipped as a minor goddess. Her name suggests connection with the Lares, as does her festival which is followed by one for the Lares. Festival date: 23 December.

ACCA LAURENTIA Seen by several sources as different from above. Also listed as a nurse of Romulus and Remus (cf above), she was the wife of Faustulus, shepherd of the flocks of Numitor or Amulius.

ACERBAS Priest of Heracles, at Tyre. (Also called Acherbas, Adherbas, Sichaeus and Sicharbas.) Husband of Dido before she founded Carthage. Killed by Pygmalion.

ACERSECOMES Surname of Apollo, meaning unshorn.

ACESIDAS *See* Idas.

ACESIS Daughter of Asclepius and Epione. Sister of Aegle, Hygieia, Iaso, Janiscus, Machaon, Panacea and Podalirius.

ACESSAMENUS (1) Father of Periboea. (2) Daughter of Eurymedon, and by Poseidon mother of Nausithous.

ACESTES Son of Crimisus and Aegesta. City of Aegeste or Aegesta (Segesta) named after him. An ally of Priam in the Trojan War, he later entertained Aeneas when he visited Sicily on his journey from Troy to Italy. Acestes helped bury Anchises, and was the winner of the archery contest in the funeral games that followed.

ACESTIUM Torch-bearer in festivals of Demeter.

ACHAEA *See* Pallas (7).

ACHAEUS Son of Poseidon and Larissa. Brother of Pelasgus and Phthius. Father of Archander and Architeles. Eponym of Achaea in Thessaly.

ACHAEUS Son of Xuthus and Creusa. Brother of Diomede, Ion, and possibly Dorus.

ACHAIA A country of Peloponnesus.

ACHARNIANS A comedy by Aristophenes.

ACHELOUS Oldest of the river gods. Son of Oceanus and Tethys. Brother of the other river gods (qv). Father of Callirrhoe, wife of Alcmeon, Castalia and Peirene. Possibly the father of the Sirens (qv) by Calliope, Melpomene or Terpsichore. He seduced Perimele, who bore him Hippodamas and Orestes.

Had the power to change shape, and became a snake and then a bull, fighting Heracles for the hand of Deianeira. Heracles broke off one of his horns. As the principal river of the mainland of South-west Greece, he swept away five nymphs who refused to pay him homage. They became the islands of Echinadia.

ACHEMENIDES A Greek who fought in the Trojan War with Odysseus. On his return trip was marooned in Sicily in the cave of Polyphemus. When Aeneas visited Sicily, he warned him of the giants on the island.

ACHERBAS *See* Acerbas.

ACHERON A river god. Son of Oceanus and Tethys, Gaea or Demeter. Brother of many rivers (*see* Rivers). According to Ovid, the father of Ascalaphus by Orphne or Gorgyra. Some versions state that he was relegated to Hades when he no longer had a use on Earth, others that he was banished to Hades by the gods for giving drinks to the Titans in their fight against the Olympians.

ACHERON River of woe. One of the five rivers of Hades. Others called Cocytus, Lethe, Phlegethon, and Styx. Charon ferried the dead across the river to Hades.

ACHILLEID Unfinished poem about Achilles, written by Statius.

ACHILLES Son of Peleus and Thetis, a Nereid. Originally called Ligyron. Married Deidameia. Father of Neoptelemus (Pyrrhus). Father of Caistrus by Penthesileia. Educated by Cheiron. As a baby, his mother dipped all but his heel in the river Styx

Achilles

3

in order to make him invulnerable to attack. She also placed him on fire embers each night to purge away his mortal parts. Only his heel remained vulnerable. He tried to avoid his obligation to go to Troy by dressing as a woman and appearing to be mad, but Odysseus found him out. Achilles took fifty ships to Troy and wore armour made by Hephaestus. He was the greatest Greek warrior there. His close friend was Patroclus. His five lieutenants were Menesthius, Eudorus, Peisander, Phoenix and Alcimedon.

He killed Tenes, a son of Apollo, who warned him of a reprisal for this act. In battle he killed Cycnus and Troilus. He killed Hector after the latter had killed Patroclus. He killed Penthesileia but fell in love with her dead body. He killed Thersites for mocking him over this. He fell in love with Polyxena, Priam's daughter, but was killed when Apollo guided the hand of Paris, Priam's son, to shoot a poisoned arrow into his heel. After his death he went not to Hades but to the White Island. Ajax and Odysseus fought for his armour, and Polyxena was sacrificed on his tomb. Epithet: Pelides (son of Peleus).

ACIDALIA Surname of Aphrodite, given to her after she bathed in the same fountain as the Graces in Boeotia.

ACIS Son of Faunus and the nymph of the River Symaethus. Brother of Dryas. Lover of Galatea but killed by Polyphemus, his rival. He became god of a stream that flows from Mount Aetna.

ACMON or ALCEMON Son of Oceanus and Theia. Brother of Passalus. They were two-tailed thievish gnomes, also called the Cercopes. Zeus turned him to stone, or into an ape, for stealing his weapons.

ACMON (1) A Greek who was turned into a bird for wounding Aphrodite in the Trojan War. (2) The Anvil. One of the three eldest Dactyli (qv). Others were Celmis and Damnameneus.

ACMONIDES A Cyclops. Son of Uranus and Gaea. Brother of Arges, Brontes, Geraestus, Polyphemus, Steropes and the Titans. Killed by Apollo. They used to forge Zeus' thunderbolts.

ACOETES Alternative spelling of Acetes.

ACONTIUS of Ceos (Cea) A poor young man who fell in love with Cydippe, the daughter of a rich Athenian noble. He wrote her love poems on an apple, orange or quince, inscribed, 'I swear by the temple of Artemis to marry no one but Acontius', and gave them to her. Inadvertently she read out the oath, and so her parents consulted the Oracle at Delphi which told them to allow the lovers to marry.

ACRIAS A suitor of Hippodameia.

ACRISIUS King of Argos. Son of Abas, king of Argos, and Ocaleia. Twin brother of Proetus and brother of Chalcodon. Married Eurydice, daughter of Lacedaemon and Sparte, though some say his wife was Aganippe. Father of Danae and Evarete. Quarrelled with his brother, even in their mother's womb, and later drove Proetus from Argos. The land was later divided into two kingdoms with Proetus ruling Tiryns.

An oracle warned Acrisius that he would be killed by a son of Danae, and he imprisoned her in an ivory tower. There she was visited by Zeus as a shower of gold, and she became the mother of Perseus. When he grew to manhood, Perseus accidentally killed his grandfather with a discus, and so the oracle was fulfilled.

ACROCORINTH The hill above the city of Corinth, the site of a temple of Aphrodite. Also associated with this hill were Briareus, Helios and Poseidon.

ACRON (1) A king killed by Romulus, after the rape of the Sabine women. (2) A friend of Aeneas, killed by Mezentius.

ACROPOLIS The citadel of any Greek

4

city, literally the highest point of the city. The famous one at Athens is 154 m above sea level and measures 300 m by 120 m. Its height is 90 m. It was the site of the palaces of Cecrops and Erechtheus. From this spot Athena and Poseidon contested for control of the city.

ACTAEA A Nereid. One of the fifty daughters of Nereus and Doris.

ACTAEON A hunter. Son of Aristaeus and Autonoe. Grandson of Cadmus. Brother of Macris. Educated and trained in hunting by Cheiron.

Actaeon spied on Artemis who was bathing naked. She turned him into a stag, and he was devoured by his own hunting dogs on the slopes of Mount Cithaeron. Cheiron erected a statue of Actaeon to appease the gods.

Actaeon

ACTAEUS First king of Attica. Father of Agraulos, the wife of Cecrops.

ACTIS One of the Heliades. Son of Helios and Rhode. Brother of Candalus, Cercaphus, Macar, Ochimus, Tenages and Triopas. With his brothers, he was the first to sacrifice to Athena. After taking part in the murder of Tenages, he left Rhodes for Egypt, where he founded Heliopolis. The Colossus of Rhodes was built in his honour.

ACTIUM A promontory on the western coast of Epirus, site of a Temple of Apollo as early as the Fifth Century BC, where Augustus Caesar beat Antony and Cleopatra in a sea battle, 2nd Sept, 31 BC, and later developed the local games to Actian Apollo.

ACTOR (1) King of Phocis. Son of Deion, king of Phocis, and Diomede. Brother of Aenetus, Asteropeia, Cephalus and Phylacus. Father of Irus, Menoetius and Polymela by Aegina, grandfather of Patroclus. He purified Peleus for the murder of his half-brother, Phocus, and then gave him one third of his kingdom, and Polymela, or some say Antigone, for a bride. (2) King of Phthia. Son of Myrmidon and Peisidice. Brother of Antiphus and Eupolemeia. Perhaps the father of Eurytion, but some claim he died childless. (3) Son of Phorbas and Hyrmina. Brother of Augeias and Tiphys. Either he or Poseidon was the father of the twins, Eurytus and Cteatus, the Molionides, by Molione. (4) A companion of Heracles in his fight with the Amazons. (5) A son of Poseidon, some say by Agamede. (6) A companion of Aeneas in his journey from Troy to Italy. (7) An Argonaut, possibly son of Hippasus. (8) Father of Echecles. (9) Some say father of Astyoche.

ADAMANTHAEA Cretan nurse of Zeus who suspended his cradle from a tree, so that he was neither in the sea, earth nor heaven.

ADAMAS Trojan son of Asius. Killed in the Trojan War by Meriones.

ADES Alternative spelling of Hades.

ADHERBAS Alternative spelling of Acherbas.

ADMETA(Admete) Daughter of Eurystheus and Antimache. She longed for the girdle of Hippolyte, and her father ordered Heracles to fetch it as one of his labours.

ADMETUS An Argonaut. First son of Pheres and Periclymene (or Clymene). Brother of Lycurgus, Idomene and Periopis. Married Alcestis. Father of Eumelus and Perimele. King of Pherae.

A member of the Calydonian Boar Hunt, he was a most hospitable man. Apollo served him as a herdsman for a year after his exile from Olympus. All Admetus' cattle bore twins. Apollo helped him to win his wife. He successfully yoked a lion and a boar to the chariot of Pelias, the father of Alcestis. On his wedding night, he forgot to pay homage to Artemis and in his bed found snakes instead of a bride; on a plea from Apollo he was forgiven. When he fell ill, Alcestis offered to die in his place.

ADONIA Greek, Phoenician and Egyptian festivals in honour of Adonis, of two to eight days in duration.

ADONIS Son of Cinyras and Cenchreis or Metharme, or of Phoenix and Alphesiboea. His mother may even have been Myrrha, daughter of Cinyras after she had had an incestuous relationship with her father. She was turned into a tree, from which a child was born.

Adonis was famous for his great beauty, and both Aphrodite and Persephone fell in love with him. As a child he was entrusted in a chest to Persephone but when she opened it she fell in love with him. Zeus decided that he should spend one third of each year with each goddess and the last part as he wished. He elected to spend it with Aphrodite, by whom he had a son and a daughter. He was killed by a boar, and from his blood sprang the anemone.

ADRASTEIA A nymph of Crete. Daughter of Melisseus, a sister of Ida and a nursemaid of Zeus.

ADRASTUS King of Argos. Son of Talaus and Lysimache, though some call his mother Eurynome or Lysianassa. Brother of Aristomachus, Astynome, Eriphyle, Mecisteus, Metidice, Parthenopaeus, Pronax and possibly Hippomedon. Married Amphithea. Father of Argeia, Aegialeia, Aegialeus, Cyanippus, Deipyle and Hippodameia.

Leader and sole survivor of the Seven against Thebes, after he was saved by his magic horse, Arion. Ten years later he was the leader of the Epigoni, but died of grief upon hearing of the death of his son, Aegialeus.

ADRASTUS (1) Son of Merops. Brother of Amphius, Arisbe and Cleite. Killed in the Trojan War by Diomedes. (2) Some say son of Polyneices and Argeia. Brother of Thersander and Timeas. (3) Father of Eurydice, the wife of Ilus.

AEA City of Colchis and home of Aeetes. The Golden Fleece was kept here.

AEACIDES Descendants of Aeacus, namely Achilles, Greater Ajax, Peleus, Telamon, Pyrrhus etc.

AEACUS King of Aegina. Son of Zeus and Aegina. Married Endeis, daughter of Cheiron. Father of Peleus, Telamon and possibly Polycrates. Grandfather of Achilles and Greater Ajax. Father of Phocus by his mistress, Psamathe.

With others, he built the walls of Troy, helped by Apollo and Poseidon. By his prayers, he helped populate his kingdom with the Myrmidons. After his death, he became a judge of the dead in Hades. The other judges were Minos and Rhadamanthys.

AEAEA Huntress of the same name changed into an island by the gods to escape the advances of the river god Phasis. The island where Odysseus stayed a year with Circe.

AEDON The nightingale. Daughter of Pandareus and Harmothoe. Sister of Cleothera (Cameiro) and Merope (Clytie). Probably the wife of Zethus of Thebes. Mother of Itylus, whom she accidentally killed, mistaking him for the eldest son of Niobe. She became a nightingale after she tried to kill herself.

AEETES King of Colchis. Son of Helios and Perseis (Perse). Brother of Circe, Pasiphae and Perses. Married Asterodeia. Father of Chalciope. Then married Eidyia. Father of Absyrtus and Medea.

He was the ruthless king of a barbaric race who lived at the eastern end of the Black Sea. He welcomed Phrixus to Colchis after the latter's escape on the ram with the golden fleece; and after Aeetes sacrificed the ram, he placed the fleece in a sacred grove of Ares. Aeetes was deposed by his brother, Perses, but Medea, or Medeias, killed Perses and restored Aeetes to the throne. When Jason and the Argonauts came for the Golden Fleece, Aeetes first gave Jason the task of harnessing fire-breathing, bronze-footed bulls to a plough, then sowing a field of dragon's teeth and finally killing the men that sprang up from the sown field. Jason succeeded but Aeetes broke his word, thus forcing Jason and Medea to steal the fleece. Aeetes was killed either by the Argonaut, Meleager, by Medea or Jason.

AEGAE Coastal city of Peloponnesian Achae (Achaia) where Poseidon had a sea palace.

AEGAEON Alternative name of Briareus, son of Uranus and Gaea. This was his mortal name, as the gods called him Briareus or Obriareus. He was one of the hundred-handed (Centimani, Hecatoncheires) and a brother of Cottus and Gyges.

AEGEAN SEA Body of water that divides Greece and Asia Minor.

AEGESTE (AEGESTA) Town founded by Acestes.

AEGEUS King of Athens. Son of Pandion and Pylia. Brother of Lycus, Nisus and Pallas. Some authors call him merely the adopted son of Pandion. Married Medea. Father of Medus. Father of Theseus by Aethra, daughter of Pittheus, though some claim Poseidon to be the father.

He offended Minos, king of Crete, so Minos made him send an annual tribute of seven young men and seven young maidens for the Minotaur to devour. One year, his son Theseus went to kill the Minotaur and it was arranged that if returning from his mission successful, Theseus would show a white flag. In fact he inadvertently showed a black one, and Aegeus, in sorrow, drowned himself in the sea. The Aegean Sea is named after him.

AEGIALE One of the Heliades. Daughter of Apollo or Helios and Clymene. Sister of Phaethon, Aegle and Aetheria, and a half-sister of Lampetie and Phaesthusa, though perhaps she may be identified with Aegle. On the death of Phaethon, like her sisters she cried for him until she was changed into a poplar and her tears became amber.

AEGIALEIA Daughter of Adrastus and Amphithea. Sister of Argeia, Aegialeus, Cyanippus, Deipyle and Hippodameia. Married Diomedes but later committed adultery with Cometes, son of Diomedes' friend, Sthenelus.

AEGIALEIA Old name for the city of Sicyon.

AEGIALEIUS Son of Inachus and Melia. Brother of Io and Phoroneus. Possibly the father of Europs. Some authorities think him the founder of Sicyon.

AEGIALEUS Eldest son of Adrastus and

7

Amphithea. Brother of Aegialeia, Argeia, Cyanippus, Deipyle and Hippodameia. One of the Epigoni, and the only one to be killed. Cyanippus may have been his son rather than his brother.

AEGIMIUS King of the Dorians. Son of Dorus and a daughter of Cretheus. Brother of Tectamus. Father of Dymas and Pamphylus. Conqueror, with the help of Heracles, of part of the land of the Lapithes.

AEGINA Daughter of Asopus and Metope. Sister of Antiope, Chalcis, Cleone, Corcyra, Ismene, Ismenus, Metope, Pelagon, Pelasgus, Plataea, Salamis, Thebe and ten others. Mother of Aeacus by Zeus who changed into a flame of fire, and of Irus, Menoetius and Polymela by Actor.

AEGINA Small Greek island in the Gulf of Aegina. Originally called Oenone, but changed to Aegina by Aeacus in honour of his mother. Home of the Myrmidons.

AEGINA, First king of Aeacus.

AEGIPAN Son of Zeus and Aex (Aega), a nymph, or of Boetis, a goat. Or this may have been an epithet of Pan, whom he resembled. He helped Hermes recover the stolen sinews of Zeus. He later became the constellation of Capricorn.

AEGIS A shield. Most commonly, the sacred shield of Zeus. It was made from the skin of the goat Amalthea (nursemaid to Zeus), and as its centrepiece bore the head of Medusa. When shown to enemies, they were turned to stone. Athena also possessed an Aegis.

AEGISTHUS King of Mycenae. Son of Thyestes and Pelopia. Married Clytemnestra, after murdering Agamemnon and Cassandra's children.

As a baby he was abandoned by his mother, and after being suckled by a goat he was found and reared by his step-father, Atreus, the brother of Thyestes. Aegisthus, sent by Atreus to kill Thyestes, recognised his father and returned to kill Atreus. He became the father of Aletes and Erigone by Clytemnestra. Aegisthus was killed by Orestes, son of Agamemnon and Clytemnestra, after reigning over his kingdom for seven years.

AEGIUM Seaport of Achaea on the Gulf of Corinth, where Agamemnon called all the Greek leaders for a council of war, prior to going to war against the Trojans.

AEGLE One of the Heliades. Daughter of Apollo or Helios and Clymene. Sister of Aegiale, Aetheria and Phaethon and a half-sister of Lampetie, Lampethusa and Phaethusa. Perhaps to be identified with Aegiale. She mourned the death of her brother, Phaethon, and was turned into a poplar. Her tears became amber.

AEGLE (Aglaea, splendour) One of the Graces. Daughter of Zeus and Eurynome. Sister of Euphrosyne, Pasithea and Thalia, although Pasithea may have been an eponym for Aegle. She is also associated with Charis, the wife of Hephaestus, which suggests closest links with Aphrodite. *See also* the Graces and Charites.

AEGLE One of the Hesperides. Some say they are daughters of Atlas and Pleione or Hesperis; others of Hesperus or Zeus and Themis. Sister of Arethusa, Erythia, Hesperia and the Hyades, Pleiades, Hyas and Calypso. The Hesperides were guardians of the Golden Apples.

AEGLE (1) Youngest daughter of Asclepius and Epione or Lampetia. Sister of Acesis, Hygieia, Iaso, Janiscus, Machaon, Panacea and Podalirius. (2) Daughter of Panopeus and Neaera. Sister of Epeius. Beloved of Theseus, for whom he forsook Ariadne.

AEGYPTUS King of Egypt. Son of Belus, king of Egypt, and Anchinoe. Twin brother of Danaus and brother of Phineus, Thronia and, possibly, Cepheus. He had fifty sons, including Cisseus, Dryas, Enceladus, Hyperbius, Idmon and Lycus.

His fifty sons married the fifty daughters of Danaus and forty-nine of the daughters murdered their husbands on their wedding night. He was also the father of a daughter, Aganippe, whom he sacrificed on the instructions of the Oracle at Delphi, to relieve Egypt of a drought.

AELLA   An Amazon slain by Heracles.

AELLO   One of the Harpies. Daughter of Thaumas and Electra. Sister of Ocypete and Podarge (Celaeno).

AEMONIDES   Italian priest of Apollo, slain by Aeneas.

AENEADES   Descendants of Aeneas.

AENEAS   Son of Anchises and Aphrodite. Brother of Lyrus. Raised by a nymph, Caieta, on Mt Ida and educated by Cheiron. Married first to Creusa, he became the father of Ascanius (Iulus). Later, in Italy, Aeneas married Lavinia, becoming the father of Aeneas Silvia (Silvius). He may also have been married to Eurydice, although this is doubtful.

Defender of Troy, he was leader of the Dardanians with Acamas and Archelous. He escaped from Troy with twenty shiploads of Trojans and his adventures on his flight to Italy are retold in the *Aeneid*. During his wanderings and search for the empire promised him, he descended into the Underworld to consult with his father and to be purged. At first his descent was hampered by the absence of the Golden Bough, but Persephone guided him to his destination.

After landing in Italy, he fought Turnus, the king, and later married Turnus' daughter, Lavinia, and founded Lavinium. Aeneas is often called the founder of the Roman race.

AENEAS, followers of   Aeneadae. Twenty shiploads of Trojans accompanied Aeneas in his flight from Troy to Italy. Thirteen of the ships were lost, but among the survivors were the *Centaurus, Chimaera, Pristis* and *Scylla*. His followers included Abas, Achates, Actor, Alcathous, Aletes, Amycus (2), Antheus, Asius, Atys, Caeneus, Caicus, Capys, Cloanthus, Clytius, Cretheus, Dares, Demophoon, Diores, Dryops, Entellus, Epytides, Eumedes, Eumelus, Euryalus, Eurytion, Gyas, Harpalycus, Helenor, Helymus, Hippocoon, Ilioneus, Iphitus, Ismarus, Ladon, Lycus, Lynceus, Merops, Misenus, Mnestheus, Nautes, Nisus, Pallas (son of Evander), Panopes, Patron, Phegus (Phlegius), Priam (grandson of King Priam), Pyrgo (nursemaid to Iulus), Sagaris, Salius, Serestes, Sergestus and Thoas. The helmsman of Aeneas' ship was called Palinurus.

AENEAS SILVIA   (Silvius)   Son of Aeneas and Lavinia. Half-brother of Ascanius (Iulus). Third in the list of mythical kings in Alba.

AENEID   Virgil's twelve-volume epic, describing Aeneas' flight from Troy to Italy.

AENETE   Daughter of Eusorus. Wife of Aeneus. Mother of Clymenus and Cyzicus.

AENETUS   Son of Deion and Diomede. Brother of Actor, Asteropeia, Cephalus and Phylacus.

AENEUS   King of Calydon. Husband of Aenete or of Eriboea. Father of Clymenus and Cyzicus.

AENIUS   A Trojan killed in the War by Achilles.

AEODE (Aoide)   Boeotian muse of song. Daughter of Uranus and Gaea. Sister of Melite and Mneme. Worshipped at Helicon.

AEOLIA   More normally a country of Asia Minor near the Aegean Sea. Some also give the name to either modern Hiera,

Lipara or Stromboli. Home of the winds and of Aeolus, god of the winds.

AEOLIA Daughter of Amythaon and Idomene or of Bias and Pero. Sister of Melampus, Perimele and Bias. Married Calydon. Mother of Epicasta and Protogeneia.

AEOLIDES Descendants of Aeolus.

AEOLUS God of the winds. Son of Hippotas. As king of Aeolia, he was also called Hippotades. Married Cyane. He had six sons and six daughters who married each other. Among his sons were Clytius and Misenus.

AEOLUS Son of Hellen and the nymph Ortheis (Orseis). Married Enarete. Father of seven sons: Athamas, Cretheus, Deion, Macareus, Perieres, Salmoneus and Sisyphus. He also had seven daughters: Alcyone, Arne, Calyce, Canace, Peisidice, Perimele and Tanagra. Brother of Xuthus and Dorus. He was the ancestor of the Aeolians. Was possibly the father of Aethlius by Protogeneia.

AEOLUS Son of Poseidon and Arne (Melanippe), daughter of Aeolus, god of the winds; or the son of Hellen and Hippe, daughter of Cheiron. Brother of Boeotus.

AEPYTUS King of Messenia. Youngest son of Cresphontes and Merope. His two brothers and his father were killed by Polyphontes, who usurped the kingship. He was reared by his maternal grandfather, Cypselus. Killed Polyphontes, thereby regaining the throne.

AEPYTUS King of Arcadia. A descendant of Stymphalus. Son of Eilatus and the father of Cypselus. Guardian of Evadne, daughter of Pitane.

AEROPE (1) Daughter of Catreus. Sister of Althaemenes, Apemosyne and Clymene. Married Pleisthenes, and later Atreus. Mother of Agamemnon, Menelaus and

possibly Anaxibia and Pleisthenes. She committed adultery with her brother-in-law, Thyestes, and bore him twin sons called Tantalus and (possibly) Aglaus or Pleisthenes. The twins were killed by Atreus and served as a meal to Thyestes. (2) Daughter of Cepheus and, less likely, Echemus. Sister of Sterope. Mother of Aeropus by Ares. She died in childbirth.

AEROPUS Son of Ares and Aerope. Father of Echemus, King of Arcadia.

AESACUS Son of Priam and Arisbe, daughter of Merops, or of Alexiroe, daughter of the river Granicus. Brother of Cassandra, Creusa, Deiphobus, Helenus, Hector, Paris, Polyxena and Troilus. Married Asterope, daughter of the river god Cebren. Merops taught him the art of prophecy. Two stories are told of his demise, both with the same ending. Either he mourned for his dead wife so greatly that he became a diver bird, or else he pursued Hesperia, daughter of Cebren, and, after she died, he mourned for her until he was turned into a diver bird.

AESCHYLUS 525/4–456 BC. Writer of about ninety Greek tragedies, seven of which survive. They are: *The Persians, The Suppliants, Prometheus Bound, Seven against Thebes* and the *Oresteia* trilogy.

AESCULAPIUS God of healing. Roman name for Asclepius. Son of Apollo (Phoebus) and Coronis. Married Epione. Father of Acesis, Aegle, Hygieia, Iaso, Janiscus, Machaon, Panacea and Podalirius. He was the physician of the Argonauts.

AESEPUS River of Ida near Troy.

AESON King of Thessaly. Eldest son of Cretheus and Tyro. Brother of Amythaon, Hippolyte, Pheres and Promachus, and half-brother of Pelias. Married Alcimede. Fathered Jason and Promachus. Either Pelias forced him to commit suicide, or Medea restored him to youth; alternatively, both events took place.

AESYETES (1) Husband of Cleomestra. Father of Antenor. (2) Father of Alcathous.

AESYMNUS Greek killed in the Trojan War by Hector.

AETHALIDES Herald of the Argonauts. Son of Hermes and Eupolemeia. He had a perfect memory. He persuaded the Lemnian women to allow the Argonauts to stay for one night. After his death, his body and memory went to Hades but his soul periodically sought a new body. It was said that eventually he became Pythagorus.

AETHER Upper air or sky. Greek god of light. Some say the son of Erebus and Nyx. Brother of Hemera, Cer, Dreams, Hypnos, Momus, Morus, Nemesis, Thanatos and Charon. Possibly father of Uranus.

AETHERIA One of the Heliades. Daughter of Apollo (Helios) and Clymene. Sister of Aegiale, Aegle and Phaethon, and half-sister of Lampetie (Lampethusa) and Phaethusa. After the death of Phaethon, she mourned for him so intensely that she became a poplar and her tears turned to amber.

AETHLIUS Founder of Elis. Son of Zeus or of Aeolus and Protogeneia. Brother of Opus. Married Calyce. Possibly father of Endymion.

AETHRA Daughter of Pittheus of Troezen. Mother of Theseus by Aegeus, king of Athens, or by Poseidon.
  She lived in Attica, but was captured by the Dioscuri and taken to Troy to be Helen's servant. She was rescued by her grandsons, Acamas and Demophoon.

AETHRA (Pleione) An Oceanid. Daughter of Oceanus and Tethys. Sister of Amphitrite, Asia, Calypso, Clymene, Doris, Europa, Hyas, the Hyades, Metis, Urania, etc. Possibly the mother, not the sister, of the Hyades, by Atlas.

AETHUSA (Arethusa) Daughter of Poseidon and Alcyone. Sister of Anthus and Hyperenor and half-sister of Hyrieus. Mother of Eleutha by Apollo.

AETIUS King of Althepia (Troezen). Son of Anthas, the previous king, and deposed by Pittheus and Troezen. His descendants founded a colony in Caria.

AETNA A volcano. Situated on the eastern coast of Sicily. At 3500 m above sea-level, it is the highest in Europe. Hephaestus (Vulcan) had his smithy there. The monster, Typhoeus, as well as Enceladus or other giants, is said to be buried beneath it.

AETNA Daughter of Briareus or possibly of Uranus. Mother of Gelon by Hymarus (Himerus). By Hephaestus, mother of the two Palici volcanoes. Thought to have given her name to the volcano.

AETOLIA Part of central Greece on the north coast of the Gulf of Corinth, named after Aetolus, son of Endymion. Divided from Acarnania by the river Achelous. Among kings in Aetolia were Hippodamas and Oeneus. Meleager slew the Calydonian Boar here.

AETOLUS King of Elis. Son of Endymion and a Naiad, or his mother may have been either Hyperippe, Iphianassa or Selene. Brother of Epeius, Eurycyda and Paeon. Married Pronoe, daughter of Phorbus. Father of Calydon and Pleuron.
  He accidentally killed Apis at the funeral games for Azan. Was succeeded to the throne by his brother, Epeius.

AEX (Aega) Daughter of Helios or Pan. Mother of Aegipan by Zeus.

AFER (Africus) The south-west wind.

AFFECTION AND FAITHFUL ATTACHMENT, Roman goddess of Pietas.

AFTERTHOUGHT An epithet of Epimetheus.

AGACLES A king of the Myrmidons. Father of Epeigeus.

AGAMEDE Daughter of Augeias. Sister of Eurytus. Married Mulius. One of the first to use herbs for healing. Some say the mother of Actor by Poseidon.

AGAMEDES The name of two men, both named king of Arcadia. (1) Son of Stymphalus. Brother of Gortys and Parthenope. (2) Son of Elatus and Laodice.

AGAMEDES An Orchomenian architect. Son of Erginus. Beheaded by his brother, Trophonius.

AGAMEMNON King of Mycenae and Argos. One of the Atreidae. Son of Atreus and Aerope, though some name his father as Pleisthenes and his mother as Cleolla. Brother of Menelaus and possibly of Anaxibia and Pleisthenes. Married Clytemnestra and fathered Chrysothemis, Electra (Laodice), Iphigeneia, Iphianassa and Orestes. Father of Chryses by his slave, Chryseis. Father of Pelops and Teledamas by Cassandra.

Commander-in-chief of the Greek forces at Troy. Took one hundred ships to the war. His herald was called Talthybios. On his return from the war, was murdered by Clytemnestra and her lover, Aegisthus.

AGANIPPE (1) Daughter of Aegyptus, king of Egypt. Sacrificed by her father on the order of the Delphic Oracle because of a drought. (2) A fountain sacred to the Muses. Located at the foot of Mt Helicon, in Boeotia. Its waters flow into the Parnassus. (3) Nymph of the fountain. Daughter of the river god, Permessus. (4) Possibly the wife of Acrisius. Either she or Eurydice was the mother of Danae.

AGAPENOR King of Tegea in Arcadia. Son of Ancaeus. Founder of the city of Paphos, and builder of the temple of Venus there. Succeeded Echemus to the throne of Tegea. Commander of Agamemnon's fleet during the Trojan War. Purchased Arsinoe, wife of Alcmeon, as a slave.

AGASSAMENUS King of Strongyle (Naxos). Husband of Pancratis.

AGASTHENES King of Elis. Son, or possibly brother, of Augeias, from whom he inherited the throne. Father of Polyxeinus. A suitor of Helen, he therefore went to the Trojan War.

AGASTROPHUS Son of Paeon. Killed in the Trojan War by Tydeides.

AGATHON (1) A son of Priam. (2) A friend of Plato and writer of Greek tragedies.

AGAVE A Nereid. One of the fifty daughters of Nereus and Doris.

AGAVE Daughter of Cadmus and Harmonia. Sister of Autonoe, Illyrius, Ino, Polydorus and Semele. Married Echion. Mother of Pentheus. Later married Lycotherses, king of Illyria, whom she murdered; the throne passed to Cadmus. Dionysus drove her mad and she then murdered her son by tearing him to pieces.

AGAVUS A son of Priam.

AGDISTIS An epithet of Cybele.

AGELAOS (Agelaus) (1) Possibly son of Heracles and Omphale. Brother of Alcaeus and Lamus. Ancestor of Croesus, king of Arcadia. (2) King of Corinth. Son of Ixion. (3) Chief herdsman of Priam, who reared Paris in defiance of an order to kill him. (4) A suitor of Penelope. (5) A Trojan killed in the Trojan War by Diomedes. (6) A Greek killed in the Trojan War by Hector.

AGENOR (1) King of Phoenicia. Son of Poseidon and Libya. Twin of Belus and brother of Lelex. Married Telephassa or Argiope. Father of Cadmus, Cilix, Demodoce, Electra, Europa, Phineus, Phoenix and Thasus, and possibly of Argus. (2) King of Argus. Son of Ecbasus or Triopas, or possibly Iasus. May have been the brother of Iasus and Pelasgus. Possibly the father of Argus Panoptes. One source has him as son of Phoroneus and brother of Jasus and Pelasgus. (3) Son of Antenor and Theano. Brother of Acamas, Archelous, Coon, Crino, Demoleon, Glaucus, Helicaon, Iphidamas, Laocoon, Laodamas, Lycaon, Polybus and Polydamas. Half-brother of Pedaeus. Father of Echeclus. One of the bravest Trojans to fight in the Trojan War. (4) Son of Pleuron and Xanthippe. One of four children. Married Epicasta. Father of Demonice, Hippodamus, Porthaon and possibly of Thestius. (5) An Agenor or Belus was the father of Anna, Dido and Pygmalion. (6) The betrothed of Andromeda, he was slain by Perseus. (7) Son of Phegeus. Brother of Arsinoe and Pronous.

AGES OF MANKIND Gold, Silver, Bronze and Iron in that order. According to Hesiod, there was a fifth, Heroic, between the Bronze and Iron.

AGLAEA (Aegle) (splendour) One of the Graces. Daughter of Zeus and Eurynome. Sister of Euphrosyne, Thalia and Pasithea, although this may have been an eponym for Aiglaia. Aglaea is also associated with Charis, wife of Hephaestus, which suggests close links with Aphrodite.

AGLAOPHEME One of the Sirens. Daughter of Achelous and Calliope, Melpomene, Sterope or Terpsichore. Sister of Molpe and Telexiepeia, and, according to some, of Peisinoe, Ligeia, Leucasia and Parthenope. *See* Sirens.

AGLAUS Twin son of Thyestes and Aerope, the wife of Atreus. He and his brother Tantalus were killed by Atreus and served as a meal to Thyestes to punish his wife for her adultery.

AGLAUS The poorest man in Psophis in Arcadia but, according to an oracle, happier than Gyges, king of Lydia.

AGNO A nymph who tended the infant Zeus and gave her name to a fountain on Mt Lycaus.

AGORIUS Son of Damasius.

AGRAULOS Daughter of Actaeus. Wife of Cecrops. Mother of Agraulos (Aglauros), Herse, Pandrosus and possibly of Erysichthon.

AGRAULOS (Aglauros) The bright one. Daughter of Cecrops and Agraulos. Sister of Pandrosus, Herse and possibly of Erysichthon. She, her mother and her sisters were entrusted by Athena with the care of Erichthonius, who was hidden in a casket. When curiosity overcame them they opened the casket, and the sight of Erichthonius drove at least two of the sisters (Herse and Aglauros?) mad, so they leapt to their death from the top of the Acropolis.

Another version of her death tells that she was turned to stone by Hermes when she failed to help him win the attentions of her sister Herse, and that it was her mother, Agraulos, and her sisters who leapt to their death from the Acropolis.

AGRIANOME Daughter of Perseon. Married Hodoedocus. Mother of Oileus.

AGRICULTURE, Roman god of Silvanus.

AGRICULTURE, goddess of Greek: Demeter. Roman: Ceres. Sabine: Vacuna.

AGRIOPE Possibly wife of Agenor, king of Phoenicia.

AGRIUS King of Calydon. Son of Porthaon and Euryte. Brother of Alcathous, Melas, Oeneus, Sterope and Leucopeus. Father of several children, including Onchestus and Thersites. Deposed his brother Oeneus from the throne and replaced him with his father. Also exiled Tydeus, son of Oeneus. Some time later, Diomedes, son of Tydeus, killed some of the sons of Agrius, and Agrius then committed suicide.

AGRIUS (1) Giant son of Gaea. Brother of Thoas and others (*see* Giants). Was defeated in battle at Phlegra either by the Fates who clubbed him to death, or he was killed by Heracles. (2) Son of Odysseus and Circe. Brother of Ardeas and Telegonus, and a half-brother of Latinus. (3) A centaur who attacked Heracles and was killed by him. (4) Possibly the father of Thersites, though he was not the same person as Agrius, king of Calydon.

AIDOS Greek personification of reverence.

AILMENTS OF WOMEN, Roman goddess of Postverta (Carmenta).

AITHON (red fire) One of the four horses of Ares. Others were Conabos, Phlogios and Phobos.

AIUS LOCUTIUS In 391 BC at dead of night on the Via Nova a voice warned Marcus Caedicius of the impending attack, by the Gauls under Brennus, on Rome. The Romans, to their loss, chose to ignore Caedicius.

AJAX, greater (Aias) Son of Telamon and Periboea or Eriboea. Half-brother of Teucer. Father of Eurysaces by his concubine, Tecmassa, daughter of Teleutas. Father of Philaeus.

Ajax was named after an eagle which appeared as an omen to Telamon. Ajax was a suitor of Helen and the tallest Greek. He led twelve ships to the Trojan War from Salamis. There he fought by the side of Ajax of Locris. He met Hector in single combat and they fought until parted by heralds. Ajax and Hector then exchanged a belt and a sword.

Ajax carried the body of Achilles from the battlefield and fought Odysseus unsuccessfully for Achilles' armour. Ajax then killed himself in a rage, but some sources claim that he was killed by Odysseus, Paris or Teucer. His squire was called Lycophron.

AJAX, lesser, of Locris Son of Oileus by his wife Eriopis, or by a nymph, Rhene.

He is described as a great hero. Frequently acted in conjunction with Greater Ajax. At the funeral games for Patroclus he lost a race with Odysseus. As a suitor of Helen, he led forty ships to the Trojan War from Locris. Two stories are told of his demise after he fought by the side of Greater Ajax. Either he dragged Cassandra from her Athenian altar and Athena caused him to be drowned; or else this insolent and conceited man escaped drowning and, climbing a rock, sat atop boasting of his escape. Poseidon split the rock with a thunderbolt and Ajax finally drowned.

ALALCOMENAE A Boeotian village where Alalcomeneus reared Athena and built a temple for her. Athena was born either here or else in Triton.

ALALCOMENEAN ATHENA Boeotian epithet of Athena, meaning Powerful Defender.

ALALCOMENEUS According to some, the first man. In his village of Alalcomenae he reared Athena.

ALALCOMENIA Son of Ogygus. Brother of Aulus and Thelyxinoea in Boeotian tradition. In Attic tradition brother of Eleusis.

ALARM, Greek god of Phobus.

ALASTOR (1) The name of one of Hades' horses used when he kidnapped Persephone and took her to the Underworld. (2) Father of Tros. (3) Sarpedon's armour bearer in the Trojan War; killed by Odysseus. (4) Husband of Harpalyce.

ALBA LONGA Very ancient city of Latium founded by Ascanius, son of Aeneas. The series of twelve or so kings of Alba, as we have them, is doubtless a late forgery. The list includes Amulius and Numitor. Alba was the parent city of Rome, and from its ruling family, the Silvian House, Romulus came to found Rome.

ALBION Son of Poseidon and Amphitrite. Brother of Benthesicyme, Charybdis, Rhode and Triton. Introduced the arts of astrology and ship-building to Britain.

ALBULA Original name of the river Tiber. Renamed after Tiberinus drowned in it.

ALBUNEA A prophetess, nymph. One of the Sibyls, she shared her name with her grove, sacred to the Muses, and a sulphurous pool nearby. She was a compiler of oracles concerning the destiny of Rome.

ALCAEUS (1) Name given to Heracles at birth, derived from (3) below. (2) Lyrical poet of Mytilene in Lesbos. Lived *c* 610–*c* 580 BC. (3) Son of Perseus and Andromeda. Brother of Electryon, Gorgophone, Heleus, Mestor, Perses and Sthenelus. Married Hipponome, daughter of Menoecius. Father of Amphitryon and Anaxo, though some say Amphitryon's mother was Laonome. Grandfather of Heracles. (*See* family tree under Perseus.) Source of patronymic of Heracles-Alcides. (4) Ruler of the isle of Thasus. Son of Androgeus. Brother of Sthenelus with whom he shared the throne. Accompanied Heracles on his quest for the girdle of Hippolyte. (5) Son of Heracles and Omphale. Brother of Agelaus and Lamus.

ALCANDER An attendant of Sarpedon, killed by Odysseus.

ALCANDRE The wife of Polybus, king of Egyptian Thebes. It was she who entertained Menelaus and Helen on their return to Egypt from the Trojan War.

ALCATHOUS King of Megara. Son of Pelops and Hippodameia. Brother of Astydameia, Atreus, Chrysippus, Copreus, Lysidice, Nicippe, Pittheus, Troezen, Thyestes and perhaps others. Married Evaechme, daughter of Megareus. Father of

Automedusa, Callipolis (whom he accidentally killed), Iphinoe, Ischepolis and Periboea. Megareus, father of Evaechme, had lost his eldest son to a lion. Alcathous killed the lion. His reward was Evaechme. Apollo helped him rebuild the walls of Megara.

ALCATHOUS (1) Son of Porthaon and Euryte. Brother of Agrius, Melas, Oeneus, Sterope and Leucopeus. He was killed by his nephew, Tydeus, or by Oenomaus. (2) Son of Aesyetes. Husband of Hippodameia, daughter of Anchises. Slain by Idomeneus in the Trojan War. (3) A friend of Aeneas, killed in the Rutulian War.

ALCEMENE *See* Alcmene.

ALCENOR (Alcanor) Together with a fellow Argive, Chromius, and a Spartan, Othryades, the three were the sole survivors of a battle between 300 Argives and 300 Spartans.

ALCESTIS Daughter of Pelias and Anaxibia or Phylomache. Sister of Acastus, Hippothoe, Pelopia and Pisidice. Married Admetus. Mother of Eumelus and Perimele.

Carried off to the Underworld by Thanatos but was returned by Persephone. She volunteered to die in her husband's place, but Heracles brought her back from the Underworld for a second time.

ALCIDAMEA Mother of Bubus by Hermes.

ALCIDES Epithet of Heracles, derived from Alcaeus.

ALCIDICE Daughter of Aleus. First wife of Salmoneus, son of Aeolus. Mother of Tyro. Died in childbirth.

ALCIMEDE Daughter of Phylacus and Clymene. Sister of Iphiclus. Married Aeson. Mother of Jason and later of Promachus.

ALCIMEDON (1) The father of Phillo. (2) Son of Laerces. One of the five lieutenants of Achilles, and one of the leaders of the Myrmidons under Patroclus.

ALCIMENES Possibly the son of Jason and Medea. Twin of Thessalus and brother of Argus, Eriopis, Mermerus, Medeias and Tisandrus.

ALCIMUS Father of Mentor.

ALCINOE Daughter of Sthenelus and Nicippe. Sister of Eurystheus and Medusa. Possibly the wife of Chalcodon, and thus the mother of Elephenor.

ALCINOUS King of the Phaecians. Son of Nausithous. Brother of Rhexenor. Married his niece, Arete. Father of Nausicaa and five sons. He offered protection to Jason and Medea when they fled from the Colchian fleet.

ALCIPPE (1) Daughter of Ares and Agraulos (Aglauros). Mother of Daedalus, Perdix and Sicyon by Eupalamus or Metion. She was raped by Halirrothius, son of Poseidon. (2) Wife of Evenus. Mother of Epistrophus, Marpessa and Mynes. (3) Possibly the mother of Evenus, Molus, Pylus, Oeneus and Thestius. (4) Spartan attendant of Menelaus and Helen. (5) A woman who gave birth to an elephant.

ALCITHOE (Alcathoe) Daughter of Minyas. Sister of Arsippe and Leucippe.

The three sisters refused to partake in the mysteries of Dionysus and so, after the god had driven them mad, Leucippe surrendered her son, Hippasus, to be torn to pieces by the three. The sisters were later turned into bats. Alcithoe was also a sister of Clymene and Periclymene.

ALCMAON Son of Thestor and Megara. Brother of Calchas, Leucippe and Theonoe. He was killed by Sarpedon after he had injured Sarpedon's friend, Glaucus.

ALCMENE (Alcemene) Daughter of Electryon and Anaxo or Eurydice. Sister of Everes and five others, and half-sister of Licymnius. Married Amphitryon. Mother

of twin sons, Heracles and Iphicles, though Zeus was the father of Heracles. After the death of Amphitryon, she married Rhadamanthys. Mother of Erythus and Gortys. She was the last mortal whom Zeus loved.

ALCMEON One of the Epigoni. Son of Amphiarus and Eriphyle. Brother of Amphilochus, Demonassa and Eurydice. Married first to Arsinoe, he fathered Clytius. By Callirrhoe, he was father of Acarnan and Amphoterus; by Manto, he fathered Amphilochus and Tisiphone.

He was the successful leader of the Epigoni on their expedition against Thebes. On his father's instructions he killed his mother, and the Furies drove him mad. Phegeus, father of Arsinoe, tried, unsuccessfully, to cure him. He was finally cured by Achelous, father of Callirrhoe. Alcmeon was murdered by the brothers of Arsinoe.

ALCON Father of the Argonaut, Phalerus. Was present on the Calydonian Boar Hunt. He was a skilled archer and helped Heracles steal the cattle of Geryon.

ALCYONE One of the Pleiades. Daughter of Atlas and Pleione. Sister of Celaeno, Electra, Maia, Merope, Sterope and Taygete. Mother of Hyrieus by Poseidon or Lycus. Mother of Anthas, Arethusa and Hypernor by Poseidon. Possibly the mother of Hyperes.

ALCYONE Daughter of Aeolus and Enarete. Sister to seven boys: Athamas, Cretheus, Deion, Macareus, Perieres, Salmoneus and Sisyphus. She also had six sisters: Arne, Calyce, Canace, Peisidice, Perimele and Tanagra. Married Ceyx, king of Thessaly (Trachis). Mother of Hippasus.

She called herself Hera to Ceyx's Zeus, and when she later drowned herself at the news of Ceyx's death, she was changed into a kingfisher, Ceyx also becoming a bird.

ALCYONE (1) Possibly the mother of Glaucus by Anthedon. (2) An epithet of Cleopatra, wife of Meleager.

ALCYONEUS One of the Giants. Son of Gaea and the blood of Uranus. *See* Giants for list of brothers.

He inhabited Pallene, a peninsula in the Aegean Sea, and twice stole the cattle of Helios. For this, Heracles tried to kill him. But Gaea revitalised him until Heracles realised that the only way to kill him permanently was to lift him off the ground (his mother).

ALECTO One of the Erinnyes. Daughter of Gaea. Sister of Megaera and Tisiphone.

ALECTOR King of Argos. (1) Son of Anaxagoras. Father of Capaneus and Iphis. (2) Possibly the father of Leitus by Cleobule.

ALECTRYON (1) Possibly the father of Leitus by Cleobule (cf Alector). (2) When Ares made love to Aphrodite, Alectryon was posted as a sentry outside the door to watch for the sunrise. But he fell asleep and the two lovers were discovered. Ares punished Alectryon by turning him into a rooster.

ALETES Son of Aegisthus and Clytemnestra. Brother of Erigone.

He became the ruler of Mycenae after Orestes murdered his parents but, in turn, was also murdered by Orestes.

ALETES King of Corinth. Son of Hippotes. He was the first of the Heraclids.

ALETES An elderly companion of Aeneas.

ALETHIA (Veritas) Daughter of Zeus. Nurse of Apollo, and Greek goddess of truth.

ALEUS King of Arcadia and Tegea. Son of Apheidas. Married Neaera, daughter of Pereus. Father of Amphidamas, Auge, Cepheus and Lycurgus. Grandfather of Ancaeus.

Attempted to murder Auge after her seduction by Heracles; and hid Ancaeus'

armour to try to prevent him from sailing with the Argonauts.

ALEUS Father of Alcidice, first wife of Salmoneus.

ALEXANDER (Alexandrus) *See* Paris.

ALEXANDRA The Spartan name for Cassandra, so called because she helped mankind with her prophecies.

ALEXANOR Son of Machaon and Anticleia. Grandson of Aesculapius. Brother of Gorgasus and Nichomachus.

ALEXIARES Son of Heracles and Hebe. Brother of Anticetus.

ALEXIROE A nymph. Daughter of the river god, Granicus. Lover of Priam. Possibly mother of Aesacus.

ALIRROTHIUS (Halirrhothius) Son of Poseidon. He accidentally killed himself when he tried to cut down an olive tree, sacred to Athena.

ALITHERSES (Halitherses, Halithersus) A soothsayer. He predicted the return of Odysseus, and warned Penelope's suitors that Odysseus would seek retribution.

ALLOPROSALLOS An epithet of Ares. Name given to Ares, because he constantly changed sides in war.

ALMOND TREE *See* Phyllis and Sangarius.

ALOEIDAE Name given to the twin giants, Otus and Ephialtes, sons of Iphimedeia and Poseidon or of Aloeus. They grew 23 cm per month or one cubit of breadth and one fathom of height, per year. At nine years of age, they fought the gods, and were killed by Apollo and Artemis.

ALOEUS Son of Uranus and Gaea, or more likely of Poseidon and Canace. If the latter, then he is brother of Epopeus, Hopleus, Nireus and Triopas. Married Iphimedeia, daughter of his brother, Triopas, and became the father of Pancratis. Later took a second wife, Eeriboea. He or Poseidon was the father of the Aloeidae.

ALOEUS King of Asopia. Son of Helios. Father of Epopeus.

ALOPE Daughter of Cercyon, king of Eleusis. Seduced by Poseidon, she mothered Hippothoon. Her father killed her and she was buried on a road between Eleusis and Megara. A spring arose from her burial mound.

ALPHEIUS (Alpheus) River god of Elis. Son of Oceanus and Tethys. Brother of the other river gods. Father of Orsilochus. He pursued the nymph Arethusa, until she was changed into a spring by Artemis. The river Alpheius joins this spring. Heracles diverted the river in order to clean the Augeian stables.

ALPHENOR One of the twelve children, six boys and six girls, of Amphion (qv) and Niobe.

ALPHESIBOEA (1) Wife of Phoenix and possibly mother of Adonis. (2) Possibly a daughter of Bias and Pero. (3) Daughter of Phegeus, identified with Arsinoe.

ALTES Father of Laothoe, wife of Priam.

ALTHAEA Daughter of Thestius and Eurythemis. Sister of Hypermnestra, Leda, Plexippus and others. Married her uncle, Oeneas. Mother of Gorge and Toxeus and of Deianeira, by Dionysus, and Meleager, by Ares or, possibly, her husband. After causing the death of Meleager, she hanged herself.

ALTHAEMENES Son of Catreus, king of Crete. Brother of Apemosyne, Aerope and Clymene. Died of grief, after killing his father, accidentally.

ALTHEPIA Original name of Troezen.

ALTHEPUS King of Oraea. Son of Poseidon and Leis, daughter of Orus. Succeeding his father to the throne, he renamed Oraea, Althepia. Later, this region became Troezen. He was succeeded to the throne by Saron.

ALTIS A sacred grove around the temple of Zeus on Mt Olympus, where the statues of Olympic champions were placed.

ALXION Either he, or Ares, was the father of Oenomaus by Harpina or Asterope.

ALYATTES Second king of Lydia of this name. Ruled in the 7th century BC, and was succeeded by Croesus.

AMALTHEA Also called Demo, Deiphobe, Demophile or Herophile. *See* Cumaean Sibyl.

AMALTHEA A Roman Sibyl. The owner, and possibly authoress, of nine books of oracular advice. She offered them to Tarquin, king of Rome, but he refused them because the price was too high. She burnt three of the books and offered the remainder for the original price. When he again refused, she burnt another three books and again offered the remainder at the original price. Tarquin this time purchased the three remaining books, which remained in the Temple of Jupiter until it was destroyed by fire in 83 BC.

AMALTHEA A goat. One of her horns flowed with ambrosia (a cornucopia), and the other with nectar. The infant Zeus was fed by her, and she herself was reared by Pan. After her death her skin was used in the Aegis.

AMALTHEA Daughter of Melissus, king of Crete. Sister of Melissa. It may have been she (cf above) who fed goatsmilk to the infant Zeus.

AMARYNCEUS An Eleian leader. Son of Pytthius. Father of Diores and Hippostratus. Shared in the government of Elis and, after his death, funeral games were held in his honour.

AMASENUS A river into which Metabus threw his daughter, Camilla.

AMATA Sister of Venilia. Married Latinus. Mother of Lavinia.

AMATHEIA A Nereid. One of the fifty daughters of Nereus and Doris.

AMAZON WOMEN Mythical female warriors of Cappadocia in Asia Minor, descendants of Ares and a naiad, Harmonia. They burned off their right breasts to facilitate the use of a bow and arrow. In the Trojan War, they aided the Trojans, after the death of Hector. Used men for breeding purposes only. Their queens included Hippolyte and Penthesileia.

AMBARVALIA Roman festivals, celebrated in May, to signify purification of the fields, during which prayers were offered to Mars.

AMBER ISLANDS Situated at the mouth of the river Eridanus. The Argonauts stopped there, on the return journey from Colchis.

AMBER, tears of *See* Heliades.

AMBRACIA City of south Epirus, the original home of Geryon.

AMBROSIA Honey-flavoured food of the gods, that gave them eternal youth. Their drink was called nectar.

AMISODAURUS A Lycian chieftain. Father of Atymnius and Maris. He reared the monster, Chimaera.

AMMON (1) Brother of Broteas. (2) Egyptian equivalent of Zeus, or Jupiter.

AMOR Boy-god of love. Son of Venus and Mars or Mercury. Roman name for Eros. (*See also* Cupid.)

AMPELUS Son of a nymph and a satyr. A great favourite of Dionysus, he was killed when he fell, in a drunken stupor, from a vine.

AMPHIANAX Epithet of Iobates.

AMPHIARUS An Argive seer. Son of Oicles and Hypermnestra. Married Eriphyle, sister of Adrastus. Father of Alcmeon, Amphilocus, Demonassa and Eurydice. He was also called Amphiorax.
He had the gift of prophecy which either came from Zeus, or was inherited from his great-grandfather, Melampus. He dethroned Adrastus. He was present on the Calydonian boar hunt, being the second to shoot the boar. One of the Seven against Thebes, and an Argonaut. Amphiarus disappeared into a split in the earth, caused by a thunderbolt from Zeus.

AMPHIBIA Epithet of Nicippe, daughter of Pelops.

AMPHICLUS A Trojan leader killed in the Trojan War by Meges.

AMPHICTYON King of Athens. Son of Deucalion and Pyrrha. Brother of Hellen, Pandora, Protogeneia and Thyia. Married Cranae, daughter of Cranaus.
After dethroning Cranaus, he ruled Attica, renaming it Athens, for twelve years, until unseated by Erichthonius. Amphictyon was the first man to mix water with wine, interpret dreams and draw omens. He founded the cult of Demeter called the Amphictyonic League.

AMPHIDAMAS King of Tegea. Son of Aleus and Neaera. Brother of Auge, Cepheus and Lycurgus. He was an Argonaut and shared his throne with his brothers.

AMPHIDAMAS Son of Lycurgus and Cleophyle or Eurynome. Brother of Ancaeus, Epochus and Iasus. Father of Antimache and Melanion.

AMPHIDAMAS (1) Father of Antibia. (2) Father of Clisonymus.

19

AMPHIDOCUS (Asphodocus) Son of Astacus. Brother of Ismarus, Leades and Melanippus. Helped defend Thebes against the Seven, and was possibly the slayer of Parthenopaeus (alternative, Periclymenus).

AMPHILOCHUS A soothsayer. Younger son of Amphiarus and Eriphyle. Brother of Alcmeon, Demonassa and Eurydice.

As a suitor of Helen, he went to the Trojan War and was in the Wooden Horse. Inherited the gift of prophecy from his father; he was one of the Epigoni. He may have helped to murder his mother at his father's command, but it is probable that his brother Alcmeon did this deed alone.

AMPHILOCHUS Son of Alcmeon and Manto. Brother of Tisiphone. He was reared by Creon, king of Corinth, and fought in the Trojan War (cf above) and founded the city of Mallus. He quarrelled with his half-brother, Mopsus, and the pair killed each other.

AMPHIMACHUS Son of Cteatus and Theronice.

A suitor of Helen, he went to the Trojan War, as one of the leaders of the Eleian forces. Was killed by Hector. His body was recovered by Menestheus and Stichius.

AMPHIMARUS Son of Poseidon. Possibly the father of Linus, by the muse, Urania.

AMPHIMEDON A suitor of Penelope.

AMPHINOME A Nereid. One of the fifty daughters of Nereus and Doris.

AMPHINOMUS Leader and most pleasing of Penelope's suitors. After he persuaded the other suitors not to murder Telemachus, the latter killed him.

AMPHION Joint king of Thebes. Son of Zeus and Antiope. Twin of Zethus. Married Niobe, daughter of Tantalus. Father of twelve children including Callirrhoe, Chloris (Meliboea), Neaera, Phthia, Phylomache, Alphenor and Dione, Amyclas, Cleodoxa, Ismenos, Broteas, Damaschthon, Ilenus, Pelops, Phaedimus, Sipylus and Tantalus (the eldest son), although different traditions offer alternative names, thus explaining the numbers of names here.

Apollo and Artemis killed eleven of the children; Chloris was the survivor, though some claim that Amyclas also survived. Hermes gave him a four-stringed lyre and he added three more strings. Because of this the walls of Thebes were built with seven gates, and music from the lyre helped the stones move, to build the walls. Amphion grew up in a shepherd's camp. He killed Dirce and Lycus to avenge the death of Epopeus, his mother's husband. He was killed by Apollo, when he raided the temple of Apollo, seeking revenge for the death of his children. He was buried at Thebes in a double tomb, with his brother, Zethus.

AMPHION An Argonaut. Son of Hyperasius or Hippasus. Brother of Asterius. He came from Pellene.

AMPHIORAX *See* Amphiarus.

AMPHISSUS A son of Apollo, by Dryope, whom he had seduced.

AMPHITHEA Daughter of Pronax. Sister of Lycurgus. Married her uncle, Adrastus. Mother of Aegialeus, Aegialeia, Argeia, Deipyle, (possibly) Cyanippus and Hippodameia.

AMPHITHEA Possibly the wife of Lycurgus (alternatively, Eurydice), and mother of Opheltes.

AMPHITHEA Wife of Autolycus and mother of Anticlea.

AMPHITHEMIS (Garamas) A Libyan chieftain. Son of Apollo and Acacallis, daughter of Minos. Brother of Miletus. Married Tritonis. Father of Caphaurus and Nasamon.

AMPHITHOE A Nereid. One of the fifty daughters of Nereus and Doris.

AMPHITRITE Greek goddess of the sea. Daughter of Nereus and Doris, or Oceanus and Tethys. Sister of forty-nine others (*see* Nereids). Married Poseidon, after he had pursued her. Mother of many, including Albion, Benthesicyme, Charybdis, Rhode and Triton.

The Dolphin constellation was placed in the sky in her honour, and she is usually regarded as the personification of the sea. Her Roman equivalent was Salacia.

AMPHITRYON Son of Alcaeus and Astydameia, Hipponome or Laonome. Brother of Anaxo. First husband of Alcmene. Father of Iphicles. (Iphicles was a twin of Heracles, the latter's father being Zeus.) He was also brother of Perimede.

He looked after the kingdom of Mycenae for his father-in-law, Electryon, while the latter was avenging his son's death. Amphitryon ransomed the stolen cattle of Electryon from Polyxenus. On the return of Electryon, Amphitryon accidentally killed him but was then purified by Creon, at Thebes. He helped kill the Teumassian fox which ate one Theban youth each month. Also at Thebes he killed Chalcodon, leader of the Euboeans in the war between Thebes and Euboea. Amphitryon himself was killed fighting Erginus.

AMPHIUS Son of Merops. Brother of Adrastus, Arisbe and Cleite. Killed in the Trojan War by Diomedes.

AMPHOTERUS (1) Son of Alcmeon and Callirrhoe. Brother of Acarnan. (2) A Lycian leader killed in the Trojan War by Patroclus.

AMPSANCTUS A small lake in the country of the Hirpini, thought to be an entrance to the Underworld because of volcanic vapours rising from it.

AMPYCUS (Ampyx) A Thessalian seer.

Son of Ares, Elatus or Titaron. Father of Mopsus, by Chloris.

AMULIUS King of Alba Longa. Son of Procas. Usurped the throne of his brother, Numitor. He killed Numitor's sons and was himself killed by Numitor's grandsons, Romulus and Remus.

AMYCLAE City of Laconia, near Sparta, founded by its first king, Amyclas. Agamemnon and Clytemnestra were buried there.

AMYCLAS One of the six sons of Amphion (qv) and Niobe. He had six sisters. When Apollo murdered the boys and Artemis all the girls except Chloris, he may also have survived.

AMYCLAS King of Amyclae, in Sparta. Son of Lacedaemon and Sparte. Brother of Eurydice. Married Diomede. Father of Argalus, Cynortas, Hyacinthus and Leaneira.

AMYCUS King of the Bebryces. Son of Poseidon and the ash-nymph, Melie. Brother of Mygdon.

He used to force visitors to box with him to the death, until he met his match in Polydeuces, who killed him with a blow on his ear or elbow.

AMYCUS (1) Name of two companions of Aeneas, both killed by Turnus. (2) Son of Ixion and Nephele.
See Ixion for relatives.

AMYMONE One of the Danaids. Daughter of Danaus and Europa. Had forty-nine sisters. Mother of Nauplius by Poseidon. Married Enceladus, son of Aegyptus.

Murdered her husband on their wedding night. After she lay with Poseidon, in drought-hit Argos, a perpetual spring gushed forth.

AMYNTOR King of Dolopians in Thessaly or of Orochomenos. Son of Ormenus or Zeus. Married Cleobule. Father of Astydameia, Crantor, Deidameia and Phoenix, although Phoenix may have been the son of Amyntor, tutor of Achilles. He was on the Calydonian boar hunt. He was killed by Heracles.

AMYTHAON Second son of Cretheus and Tyro. Brother of Aeson, Pheres and Promachus. Half-brother of Neleus. Married Idomene, daughter of Pheres. Father of Aeolia, Bias, Melampus and Perimele. With Neleus, re-established the Olympic games.

ANACREON Greek lyric poet.

ANACTORIA Original name of Miletus in Asia Minor.

ANADYOMENE Born of the sea. Epithet of Aphrodite.

ANAIDEIA The stone on Areopagus, on which the prosecutor stood.

ANAPHE A small island, north of Crete, visited by the Argonauts on their homeward journey from Colchis.

ANATOLIA A peninsula bordered by the Aegean, Black and Mediterranean Seas, now Turkey.

ANAURUS A river of south-west Thessaly, near Iolcus. Jason lost his sandal carrying Hera across it.

ANAX A giant. Son of Uranus and Gaea. *See* Giants.

ANAXAGORAS King of Argos. Son of Megapenthes. Father of Alector.

ANAXARETE A Greek princess. Beloved by Iphis, she resisted him, and he hanged himself. Watching his funeral left her so totally unmoved, that Aphrodite turned her to stone.

ANAXIBIA (1) Daughter of Pleisthenes and Cleolla or Aerope, or of Atreus and Aerope. Sister of Agamemnon and Menelaus. Mother of Pylades by Strophius I, and possibly of Antilochus, Aretus, Echephron, Peisistratus, Perseus, Stratius, Thrasymedes, Polycaste and Peisidice by Nestor. Some add Paeon as a son. (2) Daughter of Bias and Iphianassa. Possibly the wife of Pelias (alternatively, Phylomache, daughter of Amphion). Mother of Acastus, Alcestis, Hippothoe, Pelopia and Pisidice. (3) Possibly the daughter of Crisus. Sister of Astyoche and Strophius I. (Cf (1) above.)

ANAXIROE Daughter of Coronus. Married Epeius. Mother of Hyrmina.

ANAXO Daughter of Alcaeus and Hipponome. Sister of Amphitryon. Married Electryon, king of Mycenae. Mother of Alcmene and six sons, including Everes.

ANCAEUS King of Samos and an Argonaut. Son of Poseidon and Astypalea. Brother of Eurypylus. Married Samia, daughter of the river god Maeander. Father of four sons and Parthenope.

He became the helmsman of the Argo after the death of Tiphys. Told by a seer that he would not live to taste wine made from grapes that he had planted, he was later just lifting a cup to his lips when the seer said, 'There is many a slip 'twixt the cup and lips.' He then heard a boar ravaging his vineyards, put down the cup, and was killed by the boar.

ANCAEUS An Argonaut. Son of Lycurgus and Cleophyle or Eurynome. Brother of Amphidamas, Iasus and Epochus. Father of Agapenor. After Heracles, the strongest of the Argonauts. Gored to death by the Calydonian boar.

ANCHIALE (Anichale) A nymph. Either she, or Rhea, was the mother of the ten Dactyli.

ANCHIALUS A Taphian chief. Father of Mentes. As a friend of Laertes, he gave Odysseus arrow poison.

ANCHINOE Daughter of Nile. Sister of Memphis. Married Belus. Mother of Aegyptus, Danaus and Thronia, and possibly Cepheus and Phineus.

ANCHISES King of Dardania. Son of Capys and Themiste. Brother of Laocoon. Lover of Aphrodite. Father of Aeneas, Hippodameia and Lyrus.

He limped throughout his life after being struck by a thunderbolt from Zeus, after boasting of his love affair with Aphrodite. He stole some of Laomedon's stallions for stud. Rescued from the Trojan War by Aeneas, he died in Sicily, aged 80, and was buried at Eryx.

ANCHISES, funeral games of First event: ship race. Participants: Cloanthus in *Scylla* (winner); Mnestheus in *Pristis* (second); Gyas in *Chimaera* (third); and Sergestus in *Centaur* (sank).

Second event: athletics. Participants: Euryalus (first); Helymus (second); Diores (third); Nisus, Panopes, Patron and Salius.

Third event: boxing. Entellus beat Dares.

Fourth event: archery. Participants: Acestes (winner); Eurytion, Hippocoon and Mnestheus.

Junior event. Participants: Atys, Iulus and Priam.

ANCHISIA Mountain of Arcadia, where stood a shrine to Anchises.

ANCILE Sacred shield of Mars (Ares), guarded by the Roman priests, called Salii.

ANCUS MARCIUS 4th king of Rome. Son of Tullus Hostilius and grandson of Numa Pompilus. Ruled for 24 years and founded the city of Ostia.

ANCYRA Ancient city of Asia Minor, founded by Midas. Now called Ankara.

ANDANIA City of Messenia, founded by its first co-rulers, Messene and Polycaon.

ANDRAEMON King of Calydon. Captain of the Aetolians in the Trojan War. Married Gorge, daughter of Oeneus and Althaea. Father of Thoas. Possibly father of Oxylus. May have married Dryope, daughter of Eurytus, though this might have been another Andraemon. Succeeded Agrius to the throne.

ANDREAS First king of Andreis. Son of Peneius. Married Euippe, daughter of Leucon. Possibly father of Eteocles.

ANDREIS A part of northern Boeotia, renamed by Andreas.

ANDRODAMAS Son of Phlias and Chthonophyle.

ANDROGEUS Son of Minos and Pasiphae. Brother of Acacallis, Ariadne, Catreus, Deucalion, Euryale, Glaucus, Lycastus, Phaedra, Xenodice, etc. Father of Alcaeus and Sthenelus.

A famous athlete who won all the races at the Panathenaean games, using the name of Eurygyes. Was killed by the bull of Marathon on his way to race in Athens. This led to Athenians being sacrificed to the Minotaur.

ANDROMACHE Daughter of Eetion, king of Thebes. She had seven brothers. Married Hector. Mother of Astyanax. After the death of Hector, she became the concubine of Neoptolemus, mothering Molossus, Pergamus and Pielus. After the death of Neoptolemus, she married Helenus and became the mother of Cestrinus.

ANDROMEDA Daughter of Cepheus and Cassiopeia. Was betrothed to Agenor, but he was slain by Perseus. She was chained to a rock to be eaten by a sea monster after her mother boasted that Andromeda was more beautiful than the nereids, but was rescued by Perseus, who married her. Mother of Alcaeus, Electryon,

Heleus, Mestor, Perses, Sthenelus and Gorgophone. After her death, Athena transformed her into a constellation.

ANEMONE *See* Adonis.

ANGERONA An ancient Roman goddess. Festival date: 21 December (winter solstice).

ANGITIA Ancient Italic goddess of healing. Greek equivalent, Circe.

ANIGRUS A river of Elis. A centaur washing his wounds in the river caused it to have an unpleasant smell.

ANIMALS, Roman goddess associated with Bona Mater, Bona Dea, Fauna.

ANIOCHE (Eniocha) Possibly the wife of Creon of Thebes and mother of Enioche, Haemon, Megara, Menoeceus and Pyrrha. (Alternative wife of Creon, Eurydice).

ANIUS King of Delos. Son of Apollo and Rhoeo. Reared by Apollo, as his priest, after his mother placed him on the altar of Apollo at Delos. Fathered a son and three daughters: Elais (olive), Oino (wine) and Spermo (seed). They became devotees of Dionysus.

ANNA Daughter of Agenor or Belus or Mutto. Sister of Dido and Pygmalion. Unwittingly helped her sister prepare for her death.

ANNA PERENNA Ancient Roman goddess. Cf Anna. Festival date: the Ides of March.

ANOGEN Son of Castor and Hilaera.

ANTAEUS A powerful Libyan giant. Son of Poseidon and Gaea, brother of Charybdis and Ogyges. Contact with the earth made him invincible, but Heracles killed him by lifting him off his mother, Gaea (earth). Cf Alcyoneus.

ANTAEUS A friend of Turnus, killed by Aeneas.

ANTEIA The lover of Bellerophon. Anteia was Homer's name for Stheneboea, wife of Proetus.

ANTENOR A Dardanian and Trojan seer. Son of Aesyetes and Cleomestra. Married Theano. Father of fourteen sons: Coon, Demoleon, Iphidamas, Polydamas, Laodamas, Polybus, Acamas, Agenor, Archelous, Glaucus, Helicaon, Laocoon, Lycaon, Pedaeus (by a different mother), and one daughter, Crino.

He was the founder of Padua and the adviser of Priam. He suggested to Odysseus the stealing of the Palladium, and to the Trojans the return of Helen. During the Trojan War he kept up a secret correspondence with the Greeks, especially with Menelaus and Odysseus. He suggested the Wooden Horse and, after the sack of Troy, he was spared by placing a leopard skin on his door.

ANTEROS God of passion. Son of Ares and Aphrodite. Aphrodite claimed that Eros was always young. He grew quickly when Anteros was born. Brother of Deimos, Enyo, Eros, Harmonia, Pallor and Phobos. He was also the god of mutual love and tenderness.

ANTEVORTA Roman goddess of the future. Sister of Postvorta, though both were once one goddess.

ANTHAS King of Althepia (Troezen). Son of Poseidon and Alcyone. Brother of Arethusa and Hyperenor. Father of Aetius, who succeeded him.

ANTHEDON City of Boeotia, opposite Euboea. The home of Glaucus, before he became a minor sea god.

ANTHEDON Possibly the father of Glaucus, the sea god, by Alcyone.

(Alternative parentage of Glaucus, Poseidon and Nais.)

ANTHEIAS Son of Eumelus. Killed when he tried to ride the winged-dragon-drawn chariot of Triptolemus.

ANTHEIS A daughter of Hyacinth. An Athenian immigrant from Sparta, she was sacrificed by her father to palliate a plague in Athens.

ANTHEMOESSA The island of the Sirens.

ANTHESTERION Another name for February.

ANTIANEIRA (1) Daughter of Menelaus or Menetes. Mother of Echion and Erytus by Hermes. (2) Mother of Argonaut Idmon by Apollo.

ANTIBIA Daughter of Amphidamas. Possibly the wife of Sthenelus, son of Perseus. (Alternative wife, Nicippe.) *See* Sthenelus.

ANTICETUS Son of Hebe and Heracles. Brother of Alexiares.

ANTICLEIA Daughter of Autolycus and Amphithea. Married Laertes, king of Ithaca. Mother of Odysseus, possibly by her lover Sisyphus, and Ctimene. She died of grief while Odysseus fought in the Trojan War.

ANTICLEIA (Philinoe) Daughter of Iobates.

ANTICLEIA (1) Wife of Machaon. Mother of Alexanor, Gorgasus and Nichomachus. (2) Mother of Periphetes, by Poseidon or Hephaestus.

ANTIGONE Daughter of Oedipus and Jocasta or Euryganeia. Sister of Eteocles, Ismene and Polyneices. Lover of Haemon.

She performed the burial rites of Poly-neices, against the orders of Creon, and was punished by being condemned to be buried alive. She either committed suicide, or was killed by Haemon.

ANTIGONE (1) Daughter of Eurytion, king of Phthia. Married Peleus. Mother of Polydora. Killed herself, after Peleus deserted her. (2) Daughter of Pheres. Married Cometes. Mother of Asterion, an Argonaut. (3) Daughter of Laomedon. Sister of Priam. Hera changed her into a stork, for comparing their beauty.

ANTILOCHUS Eldest son of Nestor and Anaxibia or Eurydice. Brother of Aretus, Echephron, Paeon, Peisidice, Peisistratus, Perseus, Polycaste, Stratius and Thrasymedes. Possibly the father, not brother, of Paeon.

He was exposed, at birth, on Mt Ida. As a suitor of Helen, he went to the Trojan War and was a close friend of Achilles. He was buried in the same grave as Achilles and Patroclus after he died defending his father from attack by Memnon. He lives on, eternally, on White Island, the home of Heroes.

ANTIMACHE Daughter of Amphidamas. Sister of Melanion. Married Eurystheus.

ANTIMACHUS A Trojan elder. Father of Hippolochus, Hippomachus and Peisander.

Being a greedy militant, he resisted the return of Helen from Troy, recommending that the envoys of Agamemnon and Menelaus be killed instead. Later, his sons were killed in reprisal.

ANTIMACHUS A Heraclid. Son of Heracles and a daughter of Thespius. Father of Deiphontes.

ANTINOUS Son of Eupeithes. The most brutal and arrogant of Penelope's suitors, and the first to be killed by Odysseus on his return to Ithaca.

ANTION Eldest son of Periphas and Astyagyia. Consorted with Perimele, daughter of Amythaon. Possibly the father of Ixion (alternatives, Ares, Phlegyas). Antion had seven brothers.

ANTIOPE Daughter of Asopus and Metope, or of Nycteus of Thebes and Polyxo. Sister to Aegina, Cleone, Corcyra, Ismenus, Pelagon, Salamis, Ismene, Chalcis, Pelasgus, Metope, Thebe and ten others. A lover of Zeus, mothering Amphion and Zethus.

She married Epopeus, king of Sicyon, but when Lycus, brother to Nycteus, killed Epopeus, Lycus abducted and imprisoned her. Dirce, wife of Lycus, abused her cruelly until she was released, years later. She took refuge on Mt Cithaeron, and when her sons killed Dirce, and possibly Lycus, Dionysus, devotee of Dirce, drove her mad. Phocus cured her madness and married her.

ANTIOPE (Melanippe) Daughter of Ares and Otrera. Sister of Hippolyte, queen of the Amazons. Married Theseus. Possibly mother of Demophon. Theseus may have killed her when she tried to stop his marriage to Phaedra.

ANTIOPE Wife of Laocoon. Mother of either Ethron and Melanthus, or of Antiphas and Thymbraeus.

ANTIOPE Wife of Eurytus. Mother of Clytius, Iole and Iphitus.

ANTIPHAS A Trojan. Son of Laocoon and Antiope. Twin of Thymbraeus. Killed by a sea-serpent, after Laocoon defamed a temple of Apollo.

ANTIPHATES Son of Melampus and Lysippe. Brother of Abas and Mantius. Either he, or Mantius, was the father of Oicles. He was killed in the Trojan War.

ANTIPHATES King of the Lastrygonians in Sicily. A cannibal giant. When Odysseus' ships entered the port of Telepylus, the Lastrygonians crushed the ships

and ate the seamen. Antiphates ate a seaman from Odysseus' own ship, and only Odysseus' ship escaped.

ANTIPHONUS A son of Priam who went with his father to Achilles' tent to redeem the body of Hector.

ANTIPHUS Son of Thessalus. Brother of Pheidippus. Took thirty ships to the Trojan War.

ANTIPHUS Son of Priam and Hecuba. Had many brothers and sisters (*see* Priam). He was captured by Achilles, on Mt Ida, but was ransomed by his father. Killed in the Trojan War by Agamemnon.

ANTIPHUS Son of Myrmidon and Peisidice. Brother of Actor and Eupolemeia.

ANTIPHUS A friend of Odysseus, eaten by Polyphemus.

ANTIPHUS Father of Hippea, the wife of Elatus.

ANUBIS The Egyptian deity worshipped in the form of a dog. Equivalent of Hermes and Mercury.

ANVIL *See* Acmon.

ANYTUS An armed Titan. Said to have brought up Despoena and honoured in secret rites, with Despoena and Demeter.

AOEDE (Aeode) Boeotian muse of song. Daughter of Uranus and Gaea. Sister of Melete and Mneme. Worshipped at Helicon.

AONIANS The inhabitants of Aonia, later called Boeotia.

AORIS Son of Aras. Brother of Araethyrea. He ruled Phlius jointly with his sister but, after her death, he renamed the country Araethyrea.

APE *See* Cercopes, Passalus.

APELIOTES (Lips) The secondary east or south-east wind. Son of Eos and Astraeus.

APEMOSYNE Daughter of Catreus, king of Crete. Sister of Aerope, Althaemenes and Clymene.

APHAEA Epithet of Britomartis, on the island of Aegina. Britomartis was a Cretan hunting goddess, daughter of Zeus and Carme.

APHAREUS King of Messene. Son of Perieres and Gorgophone. Brother of Borus, Icarius, Leucippus and Tyndareus. Married Arene, his mother's daughter by her second husband, or Polydora, or Laocdoosa. Father of Idas, Lynceus and Peisus. Aphareus was a grandson of Perseus.

He gave refuge to two exiled princes, Neleus, son of Cretheus, and Lycus, son of Pandion. Aphareus outlived all his sons, and the rule passed to Neleus.

APHAREUS Son of Caletor. Killed in the Trojan War by Aeneas.

APHEIDAS Son of Arcas and Erato. Brother of Azan, Elatus and Hyperippe. Half-brother of Autolaus. King of Tegea, left to him by his father. Father of Pereus and Aleus, the latter succeeding him to the throne.

APHIDNA(E) Attican town, north-west of Marathon, where the Dioscuri found Helen, after her abduction by Theseus.

APHRODITE (Venus) Goddess of sensual love and beauty. Daughter of Zeus

Aphrodite

and Dione, alternatively, born of the foam of the sea, when the severed genitals of Uranus were thrown into the sea, the foam gathering round them. Some sources say the mother of Aphrodite was Eileithyia.

One of the twelve Olympians. Married Hephaestus, the fire god. She had many love affairs. By Ares, was mother of Anteros, Deimos, Eros, Harmonia and Phobos. Hephaestus discovered the lovers. By Hermes, she bore Hermaphroditus; by Poseidon, Eryx; by Dionysus, Priapus. She also coupled with mortals. By Anchises, Aeneas and Lyrus; by Adonis, a boy and a girl. Her sacred animals were a dove, sparrow, swallow, swan and turtle. Her sacred flowers were the rose and myrtle, and the apple was also sacred to her. When Paris gave her the apple of discord, she helped him win Helen. She had several epithets: 1. Acidalia (a surname) 2. Anadyomene (born of the sea) 3. Cyprian 4. Cypris 5. Cythereia 6. Eriboea (Periboea) 7. Erycina (Roman) 8. Euploios (fair voyage) 9. Paphia (sexual love) 10. Pelagia 11. Pontia (she who arose from the sea). Her girdle (cestus) gave beauty, elegance and grace to the deformed, and excited love, rekindling passion. Aphrodite was the patron of courtesans. Diomedes wounded her in the Trojan War, in which she supported Troy.

APIA Original name for Peloponnesus, after the king Apis.

APIS Ruler of Apia. Son of Phoroneus and the nymph, Teledice. Brother of Car and Niobe. Deposed and killed by Telchis and Thelxion.

APISAON Son of Hippasus. Assisted Priam against the Greeks in the Trojan War. Killed by Lycomedes.

APOLLO (Phòebus) God of prophecy, healing and music. Son of Zeus and Leto. Born on Delos.

One of the Olympians, though mostly associated with his twin sister, Artemis. Enjoyed many love affairs.

Apollo's Lovers	Children of the Union
Acacallis	Amphithemis and Miletus
Arsinoe	Eriopis
Calliope	Orpheus
Celaeno or Thyia	Delphus
Chione	Philammon
Chrysorthe	Coronus
Coronis or Arsinoe	Asclepius (Páeon)
Cyrene	Autychus, Idom (possibly) and Aristaeus
Dryope	Amphissus
Evadne	Iamus
Hecuba (possibly)	Troilus
Ocyrrhoe	Phasis
Parthenope	Lycomedes
Phthia	Dorus, Laodocus and Polypoetes
Procleia	Tenes
Psamathe	Linus
Rhoeo	Anius
Stilbe	Centaurus and Lapithus
Syllis	Zeuxippus
Thyia	Delphus
Thyria	Cycnus and Phylius

He had also love affairs with Acantha, Bolina, Clymene (*see* Heliades), Daphne, Issa and Leucothoe. He was the father of Chariclo and Cinyras (possibly), Dryops, Idmon, Melaneus, Thestor and Trophonius (possibly).

He had many epithets: 1. Acersecomes, a surname, meaning unshorn. 2. Acesius, a surname, meaning healer. 3. Cynthius (born on mount Cynthus). 4. Delius. 5. Loxias. 6. Lycius (wolf-god). 7. Moiragete (guide of the Moirae). 8. Musagetes (patron of the Muses). 9. Paean (the healing god). 10. Phoebus (shining). 11. Smintheus (mouse-god).

He was a patron of archery, music and medicine. His sacred tree was the laurel. His sacred birds were the raven and the swan. His sacred instrument was the lyre, and his sacred island was Delos. His most famous oracles were at Delphi, Delos and Tenedos. Apollo destroyed the monsters

28

Apollo

Python and the Cyclops, and for killing the latter, who were the manufacturers of Zeus' thunderbolts, he was forced to serve Admetus for one year.

Worship of Apollo was said to be very strong among the Hyperboreans. Apollo spent three months of each year with them, and the rest in Delphi. He and his sister, Artemis, shot Tityus, who had tried to rape their mother. They also shot the children of Niobe. He supported the Trojans in the war against the Greeks. His childhood nurse was called Alethia.

APOLLODORUS Mythologist of 2nd century BC, Moved from Alexandria to Athens. Among his works was the three-volume Bibliotheca (library). The extant work of this name, presenting an un-critical study of Greek Mythology, belongs to 1st or 2nd century AD.

APOLLONIUS RHODIUS 2nd or 3rd century BC Alexandrian epic poet, called

Rhodius because of his retirement to Rhodes. His most famous work was the four-volume Argonautica, the story of Jason and the Golden Fleece.

APPIADES Name applied in Roman mythology to five gods: Concordia, Minerva, Pax, Venus and Vesta. A temple was erected to them, close to the Appian Way.

APPLE OF DISCORD Eris, the goddess of Discord, arrived, uninvited, at the wedding of Peleus and Thetis and rolled a golden apple across the floor. It was inscribed 'for the fairest' and was claimed by Aphrodite, Athena and Hera. Paris was asked to judge the contest, the so-called Judgement of Paris, and he awarded Aphrodite the apple. This was the indirect cause of the Trojan War (qv).

APPLES OF THE HESPERIDES Apples from a tree that Zeus gave to Hera (or vice versa) as a wedding present. The tree was guarded by Ladon and the Hesperides. Heracles obtained three of these apples as his eleventh labour.

APSEUDES A Nereid. One of the fifty daughters of Nereus and Doris.

APSYRTUS Alternative spelling of Absyrtus (qv) the son of Aeetes and Eidyia. He was also called Phaethon.

APULEIUS 2nd century AD Roman writer and orator, born in Africa. Best known for his *Metamorphoses*, or the *Golden Ass*.

APULIA Adriatic coastal area, just north of the heel of Italy, ruled by Daunus.

AQUARIUS The water carrier. Eleventh sign of the zodiac, said to represent Cecrops, Deucalion or Ganymede.

AQUILA The eagle constellation. Represented either the eagle that carried Aphrodite's slipper to Hermes, or the eagle that took Ganymede to heaven; or was

Metope, after her transformation by Hera.

AQUILO Roman equivalent of Boreas, the Greek north wind.

ARABAS Son of Hermaon and Thronia. Eponym of Arabia.

ARABUS Son of Hermes and a Sicilian nymph. Brother of Daphnis. Father of Cassiopeia.

ARACHNE Skilful weaver of Lydia. Daughter of Idmon and Colophon.
She challenged Athena to a weaving contest, and when they finished, evenly matched, Athena destroyed Arachne's tapestry, so the girl hanged herself, but Athena turned her into a spider.

ARAE Rocks in the Mediterranean, between Africa and Sardinia, where Aeneas lost many of his ships.

ARAETHYREA Daughter of Aras. Sister of Aoris. Mother of Phlias by Dionysus or Ceisus. After the death of her father she co-ruled her country, Phlius, with her brother. When she died, Aoris renamed the country Araethyrea.

ARANTIA Another name of the country called Phlius (also called Phliasia), so called after Aras, king of the land.

ARAS King of Phlius (Arantia). Father of Aoris and Araethyrea, who jointly succeeded him to the throne of Phlius.

ARCADIA Mountainous country in the middle of Peloponnesus. Named after Arcas. Hermes was born there, Pan lived there.
Amongst the kings were: Pelasgus, Lycaon, Nyctimus, Arcas, Elatus, Stymphalus, Aepytus, Agamedes (son of Stymphalus), Agapenor, Aleus, Clymenus, Croesus, Cypselus, Echemus, another Lycaon, Lycurgus and Oicles, who was king at the time of the Trojan War. Orestes may also have been a king of Arcadia. The poorest man in Arcadia was recorded as Aglaus.

ARCAS King of the Arcadians: Ancestor and eponym. Son of Zeus and Callisto. Saved from the womb of his dead mother by Zeus, and reared by Maia. She brought him to the court of his grandfather, Lycaon, who killed him and served him to Zeus as stew. Zeus restored him to life, but destroyed the house of Lycaon. Married the Dryad, Erato. Father of Azan, Apheidas, Elatus, Hyperippe and the illegitimate Autolaus.
He succeeded Nyctimus to the throne and taught the Arcadians agriculture, breadmaking and wool spinning. After his death, Elatus succeeded to the throne and Arcas was placed among the stars as the constellation of the Little Bear, guarding his mother, the Great Bear.

ARCEISIUS Son of Zeus and Euryodia, or of Cephalus and Procris. Married Chalcomedusa. Father of Laertes.

ARCESILAUS (Polyporthes) (1) Son of Odysseus and Penelope. Brother of Telemachus. Also called Ptoliporthes. (2) King of Cyrene. Son of Battus, the next six generations of kings used alternately the names Battus and Arcesilaus. (3) A Boeotian killed in the Trojan War by Hector.

ARCHANDER Son of Achaeus. Brother of Architeles. Married a daughter of Danaus.

ARCHELOUS Son of Antenor and Theano. Brother of Acamas, Agenor, Glaucus, Helicaon, Laocoon, Coon, Polydamas, Lycaon, Demoleon, Iphidamas, Leodamas, Polybus and Crino. Halfbrother of Pedaeus. With Aeneas and Acamas, he shared the leadership of the Dardanian forces at the Trojan War.

ARCHEMORUS (start of doom) Name under which Opheltes was buried.

ARCHITELES Son of Achaeus. Brother

of Archander. Married Automate, a daughter of Danaus.

ARCHITELES Father of Eunomus who was killed by Heracles.

ARDEAS Son of Odysseus and Circe. Brother of Agrius and Telegonus, and brother or half-brother of Latinus. He became a heron.

ARDEA Coastal city, south of Rome, founded by Danae.

AREIA Daughter of Cleochus. Possibly the mother of Miletus by Apollo.

AREILYCUS Father of Prothoenor. A Trojan leader killed in the War by Patroclus.

AREILYCUS Greek in the Trojan War.

AREITHOUS Squire of Rhygmus. Both were killed in the Trojan War by Achilles.

AREIUS An Argonaut. Son of Bias and Pero. Brother of Leodocus and Talaus, and possibly Alphesiboea, Aretus and Perialces.

ARENE Daughter of Oebalus and Gorgophone. Sister of Hippocoon, and Peirene. Married her half-brother, Aphareus of Messene. Mother of Idas, Lynceus and Peisus.

ARENE City of Messene. Its rulers included Neleus and Perieres.

AREOPAGITAE Judges of the criminal court of Athens. The site was a rocky hill just to the west of the Acropolis. The accuser stood on the Anaideia. The court was called Areopagus and the first to be tried there was Ares for the murder of Halirrhothius.

ARES (Mars) God of war. Son of Zeus and Hera. Brother of Eris (Discordia). One

of the twelve Olympians, and linked with his sister and lover, Aphrodite. Brother of Arge, Eileithyia and Hebe. By Aphrodite, he was the father of Anteros, Enyo, Deimos, Harmonia, Pallor and Phobos. They were possibly the parents of Eros.

Ares' Lovers	Children of the Union
Aerope	Aeropus
Agraulos	Alcippe
Althaea	Meleager
Astynome	Calydon
Astyoche	Ascalaphus and Ialmenus
Atalanta	Parthenopaeus (possibly)
Asterope or Harpina	Oenomaus (possibly)
Chryse or Dotis	Phlegyas
Cyrene or Asterie	Diomedes
Demonice or Alcippe	Evenus, Molus, Oeneus, Pylus and Thestius
Otrera	Antiope (Melanippe), Hippolyte and Penthesileia
Pelopia or Pyrene	Cycnus
Protogeneia	Oxylus

Also the father of Ampycus, Dryas, Lycus, Melanippus, Metus (by an attendant) and Tereus.

Epithets of Ares: 1. Gradivus (leader of armies) 2. Alloprosallos. Sacred animals: the vulture and the dog. Ares sided with the Trojans in the war against the Greeks. The Aloeidae imprisoned Ares in a bronze jar for 13 months, until he was rescued by Hermes. His four horses were called Aithon (red fire), Conabos (tumult), Phlogios (flame) and Phobos (terror). Ares was the first person to be tried for the murder of Halirrhothius, at the Areopagus.

ARESTOR The husband of Mycene.

ARETE Queen of the Phaecians. Daughter of Rhexenor. Married her uncle,

31

Alcinous, over whom she exerted great influence. Mother of five boys and Nausicaa.

ARETE (1) Daughter of Dionysus. (2) Name given to the goddess of virtue.

ARETHUSA A wood nymph. Daughter of Oceanus. She was an attendant of Artemis. After being pursued by Alpheus, Artemis transformed her into a spring on the island of Ortygia near Syracuse.

ARETHUSA One of the Hesperides. Daughter of Atlas and Pleione. Sister of Aegle, Erythia and Hesperia, the other Hesperides. Sister to the Hyades, Pleiades, Hyas and Calypso.

ARETHUSA *See* Aethusa.

ARETUS Son of Nestor and Anaxibia. Brother of Antilochus, Echephron, Peisidice, Peisistratus, Perseus, Polycaste, Stratius and Thrasymedes.

ARETUS One of the fifty sons of Priam (qv). Automedon killed him, avenging the death of Patroclus.

ARETUS A famous fighter who used only a club, and was killed by Lycurgus.

ARGADES Son of Ion and Helice. Brother of Aegicores, Geleon and Hoples.

ARGALUS King of Sparta. Eldest son of Amyclas and Diomede. Brother of Cynortas, Hyacinth(us) and Leaneira.

ARGANTHOE of Cius The wife of Rhesus. She followed him to the Trojan War and died of sorrow when she discovered him, dead.

ARGE Daughter of Thespius (qv). She had forty-nine sisters. Mother of two sons by Heracles.

ARGE A beautiful huntress turned into a stag by Apollo.

ARGE A nymph. Daughter of Zeus and Hera. Sister of Ares, Eileithyia, Hebe, Eris and Hephaestus.

ARGEAS Father of Evippus and Polymelus.

ARGEIA Daughter of Adrastus and Amphithea. Sister of Aegialeia, Aegialeus, Deipyle (possibly), Cyanippus and Hippodameia. Married Polyneices. Mother of Thersander and another Adrastus.

She attended the funeral of Eteocles, and helped Antigone pile the body of Polyneices on to the pyre. Creon killed her for this, and Theseus killed Creon in retaliation.

ARGEIA Daughter of Autesion. Sister of Theras. Married Aristodemus. Was the mother of twin sons, called Eurysthenes and Procles.

ARGEIA Wife of Polybus. Mother of Argus, the builder of the Argo.

ARGEIUS Son of Licymnius and Perimede. Brother of Melas and Oeonus. Killed when helping Heracles fight Eurytas.

ARGES (the bright one) One of the Cyclops. Son of Uranus and Gaea. Brother of Brontes, Geraestus, Steropes, Polyphemus, and the Titans. Killed by Apollo.

ARGESTES The east wind.

ARGIOPE (1) Wife of Philammon. Mother of Thamyris. A nymph from Parnassus. (2) Possibly the wife of Agenor (alternatively, Telephassa), which would make her the mother of Cadmus, Cilix, Europa, Phoenix, Phineus and Thasus, and possibly Argus. May have been mother of Europa by Sidon.

ARGIPHONTES Epithet of Hermes, as the slayer of Argus Panoptes.

ARGIVES The inhabitants of Argos and Argolis. A general word for Greeks.

ARGO A ship, built at Pagasae, a seaport of Thessaly, by Argus, son of Argeia, for Jason. It was traditionally the first ship to be built.

ARGOLIS Ancient district of Peloponnesus, at the head of the Gulf of Argolis, between Arcadia and the Aegean Sea. Its principal town was Argos.

ARGONAUTS The name given to the companions of Jason who accompanied him on his quest to Colchis to seek and retrieve the golden fleece. Apollonius was the only classical writer to list them fully, but other writers mention Argonauts not in Apollonius' list. They sailed to Colchis about eighty years before the Trojan War.

Their names, in the sequence from the Argonautica, were as follows: Jason, son of Aeson and Alcimede; Orpheus, son of Oeager and Calliope; Asterion, son of Cometes and Antigone; Polyphemus, son of Eilatus and Hippea; Iphiclus, son of Phylacus and Clymene; Admetus, son of Pheres and Periclymene; Erytus and Echion, sons of Hermes and Antianeira; Aethalides, son of Hermes and Eupolemeia; Coronus, son of Caenus; Mopsus, son of Ampycus and Chloris; Eurydamas, son of Ctimenus; Menoetius, son of Actor and Aegina; Eurytion, son of Irus and Demonassa; Eribotes, son of Teleon; Oileus, son of Hodoedocus and Agrianome; Canthus, son of Canethus; Clytius and Iphitus, sons of Eurytus; Telamon and Peleus, sons of Aeacus and Endeis or Creusa; Butes, son of Teleon or Poseidon and Zeuxippe; Phalerus, son of Alcon; Tiphys (the pilot of the Argo), son of Hagnias or Phorbas and Hyrmina; Phlias, son of Dionysus or Ceisus and Araethyrea; Talaus, Leodocus and Areius, sons of Bias and Pero; Heracles, son of Zeus and Alcmene; Hylas, son of Theiodamas and Menodice; Nauplius, son of Clytoneus; Idmon, son of Apollo or Abas and Cyrene or Asteria; Castor and Polydeuces, sons of Leda by Tyndareus and Zeus; Lynceus and Idas, sons of Aphareus and Arene; Periclymenus, son of Neleus and Chloris; Amphidamas and Cepheus, sons of Aleus and Neaera; Ancaeus, son of Lycurgus and Cleophyle or Eurynome; Augeias, son of Poseidon or Phorbas and Hyrmina; Amphicn and Asterius, sons of Hyperasius; Euphemus, son of Poseidon and Europa; Erginus and Ancaeus, sons of Poseidon and Astypalea; Meleager, son of Oeneus or Ares and Althaea; Laocoon, son of Oeneus and a servant; Iphiclus, son of Thestius; Palaemon, son of Hephaestus or Lernus; Iphitus, son of Naubolus; Calais and Zetes, sons of Boreas and Oreithyia; Acastus, son of Pelias and Anaxibia or Phylomache.

Argonauts named by other authors included Actor, son of Hippasus; Autolycus, son of Deimachus; Ascalaphus and Ialmenus, sons of Ares; Caeneus, father of Phocus and Priasus; Deileon, son of Deimachus; Deucalion, son of Minos; Elatus and Glaucus; Hippalcimus, son of Itonus; Laertes, son of Arceisius and Chalcomedusa; Leitus, son of Alector and Cleobule; Penelaus, son of Hippalcimus and Asterope; Phalerus, son of Alcon; Phanus, son of Dionysus and Ariadne; Philoctetes, son of Poeas and Demonassa; Phocus and Priasus, sons of Caeneus; and Staphylus, son of Dionysus and Ariadne. Herald to the Argonauts was Aethalides, son of Hermes and Eupolemeia. Aesculapius was their physician.

ARGOS Principal town of Argolis. Among the kings of Argos were Inachus (first, reigned for sixty years), Phoroneus (second), Apis (third), Argus (fourth, reigned for seventy years and eponym of the town), Abas, Bias, Talaus, Temenus, Ceisus, Medon and through ten generations to Meltas who was deposed; Cyanippus, Cylarabes, Orestes, Iphis, Sthenelus, Acrisius, Adrastus, Agamemnon, Agenor, Gelanor, Alector, Anaxagoras, Danaus, Lynceus, Pelasgus, Melampus, Tisamenus, Crotopus, Megapenthes, Ceisus and the last king of Argos, Meltas. The citadel of Argos was called Larisa.

ARGUS King of Argos. Son of Zeus and Niobe, daughter of Phoroneus. Was the first son of Zeus by a mortal. Brother of Osiris, Pelasgus and Typhon. Married Evadne. Father of Criasus, Ecbasus, Epidaurus and Peiras. He was possibly the father of Phorbas and Tiryns (Tirynx).

The town of Argos was named after him, and he reigned for seventy years. Argus introduced grain cultivation to the town.

ARGUS Eldest son of Phrixus and Chalciope. Brother of Cytissorus, Melas, Presbon and Phrontis. Possibly the father of Magnes by Perimele.

He escaped from the court of his grandfather, Aeetes, but was shipwrecked and then rescued by the Argonauts. He persuaded Aeetes to give Jason the golden fleece.

ARGUS Son of Jason and Medea. Brother of Alcimenes, Eriopis, Medeias, Pheres, Mermerus, Thessalus and Tisandrus. He was murdered, possibly by his mother.

ARGUS An Argonaut and Thespian. Son of Argeia. Builder of the Argo.

ARGUS (1) The name of one of Actaeon's dogs. (2) The name of Odysseus' faithful dog. On Odysseus' return, after 20 years, the dog recognised him, and then died. (3) Possibly a son of Agenor.

ARGUS PANOPTES One hundred eyes, only two of which closed together. Born of the earth (Gaea), or a son of Inachus or Agenor. Possibly the father of Iasus, by Ismene. Slayer of Echidna and guardian of Io, whom Zeus had turned into a white heifer at Hera's insistence. Argus Panoptes was killed by Hermes, and Hera saw to it that his eyes were placed in the peacock's tail.

ARGYRIPA A town at Apulia, built by Diomedes after the Trojan War.

ARIADNE Daughter of Minos and

Ariadne and Dionysus

Pasiphae. Sister of Acacallis, Androgeus, Catreus, Deucalion, Euryale, Glaucus, Lycastus, Phaedra and Xenodice. She was first married to Theseus, who may have fathered some of her children, and who deserted her soon after their marriage on the isle of Naxos (Dia). Theseus had married her after she had helped him to escape from the labyrinth with the aid of a ball of thread. Married Dionysus. Mother of Ceramus, Peparethus, Phanus and Thoas by Dionysus, and possibly Oenopion and Staphylus, though most agree that their father was Theseus.

Daedalus built a dance floor for her at Cnossus. There are many traditions relating to Ariadne's death. Some say that she died heartbroken when deserted by Theseus, others that she was killed by Artemis as she gave birth to twin sons. Alternatively, she may have been killed during a fight between Dionysus and Perseus.

Dionysus set the crown he gave her at their marriage in the stars as the 'corona borealis'.

ARICIA An ancient town south-east of Rome where there was a sacred grove of Diana. Here the priest was always a murderer – killing his predecessor.

ARIES (the ram) First sign of the zodiac. Represents the ram with the golden fleece.

ARIMASPI One-eyed horsemen, inhabitants of the Scythian steppes, neighbours of the Hyperboreans. They lived near a golden stream, Arimaspias, and fought continually with griffins who collected gold from the stream, and were conquered by Alexander the Great.

ARION of Methymna 8th-7th century BC. Lyric poet, the first to use the dithyramb, and musician, who played the cithara. The crew of a ship carrying him back to the court of Periander of Corinth, from Sicily, after his having won many prizes in competitions, threw him overboard, but he was rescued by a dolphin.

ARION A fabulous horse. Son of Poseidon and Demeter who conceived him after both had become horses. Arion's right feet were human; and his harness-mate was Caerus. He could talk and this saved Adrastus' life at Thebes.

ARISBAS (1) Father of Molurus, murdered for adultery. (2) Father of Leiocritus.

ARISBE Daughter of Merops. Sister of Amphius, Adrastus and Cleite. Became the first wife of Priam. Mother of Aesacus. Later married Hyrtacus. Mother of Asius.

ARISBE (Bateia) Daughter of Teucer. Wife of Dardanus. Mother of Erichthonius and Ilus.

ARISTEAS An epic poet said to be inspired by Apollo. The accounts of his life are fabulous. His father owned a fuller's shop in the land of the Hyperboreans, and when Aristeas died, he disappeared. 340 years later his ghost appeared, commanding the people of Metapontus to raise an altar to Apollo.

ARISTAEUS Protector of beekeepers. Son of Apollo and Cyrene. Brother of Autychus. Married Autonoe, daughter of Cadmus. Father of Actaeon and Macris, and probably others.

His fondness for hunting obtained for him the names Nomus and Agreus. Born in Libya, he was raised by the Horae and, as a god, fed on nectar. Worked as a bee keeper, cheese maker and olive grower, and was the inventor of book-keeping. Aristaeus fell in love with Eurydice, but when fleeing his pursuing bees she was killed by a snake, as a result of which the gods killed all his bees. His mother told him to seek the advice of the sea god, Proteus, who instructed him to sacrifice cattle in Eurydice's memory. He then found new swarms of bees in the carcasses. He disappeared near Mt Haemus.

ARISTODEMUS A Heraclid. Son of Aristomachus. Brother of Cresphontes and Temenus. Married Argeia. Father of twin sons, Eurysthenes and Procles. Killed by a thunderbolt, or one of Apollo's arrows.

ARISTOMACHUS (1) Son of Cleodaeus. Father of Aristodemus, Cresphontes and Temenus. Killed in an unsuccessful attempt to conquer Peloponnesus. (2) A beekeeper for 58 years. (3) Son of Talaus and Lysimache. Father or brother of Hippomedon and brother of Adrastus, Astynome, Eriphyle, Mecisteus, Metidice, Parthenopaeus and Pronax.

ARISTOPHANES 5th–4th century BC Greek writer of old comedy, the only one of whom any entire works are left. His comedies, about forty in number, include *The Birds*, *The Frogs* and *The Wasps*.

ARISTOTELES Original name of Battus, son of Polymnestus and Phronime.

ARMILUSTRIUM A Roman festival of Mars. A purification of arms at the end of the fighting season. Celebrated on 19 October.

ARNAEUS The errand boy (later a beggar called Irus) of Penelope's suitors at the palace of Odysseus.

ARNE (Melanippe) Daughter of Aeolus and Hippe or Enarete. Sister of seven boys: Athamas, Cretheus, Deion, Macareus, Perieres, Salmoneus and Sisyphus, and of six girls: Alcyone, Calyce, Canace, Peisidice, Perimele and Tanagra. Mother of Aeolus II and Boeotus by Poseidon during the time he had the shape of a bull.

AROE Town on the Gulf of Patrae.

ARSINOE (Alphesiboea) (1) Daughter of Phegeus. First wife of Alcmeon. Mother of Clytius. After her brothers murdered Alcmeon, she was sold as a slave to Agapenor. (2) Daughter of Leucippus and Philodice. Sister of Hilaera and Phoebe. Mother of Eriopis by Apollo. It was sometimes said that it was she, and not Coronis,

who was the mother of Asclepius by Apollo, but it was denied by the Oracle at Delphi. (3) Orestes' nurse who allowed her son to be killed by Clytemnestra in place of Orestes.

ARSIPPE Daughter of Minyas. Sister of Alcithoe and Leucippe.

All three sisters refused to partake in the mysteries of Dionysus and were driven mad; and after killing Hippasus, son of Leucippe, were turned into bats. Arsippe had two other sisters, Clymene and Periclymene.

ARTACIA A spring in the land of the Laestrygones where the companions of Odysseus met the daughter of Antiphates.

ARTEMIS (Diana) The moon goddess, goddess of hunting. Daughter of Zeus and Leto. Sister of Apollo.

She and her companions were all avowed virgins. She is represented with a bent bow and quiver, attended with dogs, and sometimes in a chariot drawn by two white stags.

Epithets: 1. Auge, an Arcadian epithet. 2. Caryatis, the reporter of the death of Carya. 3. Lucina, the Roman goddess of childbirth. 4. Phoebe, the moon goddess. She was also called Cynthia, Delia, Hecate, Luna and Selene. As a supporter of the Trojans in the War, she withheld the wind to try to prevent the Greeks reaching Troy.

ARUNS Son of Tarquinius Superbus and Tanaquil. Brother of Lucius Tarquinius. Married Tullia, daughter of Servius Tullius. A mild man, Aruns was killed by his violent and ambitious wife.

ARUNS The soldier who killed Camilla and was slain by a dart of Artemis.

ARYBAS A native of Sidon whose daughter was abducted by pirates.

ASAEUS A Greek, slain in the Trojan War by Hector.

ASCALABUS A rude boy who was

turned into a lizard for making fun of Demeter.

ASCALAPHUS Son of the river god Acheron and Gorgyra or Orphne. After he had spied on Persephone, watching her eat pomegranate seeds that prevented her from leaving the lower world, Demeter turned him into an owl.

ASCALAPHUS Argonaut and co-ruler of Orchomenus. Son of Ares and Astyoche. Brother of Ialmenus. A suitor of Helen, he took thirty ships to Troy with his brother. He was killed by Deiphobus.

ASCANIUS (Ilus, Iulus, Julus) Son of Aeneas and Creusa. Traditional ancestor of Julius Caesar.

Succeeded his father to the throne of Lavinium and founded Alba Longa, mother city of Rome. His descendants ruled for 420 years, ending with Numitor. Ascanius took part in the First Trojan War Game (Lusus Troianus).

ASCANIUS Son of Hippotion. Brother of Morys. Eponym of Ascania.

ASCLEPIUS (Aesculapius) Greek god of healing. Son of Apollo and Coronis or, possibly, Arsinoe. Saved from the flames of his mother, destroyed for infidelity. Married Epione, daughter of Merops. Father of sons Machaon and Podalirius and daughters Acesis (remedy), Aegle, Iaso (cure), Janiscus, Hygieia (health) and Panacea (all-healing). All are probably personifications of his own powers. Cheiron taught him medicine and he was the physician of the Argonauts. He was a deified mortal. Zeus killed him with a thunderbolt, because he feared men might try to escape death altogether, and set him among the stars as Serpentarius the snake-bearer. His staff with coiled snakes is used to this day as a symbol of the medical profession.

ASIA An oceanid. Daughter of Oceanus and Tethys. Sister of many, including Callirrhoe, Clymene, Clytis, Europa, Perseis

and Styx. Either she or Clymene was the mother of Atlas, Epimetheus, Menoetius and Prometheus by Iapetos.

ASIA Another name for Hesione, the wife of Prometheus.

ASIUS (1) Son of Dymas, king of Phrygia and Evagora or Glaucippe. Brother of Hecuba. Father of Adamas. An ally of the Trojans who led the Phrygians in the Trojan War. Killed by Ajax. (2) Son of Hyrtacus and Arisbe. He led the allies of Troy from the cities bordering the Hellespont, but was killed by Idomeneus. (3) Follower of Aeneas on his journey from Troy.

ASOPIA (Sicyonia), kings of. Aloeus, Epopeus and Helius.

ASOPUS A river god. Son of Oceanus and Tethys. Brother of the other river gods. Married Metope, daughter of Ladon. Father of Ismenus, Pelagon and Pelasgus and of twenty daughters, including Aegina, Antiope, Ismenus, Cleone, Corcyra, Ismene, Metope, Plataea, Salamis and Thebe. When Zeus abducted Aegina, Asopus pursued them but was driven back by Zeus' thunderbolts. Charcoal was found in the riverbed for centuries, believed to be from thunderbolts.

ASOPUS Son of Poseidon and Eurynome. Brother of Bellerophon.

ASPARAGUS *See* Ioxus, Perigune.

ASPHODEL The flower of Hades, possibly a daffodil, more likely a weed.

ASPHODEL FIELDS The meadow of the dead, inhabited by Achilles, Agamemnon, Odysseus and Patroclus.

ASPHODICUS Another name for Amphidocus, son of Astacus.

ASS *See* Ocnus.

ASSARACUS A Trojan leader. Son of Tros and Callirrhoe. Brother of Cleopatra, Ilus and Ganymedes. Married Hieromneme. Father of Capys. Ancestor of Aeneas.

ASSES' EARS *See* Midas.

ASTACUS of Thebes Father of Amphidocus (Asphodicus), Ismarus, Leades and Melanippus.

ASTERIA Daughters of titans Phoebe and Ceus (Coeus). Sister of Leto. Married Perses. Mother of Hecate. Drowned herself and became a quail. Island of Delos (Asteria) named after her.

ASTERIA One of the fifty daughters of Danaus.

ASTERIE Daughter of Atlas. Either she or Cyrene was the mother of Diomedes of Thrace.

ASTERION A river god. Son of Oceanus and Tethys. With Cephissus and Inachus, he was a judge in the contest between Poseidon and Hera for the patronage of Argos.
The river Asterion was in Peloponnesus.

ASTERION (Asterius) An Argonaut. Thessalian son of Cometes and Antigone, daughter of Pheres.

ASTERIUS (1) Pellenian son of Hyperasius or Hippasus. Brother of Amphion. An Argonaut. (2) An Argonaut. *See* Asterion. (3) Son of Minos and Pasiphae, or of Tectamus and a daughter of Cretheus. King of Crete. Married Europa. Father of Crete. Adopted Minos, Rhadamanthys and Sarpedon, sons of Europa and Zeus. (4) Another name for the Minotaur, the strongest creature of his age.

ASTERODEIA A nymph. First wife of Aeetes and mother of Chalciope.

ASTEROPAEUS Son of Pelagon. Killed in the Trojan War by Achilles.

ASTEROPE Epithet of Sterope, one of the Pleiades. Daughter of Atlas and Pleione. Wife of Oenomaus, though perhaps his mother.

ASTEROPE The wife of Hippalcimus and mother of Penelaus.

ASTEROPE Daughter of river god Cebren. Married Aesacus.

ASTEROPEIA (1) Daughter of Deion and Diomede. Sister of Actor, Aenetus, Cephalus and Phylacus. (2) Epithet of Periboea, the wife of Icarius and mother of Penelope.

ASTIOCHE *See* Axioche.

ASTRAEA Goddess of justice. Daughter of Zeus and Themis. Sister of the Moerae and the Horae. She is sometimes called Dike, as is one of the Horae.
She left the earth during the Golden Age, to avoid the evils of mortals that occurred during the bronze and iron ages, and was placed among the stars as Virgo. She is represented as a virgin holding a pair of scales.

ASTRAEUS A Titan, son of Crius and Eurybia. Brother of Pallas and Perses. Consorted with Eos to produce the winds, Boreas, Hesperus, Notus, Phosphorus, Zephyrus, possibly Aura, and all the stars. Warred against Zeus.

ASTYAGIA Daughter of Hypseus, king of Thessaly. Sister of Cyrene, Stilbe and Themisto. Married Periphas. Mother of eight sons, the eldest being Antion.

ASTYANAX (Scamandrus) Son of Hector and Andromache. He should have become king of Troy but was killed as a child by being thrown from the walls of Troy because Odysseus warned that no descendant of Priam should survive. According to Euripides, he was killed by Menelaus but, according to Seneca, it was Pyrrhus that carried out the deed. A few sources even claim that he survived to become king.

ASTYDAMEIA (Deidameia) Daughter of Amyntor and Cleobule. Sister of Crantor and Phoenix. Some sources make her the mother of Ctesippus and Tlepolemus by Heracles.

ASTYDAMEIA Daughter of Pelops and Hippodameia. Sister of Alcathous, Atreus, Chrysippus, Copreus, Lysidice, Nicippe, Pittheus, Thyestes and Troezen. Married Acastus. Mother of Laodameia, Sterope, Sthenele and unnamed sons. Some say she fell in love with Peleus who ignored her. This caused her to seek vengeance. Others add that she was later killed by Peleus who cut up her body.

ASTYELES Father of Euthymus, though this was possibly Caecinus.

ASTYNOME Daughter of Talaus and Lysimache or Lysianassa. Sister of Adrastus, Aristomachus, Eriphyle, Hippomedon, Mecisteus, Metidice, Parthenopaeus and Pronax. Married Hipponous. Mother of Capaneus and Periboea. Also mother of Calydon and Periboea by Ares.

ASTYNOUS Son of Phaethon.

ASTYOCHE (1) Daughter of Laomedon and Strymo, or daughter of Actor and, if so, sister of Cilla, Clytius, Hesione, Hicetaon, Lampus, Priam and Tithonus. Mother of Ascalaphus and Ialmenus by Ares. (2) Daughter of Simoeis, the river god. Sister of Hieromneme. Married Erichthonius. Mother of Tros. (3) Daughter of Crisus. Sister of Strophius and possibly Anaxibia. (4) Daughter of Phylas. Mother of Tlepolemus by Heracles who had seduced her. Possibly mother of Eurpylus by Telephus.

ASTYPALEA (1) Daughter of Phoenix and Perimede. Sister of Europa. Mother of Ancaeus and Eurypylus by Poseidon. She gave her name to: (2) An island of the south-east Cyclades.

ASTYPYLUS A Trojan killed in the War by Achilles.

ATALANTA A virgin huntress. Daughter of Iasus and Clymene.

An outstanding sportswoman, she was the heroine of the Calydonian Boar Hunt and was the first to wound the boar. As a baby she was disowned by her father but was suckled by a bear sent by Artemis. Atalanta had many suitors whom she forced to race with her and when they inevitably lost she killed them, as instructed by an oracle. She wrestled with and defeated Peleus, and slew the centaurs Hylaeus and Rhoecus, when they tried to attack her. It was said that Melanion or Hippomenes won and married her by the trick of dropping golden apples and disracting her during the race. They became the parents of Parthenopaeus. Both were turned into lions for making love in a place sacred to Zeus. (Cf next entry.)

ATALANTA of Boeotia Daughter of Schoeneus, king of Scyros. She married Hippomenes (Melanion), after previously wanting to remain a virgin. This character is often confused with Atalanta, daughter of Iasus.

ATALANTA Daughter of Maenalus.

ATE According to Hesiod, daughter of Zeus and Eris. She was the goddess of evil, mischief and infatuation, and the personification of moral blindness. Was banished from heaven for raising sedition and jealousy.

ATHAMAS According to various traditions, king of Achaea, Orchomenus, Phthiotis, Thebes. Son of Aeolus and Enarete. He had six brothers: Cretheus, Deion, Macareus, Perieres, Salmoneus and Sisyphus; and seven sisters: Alcyone, Arne,

Calyce, Canace, Peisidice, Perimele and Tanagra. He married three times. By his first wife, the nymph Nephele, he was father of Helle and Phrixus; by Ino, he was father of Learchus and Melicertes; by his third wife, Themisto, his children were Erythrius, Leucon, Ptous and Schoeneus. All these children, except Leucon and Learchus, were accidentally killed by Themisto. Athamas himself killed Learchus after mistaking him for a stag. For this he was exiled to Thessaly which he renamed Athamantia.

ATHENA (Minerva) Greek goddess of war, wisdom and the liberal arts. Daughter of Zeus. Metis became pregnant with Athena and Zeus swallowed her. Athena was then born, armed and fully grown, out of Zeus' head. Possibly mother of the Corybantes by Apollo or Helios.

She lived on Olympus and at the Acropolis of Athens. Her sacred tree was the olive.

Epithets: 1. Pallas Athena 2. Parthenia 3. Parthenos (virgin goddess) 4. Polymetis (resourceful) 5. Promachus (protectress) 6. Mechanitis (patroness of undertakings) 7. Soteira 8. Tritogeneia (thrice born).

She was the patroness of Athens and many benefited from her help. 1. She gave a magic bridle to Bellerophon. 2. Helped Perseus to kill Medusa. 3. Taught Argus to build the Argo. 4. Taught Danaus to build a two-prowed ship. 5. Helped Epeius to build the wooden horse. 6. Gave dragons' teeth to Cadmus and Aeetes for them to sow in the ground. 7. Helped Heracles many times, and also Diomedes, Odysseus and Tydeus. She sided with the more civilised Greeks in the Trojan War.

ATHENA NIKE Temple of the Acropolis, dedicated to Athena, goddess of victory.

ATHENA PARTHENOS The name of a gold and ivory statue made by Phidias.

ATHENS (Attica), kings of Actaeus, Cecrops, Cranaus, Amphictyon, Ericht-

Athena

honius, Pandion, Aegeus, Theseus, Demophoon, Thymoetes, Melanthus, Codrus. Some alternatives to this sequence were as follows: Cecrops, not Actaeus, was the first king; Pandion was followed by Erechtheus; next came a second Cecrops and a second Pandion; Acamas was possibly a joint ruler with Demophoon; and Menestheus ruled Athens during the absence of Theseus; Xuthus was a possible ruler; and the last king was called Medon.

ATLANTIADES The children of Atlas, essentially the Hyades and the Pleiades.

ATLANTIDES (Pleiades) The seven daughters of Atlas and Pleione: Alcyone, Celaeno, Electra (Eudora), Maia, Merope, Sterope (Asterope) and Taygete.

ATLANTIS The mythical island-home of an advanced culture that disappeared beneath a giant tidal wave. Although many place it in mid-Atlantic, it is now generally considered to be the volcanic Mediterranean island of Santorini that destroyed Cnossus.

ATLAS King of Mauretania and master of 1000 flocks of every kind, and of beautiful fruit trees. Titan son of Iapetos and Clymene or Asia. Brother of Epimetheus, Menoetius and Prometheus. Married Pleione. Father of the Hesperides, Pleiades, and Hyades, and Hyas, Calypso and Asterie. Father of Dione. Some call Hesperis mother of the Hesperides. He supported the Titans against Zeus and was punished by having to carry the weight of the world on his shoulders. Later he was tricked into giving Heracles three Golden Apples. Perseus eventually turned him to stone.

ATREUS King of Mycenae. Son of Pelops and Hippodameia. Brother of Alcathous, Astydameia, Chrysippus, Copreus, Lysidice, Nicippe, Pittheus, Thyestes and Troezen, and perhaps others. Married Aerope. Father of Agamemnon and Menelaus. Possibly father of Anaxibia and Pleisthenes.

Sources differ as to whether Atreus or Thyestes married Pelopia, an exiled daughter of Thyestes. If Thyestes married her, then he was following the instructions of an oracle which informed him that if he were to marry his daughter the issue would avenge him on Atreus (Thyestes had been fed a meal of his own sons by Atreus, after the latter learnt of Thyestes' union with Aerope). If Atreus married Pelopia then he did so thinking her to be the daughter of Thesprotus. In this case she was already pregnant by Thyestes at the time of her marriage with Atreus. Thus it was a son of Thyestes and Pelopia, Aegisthus, who killed Atreus.

ATRIDAE Generic name of Agamemnon and Menelaus, sons of Atreus.

ATROPOS (the unbending) One of the Moirae. Daughter of Zeus and Themis. Sister of Clotho and Lachesis. She carried shears to cut the threads of life.

ATTHIS Daughter of Cranaus and Pedias. Sister of Cranae. Married Hephaestus. Mother of Erichthonius. Attica is named after her.

ATTICA The Greek peninsula which includes Athens and Eleusis.

ATTIS (Atys) Son of Nana and a fallen almond that had grown from the severed genitals of Agdistis. Attis was the consort of the Phrygian goddess, Cybele. When he castrated himself, he became a pine tree.

ATYMNIUS Son of Amisodaurus. Brother of Maris. Killed in the Trojan War by Antilochus.

ATYMNIUS Son of Zeus and Cassiopeia. Either he or Miletus was the lover of Minos.

ATYS Alternative spelling of Attis.

AUGE An Arcadian princess. Daughter of Aleus and Neaera. Sister of Amphidamas,

Cepheus and Lycurgus. Married Teuthras, after being sold to him as a slave by Nauplius. Mother of Argiope. Mother of Telephus by Heracles.

AUGE Goddess of childbirth. Arcadian epithet of Artemis.

AUGEIAN STABLES Contained 3000 cattle and remained uncleaned for thirty years until Heracles tackled the task as his sixth labour. He diverted the rivers Alpheus and Peneus to achieve this.

AUGEIAS King of Elis. Son of Phorbas or Poseidon and Hyrmina, although some claim his parents to be Helios and Naupiadame. Brother of Actor, Tiphys and, possibly, Phyleus, though probably. father of the latter. Father of Agamede and Eurytus. Probably father, rather than brother, of Agasthenes. An Argonaut and the owner of the Augeian stables, Heracles killed him when he refused to pay for their cleaning.

AULIS Port of Boeotia. 1116 ships of the Athenians, Boeotians, Lacedaemonians and Locrians were becalmed in this port on their way to the Trojan War, until Agamemnon sacrificed his daughter Iphigeneia to appease Artemis.

AULUS Son of Ogygus. Brother of Alalcomenia and Thelxinoea in Boeotian tradition. Brother of Eleusis in Attic tradition.

AURA Goddess of breezes. Daughter of Eos and, possibly, Astraeus.

AURORA Roman goddess of the dawn. Daughter of Uranus and Gaea or of Hyperion and Theia. Greek equivalent: Eos. She had a passionate love affair with Tithonus. Mother of Emathion and Memnon.

AUSON Son of Odysseus and Calypso. Eponym of Ausonia, the ancient name for Italy.

AUSTER (Notus) The south-west wind.

AUTESION Son of Tisamenus. Father of Argeia and Theras.

AUTOLAUS Bastard son of Arcas. Half-brother to Azan, Apheidas, Elatus and Hyperippe.

AUTOLYCUS A mythical thief. Son of Hermes and Chione. Married Amphithea. Father of several sons and Anticleia. An Argonaut. He taught Heracles to wrestle; seized Amyntor's helmet and stole cattle, changing the colour of their identity marks.

AUTOLYCUS An Argonaut. Son of Deimachus. Brother of Deileon and Phlogius. Married Neaera. Father of Polymede.

AUTOMEDON Charioteer of Achilles and Pyrrhus. Son of Diores. He took ten ships to the Trojan War, where he slew Ares. After Achilles' death he fought beside Pyrrhus (Neoptolemus).

AUTOMEDUSA Daughter of Alcathous and Evaechme. Sister of Callipolis, Iphinoe, Ischepolis and Periboea. First wife of Iphicles and mother of Iolaus.

AUTONOE Daughter of Cadmus and Harmonia. Sister of Agave, Illyrius, Ino, Polydorus and Semele. Married Aristaeus. Mother of Actaeon and Macris and probably others. Dionysus drove her and her sisters mad as punishment for tormenting Semele.

AUTONOUS A Greek slain in the Trojan War by Hector.

AUTOPHONUS The father of Polyphontes.

AUTYCHUS Son of Apollo and Cyrene. Brother of Aristaeus. Succeeded his mother to the throne of the city of Cyrene, in Libya.

AVENTINE One of the seven hills of Rome. The others were: Caelian, Capitoline, Esquiline, Palatine, Quirinal and Viminal.

AVENTINUS Son of Heracles and a priestess of Rhea. Supported Turnus against Aeneas.

AVERNUS Sulphurous holy lake near Cumae (which was in the Naples region), an entrance to Hades, entrusted to the care of the Sibyl. Aeneas entered Hades through one of its caves.

AXINE (Euxine) The Black or Friendly Sea.

AXIOCHE Either she or Astioche was the mother of Chrysippus by Pelops.

AXION (1) Son of Priam, killed by Eurypylus. (2) Possibly, son of Phegeus.

AXIOTHEA Another name for Hesione, wife of Prometheus.

AXIUS A river god of Macedonia, son of Oceanus and Tethys. Father of Pelegon by Periboea.

AZAN Son of Arcas and Erato. Brother of Apheidas, Erato and Hyperippe. Half-brother of Autolaus. First to have funeral games celebrated in his honour.

AZEUS Son of Clymenus. Brother of Erginus.

B

BABYLON Son of Belus. Brother of Ninus. Eponym of the city.

BACCHAE (Bacchants) Followers of Dionysus.

BACCHANALIA Festivals of Dionysus, introduced to the Greek colonies of Italy and to Rome itself, towards the end of the third century BC.

BACCHANTS (Bacchanals) Female votaries of Dionysus, also called Maenads or Bacchae.

BACCHUS (Liber) Greek god of wine. Son of Zeus and Semele. Also called Dionysus (qv) and Liber by the Romans. His name is derived from Lydia, whence came Dionysus. Also called Iacchus at the Athenian festivals. Bacchus married Ariadne and had many children. According to Milton, father of Comus by Circe (Marica).

BALIUS Immortal horse of Achilles. Son of Boreas and the Harpy, Podarge. Brother of Xanthus, his partner.

BASSARIDES Followers of Dionysus.

BAT See Alcithoe, Arsippe and Leucippe.

BATEIA Mother of the Trojan race. Daughter of Teucer, king of Phrygia. Married Dardanus. Mother of Erichthonius and Ilus, grandmother of Tros, eponym of Troy.

BATEIA A Naiad. Either she or Gorgophone was the mother of Hippocoon, Icarius and Tyndareus, by Oebalus.

BATHYCLES Son of Chalcon. Killed in the Trojan War by Glaucus. A Myrmidon.

BATON (Elato) Charioteer of Amphi-araus, who accompanied him to the war of the Seven against Thebes. Man and master were engulfed together by a thunderbolt from Zeus.

BATTLES, mother of Eris (Discordia).

BATTUS (Aristoteles) King of Cyrene. Son of Polymnestus, a Theraean noble, and Phronime, daughter of Etearchus. Father of Arcesilaus. Battus reigned for forty years and was succeeded by his son. There followed six generations of descendants who bore alternating names.

As the result of a Delphic oracle, Battus founded the city of Cyrene in Libya. He was a stammerer (his name means 'stammer'), but was cured when frightened by a lion.

BATTUS Cowherd of Neleus from Pylos. Hermes turned him to stone after he had broken a promise not to tell Apollo that Hermes had stolen his cattle.

BAUCIS Elderly peasant-woman of Bithynia. With her husband, Philemon, she offered refuge to Zeus and Hermes after others had rejected them. For this action, they escaped the Flood, and their humble cottage was turned into a marble temple with a golden roof. When they died, they were transformed into an oak and a linden tree before the doors of the temple.

BEAR See Callisto.

BEAR, Great (Ursa Major) See Arcas.

BEAR, Little (Ursa Minor) See Callisto.

BEAR MOUNTAIN The mountainous peninsula on the Mysian coast of the Sea of Marmara, inhabited by six-armed monsters which were killed by the Argonauts and Heracles.

BEAUTY, Roman goddess of Hora Quirini.

BEBRYCES Warlike Mysian tribe. They

and their king, Amycus, inhabited the eastern end of the Sea of Marmara.

BEE *See* Melissa.

BEES, Greek god and protector of Priapus.

BEETLE *See* Cerambus.

BEGINNINGS, Roman god of Janus.

BELLEROPHON (Hipponous) (1) Son of Glaucus and Eurymede. Brother of Deliades. Lover of Stheneboea (Anteia). Married Philinoe. Father of Deidameia, Hippolochus, Isander and Laodameia. Slayer of the Chimaera, he was one of the seven great slayers of monsters (qv). Conqueror of the Amazons and the Solymi. He was exiled from Ephyra for accidentally killing Bellerus, tyrant of Corinth, or his brother. Bellerophon captured Pegasus and used him on many of his adventures. When he tried to fly the wonder horse to heaven, the gods sent a gadfly to sting Pegasus, thus killing Bellerophon when he was flung to the earth (although Homer claims that he survived the ordeal and wandered around, blind, lame and friendless).
(2) Son of Poseidon and Eurynome. Brother of Asopus.

BELLERUS Tyrant of Corinth. Possibly killed by Bellerophon.

BELLONA Roman goddess of war. Often identified with Enyo, she was the sister, wife or friend of Mars or Quirinus. Her festival date: 3 June. Her temple in Rome was used to welcome foreign ambassadors.

BELUS King of the Egyptians. Son of Poseidon and Libya. Twin brother of Agenor and brother of Lelex. Married Anchinoe. Father of Aegyptus, Danaus and Thronia, and possibly the father of Cepheus and Phineus and of Lamia, by his mother, and of Babylon and Ninus (but their father may have been a different Belus).

BELUS Son of Phoenix.

BELUS Possibly father (alternatively, Agenor) of Dido, Anna and Pygmalion.

BENTHESICYME Daughter of Poseidon and Amphitrite. Sister of Albion, Charybdis, Rhode and Triton. Married an Ethiopian king and bore two daughters. She reared Eumolpus, son of Chione.

BERENICE A beautiful woman who married her own brother.

BEROE (1) Name adopted by Iris when she advised the Trojans to burn their ships. (2) An old woman of Epidaurus, nurse to Semele, possibly the mother of Dionysus by Zeus. Juno assumed her shape when she persuaded Semele not to succumb to Jupiter.

BIA (force) Daughter of the Titan, Pallas, and of Styx. Sister of Kratos, Nike and Zelos. Some sources call her a boy.
She was always at Zeus' side. Hephaestus made her bind Prometheus to a rock to punish him for stealing fire from the gods.

BIADICE Either she or Demodice was the wife of Cretheus, king of Iolcus.

BIAS King of Argos. Son of Amythaon and Idomene. Brother of Aeolia, Melampus and Perimele. Married first to Pero. Father of Areius, Leodocus and Talaus, and possibly Alphesiboea, Aretus and Perialces. Some call Aeolia his daughter. His second wife, daughter of Proetus, was Iphianassa, by whom he fathered Anaxibia.

BIAS One of the Seven Wise Men of Greece (qv), the others being Chilon, Cleobulus, Periander, Pittacus, Solon and Thales.

BIAS Father of Dardanus and Laogonus.

BIBLIS (Byblis) Daughter of Miletus and Cyanee. Sister of Caunus. When she fell in love with her brother, she was changed into a fountain.

BIRDS, expert on Halitherses, the Ithacan seer.

BIRDS, unnamed *See* Caeneus, Calais, Polycaste, Zetes.

BIRTH, Roman god of Genius.

BISTONIANS (Bistones) A Thracian tribe. Inhabitants of the southern shore of Thrace; their capital was Abdera.

BITHYNIA Area of north-west Asia Minor, bordering the Black Sea and the Sea of Marmara. Formerly called Bebrycia. Home of Baucis and Philemon.

BITON Son of Cydippe, Hera's priestess at Argos. Brother of Cleobis. With his brother he pulled their mother's chariot when she had no oxen, and for this deed was rewarded with the highest gift given to mortals, that of eternal sleep.

BODY ORGANS, goddess of Carna. She was also goddess of hinges.

BOEOTIA Greek province. Capital: Thebes.

BOEOTUS Son of Poseidon and Arne (Melanippe). Brother of Aeolus. Father of Itonus.

BOETIS A goat. Either she or Aex was the mother of Aegipan by Zeus.

BONA DEA Obscure Roman goddess of fertility. Her real name was Fauna, and she was worshipped only by women. Her festival date was 4 December at which time there were secret rites. After she married Faunus, no man ever set eyes on her except her husband. Associated with Cybele, Fatua, Ops, Rhea and Vesta.

BOREADES The sons of Boreas.

BOREAS (Aquilo) The north wind. Son of Eos and Astraeus. Had many offspring. 1. Father of the horses of Ares, by one of the Erinnyes. 2. Father of the horses of Erechtheus, by one of the Harpies. 3. Father of the immortal horses of Achilles, Balius and Xanthus, by the Harpy, Podarge. 4. Father of twelve fast horses by the twelve mares of Dardanus. 5. Father of twelve foals by a mare of Danaus (although several of these may be doublets). Boreas was renowned as a father of horses because of their speed. Father of Butes. He abducted Oreithyia and by her became the father of Calais and Zetes, Chione, Cleopatra and Haemus.

BORUS Son of Perieres and Gorgophone. Brother of Aphareus, Icarius, Leucippus and Tyndareus. Married Polydora. Stepfather of Menesthius, Polydora's son by Spercheius.

BOSPHORUS Two narrow straits that connect the Black Sea and the Sea of Marmara, and separate Europe from Asia. The Argonauts passed through it.

BOUNDARIES, Roman god of Terminus.

BRAESIA Daughter of Cinyras of Cyprus. Sister of Laogore, Mygdalion and Orsedice. After having an affair with a stranger in Cyprus, she emigrated to Egypt.

BREADMAKING, Roman god of Fornax.

BREEZES, goddess of Aura.

BRIAREUS One of the Hecatoncheiroi, the Hundred-handed. Son of Uranus and Gaea. Brother of Cottus and Gyges. Father of Aetna. Also known as Obriareus by the gods and Aegaeon by mortals. Briareus aided Zeus against the Titans.

BRISEIS Patronymic form for Hippodameia. Daughter of Brises of Lyrnessus near Troy. Achilles killed her parents, three brothers and husband, and abducted her as a concubine. When Agamemnon demanded her, Achilles withdrew from the fighting until after the death of Patroclus.

BRISES of Lyrnessus Father of Briseis. Killed by Achilles.

BRITOMARTIS Cretan nymph in service to Artemis. Daughter of Zeus and Carme. Was pursued to her death by Minos and became immortal as the goddess Dictynna (the lady of the nets). Goddess of hunters, fishermen and sailors. Known in Aegina as Aphaea.

BRIZE The gadfly sent by Hera to torture Io.

BROMIOS Epithet of Dionysus meaning 'thunderer'. Used as a surname.

BRONTES (thunder) One of the Cyclops. Son of Uranus and Gaea. Brother

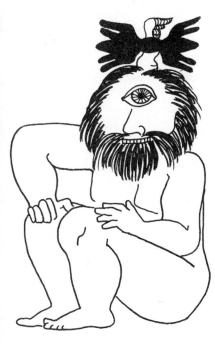

Brontes

of Arges and Steropes. He had a single eye in the centre of his forehead.

BRONZE (Brass) Third age of man. Others were gold, silver and iron.

BROOKS, goddess of Greek: Leucothea. Roman: Mater Matuta.

BROTEAS Son of Tantalus and Dione. Brother of Niobe and Pelops.
   Carved the most ancient image of the mother of the gods in a rock called Coddinus, north of Mt Sipylus. When he refused to do the same for Artemis, she drove him mad and he burned himself to death, believing himself immortal.

BROTEAS (1) One of the twelve children, six sons and six daughters, of Amphion (qv) and Niobe. (2) Brother of Amnon, a skilful, undefeated boxer.

BRYGEIANS (Bryges) A tribe of Epirus. Helped by Ares, they defeated Odysseus and the Threspotians.

BUBONA (Epona) A beautiful Roman goddess, protector of horses, cows and oxen. Daughter of a mortal and a mare.

BUBUS King of Corinth. Son of Hermes and Alcidamea. Succeeded Aeetes.

BUCEPHALUS The favourite horse of Alexander the Great. Its head resembled that of a bull, and it lived for thirty years.

BUCOLION Son of Laomedon and Calybe.

BUCOLUS Father of Sphelus.

BULL *See* Canace (Poseidon), Minos and Pasiphae.

BUPHAGOS Son of Iapetos and Thornax. Artemis shot him after he offered her violence on Mt Phobe.

BUSIRIS King of Egypt. Son of Poseidon

47

and Lysianassa. Brother of Memphis. A despot. Killed by Heracles.

BUTES An Argonaut. Son of Poseidon or Teleon and Zeuxippe. Possibly father of Eryx by Aphrodite. Father of Polycaon. On the return journey from Colchis, he jumped overboard to swim to the Sirens but was rescued by Aphrodite.

BUTES (1) Son of Boreas. Half-brother of Lycurgus, king of Thrace, against whom he plotted, and was exiled and became a pirate. After he raped Coronis, Dionysus drove him mad and he jumped in a well and was drowned. (2) Son of Pandion and Zeuxippe. Twin of Erechtheus and brother of Philomela and Procne. Married Cthonia, daughter of Erechtheus.

BUTHROTUM Port of Epirus founded by Helenus after the fall of Troy.

BUTO Egyptian goddess. Mother of the sun and moon. Equivalent to Leto and Latona.

BYBASSUS A goatherd. Father of Syrna, the wife of Podalirius.

BYBLIS (Biblis) Twin daughter of Miletus and Cyane who fell in love with her brother, Caunis, and was changed into a fountain.

C

CABEIRI (Mystic deities occurring in various parts of the ancient world) The three children of Uranus and the first earthly mortals. Or children of Camillus, son of Cabeiro, who had three daughters, perhaps called Cabeirides and three sons, Cabeiri. The Cabeiri of Samothrace were the sons of Zeus and Calliope. The Cabeiri were also ancient deities worshipped along the coast of the Aegean Sea and on the Aegean islands.

CABEIRO Daughter of Proteus and Psamathe. Sister of Eidothea (Theonoe) and Theoclymenus. Mother of Camillus, by Hephaestus.

CACA Ancient Roman goddess of the hearth. Daughter of Vulcan and Medusa. Sister of Cacus. Succeeded by Vesta.

CACUS Fire-breathing giant. Son of Vulcan and Medusa. Brother of Caca.
A three-headed, half-human, fire-breathing monster that lived in a cave on Mt Palatine in Rome. Stole some of the cattle of Geryon. Heracles found them and killed Cacus.

CADMEIA The citadel (acropolis) of Thebes.

CADMUS King of Thebes. Son of Agenor of Phoenicia and Telephassa or Argiope. Brother of Cilix, Electra, Demodoce, Phineus, Thasus, Argos (possibly), Europa and Phoenix. Married Harmonia. Father of Agave, Autonoe, Illyrius, Ino, Polydorus and Semele. The gods attended his wedding (cf Peleus).
On the advice of the Delphic oracle, he built Cadmeia. When he killed the dragon of Ares he sowed half its teeth and from these the dragon-men (or sown-men) sprang up. In Illyria, both he and Harmonia were changed into beautiful spotted snakes.

Cadmus introduced the alphabet and art of writing into Greece.

CADUCEUS The golden, snake-intertwined staff of Hermes, given in exchange with Apollo for a lyre.

CAECINUS A river god. Son of Oceanus and Tethys. Brother of the other river gods. Either he or Astyeles was the father of Euthymus.

CAECULUS Son of the sister of the Fratres Delpidii and a spark from a fire. Claimed descent from Vulcan. Founder of Praeneste, he was an ally of Turnus against Aeneas.

CAELIAN One of the seven hills of Rome. Others were: Aventine, Capitoline, Esquiline, Palatine, Quirinal and Viminal.

CAENEUS A Lapith chieftain. Son of Elatus and Hippea but born a girl known as Caenis. Brother of Polyphemus and Ischys. He changed sex after being raped by Poseidon. Father of Coronus.
When fighting broke out between the centaurs and the Lapithae, at the wedding of Peirithous and Hippodameia, Caeneus offended Zeus and was buried beneath a pile of pine trees, then was changed into a bird.

CAENEUS (1) An Argonaut, the father of Phocus and Priasus. (2) Accompanied Aeneas to Italy where he was killed by Turnus.

CAENIS Daughter of Elatus. Sister of Polyphemus. Became a man, Caeneus (qv), after being raped by Poseidon.

CAERUS A winged wonder horse, harness-mate of Arion.

CAESAR Surname of twelve Roman emperors.

CAICAS The north-east wind, born of Eos and Astraeus.

CAIETA Aeneas' old nurse.

CAISTRUS Possibly the son of Penthesileia and Achilles. A Lydian river was named after him.

CALAIS One of the Boreades and an Argonaut. Twin son of Boreas and Oreithyia. Twin of Zetes and brother of Chione, Cleopatra and Haemus.

He and Zetes accompanied the Argonauts and were given wings for rescuing Phineus from the Harpies. Calais, like his brother, was killed by Heracles and both became birds or winds.

CALCHAS Wisest of Greek soothsayers at the Trojan War. Son of Thestor and Megara. Brother of Alcmaon, Leucippe and Theonoe. Father of Cressida. Rival of Mopsus the diviner. Calchas was a priest of Apollo, and some say that he was on the Argo, but this is doubtful. Accompanied Agamemnon to Troy and made the following prophecies: 1. Troy would not fall without the help of Achilles. 2. It would take ten years for Troy to fall. 3. The Greek fleet could not sail from port until Agamemnon sacrificed his daughter, Iphigeneia, to Artemis. 4. A plague affecting the Greeks would pass only after Chryseis was returned to her father, Chryses.

Calchas advised the Greeks to build the Wooden Horse. He was told that if he met his match he would die. He challenged Mopsus to a contest and when Mopsus correctly guessed the number of figs on a tree, and Calchas could not, he died of grief.

CALETOR (1) Son of Clytius, a Trojan elder. Descendant of Dardanus. Cousin of Hector. Killed in the Trojan War by Greater Ajax. (2) Father of Aphareus.

CALLIANASSA A Nereid. One of the fifty daughters of Nereus and Doris.

CALLIANEIRA A Nereid. One of the fifty daughters of Nereus and Doris.

CALLIDICE Queen of Thesprotia. Married Odysseus, after the Trojan War. Mother of Polypoetes who succeeded to the throne.

CALLIOPE Muse of epic poetry. Daughter of Zeus and Mnemosyne. One of the nine Muses. Mother of Linus and Orpheus by Apollo or Oeagrus. Possibly mother of Rhesus by Strymon. Mother of the Cabeiri of Samothrace and the Corybantes by Zeus. Possibly the mother of the Sirens, Aglaopheme, Molpe, Peisinoe and Thelexiepeia, by Achelous.

Calliope was the Muse of epic poetry, telling of the heroes and their deeds; and she could also play any musical instrument. She arbitrated between Aphrodite and Persephone, giving Adonis to each of them for four months of the year. Often portrayed with Homer.

CALLIPOLIS Son of Alcathous and Evaechme. Brother of Automedusa, Iphinoe, Ischepolis and Periboea. Accidentally killed by his father.

CALLIRRHOE (1) Daughter of the river god, Achelous. Sister of Castalia and Peirene, and possibly the Sirens. Second wife of Alcmeon and the mother of Acarnan and Amphoterus. (2) Daughter of the river god, Scamander. Married Tros. Mother of Assaracus, Cleopatra, Ilus and Ganymedes. A fountain is named after her in Attica at the spot where she killed herself. (3) Daughter of Lycus of Libya. Lover of Diomedes. Killed herself when he deserted her. (4) Daughter of Amphion and Niobe. Killed by Artemis, together with four of her five sisters. Apollo killed five of her six brothers. (5) An Oceanid. Daughter of Oceanus and Tethys. Sister of many, including Asia, Clymene, Clytia, Europa, Perseis and Styx. (*See* Oceanus.) Married Chrysaor. Possibly mother of Cerberus, Echidna and Geryon. Mother of Cotys by Manes.

CALLISTE Original name of Thera, a volcanic island north of Crete. Now called Santorini.

CALLISTO An Arcadian goddess. Daughter of Lycaon and Cyllene or of Nycteus or Ceteus. Sister of Pallas. Mother of Arcas by Zeus. Transformed into the Great Bear constellation by Zeus, Artemis (with whom she is associated), or Hera.

CALPE (Gibraltar) Mountain of southern Spain opposite Mt Abyla in North Africa. The mountains, called the Pillars of Hercules, were erected by him after he had recovered Geryon's stolen cattle.

CALUS Another name for Perdix the inventor.

CALYBE A nymph. Mother of Bucolion by Laomedon.

CALYCE Daughter of Aeolus and Enarete. Sister of seven brothers: Athamas, Cretheus, Deion, Macareus, Perieres, Salmoneus and Sisyphus; and also of six sisters: Alcyone, Arne, Canace, Peisidice, Perimele and Tanagra. Married Aethlius. Mother of Endymion, though his father may have been Zeus.

CALYCE Daughter of Hecato. Mother of Cycnus by Poseidon.

CALYDON Son of Aetolus and Pronoe. Brother of Pleuron. Married Aeolia. Father of Epicasta and Protogeneia.

CALYDON Son of Thestius. Accidentally killed by his father.

CALYDON Son of Ares and Astynome. Turned to stone for watching Artemis bathing.

CALYDON City of Aetolia. Founded by Calydon and Pleuron, it was the scene of the Calydonian Boar Hunt.

CALYDON, kings of Porthaon, Oeneus, Agrius, Andraemon. Aeneus was also a king of Calydon.

CALYDONIAN BOAR HUNT A wild boar, possibly the offspring of Phaea, was sent by Artemis to ravage Oeneus' land after he had failed to pay her proper homage. The participants were Acastus, Admetus, Alcon, Amphiarus, Atalanta (heroine of the hunt), Castor, Jason, Meleager (who killed the boar with his bare hands), Peleus, Peirithous, Plexippus, Polydeuces, Telamon, Theseus and Toxeus.

CALYPSO Daughter of Atlas and Pleione or of Oceanus and Tethys. Sister of Hyas, the Hyades, the Hesperides, Maia and the Pleiades. The mother of Nausinous and Nauisithous by Odysseus.

When Odysseus was shipwrecked on her island home of Ogygia, she offered him eternal youth and immortality if he stayed with her, but he stayed only seven years and when he left she was heartbroken.

CAMASENA Possibly the mother of Tiberinus by Janus.

CAMEIRO Another name for Cleothera.

CAMEIRUS Son of Cercaphus and Cydippe. Grandson of Helios and Rhode. Brother of Ialysus and Lindus. Eponym of city of Cameirus on the island of Rhodes.

CAMENAE Roman divinities. Prophetic nymphs, identified with the Muses, of the spring that supplied water for the Vestal Virgins. Includes Carmenta (Postverta, Nicostrata).

CAMILLA A Volascian queen and virgin huntress. Daughter of Metabus and Casmilla, dedicated to the service of Artemis. A swift runner, she fought with one breast bare to enable her to use a bow. Sided with Turnus against Aeneas. Speared to death by the Etruscan Aruns in an ambush.

CAMILLUS Son of Hephaestus and Cabeiro. Possibly the father of the Cabeiri.

CAMPUS MARTIUS Field of Mars. Large plain outside walls of Rome where youths boxed, wrestled, rode horses and chariots, and threw the discus and javelin. Public assemblies were held here, and foreign ambassadors welcomed. It became adorned with statues and its pleasant situation made it very popular.

CANACE Daughter of Aeolus and Enarete. Sister of seven boys: Athamas, Cretheus, Deion, Macareus, Perieres, Salmoneus and Sisyphus; and of six girls: Alcyone, Arne, Calyce, Peisidice, Perimele and Tanagra. Mother of Aloeus, Epopeus, Hopleus, Nireus and Triopas by Poseidon. After committing incest with Macareus, she killed herself at her father's command.

CANCER The second labour of Heracles was to fight the Lernean Hydra. At the same time, he had to contend with Cancer the crab.

CANCER The second sign of the zodiac, representing the crab.

CANDALUS One of the Heliades. Son of Helios and Rhode. Brother of Actis, Cercaphus, Macar, Ochimus, Tenages and Triopas. Co-murderer of Tenages, he went into exile with his brothers. The first to sacrifice to Athena.

CANDAULES The last king of Lydia.

CANENS A nymph. Daughter of Janus and Venilia. She loved, and was promised in marriage, to Picus, who did not return her love. When Circe turned Picus into a woodpecker, she searched for him for six days then, not finding him, she dissolved in her own tears, so great was her grief.

CANETHUS Son of Abas. Father of Canthus.

CANTHUS An Argonaut from Euboea. Son of Canethus. Friend of Polyphemus. Killed by Caphaurus or Cephalion of Libya while trying to steal his sheep.

CAPANEUS Son of Alector. Brother of Iphis.

CAPANEUS Son of Hipponous and Astynome. Married Evadne. Father of Sthenelus.

One of the Seven against Thebes, Zeus killed him with a thunderbolt for boasting that the god could not stop him entering Thebes. Possibly resurrected by Asclepius. Capaneus was the inventor of the scaling ladder.

CAPHAREUS, Cape Rocky promontory in south-east Euboea, where Nauplius lit beacons to lure the returning Greek ships on to the rocks.

CAPHAURUS (Cephalion) A Libyan shepherd. Son of Amphithemis and Tritonis. Brother of Nasamon. Killed the Argonauts, Canthus and Eribotes, for trying to steal his sheep. Was killed by the Argonauts.

CAPITOL Famous Roman temple, dedicated to Jupiter, and citadel on the Tarpeia rock.

CAPITOLINE Smallest of the seven hills of Rome. Others are: Aventine, Caelian, Esquiline, Palatine, Quirinal and Viminal.

CAPRICORN The goat. Tenth sign of the zodiac, named after Aegipan.

CAPYS Son of Assaracus and Hieromneme. Married his cousin, Themiste. Father of Anchises and Laocoon.

CAPYS A Trojan, founder of Capua in Italy, with Aeneas. He warned of the dangers of the Wooden Horse.

CAR King of Megara. Son of Phoroneus and Cerdo, Peitho or Teledice. Brother of Apis and Niobe.

CARDEA Goddess of thresholds and door-pivots. A virgin huntress who resorted to trickery to protect her virginity. She gave control of her powers to Janus, whom she loved.

CARDYS Father of Clymenus, king of Olympia.

CARIA Region of Asia Minor: the cities of Cnidus, Halicarnassus and Miletus, Mt Latmos, where Endymion sleeps immortally, and the River Maeander.

CARIA Citadel of Megara where Demeter worshipped. Named after Car.

CARME A nymph. Daughter of Eubulus. Mother of Britomartis by Zeus. She was an attendant of Artemis and a nursemaid to Scylla.

CARMEIRUS *See* Cameirus.

CARMENTA (Nicostrata) One of the Camenae. A fountain nymph, goddess of healing and the future. Ancient Roman goddess of childbirth. Mother of Evander by Hermes. Greek equivalent: Themis. She gave oracles in verse.

CARNA Roman goddess of hearts and other body organs, also over-hinges. Festival date: 1 June.

CARNABON King of the Getae of Thrace. When he killed one of Triptolemus' snakes, Demeter's punishment was to place him in the constellation of the Serpent Holder.

CARPO (autumn) One of the Horae (qv), goddesses of the seasons. Daughter of Zeus and Themis. Worshipped with Thallo.

CARTHAGE North African city founded by Dido. Renowned for trading. Fought for supremacy with Rome for many years. Destroyed in 146 BC.

CARUTIUS Husband of Acca Larentia. Father of the Fratres Arvales. Bequeathed his estates to his wife.

CARYA A maid whom Dionysus loved. After she died, she became a walnut tree. Artemis reported the death and was given the epithet of Caryatis for doing so.

CARYA City of Laconia.

CASMILLA Wife of Metabus, king of the Volsci. Mother of Camilla.

CASSANDRA (Alexandra) Daughter of Priam and Hecuba. Sister of Aesacus, Creusa, Deiphobus, Hector, Helenus (her twin), Paris, Polyxena and Troilus, amongst others. She had eleven sisters and fifty brothers.

Apollo gave her the gift of prophecy, but her predictions were always disbelieved. She warned of the dangers of the Wooden Horse. After the fall of Troy, she fled to the sanctuary of Athena. However, Ajax found her and ravished her. In the sharing of spoils Agamemnon took her to Mycenae where she and Agamemnon were murdered by Aegisthus and Clytemnestra.

CASSIOPEIA Daughter of Arabus. Married Cepheus, king of Ethiopia. Mother of Andromeda. Mother of Atymnius by Zeus. She angered Poseidon by boasting that she was more beautiful than the Nereids, so he sent a sea-monster to ravage Ethiopia. After her death she became a constellation.

CASTALIA Daughter of the river god, Achelous. Sister of Callirrhoe and Peirene. She was the nymph of the famous spring at Delphi, on Mt Parnassus, sacred to Apollo and the Muses.

CASTALIDES Epithet of the Muses, so called because they were linked with Castalian spring.

CASTALIUS Either he or Cephisus was the father of Thyia.

CASTOR One of the Dioscuri. Son of Tyndareus and Leda. Brother of Phoebe, Philonoe, Timandra, Clytemnestra, and half-brother of Helen and Polydeuces, children of Zeus and Leda. Married Phoebe. Father of Anogen by Hilaera, Polydeuces' wife. Inseparable companion of Polydeuces, who had been conceived and born at the same time as himself, though they shared only a mother.

A great warrior and horseman, Castor taught Heracles to fence. He was an Argonaut and a member of the Calydonian Boar Hunt. Was killed by Idas. After their deaths, he and Polydeuces became the constellation, Gemini.

CATAMITUS The Roman equivalent of Ganymede, son of Tros.

CATREUS King of Crete (part). Son of Minos and Pasiphae. Brother of Acacallis, Androgeus, Ariadne, Deucalion, Euryale, Glaucus, Lycastrus, Phaedra and Xenodice. Father of Aerope, Althaemenes, Apemosyne and Clymene. Accidentally killed by Althaemenes.

CATTLE OF GERYON The tenth labour of Heracles (qv).

CATTLE OF THE SUN Sacred cattle of Apollo, living on the island of Thrincia. All the crew of Odysseus' ship were drowned at sea as punishment for killing some of the cattle.

CATTLE, Roman god of Pales. (May have been female.)

CATULLUS 1st century BC Roman lyric poet. His longest poem features the marriage of Peleus and Thetis.

CAUCASIAN EAGLE Offspring of Typhon and Echidna, as were Chimaera, Cerberus, Orthus, the Hydra, Sphinx, Crommyonian Sow, Nemean Lion and Vultures.

CAUCASUS Mountain range to which Zeus chained Prometheus. It is possible that the mountains caught fire when Phaethon's chariot came too close.

CAUNUS Twin son of Miletus and Cyanee. Brother of Byblis. He fled to Caria when his sister fell in love with him.

CEBREN Trojan river god. Probably the son of Oceanus and Tethys. Father of Asterope, wife of Aesacus and father of Oenone, wife of Paris.

CEBRIONES Bastard son of Priam. Half-brother of Hector for whom he acted as charioteer. Killed by Patroclus.

CECROPIA Original name of Attica and Athens.

CECROPS King of Attica (Athens) – many authorities state that he, not Actaeus, was the first king. Son of Gaea and brother of many. He had a man's body and a snake's tail. Married Agraulos. Father of Agraulos, Erysichthon, Herse and Pandrosus.

Ruled for fifty years and built the citadel of Cecropia. The court of Areopagus was founded during this time. He attempted to end human sacrifice, introduced olive cultivation to Athens, and organised the city into twelve tribes. Was the first to name Zeus as the supreme god, and introduced marriage rites and monogamy. Judged the contest between Athena and Poseidon for the patronage of Athens.

CECROPS Eighth king of Attica (Athens). Son of Erechtheus and Praxithea. Brother of Chthonia, Creusa, Eupalamus, Metion, Orneus, Pandorus, Procris, Oreithyia, Protogeneia and Thespius. Married Metiadusa. Father of three daughters and Pandion.

CECROPS Son of Pandion and grandson of Cecrops, king of Athens. Worshipped as a hero at Haliartus.

CEDALION Messenger sent by Hephaestus to bring Orion from Lemnos to the sun where Apollo restored his sight.

CEISUS Son of Temenus, king of Argos. Brother of Agraeus, Cerynes, Hyrnetho and Phalces. Father of Medon. Possibly father of Phlius by Araethyrea. After he seized his father's throne, his descendants ruled for ten generations, ending with Meltas.

CELAENO One of the Pleiades. Daughter of Atlas and Pleione. Sister of Alcyone, Electra, Maia, Merope, Sterope and Taygete. Mother of Lycus and Chimaereus by Poseidon. Possibly mother of Delphus by Apollo.

CELAENO A Danaid. Daughter of Danaus. Sister of Amymone, Asteria, Hypermnestra, Phylodameia and forty-five others.

CELAENO (1) Daughter of Poseidon and Ergea. (2) One of the Harpies (qv).

CELEUS King of Eleusis. Husband of Metaneira. Father of four daughters, Demophon, and possibly Abas and Triptolemus. A teacher of agriculture, he was the inventor of several agricultural tools. Co-founder (with Eumolpus) of the Eleusinian Mysteries.

CELMIS One of the three oldest Dactyli. Others were Acmon and Damnameneus.

CELMUS A playmate of the infant Zeus, turned to magnetic stone for claiming that Zeus was mortal.

CENCHREIS The wife of Cinyras and mother of Adonis and Myrrha.

CENCHRIAS Son of Peirene. Brother of Leches. Accidentally killed by Artemis. The harbour of Corinth, called Cenchreia, is named after him.

CENTAURS Inhabitants of Thessaly. Offspring of Ixion and Nephele (a cloud). Half human, half horse, they were shaped by Zeus to resemble Hera. Their father is also given as Centaurus, but he may have been the father of some only. Ixion and Nephele were not the parents of Cheiron and Pholus.

Many centaurs, including Abas, Cyllarus,

Eurytion and Nessus, fought the Lapiths at the wedding of Peirithous, after they had become inflamed by alcohol. Hylonome was a female centaur.

CENTAURUS (1) Son of Apollo and Stilbe or of Ixion and Nephele. Brother of Lapithus. Possibly the father of the other centaurs by Magnesian mares. (2) One of the ships of Aeneas.

CENTIMANI The Roman name for the Hecatoncheiroi or hundred-handed. Called Briareus (Aegaean, Obriareus), Cottus and Gyges.

CEPHALION Another name for Caphaurus, son of Amphithemis and Tritonis. Brother of Nasamon.

CEPHALUS (1) Son of Deion and Diomede. Brother of Actor, Aenetus, Asteropeia and Phylacus. Eos was enamoured of him. Married first to Procris, whom he accidentally killed. For this he was tried and convicted at the Areopagus. Banished to Taphos, he helped Amphitryon conquer the island kingdom. Later he married Clymene, becoming the father of Iphiclus. (2) Son of Hermes and Herse. Brother of Ceryx. Father of Phaethon by Hemera, although Phaethon may have been the son of Tithonus and Eos. Was the father of Tithonus by Eos. (3) Possibly the father of Arceisius.

CEPHEUS King of Ethiopia. Probably the son of Belus and Anchinoe. Married Cassiopeia. Father of Andromeda.

CEPHEUS King of Tegea and an Argonaut. Son of Aleus and Neaera. Brother of Amphidamas, Auge and Lycurgus. Father of Aerope, Echemus, Sterope and many others.

He possessed a lock of Medusa's hair, given him by Athena, which made his kingdom invincible. During his absence on the voyage of the Argonauts, he gave the lock to Sterope. Cepheus and his sons were killed aiding Heracles in a war against Hippocoon.

CEPHEUS The father of Asterope (may be a different Cepheus from above).

CEPHISUS A river god. Son of Oceanus and Tethys. Brother of the other river gods (qv). Father of Narcissus by Leiriope. Possibly the father of Thyia (alternatively, Castalius). Possibly the father of Eteocles (alternatively, Andreus).

CER Goddess of violent death. Daughter of Nyx and Erebus. Sister of Nemesis, Aether, Dreams, Hypnos, Momus, Moros, Nemesis, Charon and Thanatos.

CERAMBUS A man saved from the Flood by nymphs, who was turned into a beetle and flew to Mt Parnassus.

CERAMUS Son of Dionysus and Ariadne, and brother of Peparethus, Phanus, Staphylus and Thoas.

CERAS Cypriots who were changed into bulls.

CERBERUS Watchdog of Hades. Son of Typhon and Echidna. Brother of Chimaera, Hydra, Orthus, Caucasian Eagle, Crommyonian Sow, the Sphinx, Nemean Lion and vultures.

Represented as having a dragon's tail, fifty or one hundred heads, or with three heads and snakes springing from his neck and back. Aconite sprang from the ground after foam dripped from his mouth. Cerberus guarded the entrance to Hades and ate people who attempted to escape. He also stopped people from entering Hades while they were still alive, but Aeneas with the Sibyl of Cumae, Odysseus and Orpheus managed to do so. As his twelfth labour, Heracles brought Cerberus up from Hades.

CERCAPHUS One of the Heliades. Son of Helios and Rhode. Brother of Actis,

Cerberus

56

Candalus, Macar, Ochimus, Tenages and Triopas. Married Cydippe, daughter of Ochimus. Father of Carmeirus, Ialysus and Lindus. He or Macar was first to sacrifice to Athena.

CERCOPES Two-tailed thievish gnomes. Sons of Oceanus and Theia. Named Acmon and Passalus, they lived in Lydia. Were turned into stone or apes by Zeus for stealing his weapons.

CERCYON King of Eleusis. Son of Hephaestus. Father of Alope, whom he killed. He required all strangers to wrestle with him, and was killed by Theseus.

CERDO (the wise) Wife of Phoroneus and mother of Car, but not of Phoroneus' other children.

CEREALIA Roman festivals of Ceres.

CERES Roman goddess of agriculture. One of the twelve great Olympians. Daughter of Cronos and Rhea as Demeter. Sister of Jupiter, etc. Mother of Arion by Poseidon, and of Proserpina by Jupiter. Goddess of corn, other grains, fruit and flowers. Her festival date: 19 April, when pigs were sacrificed to her. As Demeter, the celebration of the Eleusinian mysteries was held in her honour.

CERYNEAN HIND (Stag) A stag with brazen hoofs and golden antlers, sacred to Artemis and captured by Heracles as his third or fourth labour.

CERYNES Son of Temenus, the Heraclid. Brother of Agraeus, Ceisus, Hyrnetho and Phalces.

CERYNITIA Forest of Cerynea where Heracles hunted the hind.

CERYNITIS A sacred hind.

CERYX (1) Son of Hermes and Herse. Brother of Cephalus. (2) Heraclid son of

Eumolpus and a daughter of Benthesicyme. Brother of Ismarus (Immaradus).

CESTRINUS Son of Helenus and Andromache. A half-brother to Astyanax, Pergamus, Pielus and Molossus. Founded Cestrine in Epirus.

CESTUS Aphrodite's girdle with powers of magic and love inspiration.

CETEUS Possibly the father of Callisto (alternatively, Lycaon or Nycteus).

CETO (of the fair face) Sister of Eurybia, Nereus, Phorcys, Thaumas and Crius. Daughter of Oceanus and Gaea. Married Phorcys. Mother of Echidna (alternatively, Callirrhoe), Ladon, Scylla and the Gorgons and the Graiae. She lived in the sea.

CEUS (Coeus) Son of Uranus and Gaea. Brother of the other Titans. Married Phoebe. Father of Leto and Asteria.

CEUTHONYMUS Father of Menoetes, the herdsman of Hades.

CEYX King of Trachis. Son of Eosphorus. Brother of Leuconoe. Married Alcyone. Father of Hippasus.
    Offered hospitality to Heracles after he had fled from Eurystheus, and also to Peleus on his exile. Drowned on a sea voyage to Claros and was changed into a gannet, gull or kingfisher.

CHALCIOPE (Iophossa) Daughter of Aeetes, king of Colchis, and Asterodeia. Half-sister of Absyrtus and Medèa. Married Phrixus. Mother of Argus, Cytissorus, Melas, Phrontis and Presbon, and of Thessalus by Heracles.
    After the Argonauts rescued her four shipwrecked sons, she persuaded her sister to help Jason find the Golden Fleece.

CHALCIS Daughter of Asopus and Metope. Sister of Antiope, Aegina, Cleone,

Corcyra, Ismene, Ismenus, Metope, Pelagon, Pelasgus, Plataea, Salamis and Thebe and ten others.

CHALCIS Chief city of Euboea, named after Chalcis, and last home of Aristotle.

CHALCODON King of the Abantes of Euboea. Son of Abas and Ocaleia. Brother of Acrisius and Proetus. Married either Imenarete or perhaps Alcinoe. Father of Elephenor. He was killed at Thebes by Amphitryon. His people were called Abantes.

CHALCOMEDUSA Wife of Arceisius. Mother of Laertes.

CHALCON A Myrmidon. Father of Bathycles.

CHANCE, Roman goddess of Fortuna.

CHAOS The original void. That which, in Greek mythology, preceded anything else. Sometimes called a part of the infernal regions. Out of Chaos came Gaea, Tartarus and Eros. Chaos bore Erebus and Nyx.

CHANGE, Roman god of Vertumnus.

CHARICLO A nymph. Wife of Everes and mother of Teiresias. A favourite of Athena.

CHARICLO Daughter of Apollo, Oceanus or Perses. Married Cheiron. Mother of Endeis, Theia and Ocyrrhoe (Menalippe).

CHARIS (Aegle) Goddess of delight, graces and pleasures. Wife of Hephaestus, and possibly one of the Graces. *See* Aegle.

CHARITES (Graces) Normally regarded as three in number but there are many references to others. Daughters of Zeus and Eurynome, or Helios and Aegle, or Zeus and Aphrodite, or Dionysus and Aphrodite. Attendants of Aphrodite, and the personification of beauty, friendship and grace amongst men. They were called Aglaea (Splendour, also called Charis), Euphrosyne (festivity), Pasithea and Thalia (rejoicing).

CHARON Ferryman of the dead across the Styx. Son of Erebus and Nyx. Brother of Aether, Cer, Dreams, Hypnos, Momus, Moros, Nemesis, Thanatos and Hemera. For a fare of one silver obol placed in the mouth of the corpse at burial, Charon would ferry the soul across the rivers Acheron and Styx. He was pictured as an old, dishevelled, but sturdy, man with a grey beard and a short cloak. He would not ferry the unburied until a hundred years had passed.

CHAROPS (1) Possibly the grandfather of Orpheus. He fought with Dionysus against Lycurgus. (2) Son of Hippasus. Brother of Socus. Killed in the Trojan War by Odysseus.

CHARYBDIS (1) Daughter of Poseidon and Gaea. Sister of Antaeus and Ogyges. A whirlpool at the entrance to the Straits of Messina. Together with Scylla, she guarded the straits, Charybdis on the Sicilian side, making passage through impossible. A fig tree grew over the whirlpool and Odysseus clung to it to avoid being sucked in. (2) Daughter of Poseidon and Amphitrite. Sister of Albion, Benthesicyme, Rhode and Triton.

CHEIRON An immortal Centaur. Son of Cronos and Philyra. Married Chariclo. Father of Endeis, Ocyrrhoe (Menalippe) and Theia.

A wise and kindly Centaur, famous for his knowledge of archery, medicine and music, he was teacher to Actaeon, Achilles, Asclepius, Jason, Machaon and Podalirius. He was accidentally wounded by Heracles and, although immortal, decided to die and so passed on his immortality to Prometheus. Became the constellation Sagittarius.

CHELONE A nymph who ridiculed the

wedding of Zeus and Hera and became a perpetually silent tortoise.

CHEMMIS An Egyptian city near Thebes, home of Danaus and Lynceus, whose inhabitants worshipped Perseus.

CHERSIDAMAS A Trojan killed in the War by Odysseus.

CHILDBIRTH, Roman god of Genius.

CHILDBIRTH, Greek goddesses of Artemis, Eleithyia, Hera, Parca and Themis.

CHILDBIRTH, Roman goddesses of Carmenta, Juno, Lucina, Postverta.

CHILDBIRTH, Arcadian god of Auge (Epithet of Artemis).

CHILDREN'S POTIONS, Roman goddess of Potina.

CHILON One of the Seven Wise Men of Greece (qv).

CHIMAERA Firebreathing daughter of Echidna and Typhon. Reared by Amisodaurus. Sister of Cerberus, the Hydra, the Caucasian Eagle, the Crommyonian Sow, Orthus, vultures, the Nemean lion and the Sphinx. She had three heads: that of a glowering lion, a snake and a goat; or else had the head of a lion, body of a goat and the tail of a snake. Chimaera was killed by Bellerophon.

CHIONE Daughter of Daedalion. She had many suitors. Chione was killed by Artemis, jealous of her beauty. In one day she became the mother of Autolycus by Hermes, and of Philammon by Apollo.

CHIONE Daughter of Boreas and Oreithyia. Sister of Calais, Cleopatra, Haemus and Zetes. She was seduced by Poseidon and threw their child, Eumolpus,

Chimaera

into the sea, where he was rescued by Poseidon.

CHLORIS (Meliboea) Greek goddess of flowers. (1) Daughter of Amphion and Niobe, and sole survivor when Apollo and Artemis killed her six brothers and five sisters, though one brother may have escaped. Married to Neleus, she bore him a daughter, Pero, and twelve sons including Chromius, Nestor and Periclymenus. (2) Mother of Mopsus by Ampycus. (3) Wife of Zephyrus. Chloris, known to the Romans as Flora, was a winner at the Heraean games.

CHLORIS Daughter of Teiresias. Mother of Periclymenus by Poseidon (cf above).

CHROMIUS Son of Neleus and Chloris. Brother of Pero and eleven boys, including Nestor and Periclymenus.

He and Alcenor were the sole Argive survivors in a battle between 300 Argives and 300 Spartans. Othryades was the sole Spartan survivor.

CHRYSAOR Son of Poseidon and Medusa, rising from her blood. Brother of Pegasus. Married the Oceanid Callirrhoe. Possibly father of Echidna and Geryon.

CHRYSE (Comana) (1) Daughter of Pallas. First wife of Dardanus. (2) Daughter of Halmus. Sister of Chrysogeneia. Mother of Phlegyas by Ares.

CHRYSEIS (Astynome) Daughter of Chryses, thus called Chryseis. She was captured by the Greeks at Troy and became a concubine of Agamemnon, bearing him a child, also called Chryses.

CHRYSES (1) Son of Agamemnon and Chryseis. Helped his half-brother, Orestes, kill Thoas. (2) Son of Poseidon and Chrysogeneia. Father of Minyas. King of Phlegyantis. (3) Son of Hermes. Brother of Eurymedon, Nephalion and Philocaus. Co-ruler of the Isle of Paros. (4) Father of Chryseis. A priest of Apollo Smintheus. When the Greeks refused to return his daughter to him, he prayed for vengeance which came in the form of a plague.

CHRYSIPPUS Bastard son of Pelops and Axioche or Astyoche. After he was abducted to Thebes by Laius, Hera sent the Sphinx to punish the Thebans. Chrysippus was murdered by his half-brothers, Atreus and Thyestes, or by Hippodameia, wife of Pelops.

CHRYSOGENEIA Daughter of Halmus. Sister of Chryse. Married Chryses. Mother of Minyas.

CHRYSORTHE Mother of Coronus by Apollo.

CHRYSOTHEMIS Daughter of Agamemnon and Clytemnestra. Sister of Electra, Iphigeneia and Orestes, although she may have been the same person as Iphigeneia. Married Staphylus.

CHRYSOTHEMIS A Cretan who won first prize for poetry and music in the Pythian games.

CHTHON Epithet of Gaea.

CHTHONIA (she of the earth) Daughter of Colontas, who built a sanctuary for Demeter after her father was destroyed for snubbing the goddess.

CHTHONIA (Cthonia) Daughter of Erechtheus and Praxithea. Sister of Cecrops, Creusa, Eupalamus, Metion, Orneus, Pandorus, Protogeneia, Oreithyia, Procris and Thespius. Married Butes, her father's twin.

CHTHONIUS One of the Sparti of Thebes. Either he or Hyrieus was the father of Lycus and Nycteus by Clonia. Chthonius was the brother of Echion, Hyperenor, Pelorus and Udaeus.

CHTHONOPHYLE (Cthonophyle) Daughter of Sicyon and Zeuxippe. Married Phlias. Mother of Androdamas. Mother of Polybus by Hermes.

CICONES Inhabitants of Thrace. When Odysseus was returning home from Troy, he plundered their main city, Ismarus, because they had been allies of the Trojans. In retaliation they killed six crewmen from each of Odysseus' ships.

CILISSA Orestes' nurse who sacrificed her own son in order to save Orestes' life.

CILIX Son of Agenor and Telephassa or Argiope. Brother of Cadmus, Europa, Demodoce, Electra, Argus (possibly), Phineus, Phoenix and Thasus, though Thasus may have been his son. When Europa was kidnapped, Cilix accompanied Cadmus and Phoenix to find her.

CILLA Daughter of Laomedon and

Strymo. Sister of Astyoche, Clytius, Hesione, Hicetaon, Tithonus, Lampus and Priam.

CILLAS The Olympians' name for Sphaerus, charioteer of Pelops.

CIMMERIANS Inhabitants of caves at the entrance to Hades, in Cumae. They never saw daylight, and either they or the Sibyl administered the oracle of the dead at Cumae. Odysseus visited them on his way back from Troy.

CIMON (1) Son of Miltiades. He brought the skeleton of Theseus back to Athens from Scyros. King of Athens. (2) Father of Miltiades, hero of Marathon.

CINYRAS King of Paphos in Cyprus. Son of Sandorcus of Syria, or of Paphus, Apollo or Pygmalion. Married Cenchreis or Metharme. Father of Myrrha and Adonis, although Adonis' mother may have been Myrrha. Also the father of Braesia, Laogore, Mygdalion and Orsedice.
As a suitor of Helen he should have gone to the Trojan War, but instead promised Agamemnon fifty ships. Forty-nine of the ships turned out to be of clay, but Mygdalion commanded the fiftieth. Cinyras committed suicide after his incestuous relationship with Myrrha.

CIRCE Daughter of Helios and Perseis (Perse). Sister of Aeetes, Pasiphae and Perses. She married Odysseus and bore Ardeas, Agrius and Telegonus. Then she married Telemachus, and gave birth to Latinus, though some say that this child was Odysseus' son. According to Milton the wizard, Comus, was the son of Circe and Bacchus.
A sorceress with beautiful hair, she was the sole inhabitant of the island of Aeaea, where she turned visitors into animals. It was she who turned Scylla into a monster, to spite Glaucus who preferred Scylla to herself. The Romans knew her as Marica and the Italians as Angitia. An epithet of hers was Aeaea.

CISSEUS One of the fifty sons of Aegyptus who married one of the fifty daughters of Danaus.

CISSEUS Son of Melampus, companion of Heracles. Brother of Gyas; ally of Turnus. Killed by Aeneas.

CISSEUS (1) King of Thrace. Father of Theano. (2) A river god. One of several putative fathers of Hecuba.

CITHAERON First king of Plataea. A cruel king, brother of Helicon and husband of Plataea, daughter of Asopus.
Gave his name to the mountain range that separates Attica from Boeotia. The mountains were the home of the Furies and were sacred to Dionysus and Zeus. On these slopes the infant Oedipus was left to die, and Actaeon was torn to pieces by his dogs.

CIVILISATION, Roman god of Consivius (Janus).

CLAROS Oracle of Apollo, located in Ionia. Ceyx drowned on his way to consult this oracle.

CLASHING ROCKS (Symplegades) Situated one on either side of the northern entrance to the Bosphorus. The Argonauts were the first to pass successfully between them.

CLEEIA One of the Hyades. Daughter of Atlas and Pleione. *See* Atlas and the Hyades.

CLEIO Muse of history. Alternative spelling of Clio (qv), one of the nine Muses. Daughter of Zeus and Mnemosyne. Mother of Hyacinth by Pierus. She mocked Aphrodite for her infatuation with Adonis. Possibly mother of Orpheus by Oeagrus.
Her symbols were a wreath of laurel and a scroll. She is often depicted with a writing implement and with Cadmus, who introduced Phoenician lettering into Greece.

CLEITE Daughter of Merops. Sister of Adrastus, Arisbe and Amphius. Married Cyzicus, king of the Doliones.

After the Argonauts killed her husband, she committed suicide. The wood nymphs were so affected by this tragedy that they wept profusely, their tears becoming a fountain which was named after her.

CLEITUS (1) Son of Mantius. Brother of Polypheides. Carried off by Eos, because of his beauty. (2) Son of Peisenor. Squire of Polydamas. Killed in the Trojan War by Teucer.

CLEOBIS Son of Cydippe, the priestess of Hera at Argos. Brother of Biton. He and his brother were awarded the highest gift attainable by mortals, that of eternal sleep, in return for services rendered to their mother, when they pulled her ox-cart to the temple in the absence of oxen.

CLEOBULE Wife of Amyntor. Mother of Crantor, Deidameia (Astydameia) and Phoenix.

CLEOBULE The mother of Leitus by either Alector, Electryon or Lacritus.

CLEOBULUS (1) One of the Seven Wise Men of Greece (qv). Others were Bias, Chilon, Periander, Pittacus, Solon and Thales. (2) A Trojan leader killed in the Trojan War by Greater Ajax.

CLEOCHARIA Naiad mother of Eurotas, Polycaon, Therapne, and Myles, by her husband, Lelex.

CLEOCHUS Father of Areia.

CLEODAEUS Son of Hyllus and Iole. Father of Aristomachus. A Heraclid.

CLEODORA A Danaid. One of the fifty daughters of Danaus who married the fifty sons of Aegyptus. Sister of Amymone, Asteria, Celaeno, Hypermnestra and Phylodameia, among others.

CLEODORA A nymph. Wife of Cleopompus. Mother of Parnassus by Poseidon.

CLEODOXA Daughter of Amphion and Niobe. Sister of five girls and six boys all killed by Artemis and Apollo, except Chloris (and perhaps one brother). Sisters and brothers were: Amyclas, Alphenor, Callirrhoe, Chloris, Broteas, Damaschthon, Ismenos, Ilenus, Meliboea, Neaera, Pelops, Phthia, Phylomache, Sipylus and Tantalus. (Different authorities name different children, hence length of list).

CLEOLLA Daughter of Dias. Married Pleisthenes. Mother of Anaxibia and, possibly, Agamemnon and Menelaus.

CLEOMESTRA The mother of Antenor by her husband, Aesyetes.

CLEONE Daughter of the river god, Asopus, and Metope. Sister of Aegina, Antiope, Chalcis, Corcyra, Ismene, Ismenus, Metope, Pelagon, Pelasgus, Plataea, Salamis, Thebe and ten others. The town of Cleonae, between Argos and Thebes, was named after her.

CLEOPATRA Daughter of Boreas and Oreithyia. Sister of Calais, Chione, Haemus and Zetes. Married Phineus. Possibly the mother of Pandion and Plexippus by her husband.

CLEOPATRA Daughter of Idas and Marpessa. Married Meleager. Mother of Polydora.

Persuaded her husband to save Aetolia from the Curetes. Hanged herself or died of grief after her husband's death.

CLEOPATRA (1) Daughter of Tros and Callirrhoe. Sister of Assaracus, Ganymedes and Ilus. (2) The name of seven queens of Egypt. (3) A Danaid. One of the fifty daughters of Danaus who married one of the fifty sons of Aegyptus. She killed her husband on her wedding night.

CLEOPHYLE Either she or Eurynome

was the wife of Lycurgus and mother of Amphidamas, Ancaeus, Epochus and Iasus.

CLEOPOMPUS The husband of Cleodoxa.

CLEOSTRATUS A youth rescued by his lover, Menestratus, from the dragon that annually attacked the city of Thespiae.

CLEOTHERA (Cameiro) Daughter of Pandareus and Harmothoe. Sister of Aedon and Merope (Clytie).
After her parents were killed by Zeus, she was raised by Athena. Later, she and Merope were abducted by the Harpies and became servants of the Erinnyes.

CLIO *See* Cleio.

CLISONYMUS Son of Amphidamas. Killed during a dice game with Patroclus.

CLITE Wife of Cyzicus. *See* Cleite.

CLOANTHUS Winner of the boat race in the funeral games of Anchises.

CLONIA A nymph, the mother of Lycus and Nycteus by Hyrieus or Chthonius.

CLONIUS A Greek ally killed in the Trojan War by Agenor.

CLOTHO (The spinner) Youngest of the Moirae. Daughter of Zeus and Themis. Sister of Atropos and Lachesis. Pictured as carrying a spindle and spinning the threads of life.

CLOUD *See* Nephele.

CLYMENE Daughter of Oceanus and Tethys. Sister of Asia, Callirrhoe, Clytia, Doris, Eidyia, Electra, Europa, Meliboea, Metis, Perseis, Pleione, Proteus and Styx. Married Iapetos. Mother of Atlas, Epimetheus, Monoetius and Prometheus.

CLYMENE Daughter of Minyas. Sister of Alcithoe, Arsippe, Leucippe and Peri-

clymene. Possibly second wife of Cephalus. Mother of Iphiclus by Phylacus or Cephalus. Possibly mother of Atalanta by Iasus. Mother of Alcimede by Phylacus.

CLYMENE Daughter of Catreus. Sister of Aerope, Althaemenes and Apemosyne. Married Nauplius. Mother of Nausimedon, Oeax and Palamedes.

CLYMENE A Nereid. One of the fifty daughters of Nereus and Doris.

CLYMENE (1) Mother of Promachus and Tlesimenes by Parthenopaeus. (2) Helen's servant, abducted with her by Paris. (3) Wife of Dictys. (4) Mother of the Heliades and Phaethon by Apollo or Helios.

CLYMENUS King of Arcadia. Father of Harpalyce with whom he had incestuous relations even after her marriage to Alastor. He cut up their baby, then hanged himself.

CLYMENUS King of Boeotian Orchomenus. Son of Presbon. Father of Azeus, Erginus and three other sons. Killed in a fight with the Thebans, by Perieres, his death being avenged by Erginus.

CLYMENUS (1) King of Olympia. Cretan son of Cardys. A descendant of Heracles, he came to Crete fifty years after the Flood. Restored the Olympic Games. Overthrown by Endymion. (2) Son of Aeneus, king of Calydon, and Aenete. Brother of Cyzicus. (3) Father of Eurydice, wife of Nestor.

CLYTEMNESTRA Daughter of Tyndareus and Leda. Sister of Castor, Phoebe, Philonoe, Timandra. Half-sister of Polydeuces and Helen (who were fathered by Zeus). Married Agamemnon. Mother of Electra (Laodice), Chrysothemis, Iphigeneia (Iphianassa), and Orestes. After she plotted to murder Agamemnon, she married her co-conspirator, Aegisthus; became mother of Aletes and Erigone. Clytemnestra had been given in marriage to Tantalus, but

Agamemnon murdered him and their baby. In her turn, Clytemnestra murdered Cassandra, concubine of Agamemnon, when they returned from Troy, and was herself killed by her son, Orestes.

CLYTIA An Oceanid. Daughter of Oceanus and Tethys. Sister of Asia, Callirrhoe, Clymene, Europa, Perseis, Styx, etc.
   She was the lover of Apollo and, when she was deserted by him, changed into a heliotrope. Heliotropes show their devotion by always facing the sun.

CLYTIE Alternative name for Merope, daughter of Pandareus and Harmothoe.

CLYTIUS A Trojan elder. Son of Laomedan and Strymo. Some sources name his mother as Leucippe or Placia. Brother of Astyoche, Cilla, Hesione, Hicetaon, Lampus, Priam and Tithonus. Father of Caletor. The only one of Laomedon's sons to survive when Heracles sacked Troy.

CLYTIUS An Argonaut. Son of Eurytus and Antiope. Brother of Iole and Iphitus. Was present on the Calydonian Boar Hunt. Clytius was killed by Aeetes.

CLYTIUS Son of Aeolus and Cyane. Had six sisters, including Melanippe, and five brothers, including Metapontus and Misenus. Married one of his sisters. A follower of Aeneas, he was killed by Turnus.

CLYTIUS (1) A giant, son of Uranus and Gaea. Killed by Hecate or Hephaestus. (2) Son of Alcmeon and Arsinoe. (3) A follower of Turnus. (4) Father of Dolops.

CLYTIUS Son of Dolops. Killed by Hector.

CLYTONEUS Descendant of Nauplius the navigator. Father of Nauplius the Argonaut.

CNIDUS Ancient city of Asia Minor where Praxiteles made the first nude statue of Aphrodite, sacred to the city.

CNOSSIA A nymph. Mother of Xenodamus by Menelaus.

CNOSSUS (Knossos) Principal city of Crete, site of the Minoan palaces. Cnossus is linked with Minos and Pasiphae, the Minotaur and the labyrinth, and is thought by many to be the site of Atlantis, the lost city.

COCALUS King of Camicus in Sicily. After Daedalus was given refuge in Sicily by Cocalus, the king's daughters drowned Minos in boiling water when he came in pursuit of Daedalus from Crete.

COCYTUS A river god. Son of Oceanus and Tethys. Brother of the other river gods. Father of Mentha. The river of wailing. One of the five rivers of Hades. Others were the Acheron, Lethe, Phlegethon and Styx.

CODRUS King of Athens. Son of Melanthus. Married an Athenian woman though he himself was a Messenian refugee. Father of Medon and others, who founded most of the cities of Ionia.

COELUS Epithet of Uranus. Son and, later, husband of Gaea. Father of the Titans.

COERANUS Father of Polyeidus.

COEUS (Ceus) A Titan. Son of Uranus and Gaea. Brother of the other Titans. Married his sister, Phoebe. Father of Asteria and Leto.

COLCHIS Asian country, situated at the eastern end of the Black Sea, visited by the Argonauts because the golden fleece was here. The birthplace of Medea.

COLCHIS, kings of Absyrtus, Aeetes (king at the time of the Argonauts), Medus and Perses.

COLONTAS   Father of Chthonia. Burnt to death in his own home for refusing to entertain Demeter.

COLOPHON   Mother of Arachne by Idmon.

COLOSSUS AT RHODES   One of the Seven Wonders of the World (qv) it was a bronze statue of the sun god, Helios, thirty metres or seventy cubits high. Built to honour Actis, son of Helios, it guarded the entrance to the harbour at Rhodes and was destroyed by an earthquake in 224 BC.

COMAETHO   Priestess of Artemis Triclaria at Patrae. Slept with her lover, Melanippus, in the holy shrine, so both were sacrificed to Artemis.

COMAETHO   Daughter of Pterelaus, king of the Taphians. She had six brothers. She fell in love with Amphitryon and helped him capture her father's city by cutting off the golden thread of hair from her father's head, thus destroying the city's invincibility. Amphitryon executed her.

COMANA   Another name for Chryse.

COMATAS   Goatherd and servant of the Muses on Mt Helicon. After he had sacrificed a goat, he was imprisoned in a chest but the Muses rescued him.

COMETES   Son of Sthenelus, the friend of Diomedes. Brother of Cylarabes, king of Argos. Married Antigone. Father of Asterion. Committed adultery with Aegialeia, wife of Diomedes.

COMMERCE, Roman god of   Mercury.

COMPITALIA   Roman feast of Lares. Celebrated on 12 January and 6 March.

COMUS   According to Milton, son of Circe (Marica) and Bacchus. Roman god of drinking, eating, laughter, nocturnal entertainments and revelry

CONABOS (tumult)   One of the four horses of Ares. Others were Aithon, Phlogios and Phobos.

CONCORDIA   Roman goddess of harmony and peace. With Pax and Salus, she was also the goddess of unity.

CONSCIENCE, Greek personification of   Aidos.

CONSENTES   Roman name for the twelve Greek Olympians.

CONSIVIUS (the sower)   Epithet of Janus, as the Roman god of civilisation.

CONSUS   Italian god of councils and counsel. Called Poseidon Hippios by the Greeks and Equestrian Neptune by the Romans, Consus was introduced into Italy by Evander. His feast days were 21 August and 15 December. His temple in the Circus Maximus was covered, to show that councils should be secret.

CONVALESCENCE, Greek god of   Teesphorus.

COON   Eldest son of Antenor. Brother of Acamas, Agenor, Archelous, Glaucus, Helicaon, Lycaon, Laocoon, Polybus, Demoleon, Iphidamas, Laodamas, Polydamas and Crino. Half-brother of Pedaeus. Killed in the Trojan War by Agamemnon.

COPIA (abundance)   Roman goddess of wealth and plenty. Handmaiden of Fortuna, she carried the cornucopia.

COPREUS   Herald of Eurystheus. Son of Pelops and Hippodameia. Brother of Alcathous, Astydameia, Atreus, Chrysippus, Lysidice, Nicippe, Pittheus, Thyestes and Troezen, and others. Father of Periphetes. Was once the owner of Arion. Killed by Heracles who threw him from the walls of Tiryns.

CORA   Epithet of Persephone, daughter of Demeter and wife of Hades.

CORAX King of Sicyon. Son of Coronus. Brother of Lamedon. Epopeus deposed him and succeeded to his throne.

CORCYRA Daughter of Asopus and Metope. Sister of Aegina, Antiope, Cleone, Chalcis, Ismene, Pelasgus, Ismenus, Pelagon, Plataea, Salamis, Metope, Thebe and ten others. Abducted by Poseidon to Isle of Corcyra (Corfu) or to Black Corcyra (Korcula) where she gave birth to Phaex. Alcinous is possibly a descendant of Poseidon and Corcyra.

CORCYRAEAN BULL The bull of Corcyra (Corfu) that bellowed, so preventing the fishermen catching fish, until it was sacrificed to Poseidon.

CORE (Kore) Daughter of Zeus and Demeter. An epithet of Persephone. Festivals called Correia were held in her honour in Greece.

CORESUS A priest of Dionysus at Calydon who committed suicide rather than sacrifice Callirrhoe, whom he loved.

CORINTH Vastly wealthy ancient city of Argos on the Isthmus and Gulf of Corinth. Founded by Sisyphus. Received its name from Corinthus, son of Peplops. Destroyed by the Romans 146 BC.

CORINTH, kings of Corinthus, Jason (consort of Medea), Sisyphus, Ornytion, Thoas. Also Aletes, Creon, Agelaos, Bunus, Corythus, Glaucus and Polybus.

CORINTHUS King of Corinth. Son of Marathon or Peplops. Brother of Sicyon. Father of Sylea. He had no sons, so his rule passed to Medea (and Jason).

CORINTHUS A son of Zeus.

CORN, Roman god of Robigus.

CORN, Greek goddess of Demeter.

CORN, Roman goddesses of Ceres, Robigo.

CORNUCOPIA Horn of plenty. The horn of the goat Amalthea. Carried by Copia, it was perpetually filled with food and drink.

COROEBUS Son of Mygdon. Suitor of Cassandra. Killed by Diomedes or Neoptolemus.

COROEBUS A hero of Argolis. Killed the snake Poene, sent by Apollo. Later he built a temple to Apollo on Mt Geranis after consulting an oracle as to how to cure a plague that ravaged Argolis.

CORONA BOREALIS The constellation of 'northern lights'. Represents Ariadne's crown.

CORONEUS of Phocis Father of Coronis.

CORONIDES Name given to the two daughters of Orion, Menippe and Metioche. Given beauty by Aphrodite and skill in weaving by Athena, they killed themselves to stop a plague in Orchomenus.

CORONIS A Thessalian princess. Daughter of Phlegyas, king of Orchomenus. Sister of Ixion. She consorted with Apollo and gave birth to Asclepius. Later she was unfaithful and as she prepared to marry Ischys, son of Elatus of Arcadia, she was killed by Apollo or Artemis.

CORONIS Daughter of Coroneus of Phocis. Poseidon fell in love with her and Athena transformed her into a white crow. After she brought bad news to Athena, the goddess turned her permanently black.

CORONIS (1) Daughter of Ares. Attacked by Apollo. (2) Daughter of Atlas and Pleione. One of the Hyades (qv).

CORONUS King of Sicyon. Son of

Apollo and Chrysorthe. Father of Corax and Lamedon. Deposed by Epopeus.

CORONUS Founder of Coroneia. Son of Thersander. Brother of Haliartus. The two boys were adopted by King Athamas when they were exiled from Corinth to Orchomenus.

CORONUS Argonaut and leader of the Lapiths. Son of Caeneus. Father of Leonteus and Lyside. Killed by Heracles.

CORONUS Father of Anaxiroe, the wife of Epeius.

CORUS The north or north-west wind.

CORYBANTES According to Ovid, people born out of rainwater. Others called them children of Apollo and Thalia or Athena, Helios and Athena, Zeus and Calliope, Corybas or Cronos and Rhea. Still others called them divine beings, associating them with the Curetes. They were the male attendants of Phrygian Cybele. Also called Galli. They provided music for the goddess' orgiastic dances.

CORYBAS Son of Iasus and Cybele. Possibly father of the Corybantes.

CORYDON Shepherd or swain of Arcadia.

CORYNETES Another name for Periphetes, son of Hephaestus and Anticleia.

CORYPHAEUS The chorus leader in Greek tragedy.

CORYTHUS Son of Paris and Oenone. Brother of Daphnis. He guided the Greeks to Troy. His father killed him when Corythus, too, fell in love with Helen.

CORYTHUS (1) King of Laconia who foster-fathered Parthenopaeus and Telephus. (2) A king of Corinth.

COS (Kos) Aegean island near the place where Hera shipwrecked Heracles.

COTHONEA The wife of Eleusis and mother of Triptolemus.

COTTUS One of the Hecatoncheiroi. Son of Uranus and Gaea. Brother of Briareus (Aegaeon, Obriareus), and Gyges.

COTYS (Cotytto) (1) A king of Thrace. (2) Son of Manes and Callirrhoe. (3) Another name for the father of Asia (Hesione). (4) Thracian goddess. Accepted into Greece, her worship was linked with debauchery.

COUNCILS AND COUNSEL, gods of Greek: Poseidon Hippios. Roman: Equestrian Neptune. Italic: Consus.

COW *See* Io.

COWS, protector of Bubona (Epona).

CRAB Ally of the Hydra against Heracles, it bit his toe. Hera turned it into the constellation Cancer.

CRAFTSMEN, goddesses of Greek: Athena. Roman: Minerva.

CRANAE Daughter of Cranaus and Pedias. Sister of Atthis. Married Amphicyton.

CRANAUS King of Athens. Son of Gaea. Married Pedias of Sparta. Father of Atthis and Cranae. The Biblical Flood occurred during his reign. Deposed by his son-in-law, Amphictyon.

CRANTAEIS (Crantaiis) Epithet of Hecate. Mother of Scylla by Phorcys.

CRANTOR Son of Amyntor and Cleobule. Brother of Deidameia (Astydameia) and Phoenix. Killed in the battle between the Lapiths and Centaurs, fighting beside Peleus.

CRATUS A Titan. Son of Uranus and Gaea. Blinded Prometheus on the orders of Hephaestus.

CRATUS (strength) (Kratos) Son of Pallas and Styx. Brother of Bia (force and violence), Nike (victory) and Zelos (Emulation).

CRAUGASUS The father of Philonome.

CREON King of Corinth. Son of Lycaethus or Sisyphus. Father of Glauce (Creusa). Burned to death with his daughter.

CREON King of Thebes. Son of Menoeceus. Brother of Hipponome and Jocasta. Married Eurydice or possibly Anioche. Father of Enioche, Haemon, another Menoeceus, Pyrrha and Megara. Refused burial to Polyneices, thus leading to the death of Antigone and the suicide of his own son, Haemon. Was killed by Theseus.

CREONTIDAS Son of Heracles and Megara. Brother of Deicoon and Therimachus. Killed by Heracles.

CRES Eponym of Crete and father of Talus, guardian of Crete.

CRESPHONTES King of Messenia. One of the Heraclids. Son of Aristomachus. Brother of Aristodemus and Temenus. Married Merope, daughter of Cypselus. Father of Aepytus and two others.

CRESSIDA Not strictly a mythological character, but the medieval mythical daughter of Calchas. Mistress of Troilus. Cf Chryseis.

CRETAN BULL A bull sacred to Poseidon, sent to Minos. Father of the Minotaur by Pasiphae. Captured by Heracles as his seventh labour, but later released. This same bull caused havoc at Marathon until killed by Theseus.

CRETE Daughter of Asterius and Europa.

CRETE Daughter of Deucalion. Sister of Idomeneus.

CRETE Largest of the Aegean islands. Kings were: Tectamus, Asterius, Minos, Deucalion, Idomeneus, Leucus. Other kings were Melissus and Rhadamanthys.

CRETHEIS Wife of Acastus. Mother of Sterope. Possibly the same person as Hippolyte or Astydameia, she was killed by Peleus for falsely telling his wife that he had attempted to rape her.

CRETHEUS First king of Iolcus. Son of Aeolus and Enarete. Had six brothers: Athamas, Deion, Macareus, Perieres, Salmoneus and Sisyphus; and seven sisters: Alcyone, Arne, Calyce, Canace, Peisidice, Perimele and Tanagra. First married Sidero, widow of Salmoneus. His second wife was Tyro, daughter of Salmoneus and Sidero. Father of Aeson, Amythaon, Pheres and Promachus. Finally married Demodice or Biadice. Founder of Iolcus.

CRETHEUS A follower of Aeneas killed by Turnus.

CREUSA Daughter of Priam and Hecuba. Sister of Aesacus, Cassandra, Deiphobus, Hector, Helenus, Paris, Polyxena and Troilus. Married Aeneas. Mother of Ascanius (Iulus). During the Trojan War, she was captured by the Greeks but rescued by Aphrodite and Cybele. When Aeneas fled from Troy, Creusa disappeared.

CREUSA Youngest daughter of Erechtheus and Praxithea. Sister of Cecrops, Chthonia, Eupalamus, Metion, Oreithyia, Orneus, Pandorus, Protogeneia, Procris and Thespius. Married Xuthus. Mother of Achaeus, Diomede and Ion, and, according to some, Dorus. Mother of Janus by Apollo, after he had raped her. Some say that Ion was also their child.

CREUSA (1) Another name for Glauce, daughter of Creon. Burned to death with her father. (2) A Naiad, mother of Hypseus and Stilbe. (3) The wife of Peneius and mother of Hypseus. (4) Possibly the mother of Telamon. (5) One of the Nereids (qv). (6) One of the Danaids (qv).

CRIASUS Son of Argus and Evadne. Brother of Ecbasus, Epidaurus and Peiras.

CRIMISUS A river god. Son of Oceanus and Tethys. Married Egesta, daughter of Hippotes. Father of Acestes.

CRINO Daughter of Antenor and Theano. Her thirteen brothers were Archelous, Acamas, Agenor, Coon, Glaucus, Helicaon, Polybus and Polydamas, Laocoon, Lycaon, Iphidamas, Demoleon and Laodamas. Half-sister of Pedaeus.

CRISUS (Crissus) Son of Phocus and Endeis. Brother of Panopaeus. May have been father of Strophius, Astyoche and Anaxibia. After murdering their father he and Panopaeus emigrated to Phocis from Aegina, their home.

CRITICISM AND PLEASANTRY, Greek god of Momus.

CRIUS Titan son of Uranus and Gaea. Brother of Ceto, Eurybia, Nereus, Phorcys and Thaumas. Married Eurybia. Father of Astraeus, Pallas and Perses.

CROCALE A nymph. Diana's hairdresser when Actaeon spied on her while bathing.

CROCUS A beautiful youth in love with the nymph, Smilax. Because of his impatience, both were turned into flowers or yew trees.

CROESUS King of Lydia. The richest man in the world. Much of his money was said to have been inherited from his predecessor, Midas. Croesus gave much gold to the oracle at Delphi. He was a patron of Aesop.

CROMMYONIAN SOW (Phaea) Offspring of Typhon and Echidna, as were Cerberus, Chimaera, Orthus, the Hydra, Caucasian Eagle, Nemean Lion, Sphinx and Vultures. A savage sow, that ravaged the countryside of Corinth, killed by Theseus. Possibly the mother of the Calydonian Boar.

CRONIA Attican festivals in honour of Cronos.

CRONOS (Kronos) Greek god of the world and time. One of the Titans. Youngest son of Uranus and Gaea. Married his sister, Rhea. Father of Hades, Hera, Hestia, Demeter, Poseidon and Zeus. Father of Cheiron by Philyra. Possibly father of the Corybantes by Rhea.

He castrated his father with a sickle given him by his mother. From then on, the heavens and earth developed separately. Cronos swallowed his sons to prevent them replacing him as supreme god, but Hera saved Zeus by substituting a stone for him. When Zeus replaced him, Cronos vomited the others out, and all his sons waged war against him. Cronos was known as Saturn to the Romans.

CROPS, Divinities of Greek: Demeter Roman: Faunus, Ceres.

CROTOPUS King of Argos. Father of Psamathe, the possible mother of Linus.

CROTUS Son of Pan and Eupheme. He became the constellation Sagittarius.

CROW Sacred bird of Apollo, originally white, but was turned black because it told tales of Coronis' infidelity.

CTEATUS A Molionid. Son of Actor or Poseidon and Molione. Twin of Eurytus. Married Theronice, twin daughter of Dexamenus. Father of Amphimachus.

CTESIPPUS A suitor of Penelope, killed by Eumaeus.

CTESIPPUS A son of Heracles and Deianeira.

CTESIUS Son of Ormenus, king of the island of Syria. The father by Panthia of Eumaeus, the swineherd of Laertes.

CTESON Son of Lelex, king of Megara. Father of Pylas.

CTHONIA (Chthonia) Daughter of Erechtheus and Praxithea. Sister of Cecrops, Creusa, Eupalamus, Oreithyia, Orneus, Pandorus, Metion, Procris, Protogeneia and Thespius. Married her father's twin, Butes.

CTHONOPHYLE (Chthonophyle) Daughter of Sicyon and Zeuxippe. Married Phlias, son of Dionysus. Mother of Androdamas. Mother of Polybus by Hermes.

CTIMENE Daughter of Laertes and Anticleia. Sister of Odysseus. Married Eurylochus.

CTIMENUS The father of Eurydamas.

CUCKOO *See* Hera.

CUMAEAN SIBYL (Deiphobe) A famous prophetess. Also called Amalthea, Demo, Demophile or Herophile. Daughter of Glaucus. Apollo gave her a lifespan equivalent to the grains of sand in her hand, plus her powers of prophecy, but she forgot to ask for perpetual beauty. She lived in Cumae, sixteen kilometres west of Naples, in a cave with a hundred openings. When Aeneas sought her help she was 700 years old.

CUPID Son of Mars and Venus, or Mercury and Diana, or Mercury and Venus. Lover of Psyche and father of Voluptas. Also called Amor. Roman equivalent of Eros, god of love. Depicted with wings.

CURETES Early inhabitants of Crete. Semi-divine beings associated with the Corybantes. Possibly daughters of Hecaterus by a daughter of Phoroneus. Among the leaders of this group were Dorus, Laodocus and Polypoetes, sons of Apollo and Phthia. These three were killed by Aetolus. Their knowledge of all the arts was extensive. They prevented Cronos from finding the hidden infant Zeus, but Zeus was later to kill them for abducting Epaphus.

CYANE A Sicilian nymph. A nymph, turned into a fountain by Hades for trying to prevent the abduction of Persephone.

CYANE A Syracusan nymph who offered her father as an altar sacrifice after he had assaulted her.

CYANE Daughter of Liparus. Married Aeolus. Mother of six sons and six daughters who married each other.

CYANEE Daughter of Maeander. Sister of Samia. Married Miletus. Mother of twin sons, Byblis and Caunus.

CYANIPPUS King of Argos. Son of Adrastus and Amphithea. Brother of Aegialeia, Aegialeus, Argeia, Deipyle and Hippodameia. Some authorities call Aegialeus his father, not his brother.

CYATHUS Another name for Eurynomous, son of Architeles.

CYBELE (Cybebe) Phrygian mother-goddess. Identified with Rhea, Demeter and Bona Dea. The Romans also called her Magna Mater and Mater Turrita. Also called Ops and Dindymene. Her epithet was Agdistis.
Possibly born the hermaphrodite child of Zeus, her male genitals were cut off by the other gods, though most authorities call her the daughter of Meion and Dindyme or of Uranus and Gaea. Mother of Midas by Gordius. All sources acknowledge the love of Attis and Cybele. She enjoined on him perpetual celibacy. The violation of his promise was punished by self-castration. A protectress of cities, she was the first to build city walls. Her attendants were the Corybantes, and she rode a chariot drawn by lions. Festival date: 4 April.

Cybele

CYCHREUS (Cynchreus) First king of Salamis. Son of Neptune and Salamis. Father of Glauce. He left his kingdom to Telamon, who may have been his grandson.

CYCLOPS One-eyed monsters. Sons of Uranus and Gaea. Called Arges (bright one), Brontes (thunder) and Steropes (lightning). Other Cyclops were called Geraestus and Acmonides; the latter's task was to forge Zeus' thunderbolts. Brothers of the Titans. They are said to have lived in or under Mt Aetna and to have been workmen of Hephaestus. Thrown into Tartarus, first by Uranus, later by Cronos, Zeus freed them and they helped him to become leader of the gods. The Cyclops gave to Poseidon his trident, to Zeus his thunder and lightning, and a cap of invisibility to Hades. When Zeus killed Asclepius with a thunderbolt, Apollo killed the Cyclops.

CYCNUS King of Colonae near Troy. Son of Poseidon and Calyce. Abandoned by his parents, he was reared by a swan. Married first Procleia, daughter of Laomedon. Father of Hemithea and Tenes. Then married Philonome, daughter of Craugasus. Philonome fell in love with Tenes, but when he did not respond she lied about him to Cycnus. Cycnus then set his children afloat in a chest, but he killed Philonome when he discovered she had lied to him. Cycnus was invincible, and when Achilles threatened finally to overcome him, his father turned him into a swan.

CYCNUS King of the Ligurians. Son of Sthenelus, king of the Ligurians. Father of Cinyras and Cupavo. A musician and close friend of Phaethon. When Phaethon died, Cycnus so grieved for him that Apollo changed him into a swan.

CYCNUS Son of Apollo and Thyria. Brother of Phylius. Committed suicide after losing the friendship of Phylius and was changed into a swan. His mother followed him.

CYCNUS Son of Ares and Pelopia or Pyrene. (May have been two different people with the same father.) After wounding Heracles, was killed by the latter, and turned into a swan.

CYDIPPE An attendant from Cyrene.

CYDIPPE Daughter of Ochimus and Hegetoria. Married her uncle, Cercaphus. Mother of Cameirus, Ialysus and Lindus.

CYDIPPE (1) A priestess of Hera. Mother of Biton and Cleobis. (2) The daughter of a rich noble who, because of a trick, married the poor Acontius (qv).

CYDON Son of Hermes or Tegeates and Acacallis.

CYLARABES King of Argos. Son of Sthenelus. Brother of Cometes. Succeeded Cyanippus to the throne.

CYLLARUS A Centaur. Son of Ixion and Nephele. The most beautiful of the Centaurs, he fell in love with Hylonome and, so great was their love, she committed suicide after he was killed by the Lapiths.

CYLLENE (1) Nymph of Mt Cyllene in Arcadia. Nurse to the baby Hermes. (2) The wife of Pelasgus, king of Arcadia. Mother of Lycaon. (3) Mother of Callisto by Lycaon, Nycteus or Ceteus.

CYLLENEIUS Epithet of Hermes.

CYMODOCE A Nereid. One of the fifty daughters of Nereus and Doris.

CYMOTHOE A Nereid. One of the fifty daughters of Nereus and Doris.

CYNCHREUS (Cychreus) First king of Salamis. Son of Neptune and Salamis. The father of Glauce, wife of Telamon.

CYNORTAS King of Sparta. Son of Amyclas and Diomede. Brother of Argalus, Hyacinthus and Leaneira. Father of Perieres and Oebalus. Succeeded Argalus to the throne.

CYNOSURA (Ursa minor) Nymph of Mt Ida in Crete and nursemaid to the infant Zeus. Was transformed into a star.

CYNTHIA Goddess of the moon. Roman epithet of Diana. Born on Mt Cynthus, in Delos.

CYNTHIUS Epithet of Apollo who was born on Mt Cynthus.

CYNTHUS Mountain on the isle of Delos and birthplace of Apollo and Artemis (Diana).

CYPARISSUS A youth beloved of Apollo, turned into a cypress tree for killing one of Apollo's favourite stags.

CYPRIS Cypriot epithet of Aphrodite.

CYPSELUS King of Basilis in Arcadia. Descendant of Stymphalus. Father of Merope whom he married to Cresphontes by force. After Cresphontes was killed by Polyphontes, Cypselus raised his grandson, Aepytus.

CYPSELUS (1) A Corinthian who killed the Bacchiadae. (2) Son of Aepytus, grandson of Merope. Succeeded his stepfather as king of Arcadia.

CYRENE A nymph, queen of Libya. Daughter of Hypseus and Chlidanope. Sister of Astyagyia, Stilbe and Themisto. Mother of Aristaeus and Autychus by Apollo. Mother of Idmon by Apollo or Abas. Mother of Diomedes by Ares.

Gave her name to the city of Cyrene. Succeeded Eurypylus to the throne after she had killed a savage lion.

CYRENE, kings of A city in Libya. Six alternate generations of kings called either Battus or Arcesilaus ruled the city.

CYTHEREIA   Epithet of Aphrodite.

CYTISSORUS Son of Phrixus and Chalciope. Brother of Argus, Melas, Presbon and Phrontis. Aided the Argonauts by helping them to capture the fleece and then escape from Colchis.

CYZICUS King of the Doliones, a Mysian tribe. Son of Aeneus and Aenete. Brother of Clymenus. Married Cleite, daughter of Merops. They had no children. Killed by Jason and the Argonauts on their way to Colchis.

D

DACTYLI (fingers) Their number seems to have originally been three. Acmon, Celmis and Damnameneus were the eldest Dactyli. Others were then added. They introduced fire and the forging of copper and iron into Crete. Another tradition says they were the ten children of Rhea or the nymph, Anchiale. There were five boys (or perhaps six) called by some Epimedes, Heracles, Iasus, Idas (Acesidas) and Paeonaeus, and five girls with secret names, all born on Mt Ida. Heracles established the Olympic games. Some say there were thirty-two Dactyli who were magicians and twenty counter-magicians.

DAEDALION Brother of Ceyx. Father of Chione. When Chione died, he committed suicide and Apollo changed him into a hawk.

DAEDALUS Athenian inventor. Son of Metion or Eupalamus and Alcippe or Merope. Brother of Perdix and Sicyon. Father of Icarus. A master craftsman, he was nevertheless jealous enough of his talents to murder his nephew and pupil Talos, and so was exiled from Athens. He went to Cnossus and built the labyrinth for the Minotaur. He also designed the hollow cow in which Pasiphae lay when she conceived the Minotaur. Among his other inventions were the axe, level, wimble, wedge, and sails for ships. Daedalus and Icarus escaped from Minos by tying feathers joined with wax to their arms, and flying. Icarus was killed when he flew too close to the sun and the wax melted. Daedalus sought refuge in Sicily with Cocalus.

DAEMON Two ancient spirits presiding over people and places, one good, one bad.

DAMASCHTHON One of the twelve children (six boys) of Amphion and Niobe.

DAMASIUS Son of Penthilus. Brother of Echelas. Father of Agorius.

DAMASTES (Polypemon, the stretcher) Real name of Procrustes. Father of Sinis, the pine-bender, by Sylea. Killed by Theseus.

DAMASTOR A Trojan. Father of Tlepolemus. Killed by Patroclus.

DAMASUS One of the Lapithes. Killed by Polypoetes.

DAMISISTRATUS King of Plataea. The man who buried the body of Laius, king of Thebes, at the foot of Mt Parnassus.

DAMNAMENEUS One of the three eldest Dactyli. The others were Acmon and Celmis.

DANAE Daughter of Acrisius and Eurydice, daughter of Lacedaemon. Some say that her mother may have been Aganippe and her father Teutanias. Sister of Evarete. Mother of Daunus by Pilumnus.

Danae was imprisoned in a bronze tower by her father, because an oracle claimed that a son born to her would cause her father's death. However, Zeus visited her in the form of a golden shower and she became the mother of Perseus. Years later, Perseus accidentally killed Acrisius with a discus, so fulfilling the prediction.

DANAIDS (Danaidae) The fifty daughters of Danaus who married the fifty sons of Aegyptus. They included Celaeno, Erato, Eurydice, Glauce and Hypermnestra. All except Hypermnestra murdered their husbands on their wedding night.

DANAUS King of Libya. Son of Belus and Anchinoe. Twin brother of Aegyptus and brother of Thronia and possibly Cepheus (Phineus). Father of fifty daughters, the Danaids, including Amymone, Asteria, Astioche, Celaeno, Cleodora, Cleopatra, Creusa, Erato, Eurydice, Glauce, Hypermnestra, Phylodameia and Polydore. He was succeeded to the throne by Lynceus.

DAPHNE Daughter of the river god Ladon, or of the river god Peneius. Sister of Metope. Transformed into a laurel tree by her father to foil Apollo's overtures of love.

DAPHNE Another name for Manto, daughter of Teiresias.

DAPHNIS Son of Hermes and a Sicilian nymph. Abandoned at birth, he was reared by a shepherd. Pan taught him to sing and play the flute. He was the inventor of bucolic poetry. A Naiad, variously called Lyce, Nais, Nomia, Xenea or, more probably, Piplea, fell in love with him and made him promise to associate with no other woman – though he may have won his wife in competition with Literses. He was blinded by the Muses when he broke this promise. Daphnis died of grief after the death of some of his dogs and was raised to heaven.

DAPHNIS (1) Son of Paris and Oenone. Brother of Corythus. (2) A shepherd on Mt Ida, turned to stone by a jealous nymph.

DARDANIA, kings of Dardanus, Ilus, Erichthonius, Assaracus.

DARDANUS Prime ancestor of the Trojans. Son of Zeus and Electra. Brother of Iasion. Married first to Chryse, daughter of Pallas. After her death, married Bateia (Arisbe), daughter of Teucer. Father of Erichthonius and Ilus. Father of Herophile by Neso.

The favourite son of Zeus by a mortal, Dardanus built a city at the foot of Mt Ida, later named Troy. He taught his subjects to worship Athena and gave them the Palladium.

DARDANUS King of the Scythians. The father of Idaea.

DARDANUS Son of Bias. Brother of Laogonus. Both brothers were killed in the Trojan War by Achilles.

DARDANUS, mares of The mares of twelve horses so swift that no one could catch them. Their sire was Boreas, who had taken the shape of a horse. Among the offspring were Xanthus and Balius.

DARES A warrior-friend of Aeneas on his journey to Italy, killed by Turnus.

DASCYLUS King of the Mariandynians. The father of Lycus. Heracles aided him in his battles.

DASCYLUS Son of Lycus, king of the Mariandynians. Accompanied Jason and the Argonauts as far as Thermodon.

DAULIS A city of Phocis, twelve miles east of Delphi. Also the nymph of the city.

DAUNUS King of Rutulia. Son of Pilumnus and Danae. Married Venilia. Father of Juturna (Iuturna) and Turnus. His sword was a gift from Vulcan.

DAUNUS Son of Lycaon. Brother of Iapyx and Peucetius. Founder of a kingdom in southern Italy.

DAWN, goddess of Greek: Eos. Roman: Aurora.

DEA DIA Roman goddess of the fields. Revered by the Fratres Arvales. She had three feast days in May.

DEAD, Roman goddess of the Mania.

DEATH, Personification of Thanatos.

DEATH, goddesses of Cer (violent death), Libitina (Roman), Mors.

DECIMA (tenth month) One of the three Parcae (fates). Companion of Nona and Parca.

DEER *See* Iphigeneia.

DEGMENUS An Eleian archer. Because Degmenus was unsuccessful in single

75

combat against Pyraechmes, Oxylus replaced Dius as king of Elis.

DEIANEIRA Daughter of Dionysus or Oeneus and Althaea. Half-sister of Gorge, Meleager and Toxeus. Second wife of Heracles. Mother of Ctesippus, Hyllus, Macaria, and one other.

After accidentally killing Heracles by giving him the poisoned cloak of Nessus, she committed suicide; and Artemis changed her into a guinea-fowl.

DEIANEIRA *See* Achelous.

DEICOON Son of Heracles and Megara. Brother of Creontidas and Therimachus. Killed by Heracles.

DEIDAMEIA (Astydameia) (1) Daughter of Lycomedes of Scyros. Lover of Achilles. Mother of Neoptelemus (Pyrrhus). After the death of Achilles, her son gave her as wife to Helenus. (2) Daughter of Bellerophon and Philonoe. Sister of Hippolochus, Isander and Laodameia. Married Evander. Mother of Dyna, Pallantia, Pallas, Roma and Sarpedon II. (3) Daughter of Amyntor and Cleobule. Sister of Crantor and Phoenix.

DEILEON An Argonaut. Son of Deimachus. Brother of Autolycus and Phlogius.

DEIMACHUS (1) Father of Autolycus, Deileon and Phlogius. (2) Father of Enarete, wife of Aeolus.

DEIMOS (fear) Son of Ares and Aphrodite. Brother of Terror (Pallor), Anteros, Enyo, Eros, Harmonia and Phobos. Accompanied Ares and Phobos into battle.

DEINO One of the Graiae. Daughter of Phorcys and Ceto. Sister of Enyo and Pephredo. The Graiae had one eye and one tooth which they shared and passed among them. They were guardians of the Gorgons.

DEIOCHUS A Greek captain killed in the Trojan War by Paris.

DEION King of Phocis. Son of Aeolus and Enarete. Had six brothers: Athamas, Cretheus, Macareus, Perieres, Salmoneus and Sisyphus; and seven sisters: Alcyone, Arne, Calyce, Canace, Peisidice, Perimele and Tanagra. Married Diomede. Father of Actor, Aenetus, Asteropeia, Cephalus and Phylacus.

DEIONE Possibly the mother of Miletus by Apollo.

DEIONEUS Either he or Eioneus was the father of Dia.

DEIOPE Priestess of Demeter at Eleusis. The mother of Eumolpus by Musaeus.

DEIOPITES Son of Priam slain in the Trojan War by Odysseus.

DEIPHOBE Epithet of the Cumaean Sibyl. Daughter of Glaucus, she led Aeneas to the Underworld.

DEIPHOBUS Son of Priam and Hecuba. Brother of Aesacus, Cassandra, Creusa, Hector, Helenus, Paris, Polyxena and Troilus.

Next to Hector, he was bravest amongst the Trojans. He married Helen by force after the death of Paris, but was slain by her former husband, Menelaus. His body was never found.

DEIPHOBUS Son of Hippocoon. He had eleven brothers and all were killed with their father, by Heracles.

DEIPHONTES A Heraclid. Son of Antimachus. Married Hyrnetho, daughter of Temenus. Father of three sons and one daughter. Chief adviser to Temenus until replaced by his brothers-in-law, Temenus' own sons.

DEIPYLE Daughter of Adrastus and Amphithea. Sister of Aegialeia, Aegialeus, Argeia, Hippodameia and possibly Cynanippus. Married Tydeus. Mother of Diomedes.

DEIPYLUS (1) Son of Polymnestor and Ilione. (2) Son of Tlepolemus and Polyxo. (3) Possibly son of Jason and Hypsipyle, hence brother of Euneus, Thoas and perhaps Nebrophonus, if this is not a doublet for Deipylus.

DEIPYRUS A Greek killed in the Trojan War by Helenus.

DELIA Epithet of Diana (Artemis), originating from Delos, her birthplace.

DELIADES Son of Glaucus and Eurymede. Accidentally killed by his brother, Bellerophon.

DELIGHT (Voluptas) Daughter of Eros and Psyche.

DELIGHT, goddess of Charis.

DELIUS Epithet of Apollo, originating from Delos, his birthplace.

DELIVERANCE, god of Greek: Soter.

DELOS Aegean island, the birthplace of Apollo and Artemis (on Mt Cynthos). Delos was also the home of Anius, its king.

DELPHI On the slopes of Mt Parnassus in Phocis. The home of the most famous oracle of Apollo. Named after Delphus, son of Apollo. The temple of Apollo there was built and destroyed many times.

DELPHUS Son of Apollo and Celaeno or Thyia. Eponym of Delphi.

DELPHINIUS Epithet of Apollo.

DELPHYNE A dragon-woman. Guardian of the sinews of Zeus, which were stolen by Aegipan and Hermes. She was killed by Apollo, at Parnassus.

DELUGE (Flood) Sent by Zeus at the end of the iron age, to destroy mankind. Only Deucalion and Pyrrha survived,

having taken refuge (perhaps in an ark-like structure) on Mt Parnassus, which remained above the water-line.

DEMARATUS An exiled Corinthian. Father of Tarquinius Priscus.

DEMETER (Ceres) Greek goddess of agriculture and one of the great divinities of the Greeks. Daughter of Cronos and Rhea. Sister of Hades, Hera, Hestia, Poseidon and Zeus. Mother of Persephone by Zeus. Mother of Plutus and Philomelus by Iasion. Mother of the horse, Arion, by Poseidon. Mother of the unnamed goddess referred to as 'mistress' (Despoena). Possibly mother of Iacchus. Epithet: Deo.

Called the fruitful with the yellow locks, she was swallowed by her father but rescued by Zeus. As Doso, she was nursemaid of Demophon. She gave Pelops an ivory

Demeter

shoulder after unwittingly eating part of his. Left Olympus and refused to return after Hades abducted her daughter, Persephone.

DEMIOS (Deimos) Son and attendant of Ares and Aphrodite. Brother of Terror, Panic, Fear, Alarm (Phobos), Trembling and Eris (goddess of discord and strife). Also called dread.

DEMO Epithet of the Cumaean Sibyl.

DEMODICE Possibly the wife of Cretheus, king of Iolcus. Alternatively his wife may have been Biadice.

DEMODOCE Daughter of Agenor and Telephassa or Argiope. Sister of Cadmus, Cilix, Electra, Europa, Phineus, Phoenix, Thasus, and possibly Argus.

DEMODOCUS The famous minstrel of the *Odyssey* who delighted the guests at the court of Alcinous of Phaeacia, telling of the deeds of the Greeks.

DEMOLEON Son of Antenor and Theano. Brother of Acamas, Agenor, Archelous, Coon, Crino, Glaucus, Helicaon, Iphidamas, Laocoon, Laodamas, Lycaon, Polybus and Polydamas. Half-brother of Pedaeus. Killed in the Trojan War.

DEMONASSA (1) Daughter of Amphiarus and Eriphyle. Sister of Alcmeon, Amphilochus and Eurydice. Married Thersander. Mother of Tisamenus. (2) Wife of Irus and mother of Eurytion and Eurydamas. (3) Wife of Poeas and mother of Philoctetes.

DEMONICE Daughter of Agenor and Epicasta. Sister of Hippodamus and Porthaon, and possibly Thestius. Mother of Evenus, Molus, Pylus and Thestius, by Ares.

DEMOPHILE Epithet of the Cumaean Sibyl.

DEMOPHON Joint king of Melos. Son of Theseus and Phaedra or Theseus' mistress, Antiope. Half-brother or brother of Acamas. Possibly the father of Munitus (alternatively Acamas) by Laodice, daughter of Priam.

He was in the Wooden Horse and obtained the Palladium for Athens. At the fall of Troy, he fell in love with Laodice. On his way home from Troy he visited Thrace and fell in love with, and possibly married, Phyllis. She committed suicide after he deserted her, although some say Athena turned her into an almond tree out of sympathy with the girl's distress and that when he returned he was prostrate with grief to find a tree instead of his expected lover. First man to be tried by the Areopagus, for murdering an Athenian while taking the Palladium from Diomedes.

DEMOPHON (1) A companion of Aeneas on his journey to Italy. Killed by Camilla. (2) Son of Celeus, king of Eleusis, and Metaneira. He had four sisters. Was nursed by Doso (Demeter). Doso placed him nightly in burning embers to make him immortal, but he burned to death when his mother interrupted the ceremony.

DEMUCHUS Trojan son of Philetor. Tall and handsome, he was killed in the Trojan War by Achilles.

DENDRITES Epithet of Dionysus, 'he of the trees'.

DEO Epithet of Demeter.

DESIRE, god of Himeros (Pothos).

DESPOENA ('Mistress') Daughter of Poseidon and Demeter, conceived when they assumed the shape of horses. Her real name was unknown outside the secret rites held for her in conjunction with those for Anytus and Demeter.

DESTINY With the Fates, an ancient god not subject to Zeus.

DESTINY, goddess of Necessitas.

DEUCALION King of Pherae in Thessaly. Son of Prometheus and Hesione or Pronoea. Married Pyrrha. Father of Amphictyon, Hellen, Pandora, Protogeneia and Thyia.

A divine command ordered him to build an ark, so he and his wife survived the nine-day Deluge that destroyed all mankind, the ark finally coming to rest on Mt Parnassus. They offered sacrifices to Phyxios (Zeus), god of escape. Deucalion and Pyrrha repopulated the earth by throwing stones picked up from Gaea, Mother Earth, those thrown by Deucalion becoming men and those thrown by Pyrrha, women.

DEUCALION An Argonaut. Son of Minos and Pasiphae. Brother of Acacallis, Androgeus, Ariadne, Catreus, Glaucus, Euryale, Lycastus, Phaedra and Xenodice. He was the father of Crete and Idomeneus by his wife, and also of a bastard son, Molus. Took part in Calydonian Boar Hunt.

DEXAMENE A Nereid. One of the fifty daughters of Nereus and Doris.

DEXAMENUS King of Olenus. Father of Theraephone and Theronice (twin daughters), and of Eurypylus and Mnesimache.

DIA A Lapith. Daughter of Deioneus or Eioneus. Married Ixion. Mother of Peirithous, although the father may have been Zeus.

DIA (1) Aegean island, also called Naxos, where Ariadne married Dionysus after she had been abandoned there by Theseus. (2) Island in the Black Sea, also called the Island of Ares, where the Argonauts were attacked by bronze-feathered birds.

DIANA Roman goddess of forests and groves. Daughter of Jupiter and Latona. Sister of Phoebus. Her dedication day was 13 August. Greek equivalent: Artemis.

Diana

DIAS Father of Cleolla, the wife of Pleisthenes.

DIASIA Festival of Zeus held in February or March at Athens.

DICE (Dike) One of the Horae. Daughter of Zeus and Themis. Like her mother, often called Justice. Sister of Eirene and Eunomia, the other Horae (or Seasons).

DICTE, Mount The home of the Harpies, according to some sources, and possibly the birthplace of Zeus (alternatively, this was Mt Ida). Mt Dicte is in central Crete.

DICTYNNA Ancient Eastern Cretan goddess. Usually called Britomartis. A follower of Artemis. Inventor of fishermen's nets.

DICTYS Son of Magnes and a Naiad. Brother of Polydectes. Married Clymene. A fisherman of Seriphus in Crete, Dictys was made king of Seriphus by Perseus. Went to the Trojan War as the diarist of Idomeneus.

DIDO (Elissa) Daughter of Mutto or Belus, king of Tyre, or Agenor. Sister of Anna and Pygmalion. Married her uncle, Acherbas (Acerbas, Sicharbas) before she founded Carthage.

Pygmalion murdered her husband for his money. Dido was the founder of Carthage, the area of the city being marked out by her cutting up a single cow hide into strips. Aeneas visited her on his journey to Italy and she fell in love with him. After he left her she committed suicide on a funeral pyre, cursing the Trojans as she died.

DII (Di) Roman name for the twelve great Greek gods: Ceres (Demeter), Mars (Ares), Phoebus (Apollo), Diana (Artemis), Mercury (Hermes), Venus (Aphrodite), Jupiter (Zeus), Minerva (Athena), Vesta (Hestia), Juno (Hera), Neptune (Poseidon) and Vulcan (Hephaestus).

DIKE (Dice, Justice) One of the Horae. Daughter of Zeus and Themis. Sister of Eirene and Eunomia. Astraea, another daughter of Zeus and Themis, was also called Dike.

DINDYME Putative mother of Cybele by Meion or Zeus.

DINDYMENE (Ops) Epithet of Cybele, mother of the gods.

DEINO (Dino) One of the Graeae.

DIOGENEIA The wife of Phrasimus and mother of Zeuxippe and Praxithea.

DIOMEDE (1) Daughter of Xuthus and Creusa. Sister of Achaeus and Ion, and possibly Dorus. Married Deion. Mother of Actor, Aenetus, Asteropeia, Cephalus and Phylacus. (2) The wife of Amyclas and

Dike

mother of Argalus, Cynortas, Leaneira and Hyacinthus.

DIOMEDEIA Wife of Iphiclus. Mother of Podarces and Protesilaus.

DIOMEDES (Tydides) King of Aetolia. Son of Tydeus and Deipyle. Married Aegialeia, but lover of Callirrhoe, daughter of Lycus.

Went with Acamas to Troy to threaten war if Helen was not returned. As a suitor of Helen he took eighty ships to Troy from Argos with Euryalus and Sthenelus. After Achilles, he was the greatest Greek hero at Troy, killing Dolon, Rhesus and Pandorus, and wounding Aeneas, Ares and Aphrodite. When Pandorus wounded him, he was cured by Athena. He was the only Greek to help Nestor after his horses were killed. Diomedes was one of those in the Wooden Horse at Troy. He was one of the Epigoni. He stole the horses of Rhesus and, together with Odysseus, stole the Palladium. Because of his love affair with Callirrhoe, Athena caused Diomedes' wife to be unfaithful in revenge. He then left Argos and married Evippe, daughter of Daunus. Athena made him immortal.

DIOMEDES King of the Bistones of Thrace. Son of Ares and the nymph Cyrene, or Asterie.

He owned horses that fed on human flesh; and the eighth labour of Heracles was to kill them. Heracles then forced Diomedes to eat the dead horses.

DION King of Sparta. Father of Carya, Lyco and Orphe by his wife, Iphitea. Apollo gave his daughters the power of prophecy.

DIONE Daughter of Atlas or Oceanus and Tethys, or of Uranus and Gaea. Married Tantalus. Mother of Broteas, Niobe and Pelops. Possibly mother of Aphrodite by Zeus.

DIONYSIA Athenian festivals in honour of Dionysus.

DIONYSUS (Bacchus) God of wine and ecstasy. Son of Zeus and Semele or Demeter. Youngest of the twelve Olympians. Married Ariadne. Father of Hymen, possibly by Aphrodite. Father of Deianeira by Althaea, wife of Oeneus; of Phlius by Araethyrea; of Narcaeus by Physcoa, an Eleian; and of Arete. By Ariadne he also had six sons: Oenopion, Ceramus, Phanus, Peparethus, Staphylus and Thoas. May have been father of Iacchus and, by Aphrodite, Priapus and possibly the Charites.

At birth Dionysus was snatched from the body of his dead mother and reared by

Dionysus

Athamas and Ino, and later by Macris. His nurses were the Hyades. He was taught the art of agriculture by Aristaeus. His followers were called Bacchants and Maenads. Dionysus gave Midas his golden touch.

His epithets were: 1. Iacchus, (at the Athenian festivals of Bacchus). 2. Bromius, (thunderer). 3. Lenaeus. He was known to the Romans as Liber. His sacred fish was the dolphin.

DIORES Son of Amarynceus. Brother of Hippostratus. Father of Automedon. One of the leaders of the Eleian forces at Troy. Killed by Pierous.

DIORES Friend of Aeneas killed by Turnus.

DIOSCURI (Tyndaridae) The 'Gemini' (twins), Castor and Polydeuces (Pollux), sons of Tyndareus and Leda, though some traditions have Zeus as the father of Polydeuces, and others make Zeus father of both. They married their cousins, Phoebe and Hilaera. Three great events mark their fabulous lives: (1) Their expedition against Athens; (2) Their part in the expedition of the Argonauts; (3) Their battle with the sons of Aphareus.

DIOUNSIS Name by which the people of Thrace and Phrygia knew Dionysus. They called his mother Zemelo.

DIRAE Heavenly name for Alecto, Megaera and Tisiphone, the three Furies (Erinnyes), daughters of Gaea. Known in hell as the Furies.

DIRCE The wife of Lycus, brother of Nycteus, regent of Thebes. Mother of another Lycus. Antiope was given to Dirce, daughter of Nycteus, as a slave, after Lycus killed Epopeus, her husband. Antiope and

Dioscuri

Epopeus' children killed her by tying her to the tail or horns of a mad bull. She became a fountain.

DIS or DIS PATER   God of the Underworld. Roman equivalent of Pluto, Hades, etc. Husband of Persephone.

DISCORDIA   Goddess of strife and discord. Daughter of Zeus and Hera. Twin of Ares and sister of Arge, Eleithyia, Hebe and Hephaestus.

DITHYRAMB(US)   (1) Epithet of Bacchus. (2) A wild song sung by the Bacchanals.

DIUS   King of Elis. A king who resisted Oxylus during a Heraclid invasion of his land. He put up an archer, Degmenus, in single combat with Pyraechmes, the slinger of Oxylus, and lost his kingdom.

DIUS   Bastard son of Priam.

DIUS FIDIUS   Sabine god of the sky. Roman god invoked in oaths, cf Jupiter.

DODONA   The most ancient oracle of Zeus in Greece, built by Deucalion after the flood. It was centred on an oak tree.

DODONIDES   Epithet of the Hyades.

DOG   Favourite animal of Ares. *See also* Hecuba.

DOG STAR (Sirius)   *See* Maera.

DOLICHE (Icaria)   Island in the Aegean Sea where the body of Icarus was washed ashore.

DOLIONES   A Mysian tribe. People from the peninsula of Cyzicus who offered hospitality to the Argonauts.

DOLIUS   The faithful old retainer of Odysseus and Penelope who looked after Laertes for twenty years. He was the father of Melantho, Melanthus and six other sons.

Dolius helped repulse the relatives of Penelope's suitors.

DOLON   A Trojan spy. Son of Eumedes or Eumelus. Father of another Eumedes. Killed by Odysseus or Diomedes.

DOLOPS   Son of Lampus, a Trojan elder. Father of Clytius. Killed in the Trojan War by Menelaus.

DOLOPS   Greek son of Clytius. Killed in the Trojan War by Hector.

DOLPHIN   Sacred fish and symbol of Dionysus.

DOLPHIN   *See* Acetes, Amphitrite.

DOORS, Roman god of   Janus.

DOOR-PIVOTS, goddess of   Cardea.

DORIANS   A major Greek race, descendants of Dorus.

DORIS   A sea-goddess. Daughter of Oceanus and Tethys. Sister of Eidyia, Electra, Clymene, Meliboea, Metis, Perseis, Pleione, Proteus, Styx, Europa, Clytia and Callirhoe, the rivers and the fountains. Married Nereus. Mother of fifty daughters called Nereids or Dorides. May have been mother of Amphitrite, Galatea and Thetis.

DORIS   A Nereid. One of the fifty daughters of Nereus and Doris.

DORODOCHE   Another name for Periboea, wife of Icarius and mother of Penelope.

DORUS   (1) Son of Hellen and Ortheis. Brother of Aeolus and Xuthus. Father of Aegimius and Tectamus. Eponym of the Dorians. (2) Son of Apollo and Phthia. Brother of Laodocus and Polypoetes. Father of Xanthippe. Killed by Aetolus, father-in-law of Xanthippe. (3) Son of Xuthus and Creusa. Brother of Achaeus, Diomede and

Ion. This is probably another tradition referring to (1).

DORYCLUS Bastard son of Priam. Killed in the Trojan War by Greater Ajax.

DOSO Nursemaid of Demophon, son of Metaneira. Doso was really Demeter in disguise.

DOTIS Possibly the mother of Phlegyas (alternatively, Chryse) by Ares.

DOTO A Nereid. One of the fifty daughters of Nereus and Doris.

DOVES Elais, Oino and Spermo were all turned into white doves by Dionysus after their capture by Agamemnon and the Greeks at Troy. *See also* Aphrodite.

DRAGON *See* Aeetes, Cadmus.

DRANCES Friend of Latinus and enemy of Turnus who advised peace with Aeneas.

DREAD, Greek god of Phobus.

DREAMS, gods of Morpheus, Phantasos. *See* Oneiroi.

DREAMS (Oneiroi) Children of Nyx or Hypnos or Erebus, as were Aether, Cer, Hemera, Hypnos, Momus, Moros, Nemesis, Thanatos and Charon. They guarded the entrance to the Underworld.

DRINKING, Roman god of Comus.

DRYADES (Hamadryads) Woodland nymphs who lived in trees and died with them.

DRYAS (1) Son of Ares, present on the Calydonian Boar Hunt. (2) Centaur present at the wedding of Peirithous. (3) Daughter

of Faunus. Her mother may have been Marica. Sister of Acis. She so hated man that she never appeared in public. (4) One of the fifty sons of Aegyptus murdered by his wife, Eurydice, on their wedding night. (5) Son of Lycurgus. Brother of Phyllis. Dionysus made him mad for showing disrespect. (6) Father of Lycurgus, king of the Edonians. Killed with Eteocles during the Theban war.

DRYOPE Daughter of Eurytus. Gave birth to Amphissus after her seduction by Apollo. Married Andraemon. Soon after, having plucked the flowers of the lotus tree, she was changed into a lotus or poplar.

DRYOPE (1) Nymph of a fountain called Pegae. Falling in love with Hylas, she drew him into the fountain. (2) A woman of Lemnos whose body Aphrodite possessed, then incited the women of Lemnos to kill their menfolk. (3) Arcadian nymph, daughter of Dryops and Polydore. Possibly the mother of Pan by Hermes.

DRYOPS (1) Father of Dryope by Polydore. (2) Son of Priam. (3) Son of Apollo. (4) A companion of Aeneas in Italy. Killed by Clausus.

DUTY, Roman goddess of Pietas.

DYMAS King of Phrygia. Son of Aegimius. Brother of Pamphylus. Married Evagora or Glaucippe. Father of Asius and Hecuba. Killed by the Dorians during the invasion of the Peloponnesus.

DYMAS A Trojan who disguised himself as a Greek during the Trojan War and was killed by the Trojans.

DYNAMENE A Nereid. One of the fifty daughters of Nereus and Doris.

E

EAGLE The sacred bird of Zeus, which he often sent as an omen.

EAGLE *See* Ajax, Nisus, Prometheus.

EARTH, goddesses of Greek: Cora, Core, Demeter, Gaea, Gaia, Ge, Kora, Kore, Persephone, Rhea.
Roman: Ceres, Libera, Ops, Proserpina (Proserpine), Tellus, Terra, Terra Mater.
Phrygian: Cybebe, Cybele.

EATING, Roman god of Comus.

ECBASUS Son of Argus and Evadne. Brother of Criasus, Epidaurus and Peiras.

ECHECLES Son of Actor. Married Polymele, daughter of Phylas.

ECHECLUS Son of Agenor. Killed in the Trojan War by Achilles

ECHELAS Son of Penthilus. Brother of Damasias.

ECHEMUS King of Arcadia. Son of Aeropus. Married Timandra, who later deserted him.
Winner of a wrestling event in the Olympic games. Succeeded Lycurgus to the throne. Slew Hyllus in a battle defending Peloponnesus against the Heraclids.

ECHEPHRON Son of Nestor and Eurydice or Anaxibia. Brother of Antilochus, Aretus, Peisidice, Peisistratus, Perseus, Polycaste, Stratius and Thrasymedes.

ECHEPOLUS A rich Sicyonian. One of Helen's suitors, he gave Agamemnon the gift of a horse to avoid his obligation to go to the Trojan War.

ECHETUS King of Epirus. A cruel king who first blinded his daughter for yielding to her lover, and then jailed her, making her undergo forced labour.

Eagle

ECHIDNA A monster (half nymph, half snake) who, though mortal, never grew old. Daughter of either Chrysaor and Callirrhoe, Phorcys and Ceto, Tartarus and Gaea, or Styx and Peiras. Sister of Geryon if father Chrysaor; or, if Phorcys was her father, sister of Ladon, Scylla, Gorgons and Graiae. Alternatively, if Tartarus was her father, Typhoeus was her brother. Married Typhon. Mother of these monsters: Caucasian Eagle, Cerberus, Crommyonian sow, Chimaera, Geryon, Hydra of Lerna, Ladon the dragon, Nemean lion, Orthus the dog, the Sphinx and the Vultures. The Sphinx and the Nemean lion were possibly her children by Orthus, and she may also have been the mother of three children by Heracles. She was killed by Argus Panoptes in her ship.

ECHINADIAN ISLANDS (Strophades) Islands formed from five nymphs who refused to pay homage to Achelous, principal ruler of south-west Greece, and were swept away by him.

ECHION An Argonaut, Son of Hermes and Antianeira. Brother of Erytus or Eurytus. Unsurpassed in cunning, he threw the first spear in the Calydonian Boar Hunt. In the Wooden Horse at Troy.

ECHION One of the Sparti. When Cadmus sowed the teeth of the sacred dragon of Ares, the five survivors of this crop were: Echion, Cthonius, Hyperenor, Pelorus and Udaeus. Echion married Agave, daughter of Cadmus, and became father of Pentheus.

ECHIUS (1) Father of Mecisteus. Killed in the Trojan War by Polites. (2) A Lycian killed in the Trojan War by Patroclus.

ECHO Nymph of Mt Helicon. Daughter of Gaea. Attendant of Hera. Fell in love with Narcissus and Pan. Hera suspected her of conspiring to conceal one of Zeus' dalliances, and took from her the power of normal speech, leaving her able only to reply to others, and unable to remain silent after others spoke. When Narcissus spurned her love, she wasted away.

ECSTASY, god of Greek: Dionysus (Bacchus). Roman: Liber.

EDONUS Possibly the son of Poseidon and Helle. If so, brother of Paeon. His tribe, the Edoni, inhabited that part of Thrace near Mt Pangaeus.

EERIBOEA Second wife of Aloeus. Stepmother of Ephialtes and Otus, and, possibly, the mother of Ajax, son of Telamon.

EETION (1) King of Hypoplacian Thebes. Father of seven sons and Andromache. He and his sons were killed by Achilles in a single day. (2) Father of Podes.

EGERIA Obscure Roman goddess or nymph. Mistress and later second wife of Numa Pompilius, second king of Rome.

She was so disconsolate at his death she melted into tears. Diana changed her into a fountain. As a goddess, she was protectress of unborn babies.

EGESTA Daughter of Hippotes. Married the river god Crimisus. Mother of Acestes.

EIDOTHEA (1) Daughter of Proteus, the old man of the sea. Lived on Pharos. (2) A nymph who helped to educate Zeus. (3) Daughter of Proteus and Psamathe. Cf (1) and (2).

EIDYIA (Idyia) Daughter of Oceanus and Tethys. Sister of Clymene, Doris, Electra, Meliboea, Metis, Perseis, Proteus, Pleione, Europa, Clytia, Styx, Callirrhoe and Asia. Second wife of Aeetes, king of Colchis. Mother of Absyrtus and Medea.

EILATUS King of the Arcadians of Phaesane. Son of Merope. Father of Aepytus.

EIONEUS (1) Son of Magnes. Brother of Pierus and Hymenaeus. Possibly father of Dia, wife of Ixion. Suitor of Hippodameia and killed by her father, Oenomaus. (2) Possibly father of Rhesus (alternatively Strymon) by Calliope.

EIRENE (Peace) Goddess of peace. Daughter of Zeus and Themis. One of the Horae and sister of Dike and Eunomia. Known to the Romans as Pax.

ELAIS (olive) Daughter of Anius. Sister of Oino and Spermo. Devotee of Dionysus. She had the ability to produce olive oil from the ground by touch.

ELARA (Elare) Daughter of Orchomenus. Mother of Tityus by Zeus.

ELATO Another name for Baton, charioteer of Amphiarus, killed by a thunderbolt from Zeus.

ELATUS King of Arcadia. Son of Arcas and Erato. Brother of Apheidas, Azan and Hyperippe. Half-brother of Autolaus. Married Laodice, daughter of Cinyras. Father of Stymphalus. Founder of Elateia in Phocis. Aided the people of Phocis against the Phlegyans.

ELATUS (1) Father of several Argonauts. (2) Possibly father of Ampycus. (3) Suitor of Penelope. (4) An ally of Priam. (5) An Arcadian Lapith chieftain. Father of Caenis, Ischys and Polyphemus, by Hippea.

ELECTRA One of the Pleiades. Daughter of Atlas and Pleione. Sister of Alcyone, Celaeno, Maia, Merope, Sterope and Taygete. Mother of Dardanus and Iasion by Zeus. She lived on the island of Samothrace.

ELECTRA Daughter of Oceanus and Tethys. Sister of the Oceanides: Pleione, Styx, etc. (*see* Oceanus). Married Thaumas, son of Pontus and Gaea. Mother of Iris, the Harpies and the gusts of winds.

ELECTRA (Laodice) Daughter of Agamemnon and Clytemnestra. Also called Laodice. Sister of Chrysothemis, Iphigeneia and Orestes. She incited Orestes to kill their mother because of Clytemnestra's infidelity with Aegisthus, and to avenge their father's murder. With Orestes she held to ransom Hermione, daughter of Menelaus and Helen. Later married Pylades by whom she became mother of Medon and Strophius.

ELECTRA (1) Daughter of Agenor and Telephassa. Sister of Cadmus, Cilix, Europa, Demodoce, Phineus, Thasus and Phoenix. (2) An attendant of Helen.

ELECTRYON King of Mycenae. Son of Perseus and Andromeda. Brother of Alcaeus, Heleus, Perses, Sthenelus, Gorgophone and Mestor. Married Anaxo, daughter of Alcaeus. Father of six sons, including Everes, and one daughter, Alcemene. Father of Licymnius by Midea of Phrygia, and possibly of Leitus by Cleobule. Electryon was accidentally killed by Amphitryon.

ELEITHYIA Daughter of Zeus and Hera. Sister of Ares, Arge, Discordia, Hebe and Hephaestus. Roman equivalent: Lucina.

ELEIUS King of Elis. Son of Poseidon and Eurycyda. Succeeded his uncle, Aetolus, to the throne.

ELEPHENOR King of the Abantes of Euboea. Son of Chalcodon and Imenarete or perhaps Alcinoe. After giving refuge to the exiled Acamas and Demophon, all three went with forty ships to Troy where Elephenor was killed by Agenor.

ELEUSINIAN MYSTERIES Founded jointly by Eumolpus and Celeus, these most famous of ancient mystery rites consisted of fasts, dramas and purifications, as well as religious rites in honour of Demeter and Persephone. Most famous celebration was at Athens.

ELEUSIS (ELEUSINUS) Son of Ogygus. Brother of Alalcomenia and Aulus, and Thelxinoea in Boeotian tradition. Married Cothonea. Father of Triptolemus.

ELEUSIS Greek town, twenty-five kilometres west of Athens, near the Isthmus of Corinth. Site of the Eleusinian Mysteries, founded by Eumolpus, where Demeter taught her rites.

ELEUSIS, kings of Celeus, Cercyon, Hippothoon, Ogygus.

ELGIN MARBLES Sculptures of many of the Greek gods and heroes which once formed parts of the pediment, metopes and frieze of the Parthenon, and which were removed in the last century from Athens to the British Museum.

ELICIUS God of thunder and lightning. Epithet of Jupiter.

ELIS City and country of the Peloponnesus. Founded by Aeolus, Aethlius or Endymion. Olympia was in Elis; thus Elis was the home of the Olympic Games for centuries. Pisa was also in Elis until Pelops made it independent. Famed for its horses.

ELIS, kings of Endymion, Epeius, Aetolus, Eleius, Augeias, Phyleus, Agasthenes, Oxylus, Laias (the last).

Dius, Iphitus and Polyxeinus were also kings of Elis and possibly ruled between Agasthenes and Oxylus.

ELISSA Another name for Dido, founder of Carthage. Daughter of Agenor, or Belus.

ELPENOR The youngest member of Odysseus' crew. When drunk he fell off the roof of Circe's palace and was killed. His ghost met Odysseus in the underworld and asked him for a proper funeral. It was also said of him that Circe gave him a potion that changed him into a pig and that later he regained human form.

ELPIS (hope) All that remained in the box after Pandora lifted its lid.

ELYMUS A friend of Priam who returned to Sicily after the Trojan War and founded Elyma.

ELYSIAN FIELDS (Elysium, Blessed Isles, White Island) Some place these islands to the north of Africa. Ruled by Cronos or Rhadamanthys. Home of the Blessed after death, including the deified mortals: Cadmus, Diomedes, Menelaus and Peleus.

EMATHION King of Arabia. Son of Tithonus and Eos. Brother of Memnon and perhaps Phaethon. Killed by Heracles.

EMPUSA Hecate's hobgoblins who had one donkey-shaped foot and one made of brass. They withdrew when insulted or abused. Sent by Hecate to frighten foreign travellers.

ENARETE Wife of Aeolus of Magnesia. Mother of seven sons: Athamas, Cretheus, Deion, Macareus, Perieres, Salmoneus,

Sisyphus; and seven daughters: Alcyone, Arne, Calyce, Canace, Peisidice and Perimele.

ENCELADUS Most powerful of the giants. Son of Gaea. He fled from Phlegra to Sicily where some say he was killed by Heracles, others by Athena who buried him. Mt Aetna was placed on top of his body and when he turned over, an earthquake occurred and when he hissed, the volcano erupted. Some sources claim that he was killed by a thunderbolt from Zeus.

ENDEIS (1) Daughter of Cheiron and Chariclo. Sister of Ocyrrhoe (Menalippe) and Theia. Married Aeacus. Mother of Peleus and Telamon. (2) Mother of Crisus, Naubolus and Panopaeus by Phocus.

ENDINGS, Roman god of Janus.

ENDYMION King of Elis. Son of Aethlius or Zeus and Calyce. Married a Naiad. Father of Aetolus, Epeius, Eurycyda and Paeon. Father of the festival at Olympia, he begged Zeus for perpetual youth and was granted perpetual sleep during which some claim he became father of fifty daughters by Selene.

ENIOCHA *See* Anioche.

ENIOCHE Son of Creon and Anioche or Eurydice. Brother of Haemon, Megara, Menoeceus and Pyrrha.

ENNOMUS A Trojan killed in the War by Achilles.

ENODIA Epithet of Hecate.

ENOPS Father of Satinus by a nymph.

ENTELLUS Winner of the boxing contest at the funeral games of Anchises.

ENTERPRISES, Greek goddess of Praxidice, who saw that enterprises were justly carried out.

ENYALIUS God of war. A companion of Ares, or his epithet. A brother of Enyo.

ENYO (1) Daughter of Phorcys and Ceto. Sister of Deino and Pephredo. One of the Graiae. (2) Greek goddess of war, entering battle with Ares. Identified with Roman Bellona. Daughter of Ares and Aphrodite. Sister of Anteros, Deimos, Eros, Harmonia, Pallor and Phobos.

EOS Goddess of dawn. Daughter of the Titans Hyperion (or Pallas) and Theia or of Euryphaessa. Sister of Helios and Selene. Mother of Emathion, Memnon and Phaethon with her consort, Tithonus; and some say she was mother of Phaethon and Tithonus by Cephalus; of Aura, Eosphorus (morning star), Phosphorus and of the winds and stars, by Astraeus. Lover of Cleitus whom she abducted.

Eos announced her brother, Helios, each morning and accompanied him across the sky. Eos was also called Aurora by the Romans.

EOSPHORUS (Lucifer) The morning star. Son of Eos and Astraeus. Brother of the other stars. Father of Ceyx and Leuconoe.

EPALTES Lycian killed in the Trojan War by Patroclus.

EPAPHUS King of Egypt. Son of Zeus and Io. Married Memphis. Father of Libya and Lysianassa. Founder of the city of Memphis. Identified with the Egyptian god, Apis.

EPEIGEUS Ruler of Budeion. Son of the Myrmidon Agacles. Killed in the Trojan War by Hector.

EPEIUS King of Elis. Son of Endymion and a Naiad. Brother of Aetolus, Eurycyda and Paeon. Married Anaxiroe, daughter of Coronus. Father of Hyrmina. Won his throne in a foot race with his two brothers. Was succeeded by Aetolus.

EPEIUS Phocian leader at Troy. Son of Panopeus and Neaera. Brother of Aegle. Founder of Pisa, he designed and built the Wooden Horse after bringing thirty ships to Troy. Epeius won the boxing event at the funeral games of Patroclus.

EPHIALTES One of the Aloeidae. Son of Poseidon or Aloeus and Iphimedeia. Twin of Otus. They grew one cubit of breadth and one fathom of height each year. At nine years of age they warred against the gods. Ephialtes was killed by Apollo. He was possibly the same Ephialtes as the giant son of Uranus and Gaea, who was shot in the left eye by Apollo and the right eye by Heracles.

EPHIALTES Name of the Greek who betrayed the Spartans at Thermopylae.

EPHYRA An Oceanid. Daughter of Oceanus and Tethys. The first person to live on Ephyraea, the Isthmus of Corinth.

EPHYRAEA The wife of Epopeus, king of Asopia. Mother of Marathon.

EPICASTA Daughter of Calydon and Aeolia. Sister of Protogeneia. Married Agenor. Mother of Demonice, Porthaon, Hippodamus and Thestius.

EPICASTA Another name for Jocasta, daughter of Menoeceus.

EPICLES Friend of Sarpedon. Killed in the Trojan War by Greater Ajax.

EPIDAURUS Son of Argus and Evadne, according to the Argives. The Eleians believed his father was Pelops, and the Epidaurians knew him as the son of Apollo. Brother of Criasus, Ecbasus and Peiras.

EPIDAURUS Town in Peloponnesus, north of Argos, the home of Periphates. Here was a famous statue of Asclepius. Kings included Pityreus and Deiphontes.

EPIGONI Sons of the Seven against Thebes. They were: Aegialeus and Cyanippus, sons of Adrastus; Alcmeon (their leader) and Amphilochus, sons of Amphiarus; Sthenelus, son of Capaneus; Polydorus, son of Hippomedon; Euryalus, son of Mecisteus; Promachus, also known as Tlesimenes, son of Parthenopaeus. (Eteocles left no sons.) The Epigoni were helped by Diomedes, son of Tydeus and Thersander, and possibly by his two brothers, Adrastus and Timeas, sons of Polyneices.

The Epigoni marched on Thebes ten years after the Seven but, unlike their fathers, they were successful. Aegialeus was the only one killed, whereas his father had been the sole survivor of the Seven. The war of the Epigoni became the subject of epic and tragic poems.

EPIMEDES (one of the Dactyli) Son of Rhea or Anchiale. Brother of Heracles, Iasius, Idas, Paeonaeus and five sisters.

EPIMELIOS Epithet of Hermes, the guardian of flocks.

EPIMENIDES The Rip Van Winkle of mythology. This Cretan shepherd, who was a poet and prophet and possibly one of the seven wise men of Greece, taught religion and worked miracles. Searching for lost sheep, he fell asleep for fifty-seven years. Was said to have attained great age.

EPIMETHEUS Son of Iapetos and Clymene or Asia. Brother of Atlas, Menoetius and Prometheus. Married Pandora. Father of Pyrrha, the first woman born of a mortal. It was he who opened Pandora's box. His epithet was Afterthought.

EPIONE Daughter of Merops. Perhaps sister of Arisbe, Cleite, Amphius and Adrastus, although their fathers may not be the same Merops. Married Asclepius. Mother of Acesis, Aegle, Hygieia, Iaso, Janiscus, Machaon, Panacea and Podalirius.

EPISTROPHUS (1) Son of Evenus and Alcippe. Brother of Marpessa and Mynes. (2) Son of Iphitus. Brother of Schedius. Went to the Trojan War.

EPIUS Winner of the boxing event at Patroclus' funeral games, defeating Euryalus.

EPOCHUS Son of Lycurgus and Cleophyle or Eurynome. Brother of Amphidamas, Ancaeus and Iasus.

EPONA (Bubona) Roman goddess, protectress of cattle and horses, she was a daughter of a man and mare.

EPOPEUS King of Sicyon. Son of Poseidon and Canace. Brother of Aloeus, Hopleus, Nireus and Triopas. Married Antiope who was pregnant by Zeus. Killed by Lycus, Antiope's uncle.

EPOPEUS (1) Son of Aloeus. (2) King of Lesbos. Father of Nyctimene, whom he raped. (3) King of Asopia. Married Ephyraea. Father of Marathon.

EQUESTRIAN NEPTUNE *See* Consus.

ERATO Muse of love lyrics and bridal songs. Daughter of Zeus and Mnemosyne. One of the nine Muses (qv). Her symbol was a lyre.

ERATO A Dryad. Wife of Arcas of Arcadia. Mother of Apheidas, Azan, Elatus and Hyperippe.

ERATO (1) One of the Danaids, daughters of Danaus. (2) One of the Nereids, daughters of Nereus.

EREBUS The underworld darkness below Hades, through which all the dead must pass. Erebus was born of Chaos and Darkness, and was the brother of Nyx. Father of Aether, Cer, Dreams, Hypnos, Momus, Moros, Nemesis, Thanatos, Charon and Hemera, by Nyx.

ERECHTHEUM The fifth century BC temple to Athena at the Acropolis. In the courtyard grew her sacred olive tree.

ERECHTHEUS I (Erichthonius) 4th or 5th king of Athens. Son of Hephaestus, whose seed fell on Mother Earth (Gaea) when he tried to rape Athena. Erechtheus was deformed, having the tail of a snake. Some nominate Attis as his mother. He married the Naiad, Praxithea, and was father of Pandion, who succeeded him on the throne, he himself having succeeded Amphictyon. Erechtheus was reared at the Acropolis by Athena. Was the inventor of chariots and chariot-harnesses, and founded the Panathenaic festival.

ERECHTHEUS II (Erichthonius) 6th or 7th king of Athens. Son of Pandion and Zeuxippe. Twin of Butes and brother of Philomela and Procne. Grandson of Erechtheus I. Married Praxithea. Father of Cecrops, Chthonia, Creusa, Eupalamus, Metion, Oreithyia, Orneus, Pandorus, Procris, Protogeneia and Thespius. Although more are named, it is agreed by most sources that Erechtheus had only four daughters. Some names are doublets. Also the father of Merope.

In order to defeat the Eleusinians, he consulted an oracle which told him to sacrifice his daughters. After killing the youngest, the others committed suicide. He may have been the first to introduce the Eleusinian Mysteries. There can be little doubt that the names Erechtheus and Erichthonius are identical, and it is possible that Erechtheus I and II were the same person.

ERGEA Mother of Celaeno by Poseidon.

ERGINUS King of Boeotian Orchomenus. Son of Clymenus. Brother of Azeus. Father of Agamedes and, possibly, Trophonius, though Apollo was the alternative father.

The Thebans killed his father and, after a war, they were forced to give Erginus one hundred bulls a year for twenty years

in compensation. Heracles, however, reversed the process, demanding 200 bulls a year, and possibly killing Erginus.

ERGINUS An Argonaut from Miletus. Son of Poseidon or Clymenus. May have been the same person as above. After the death of Tiphys, he steered the Argo.

ERIBOEA (Eeriboea, Periboea) (1) Wife of Aeneus. Possibly mother of Clymenus and Cyzicus. (2) Wife of Aloeus, step-mother of Ephialtes and Otus. (3) Wife of Polybus. Reared Oedipus as her own child. (4) Mother of Penelope. (5) Mother of Telamonian (Greater) Ajax. (6) Epithet of Aphrodite. (7) Epithet of Juno.

ERIBOTES (Eurybates) An Argonaut. Son of Teleon. He and Canthus were killed trying to steal sheep from Caphaurus.

ERICHTHONIUS King of Dardania. Son of Dardanus and Arisbe (Bateia), daughter of Teucer. Younger brother of Ilus. Married Astyoche. Father of Tros. With 3000 horses to his name, he became the world's richest man.

ERIDANUS River god of a mythical river. Son of Oceanus and Tethys. The river was that into which Phaethon fell from his chariot (possibly the river Po).

ERIGONE Daughter of Aegisthus and Clytemnestra. Sister of Aletes. In an adulterous liaison with Orestes, husband of Hermione, she bore Penthilus and, possibly, Tisamenus. Later she brought Orestes to trial for the murder of her mother and committed suicide after he was acquitted.

ERIGONE Daughter of Icarius of Athens. Owned a dog, Maera, who discovered the burial place of her murdered father. Erigone hanged herself out of grief, and became the constellation Virgo. Bacchus deceived her by changing himself into a beautiful grape.

ERINNYES (Eumenides) Daughters of Gaea and the blood of the castrated

Uranus. Called Alecto, Megaera and Tisiphone. They avenge fathers and, occasionally, mothers, against disloyal children. The Romans knew them as the Furies. Because they punished crimes not only after death but also on earth, they were considered as ruling fate. They also prevented men learning too much about the future.

ERIOPIS Daughter of Jason and Medea. Sister of Alcimenes, Argus, Medeias, Mermerus, Pheres, Thessalus and Tisandrus.

ERIOPIS Daughter of Apollo and Arsinoe. Sister or half-sister of Asclepius. Married Oileus, king of Locris. Mother of Locrian (Lesser) Ajax.

ERIPHYLE Daughter of Talaus and Lysimache or Lysianassa. Sister of Adrastus, Aristomachus, Astynome, Mecisteus, Metidice, Parthenopaeus and Pronax, and possibly Hippomedon. Married Amphiarus. Mother of Alcmeon, Amphilochus, Demonassa and Eurydice. Her acceptance of bribes led to her and her husband's death at the hand of their son.

ERIS Goddess of discord and strife. Daughter of Zeus and Hera. Sister of Ares. The mother by Zeus of Ate. The personification of strife, Eris was also responsible for lies and falsehoods, battles and murders. It was her action in rolling the Golden Apple (qv) that ultimately led to the Trojan War. Eris was known as Discordia to the Romans. A goddess who inspired heroes to compete against each other in noble deeds. She and Athena inspired Heracles.

EROS God of love. Born of Chaos with Gaea and Tartarus. Later known as the son of Aphrodite and Ares or Hephaestus which would make him a brother of Anteros, Deimos, Enyo, Harmonia, Pallor and Phobos.

The most beautiful of the gods, he was attended by Himeros (Desire) and Pothos (Longing), as was Aphrodite. Father of Delight by Psyche. Some authorities call him a brother of Anteros. His gold-tipped arrows caused god and mortal alike to fall in love. Known to the Romans as Amor.

ERULUS King of Italy. Son of Feronia, goddess of orchards. She gave him three arms and three lives, but he lost all three lives in a single day to Evander.

ERYCINA Roman epithet of Aphrodite.

ERYLAUS Lycian killed in the Trojan War by Patroclus.

ERYMANTHIAN BOAR The giant boar of Mt Erymanthus, captured by Heracles as his fourth labour.

Eris

Eros

ERYMAS (1) A Trojan leader killed in the Trojan War by Penelaus. (2) A Lycian killed in the Trojan War by Patroclus.

ERYSICHTHON (1) Son of Cecrops and Agraulos. Brother of Agraulos, Herse and Pandrosus. He died childless. (2) Son of Triopas and Hiscilla of Thessaly. Brother of Iphimedeia, Messene and Phorbas. Father of Mestra (Metra) whom he sold into prostitution for food. He desecrated the sacred grove of Demeter, and she punished him by condemning him to be hungry no matter how much he ate. He died of hunger, eating his own legs.

ERYTHEIS (Erythia) One of the Hesperides. Daughter of Atlas and Pleione, though some distinguish her from Erythia, making her the daughter of Atlas and

Hesperis. Sister of Aegle, Arethusa and Hesperia. Was a guardian of the Golden Apples.

ERYTHIA (1) A daughter of Geryon. (2) The island where Geryon was buried. (3) *See* Erytheis.

ERYTHRAS Son of Leucon. Brother of Evippe. Suitor of Hippodameia and killed by her father.

ERYTHRIUS Son of Athamas and Themisto. Brother of Leucon, Ptous and Schoeneus.

ERYTHUS Son of Rhadamanthys and Alcmene. Brother of Gortys.

ERYTUS (Eurytus) An Argonaut. Son of Hermes and Antianeira. Brother of

Echion. May have been on the Calydonian Boar Hunt.

ERYX Sicilian mountain, burial place of Anchises and Eryx, son of Poseidon.

ERYX King of north-west Sicily. Son of Poseidon or Butes and Aphrodite. Half-brother of Aeneas. Was a boxer or wrestler who killed all those he beat until Heracles killed him. Eponym of both a city and a mountain.

ESCAPE, god of Phyxios, an epithet of Zeus.

ESQUILINE One of the seven hills of Rome, and place where criminals were executed. Other hills: Aventine, Caelian, Capitoline, Palatine, Quirinal and Viminal.

ETEARCHUS King of Oaxus, in Crete. The father of Phronime by his first wife. His second wife persuaded him that Phronime was unchaste so he threw her in the sea, but she was rescued by Themison, a Theraean trader.

ETEOCLES King of Thebes. Son of Oedipus and Jocasta or Euryganeia. Brother of Antigone, Ismene and Polyneices. Father of Laodamas. He and his brother agreed to rule Thebes jointly. Eventually this scheme failed, leading to the war of the Seven against Thebes. When many of the heroes had fallen the brothers decided on single combat, but both fell.

ETEOCLES King of Boeotian Orchomenus. Son of Andreus or Cephisus and Evippe. He died childless. The first man to name, and sacrifice to, the Graces. He succeeded Andreus to the throne and was succeeded by Halmus.

ETEOCLUS Son of Iphis. Brother of Evadne. A man of high integrity and one of the Seven against Thebes, he was killed by Leades or Megareus.

ETHRON Son of Laocoon and Antiope. Brother of Melanthus.

ETNA, Mount Sicilian volcano, site of the forge of Hephaestus. *See* Aetna.

EU(V)AEMON Husband of Ops. Father of Eurypylus of Thessaly.

EU(V)ANTHES Father of Maron, priest of Apollo.

EUBOEA (1) Second largest island in the Aegean Sea, and home of the Abantes. Chief city: Chalcis. (2) One of the fifty daughters of Thespius. (3) Hera's nurse. (4) Mistress of Hermes.

EUBOEA, kings of Abas and Chalcodon.

EUBULUS Swineherd of Eleusis. Father of Carme, the mother of Britomartis who witnessed the abduction of Persephone.

EUCHENOR A wealthy Corinthian, grandson of Polyeidus. Killed by Paris at Troy.

EUDORA (1) One of the Hyades. Daughter of Atlas and Pleione. Sister of Cleeia, Coronis, Phaeo and Phaesyle, and of the Hesperides, the Pleiades, Calypso and Hyas. (2) One of the Nereids. (3) Possibly one of the Atlantides.

EUDORUS Son of Hermes and Polymele. Raised by his grandfather, Phylas. Friend of Achilles and one of the five commanders of the Myrmidons in the Trojan War.

EU(V)IPPE (1) Daughter of Leucon. Sister of Erythras. Married Andreus. Possibly mother of Eteocles. (2) Wife of Pierus, king of Pelia. Mother of the nine Pierides.

EU(V)IPPUS (1) Son of Megareus and Iphinoe. Brother of Euacheme, Hippomenes and Timalcus. (2) A Lycian killed in the Trojan War by Patroclus.

EUMAEUS Son of Ctesius and Panthia. Chief swineherd of Laertes and, later, Odysseus. Recognised Odysseus on his return from exile and helped him slay Penelope's suitors.

EUMEDES (1) Father of Dolon (alternatively Eumelus). Killed in the Trojan War. (2) Son of Dolon. Accompanied Aeneas to Italy where he was killed by Turnus.

EUMELUS Son of Admetus and Alcestis. Brother of Perimele. Married Iphthime. Possibly the father of Dolon (cf Eumedes). Took eleven ships to Troy from Pherae, Boebe, Glaphyrae and Iolcus, and had the swiftest Greek forces in the Trojan War. Won the chariot race at the funeral games of Achilles.

EUMELUS (1) Father of Antheias. Aboriginal king of Patrae in Achaea and founder of the city of Aroe. Triptolemus taught him corn cultivation. (2) Follower of Aeneas who warned him that Trojan women were setting fire to their ships.

EUMENE *See* Eupheme.

EUMENIDES Another name for the Erinnyes or Furies.

EUMOLPUS Thracian ally of Eleusis. Son of Poseidon and Chione, but raised by his half-sister, Benthesicyme, one of whose daughters he married. He tried to rape his sister-in-law and was banished to the court of Tegrius, king of Thrace. There he plotted against the king and was exiled to Eleusis, but was later recalled and succeeded to the throne of Thrace.

With Celeus, was the co-founder of the Eleusinian Mysteries and the priesthood remained in his family for 1200 years.

Eumolpus was the father of Ismarus or Immaradus and Ceryx. Was killed in a war against Erechtheus, king of Athens, when he

tried to sieze that throne. Some traditions attribute to him a son, Phorbas.

EUMOLPUS Son of Musaeus and Deiope. Sometimes said to be founder of the Eleusian Mysteries.

EUNEUS King of Lemnos. Son of Jason and Hypsipyle. Brother of Deipylus, Nebrophonus and Thoas. Bought by Lycaon and ransomed by Eetion.

EUNOMIA Goddess of lawfulness and good order. One of the Horae. Daughter of Zeus and Themis. Sister of Dike and Eirene.

EUNOMUS (Cyathus, Eurynomous) Son of Architeles. Cup-bearer of Oeneus. Killed by Heracles.

EUPALAMUS (1) Son of Erechtheus and Praxithea. Brother of Chthonia, Creusa, Cecrops, Metion, Orneus, Pandorus, Procris, Protogeneia, Oreithyia and Thespius. Possibly the father of Daedalus and Perdix (alternatively Metion) by Alcippe. (2) The father of Metiadusa.

EUPEITHES An Ithacan prince. Father of Antinous. Also a pirate. Odysseus saved his life. Was killed by Laertes.

EUPHEME (Eumene) Mother of Crotus by Pan.

EUPHEMUS An Argonaut. Son of Poseidon and Europa or Mecionice. Father of Eurybatus.

He was the divinely appointed ancestor of the expelled Greek colonists of Cyrene in North Africa. Euphemus could run across water without getting his feet wet. Took part in the Calydonian Boar Hunt.

EUPHORBUS Son of Panthous and Phrontis. Brother of Hyperenor and Polydamas.

Either he or Hector was the slayer of Prosetilaus, the first Greek to land at Troy at the start of the War. He was the first to wound Patroclus. He was killed by Menelaus, but legend has it that he was reincarnated as Pythagorus.

EUPHROSYNE (Joy, festivity) One of the Graces. Daughter of Zeus and Eurynome. Sister of Aglaea, Pasithea and Thalia. *See also* Graces, Charites.

EUPOLEMEIA Daughter of Myrmidon and Peisidice. Sister of Actor and Antiphus. Mother of Aethalides by Hermes.

EURIPIDES circa 480–406 BC. One of the three great Greek writers of tragedy. Only nineteen of his plays survive: *Alcestis, Andromache, Bacchae, Cyclops, Electra, Hecuba, Helen, Heracles, Heraclidae, Hippolytus, Ion, Iphigeneia in Aulis, Iphigeneia in Tauris, Medea, Orestes, Phoenissae, Rhesus, Suppliants,* and *Trojan Women*.

EUROPA Daughter of Agenor and Telephassa or Argiope, or of Sidon and Argiope. Sister of Cadmus, Cilix, Demodoce, Electra, Phineus, Phoenix and Thasus, and possibly Argus. Married Asterius. Mother of Crete; also of Minos, Rhadamanthys and Sarpedon by Zeus when he took the shape of a white bull. Mother of Phaestus by Talus or Zeus.

Europe was named after her. Zeus gave her Laelaps as a watchdog and also the bronze giant, Talus.

EUROPA (1) Daughter of Phoenix and Perimede. Sister of Astypalea. (2) Daughter of Poeciles. Sister of Membliarus. Was kidnapped. (3) Daughter of Tityus. Possibly mother of Euphemus by Poseidon. (4) An Oceanid. Daughter of Oceanus and Tethys. Sister of Callirrhoe, Clytia, Perseis, Asia, Styx, etc (*see* Oceanus). (5) Mother

Europa

of the Danaids, the fifty daughters of Danaus.

EUROPS Possibly the son of Aegialeius.

EUROTAS King of Laconia. Son of Lelex and the Naiad Cleocharia. Brother of Polycaon, Therapne and Myles, though some place Myles as his father. Father of Sparte, wife of Lacedaemon and Tiasa. May have been a river god originally, as the River Riasa was named after his daughter.

EURUS (Volturnus) The south-east wind. Son of Astraeus and Eos. *See* Winds.

EURYAE (Euryale) A Gorgon. Daughter of Ceto and Phorcys. Sister of Medusa and Stheno, and of the Graiae, Scylla and Ladon.

EURYALE (1) A queen of the Amazons. (2) *See* Euryae, above. (3) A daughter of Minos and Pasiphae. Sister of Acacallis, Androgeus, Ariadne, Catreus, Deucalion, Glaucus, Lycastus, Phaedra and Xenodice. Mother of Orion by Poseidon or Hyrieus. (4) A daughter of Proetus, possibly by Eurydice.

EURYALUS An Argonaut. Son of Mecisteus. One of the Epigoni. An Argive leader at the Trojan War. A follower of Diomedes, they were co-guardians of Cyanippus. In the funeral games of Patroclus, Epius beat him at boxing.

EURYALUS Companion of Aeneas on his journey to Italy. He and his close friend, Nisus, died together at the hands of the Rutuli.

EURYBATES (Eribotes) An Argonaut. Son of Teleon. He and Canthus were killed trying to steal the sheep of Caphaurus.

EURYBATES An Ithacan herald. Quick-witted servant of Agamemnon and Odysseus at Troy. He and Talthybios went to Achilles' tent to fetch Briseis.

EURYBATES (1) Argive warrior, a frequent victor at the Nemean Games. (2) Imaginary person invented by the disguised Odysseus when he reassured his wife, Penelope, that he was still alive after twenty years' absence.

EURYBATUS Son of Euphemus. Slayer of Lamia, the monster of Crissa.

EURYBIA (1) Titan daughter of Oceanus and Gaea. Sister of Ceto, Crius, Nereus, Phorcys and Thaumas. Married Crius. Mother of Astraeus, Pallas and Perses. Called 'flint-hearted' by Hesiod. (2) Mother of Lucifer. (3) Daughter of Thespius.

EURYCLEIA Daughter of Ops. Bought for twenty oxen by Laertes as a nurse for Odysseus. When Odysseus returned after his journeyings she recognised him by a scar on his thigh.

EURYCYDA Daughter of Endymion and a Naiad. Sister of Aetolus, Epeius, Naxus and Paeon. Mother of Eleius by Poseidon.

EURYDAMAS (1) Son of Ctimenus. (2) Trojan interpreter of dreams. (3) A suitor of Penelope. (4) Son of Irus and Demonassa. Brother of Eurytion. An Argonaut.

EURYDICE Daughter of Lacedaemon and Sparte. Sister of Amyclas. Married Acrisius, son of Abas. Mother of Danae and Evarete also known as Anticleia or Cassandra. Possibly mother of Euryale by Proetus.

EURYDICE The Dryad wife of Orpheus. Bitten by a snake when fleeing from Aristaeus, she died and descended to the Underworld. Was almost rescued by Orpheus, but she was condemned to eternal death when he disobeyed Hades' instructions and turned to look back at her before they reached the light of day.

EURYDICE (1) Daughter of Adrastus. Married Ilus. Mother of Laomedon and Themiste. (2) Daughter of Actor. (3) Possibly the wife of Aeneas, but unlikely. (4) Possibly the mother of Alcmene and six sons, including Everes and Electryon. (5) Daughter of Amphiarus and Eriphyle. Sister of Alcmeon, Amphilochus and Demonassa. (6) Daughter of Clymenus. Wife of Nestor. (7) Wife of Creon of Thebes. Mother of Enioche, Haemon, Megara, Menoeceus and Pyrrha. Killed herself after Haemon committed suicide. (8) One of the Danaids. Wife of Dryas, whom she murdered. (9) Possibly the wife of Lycurgus (cf Amphithea). Mother of Opheltes.

EURYGANEIA Possibly the wife of Oedipus and mother of Antigone, Eteocles, Ismene and Polyneices.

EURYGYES Pseudonym used by Androgeus in the Athenian Games.

EURYLOCHUS An aggressive member of Odysseus' crew, the only one not to taste Circe's potions. Married Ctimene, sister of Odysseus. Zeus killed him after he and others stole cattle belonging to Helios.

EURYMACHUS Son of Polybus. An Ithacan noble, he was the favourite suitor of Penelope. Was killed by Odysseus.

EURYMEDE (Eurynome) Daughter of Nisus. Sister of Scylla and Iphinoe. Married Glaucus of Corinth. Mother of Bellerophon and Deliades.

EURYMEDON Co-ruler of isle of Paros. Son of Hermes. Brother of Chryses, Nephalion and Philocaus.

EURYNOME An Oceanid. Daughter of Oceanus and Tethys. Mother of the Graces, by Zeus. According to Apollonius Rhodius, she was an ancient goddess ruling Olympus with Ophion, before Cronos. She withdrew to the sea and is depicted as a mermaid.

EURYNOME (1) Possibly the mother of Ancaeus, Amphidamas, Iasus and Epochus (cf. Cleophyle), by Lycurgus. (2) Another name for Eurymede. (3) Daughter of Iphitus. Possibly mother of Adrastus by Talaus. (4) Mother of Leucothoe by Orchamus. (5) Daughter of Nisus. Mother of Asopus, Bellerophon (2) by Poseidon. Athena taught her wisdom and wit. (6) An attendant of Penelope.

EURYNOMOUS (Eunomus) Son of Architeles.

EURYNOMUS Father of Orsinome, wife of Lapithus.

EURYODIA Possibly the mother of Arceisius by Zeus.

EURYPHAESSA A Titan. She and Theia, wife of Hyperion, may have been one and the same. Mother of Eos, Helios and Selene.

EURYPYLUS A Trojan ally. Son of Telephus and Astyoche (Laodice). Father of Grynus.

Leader of the Mysian forces in the Trojan War, he killed Machaon and Penelaus, and was killed by Neoptolemus as he was about to set fire to the Greek ships.

EURYPYLUS Son of Evaemon and Ops. A suitor of Helen, he took forty ships to Troy from Thessaly. Was in the Wooden Horse and was also wounded by Paris after killing Axion, son of Priam. During the fall of Troy, he found a chest, made by Hephaestus, inscribed with an image of Dionysus, which drove him mad. The Delphic Oracle sent him to Aroe in search of a cure.

He was the Libyan king who gave his throne to Cyrene after she killed a lion that had ravaged Libya.

EURYPYLUS King of Cos. Son of Poseidon and Astypalea. Brother of Ancaeus. Killed by Heracles.

EURYPYLUS (1) Trojan lover of Cassandra, killed by Pyrrhus. (2) Son of Dexamenus. Brother of Mnesimache, Theraephone and Theronice.

EURYSACES Son of Greater Ajax and Tecmassa.

EURYSTHENES Son of Aristodemus and Argeia. Twin of Procles. Raised by his uncle, Theras, after his father's premature death.

EURYSTHEUS King of Mycenae and Tiryns. Son of Sthenelus and Nicippe. Grandson of Perseus. Brother of Alcinoe and Medusa. Married Antimache. Father of Admeta (Admete). He was a weakling as a child, because Hera had precipitated his birth after a seven-month pregnancy, because the younger between him and Heracles was doomed to be subservient to the other. He set Heracles his twelve labours, never dealing with him directly but always through the herald, Copreus. When Heracles brought back the skin of the Nemean lion, it so terrified Eurystheus that he hid in a bronze jar. Eurystheus was killed either by Hyllus, Heracles' son, or by Iolaus.

EURYTAS *See* Eurytus.

EURYTE Daughter of Hippodamas. Married Porthaon. Mother of Agrius, Alcathous, Melas, Oeneus and two others. Mother of Halirrhothius by Poseidon.

EURYTHEMIS Wife of Thestius. Mother of Althaea, Leda, Hypermnestra, Plexippus and others.

EURYTION An Argonaut and king of Ohthia. Son of Irus and Demonassa. Brother of Eurydamas. Father of Antigone. Accidentally killed by Peleus.

EURYTION (Eurytus) A Centaur who attempted, when drunk, to break up the marriage feast of Peirithous and Hippodameia. He later forced Mnesimache into

marriage but when he came to collect his bride, Heracles killed him.

EURYTION (1) A Centaur killed at the wedding of Peirithous and Hippodameia. (2) A son of Actor. (3) Son of Lycaon and Zeleia. Brother of Pandarus. Companion of Aeneas in Italy, and a skilled archer. (4) A king of Sparta. (5) Herdsman of Geryon, king of Erythia. He and his dog, Orthus, were killed by Heracles during his tenth labour.

EURYTUS (Eurytas) King of Oechalia. Son of Melaneus and Oechalia. Father of Dryope by his first wife; and of Clytius, Iole and Iphitus by his second wife, Antiope. After teaching Heracles to use a bow, Heracles killed him when he refused to give him Antiope.

EURYTUS (Eurytas) A Molionide. Twin son of Actor or Poseidon and Molione. Brother of Cteatus. Married Theraephone, twin daughter of Dexamenus, king of Olenus. Father of Thalpius.

EURYTUS (Erytus) An Argonaut. Son of Hermes and Antianeira. Brother of Echion. Eurytus at the Calydonian Boar Hunt is identified with him.

EURYTUS (1) Son of Augeias. Brother of Agamede. (2) A giant who was killed, battling with the gods, by Dionysus' thyrsus.

EUSORUS Father of Aenete, wife of Aeneus.

EUTERPE Muse of lyric poetry. Daughter of Zeus and Mnemosyne. One of the nine Muses. Possibly the mother of Rhesus by Strymon and, because of her love of wild music, associated with Bacchus. Her symbol was the flute, which she may have invented.

EUTHYMUS Son of Astyeles or Caecinus. Winner of several boxing events in the Olympic Games. Winner of a fight with the ghost of Lycus or Polites, crewman of Odysseus.

EUXINE (Axine)   The Black Sea.

EVADNE   Daughter of Poseidon and Pitane. Reared by Aepytus. Mother of Iamus by Apollo.

EVADNE   Daughter of Iphis. Sister of Eteoclus. Married Capaneus. Mother of Sthenelus. Immolated herself on her husband's funeral pyre.

EVADNE   Daughter of Strymon and Neaera. Married Argus, king of Argos. Mother of Criasus, Ecbasus, Epidaurus and Peiras.

EVAECHME   Daughter of Megareus. Married Alcathous. Mother of Automedusa, Callipolis, Iphinoe, Ischepolis and Periboea.

EVAGORA   Possibly mother of Asius and Hecuba by her husband, Dymas.

EVANDER (Evandrus)   Italian settler from Arcadia. Son of Sarpedon and Laodameia, or of Hermes and Carmenta (Themis). Married Deidameia, sister of Laodameia. Father of Pallantia, Pallas, Dyna, Roma and Sarpedon II.

He introduced Greek gods and the Greek alphabet into Italy, also the flute, lyre and triangular harp. Built the city of Pallanteum on the Palatine Hill outside Rome. Helped Aeneas overcome the Rutuli. He killed Erulus (qv) three times in one day. Acetes was his attendant.

EVANIPPE   Mother of Polydorus by Hippomedon.

EVARETE   Daughter of Acrisius and Eurydice. Sister of Danae. Married Oenomaus. Mother of Hippodameia and Leucippus.

EVENUS   Son of Ares and Demonice or Alcippe. Brother of Molus, Pylus, Oeneus and Thestius. Married Alcippe. Father of Epistrophus, Marpessa and Mynes. Committed suicide after Idas abducted Marpessa.

EVERES   Son of Electryon and Anaxo. Brother of Alcmene and five boys. Father of Teiresias by Chariclo. Only one of the six sons not killed when they tried to recover their father's stolen cattle.

EVIL, goddess of   Ate, Eris, Discordia.

F

FAITHFULNESS, Roman goddess of Fides.

FAMA Roman goddess of fame. Was also the goddess of rumours. Was expelled from heaven by Jupiter. The Greeks called her Pheme.

FAMILY HARMONY, Roman goddess of Verplaca.

FARMING, Roman goddess of Bona Dea, Bona Mater, Fauna, Ceres.

FATAE One of the three fates.

FATE, Greek Divinity of Moira.

FATES (Fata, Parcae) Daughters of Nyx, Zeus and Themis, or of Necessitas. According to Hesiod, they were called Atropos, Clotho and Lachesis. The Parcae were also called Decima, Parca and Nona. Known to the Greeks as the Moirae, they supported the gods in their war with the Giants, killing Agrius and Thoas.

FATHER OF MANKIND Name given to Iapetos.

FAUNA (Bona Mater) Goddess of animals, farming, fertility, nature. Real name of the Roman goddess, Bona Dea. Wife, and possibly sister, of Faunus. After her marriage she never set eyes on another man. She was probably considered mother of Latinus, son of Heracles. Festival date: 4 December.

FAUNS (fauni) Woodland nymphs. Roman equivalent of Satyrs.

FAUNUS God of crops, fertility and flocks. Son of Picus. Husband or brother of Fauna, though some call his wife Marica, a water nymph. Father of Acis and Dryas, by a water nymph, Marica. The Greeks called him Pan. Possibly father of Stercutus.

FAUSTULUS Husband of Acca Larentia (or Acca Laurentia), and chief shepherd of Amulius or Numitor. He found and raised the abandoned Romulus and Remus.

FAVONUS The Roman west wind. The Greeks called it Zephyrus. *See* Winds.

FEAR, god of Phobos, son of Ares.

FEBRUUS (Februa) Italian god of purification. February was his sacred month.

FELICITAS Roman divinity of happiness among individuals and nations.

FERALIA Feast of the Manes.

FERONIA Roman goddess of groves, orchards and woodland. Mother of Erulus.

FERTILITY, gods of Greek: Cronos, Pan, Priapus. Roman: Saturn, Faunus.

FERTILITY, Roman goddess of Bona Dea, Fauna. Also called Cybele, Fatua, Ops, Rhea, and Libera.

FERTILITY, Greek goddess of Io.

FIDES Roman goddess of faithfulness, honesty and oaths. More ancient than Jupiter, she was first worshipped by Numa Pompilius. Her festival date: 1 October.

FIELDS, Roman goddess of Dea Dia.

FIELDS OF MOURNING That part of the Underworld inhabited by the souls of suicides, including Dido.

FIGS *See* Calchas, Mopsus.

FINANCE, Roman goddess of Juno Moneta.

FIRE, god of Greek: Hephaestus. Roman: Vulcan.

FIRE, the river of Phlegethon. One of the five rivers of the Underworld.

FLOCKS, god of Greek: Pan. Roman: Faunus, Pales (though latter may be a goddess).

FLOOD (Deluge) At the end of the iron age, Zeus flooded the earth destroying everyone except Deucalion and Pyrrha. Only Mt Parnassus stayed above water.

FLORA (Chloris) Roman goddess of gardens and flowers. Wife of Zephyrus. He gave her perpetual youth. Her spring festival, between 28 April and 1 May, was called Floralia. Titus Tatius introduced her cult during the age of Romulus. Also a goddess of love.

FLOWERS, goddess of Greek: Demeter, Chloris. Roman: Ceres, Flora.

FLY-CATCHER of Alipherus in Arcadia Revered as a hero and called Myagro.

FONTUS Roman divinity of springs. Son of Janus and Juturna. His festival date: 13 October.

FORESTS, goddess of Greek: Artemis. Roman: Diana.

FORETHOUGHT Epithet of Prometheus.

FORNAX Roman goddess of bread-making. Her festival date was 17 February (or earlier). Her worship was initiated by Numa Pompilius.

FORTUNA Roman goddess of chance, fortune and luck. Known to the Greeks as Tyche. Her festival date: 24 June. Her symbol: a wheel of fortune.

Fortuna

FORTUNA (1) One of the Parcae. *See* Fates. (2) Daughter of Oceanus (cf above).

FORTUNE, goddess of Greek: Tyche. Roman: Fortuna.

FOUNTAIN *See* Biblis, Cyane, Egeria, Peirene, Rhodope.

FOUNTAINS Children of Oceanus and Tethys.

FOUR AGES OF MANKIND Gold, Silver, Bronze and Iron.

FRANKINCENSE *See* Leucothoe.

FRATRES ARVALES The twelve sons of Carutius and Acca Larentia.

FRAUS Roman divinity of treachery. Daughter of Orcus and Nyx.

FRUIT, goddess of Greek: Demeter. Roman: Ceres.

FRUIT TREES, Roman goddess of Pomona.

FULGORA Roman goddess of lightning. Protectress from thunderstorms.

FUNERALS, Roman goddess of Naenia.

FURIES (Poenae) Roman goddesses of vengeance. Daughters of Gaea (Terra), they lived in Erebus. Known to the Greeks as Eumenides or Erinnyes. Named Alecto, Megaera and Tisiphone. Known in hell as the Furies and in heaven as the Dirae.

FURINA Roman goddess of robbers. May have been one of the Furies, but was certainly an ancient Roman deity with a grove at Rome.

FUTURE, Roman goddess of the Antevorta, Carmenta (Nicostrata), Postverta (cf Antevorta).

G

GADFLY *See* Io.

GAEA (Ge, Gaia) Goddess and personification of the earth. Born of Chaos with Eros and Tartarus. Married Uranus, whom she had conceived alone, together with Pontus and Ourea. By Uranus was the mother of Cronos, Pallas, Oceanus, (possibly) of Polyphemus, the Cyclops and the Titans. From the blood and spilled semen of Uranus she produced the Erinnyes, the Giants, the Meliae and Aurora; from the severed genitals of Uranus, she became the mother of Aphrodite.

By Hephaestus, she was mother of Erichthonius; by Oceanus, of Ceto, Crius, Eurybia, Nereus, Phorcys and Thaumas; possibly by Tartarus, of Echidna and Typhoeus; by Poseidon, of Ogyges, Charybdis and Antaeus. She was also the mother of Cecrops, Cranaus, Echo, Palaechthon, Rumor, (possibly) Arion, and the snake that guarded the Golden Fleece.

An epithet was Titaea. She was known to the Romans as Terra or Tellus. Gaea was the first god to prophesy at Delphi.

GALANTHIS (Galen) Theban attendant of Alcmene. Present at Heracles' birth as Eleithyia's assistant. The goddess later changed her into a weasel.

GALATEA A Nereid. One of the fifty daughters of Nereus and Doris. She lived in the waters of Sicily and fell in love with Acis. She was inadvertently the cause of her beloved's death, as Acis was killed by Polyphemus (an admirer of Galatea) in a fit of jealousy.

GALATEA The sculptor, Pygmalion, hated women but carved an ivory statue which was so beautiful he fell in love with it. It was brought to life by Aphrodite and named Galatea. Pygmalion and Galatea became the parents of Paphos.

GALEN *See* Galanthis.

GANNET *See* Ceyx.

GANYMEDA Goddess of youth. Daughter of Zeus and Hera. Epithet of Hebe. Mother of Alexiares and Anticetus by Heracles. Was the cup-bearer of the gods prior to Ganymede.

GANYMEDE Cup-bearer of the gods. Son of Tros and Callirrhoe. Brother of Assaracus, Cleopatra and Ilus.

Known to the Romans as Catamitus. Zeus abducted him from Troy on an eagle to succeed Hebe as cup-bearer on Olympus. He became the constellation Aquarius.

GARAMAS Another name for Amphithemis or the third son of Acacallis.

Ganymede

GARDENS, god of Greek: Priapus. Roman: Vertumnus.

GARDENS, Roman goddess of Flora, Pomona.

GARDEN OF THE HESPERIDES
Garden of Atlas guarded by the three Hesperides and Ladon, where the Golden Apples grew. Gaea gave it to Hera and Hera in turn gave it to Zeus on their wedding day. Heracles was charged to bring back an apple as his eleventh labour; Eris rolled an apple at the wedding of Peleus and Thetis; Paris used one for his Judgement; Hippomenes defeated Atalanta using three of them.

GARGAPHIA A shaded valley, near Plataea, sacred to Diana, where Actaeon was torn to pieces by his own dogs.

GARGARUS Highest point of Mt Ida in Phrygia.

GASTEROCHEIRES The seven Cyclops who built the walls of Tiryns.

GATE OF HORN Gate through which pleasant dreams passed on their way from Hypnos to people.

GATE OF IVORY Gate through which unpleasant dreams passed on their way from Hypnos to people.

GATES (PILLARS) OF HERACLES
A pair of mountains, Abyla in North Africa and Calpe in southern Spain (Gibraltar), which guard the entrance to the Mediterranean.

GE *See* Gaea.

GEBELEIZIS Another name for Salmoxis, a Thracian god of the Cetae.

GEGENEES Earth-born six-armed giants who inhabited Bear Mountain on the Mysian coast and who were killed by the Argonauts.

GELANOR King of Argos deposed by Danaus.

GELEON Son of Ion and Helice. Brother of Aegicores, Argades and Hoples.

GELON Son of Hymarus and Aetna.

GEMINI (Dioscuri, the twins) The third sign of the zodiac.

GENIUS (Iovialis) Roman god of life and being. A spirit that exists in all people from birth until death. Every man, beast, etc had such a genius to himself.

GENIUS IOVALIS Father of Tages.

GENIUS LOCI The presiding spirit of a place or building.

GERAESTUS A Cyclops. Son of Uranus and Gaea. Brother of Acmonides, Arges, Brontes, Polyphemus and the Titans. Killed by Apollo. Daughters of Hyacinth were sacrificed on his grave.

GERYON King of Erythia (Cadiz). Son of Chrysaor and Callirrhoe. Brother of Echidna. Father of Erythia. He lived at Gades, 40 kilometres from the Spanish side of the Pillars of Heracles, and had either three heads or three lower parts to his thorax.
Geryon owned many flocks which were guarded by Eurythion and his dog, Orthus, but were stolen by Heracles as his tenth labour; and he killed Geryon in the process.

GIANTS Sons of Uranus and Gaea, born when the blood of Uranus fell on the earth. Possibly had snakes for feet. Called Agrius, Alcyoneus, Aloeus, Antaeus, Anax, Clytius, Cyclopes, Enceladus, Ephialtes (cf Ephialtes), Gration, Hecatoncheiroi, Hippolytus, Mimas, Pallas, Polybotes, Porphyrion (their leader), Rhoetus, Thoas, Thoon and Tityus.
They fought the gods on Mt Olympus and many were killed by Heracles and

Dionysus, Heracles despatching the wounded with his arrows. When dead, Enceladus was buried under Mt Aetna, Mimas under Mt Vesuvius and Polybotes under part of the isle of Cos, forming the new island of Nisyros.

GIRDLE OF VENUS (Cestus) A special girdle that gave both mortal and immortal women great sexual attraction.

GLAUCE (Creusa) Daughter of Creon of Corinth. Married Jason, but when at her wedding she put on the robes given her by Medea, Jason's divorced wife, they burst into flames and she, her father, and many guests were burned to death. Jason was saved by jumping out of a window.

GLAUCE (1) Daughter of Cynchreus, king of Salamis. Mother or first wife of Telamon. (2) One of the Danaids. (3) One of the Nereids.

GLAUCIPPE Possibly mother of Asius and Hecuba, by Dymas.

GLAUCUS A minor sea-god. Son of Poseidon and Nais, or of Anthedon and Alcyone, Glaucus was originally a fisherman but he grew a tail after eating a magic herb which brought his fish back to life when thrown on it. Glaucus fell in love with the lovely virgin, Scylla. When she repulsed him, she was changed into a monster. He assisted the Argonauts.

GLAUCUS Son of Minos and Pasiphae. Brother of Acacallis, Androgeus, Ariadne, Catreus, Deucalion, Euryale, Lycastus,

Phaedra and Xenodice. Smothered in a honeypot, but was revived by Polyeidus.

GLAUCUS of Corinth King of Ephyra. Son of Sisyphus and Merope, daughter of Atlas. Brother of Halmus, Ornytion and Thersander. Married Eurymede. Father of Bellerophon and Deliades. He owned horses which ate only human flesh. When he refused to let them mate, he angered Aphrodite, who saw to it that they trampled him to death at the funeral games of Pelias. His ghost, called Taraxhippos, haunted a mound at the Isthmian Games.

GLAUCUS Son of Antenor and Theano. Brother of Acamas, Agenor, Archelous, Coon, Demoleon, Iphidamas, Laodamas, Polybus, Crino, Helicaon, Laocoon, Lycaon and Polydamas. Half-brother of Pedaeus. In the Trojan War, his life was saved by Odysseus and Menelaus, but he was later killed by Agamemnon.

GLAUCUS Co-leader of the Lycian army at Troy. Son of Hippolochus. An ally of the Trojans, he exchanged armour with Diomedes when they discovered their grandfathers' friendship. Was killed by Salaminian Ajax, fighting for the corpse of Achilles. His co-leader was Sarpedon.

GLAUCUS (1) Son of Aepytus, king of Messenia. (2) Father of Deiphobe, the Cumaean Sibyl.

GNOME *See* Cercopes.

GOAT *See* Amalthea, Chimaera.

GODS

Greek name	Roman name	God of
Apollo	Apollo	music and poetry
Aphrodite	Venus	love and beauty
Ares	Mars	war
Artemis	Diana	chastity and hunting
Athena	Minerva	wisdom, war and liberal arts
Cronos	Saturn	time
Demeter	Ceres	agriculture

Greek name	Roman name	God of
Dionysus	Bacchus	wine and revelry
Gaea	Terra	earth
Hades	Pluto	underworld
Helios	Sol	sun
Hephaestus	Vulcan	fire
Hera	Juno	heaven and childbirth
Hermes	Mercury	messenger of the gods
Hestia	Vesta	fire
Poseidon	Neptune	sea
Rhea	Cybele	earth
Selene	Luna	moon
Uranus	Coelus	heaven
Zeus	Jupiter	supreme god

GOLDEN AGE First of the four ages of man, followed by Silver, Bronze and Iron. A peaceful age with no women.

GOLDEN APPLES Apples that grew in the Garden of the Hesperides. At the Judgement of Paris, one was awarded as a beauty prize; another was rolled by Eris at the wedding of Peleus and Thetis; three apples were used by Hippomenes to defeat Atalanta. One of Heracles' labours was to collect an apple from the Garden.

GOLDEN BOUGH Sacred to Persephone, it grew on a tree near Cumae. Aeneas used it as a passport into the Underworld so that Charon would ferry him across the Styx.

GOLDEN FLEECE The fleece of the ram, offspring of Poseidon and Theophane, which could speak and fly, and which was rescued by Phrixus from his father, Athamas. Phrixus and Helle escaped from Boeotia on it and, though his sister died on the journey, Phrixus reached Colchis, where he sacrificed the ram, and placed the pure gold fleece in a sacred grove guarded by a snake. The ram became the constellation, Aries.

The saga of the Argonauts was the quest for the Golden Fleece.

GOOSE *See* Nemesis.

GORDIUS Father of Midas, king of Phrygia, by Cybele. Tied the Gordian knot. An oracle declared that whoever untied the knot should rule over Asia. Alexander the Great did so.

GORGASUS Son of Machaon and Anticleia. Brother of Alexanor and Nichomachus. A doctor.

GORGE Daughter of Oeneus and Althaea. Sister of Toxeus and half-sister of Deianeira and Meleager. Married Andraemon. Mother of Thoas. Possibly mother of Tydeus (alternatively, Periboea) by Oeneus.

She was so distressed by the death of Meleager that Artemis changed her into a guinea-fowl, although some sources state that she alone was spared this fate.

GORGONS Daughters of Ceto and Phorcys. Called Euryae, Medusa and Stheno; only Medusa was mortal. Sisters of Echidna, Ladon, Scylla and the Graiae. Some nominate Gaea as their mother. Medusa was the mother of Chrysaor and Pegasus who rose from her blood.

To look upon them would turn people to stone. Medusa was killed by Perseus and her body buried in the market-place of Argos; her head was set in the Aegis by Perseus.

GORGOPHONE Daughter of Perseus

Gorgon

possibly wife of Hephaestus and the youngest, Pasithea, was promised in marriage to Hypnos. Others were called Euphrosyne and Thalia.

GRADIVUS Epithet of Mars, Roman god of war, as leader of armies.

GRAECUS Son of Zeus and Pandora.

GRAIAE (Graeae) Daughters of Phorcys and Ceto. Sisters of Echnidna, Ladon, Scylla and the Gorgons. They were called Deino, Enyo and Pephredo, and all were born as old hags with only one eye and one tooth between them. Perseus stole both eye and tooth after being directed to them for information.

GRAIN, Roman god of Robigus.

GRAIN, goddes of Greek: Demeter. Roman: Ceres, Robigo.

GRANICUS A river god. Son of Oceanus and Tethys. Father of Alexiroe. Also, Granicus was a river of Ida near Troy.

GRASSHOPPER *See* Tithonus.

GRATION Son of Gaea. He was a giant killed by Heracles in the war with the gods, after Artemis had wounded him.

GREAT BEAR (Ursa Major) Callisto was changed into this constellation and her son, Arcas, became Ursa Minor.

GRIFFINS These mute creatures had the head and wings of an eagle, and the body of a lion. They took gold from the stream Arimaspias. Neighbours of the Hyperboreans, they belonged to Zeus.

GROVES, goddess of Greek: Artemis. Roman: Diana, Feronia.

GRYNUS Son of Eurypylus. An ally of the Greeks in the Trojan War, he enlisted the aid of Pergamus against his enemies. He went on to build Gryneium.

and Andromeda. Sister of Alcaeus, Electryon, Heleius, Mestor, Perses and Sthenelus. Married Perieres of Messene. Mother of Aphareus, Borus, Icarius, Leucippus and Tyndareus. After the death of Perieres, she married Oebalus, becoming the first widow to remarry. Mother of Arene, Hippocoon and Peirene.

GORGYRA Possibly the wife of Acheron; if so, mother of Ascalaphus.

GORTYS (1) Son of Rhadamanthys and Alcmene. Brother of Erythus. (2) Son of Stymphalus. Brother of Agamedes and Parthenope.

GRACES (Charites) Normally regarded as three in number but there are many references to others. Personifications of beauty and grace. Daughters of Zeus and Eurynome, or of Zeus or Dionysus and Aphrodite. Grace or Charis (Aglaea) was

GUINEA FOWL *See* Deianeira, Gorge.

GUNEUS Father of Laonome, possibly mother of Amphitryon.

GUNEUS King of Cyphus, near Dodona in Epeirus. Son of Octyus. He took twenty-two ships to the Trojan War. Founded a town in Libya.

GYAS Son of Melampus. Brother of Cisseus. Accompanied Aeneas to Italy. Took third place in the boat race at Anchises' funeral games.

GYGES (1) One of the Hecatoncheroi. Son of Uranus and Gaea. Brother of Briareus (Aegaeon, Obriareus) and Cottus. The Hecatoncheroi were also known as the Centimani or hundred-handed. (2) A king of Lydia. According to an oracle, he was less happy than Aglaus, the poorest man in Arcadia.

GYRTIAS Father of Hyrtius.

H

HADES King of the Underworld. Son of Cronos and Rhea. Brother of Poseidon, Demeter, Hera, Hestia and Zeus. Married Persephone, whom he abducted. Hades was swallowed at birth by his father, but was rescued by Zeus. Also called Ades, Aides, Aidoneus, Dis, Orcus, Pluto, Pluton.

HADES, dog of Cerberus.

HADES, flower of Asphodel.

HADES, house of The abode of the dead.

HADES, Judges of Aeacus, Minos and Rhadamanthys.

HADES, rivers of Acheron, Cocytus, Lethe, Phlegethon and Styx.

HAEMON (1) A son of Creon. Father of Maeon. Killed by the Sphinx (cf below). (2) Youngest son of Creon and Anioche or Eurydice. Brother of Enioche, Megara, Menoeceus and Pyrrha. Lover of Antigone, they died together. (3) Son of Thoas. Father of Oxylus, Thermius and possibly Iphitus. (4) Father of Laerces.

HAEMUS Son of Boreas and Oreithyia. Brother of Calais, Chione, Cleopatra and Zetes. Married Rhodope. When they assumed the names of Zeus and Hera they were changed into mountains.

HAEMUS The Balkan mountains of Thrace. *See above.*

HALIA (sea-woman) Daughter of Pontus, Poseidon or Uranus, and Thalassa. Sister of the Telchines. Mother of Rhode and six sons. Some say that it was she, not Ino, who was deified as Leucothea.

HALIARTUS Son of Thersander. Brother of Coronus.

HALIE (the ox-eyed) A Nereid. One of the fifty daughters of Nereus and Doris.

HALIRRHOTHIUS Son of Perieres and Gorgophone. Brother of Borus, Pisus, Aphareus, Icarius, Leucippus and Tyndareus.

HALIRRHOTHIUS Son of Poseidon and Euryte. After he raped Alcippe, was murdered by her father, Ares. This led to the first trial for murder.

HALITHERSES An Ithacan seer. An expert on birds, he was a friend of Odysseus and Penelope and warned Penelope's suitors of Odysseus' impending return.

HALMUS King of Boeotian Orchomenus. Son of Sisyphus and Merope. Brother of Glaucus, Ornytion and Thersander. Father of Chryse and Chrysogeneia. Succeeded Eteocles to the throne.

HALYS A river god. Son of Oceanus and Tethys. Unsuccessful suitor of Sinope.

HAMADRYADS Tree nymphs who died with their trees.

HAMMON Possibly father of Iarbas, king of Gaetulia.

HAPPINESS, Roman divinity of Felicitas.

HARBOURS, god of Greek: Melicertes. Roman: Portunus.

HARMONIA (Hermione) Daughter of Ares and Aphrodite or Zeus and Electra. Sister of Anteros, Deimos, Enyo, Eros, Pallor and Phobos. Married Cadmus of Thebes. Mother of Agave, Autonoe, Illyrius, Ino, Polydorus and Semele.

Owner of a beautiful necklace or robe, made for her by Hephaestus, which inspired evil in her children. She was turned into a snake by Ares.

HARMONY, Roman goddess of Concordia, Pax. Salus.

HARMOTHOE Wife of Pandareus. Mother of Aedon, Cleothera (Cameiro), and Merope (Clytie). She and her husband were killed by Zeus.

HARPALION Paphlagonian son of Pylaemenes. Assisted Priam in the Trojan War. Killed by Meriones.

HARPALYCE Daughter of Harpalycus, king of Thrace. A huntress who preyed upon peasants.

HARPALYCE Daughter of Clymenus. She continued an incestuous relationship with her father even after her marriage to Alastor. When she served the child of this relationship to her father as a meal, he killed her, and she became an owl.

HARPALYCUS (1) Friend of Aeneas, killed by Camilla. (2) Son of Hermes and father of Harpalyce. Taught Heracles to box.

HARPIES Daughters of Thaumas and Electra or Poseidon and Gaea. Usually three in number, they were given many names, but normally were called Aello, Celaeno (Podarge) and Ocypete. Sisters of Iris.

Early myths call them beautiful and they varied in number, but later myths depict them as ugly bird-like monsters with large claws. They always stank, were perpetually hungry and Zeus sent them continually to take the food away from Phineus. Podarge became the mother of Balius and Xanthus, immortal horses of Achilles, by Boreas. The Harpies were killed by Calais and Zetes. Their abode was either the Strophades islands or a place in Crete.

Harpies

HARPINA Possibly the mother (cf Asterope) of Oenomaus by Alxion or Ares.

HARVESTS, goddess of Greek: Rhea. Roman: Ops.

HAWK *See* Daedalion.

HEALING, god of Greek: Apollo, Asclepius, Thanatos. Roman: Aesculapius, Apollo.

HEALING, goddess of Greek: Iaso. Roman: Angitia, Carmenta.

HEALTH, goddess of Greek: Hygeia, Panacea. Roman: Salus.

HEARTH, Roman goddess of the Vesta, but preceded by Caca.

HEARTS, Roman goddess of Carna. Also goddess of other body organs.

HEBE (Ganymeda) Goddess of eternal youth. Daughter of Zeus and Hera. Sister of Ares, Arge, Eleithyia, Eris and Hephaestus. Mother of Alexiares and Anticetus by Heracles.
  Cup-bearer of the gods on Olympus until she indecently exposed herself at a festival and was replaced by Ganymede. Restored to youth by Iolaus. Known to the Romans as Juventas.

HEBRUS River of Thrace, bordered with golden sands, into which the Bacchants threw the dismembered body of Orpheus.

HECALE An old woman who gave refuge to Theseus before he captured the Marathonian Bull.

HECATE Goddess of the Underworld. Daughter of Perses and Asteria, although others describe her as daughter of Zeus and Demeter. She taught magic to her priestess, Medea, and is often pictured carrying a torch. Hecate was the epithet often used by Luna, the moon-goddess, Diana, the earth-goddess and Persephone, the goddess of the

Hecate

Underworld. Her epithets were Enodia, the wayside goddess, and Trioditis, meaning the goddess of the meeting of three routes. Crantaeis was also possibly an epithet of Hecate.

HECATERUS Possibly the father of the Curetes, mountain nymphs, and Satyrs, by a daughter of Phoroneus.

HECATO Father of Calyce, mother of Cycnus.

HECATOMB Ancient Greek sacrifice of a large number of cattle or people.

HECATONCHEIRES *See* Hecatoncheroi.

HECATONCHEIROI (Centimani, Hekatoncheires) Titan sons of Uranus and Gaea, they had one hundred hands and fifty heads. Called Briareus (Aegaeon Obriareus), Cottus and Gyges.

Uranus feared their strength and imprisoned them in Tartarus from where Zeus rescued them and brought them to Olympus, where they fed on ambrosia and nectar. In return, they allied themselves to the gods against the Titans.

HECTENES Theban aboriginal tribe, whose king was Ogygus, which was destroyed by plague.

HECTOR Eldest son of Priam and Hecuba. Brother of Aesacus, Cassandra, Creusa, Deiphobus, Helenus, Paris, Polydorus, Polyxena and Troilus, amongst others. Married Andromache. Father of Astyanax (Scamandrius).

Leader of the Trojan forces in the Trojan War, he killed thirty-one Greeks, including Patroclus, before being himself killed by Achilles. His squire was Molion.

HECUBA (Hecabe) Daughter of Dymas of Phrygia and Evagora or Glaucippe; or of the river god Cisseus; or of the river

god Sangarius and Metope. Sister of Asius. Second wife of Priam. Mother of nineteen of his children, though some say she was the mother of fifty sons and twelve daughters. Her children included Aesacus, Antiphus, Cassandra, Creusa, Deiphobus, Hector (eldest), Helenus, Isus, Paris, Polydorus (youngest), Polyxena, Laodice and Troilus. Possibly mother of Troilus by Apollo.

After the fall of Troy she was given to Odysseus as a slave. Having blinded and killed the sons of Polymnestor in revenge for his killing Polydorus, she was changed into a dog.

HEGETORIA A nymph. The wife of Ochimus, a Heliade. Mother of Cydippe.

HELEIUS (Heleus) Co-ruler of the Taphian islands. Son of Perseus and Andromeda. Brother of Alcaeus, Electryon, Gorgophone, Mestor, Perses and Sthenelus. Ruled with Cephalus.

HELEN Queen of Sparta. Daughter of Zeus and Leda or Nemesis. Step-daughter of Tyndareus. Married Menelaus. Mother of Hermione, Pleisthenes and possibly Nicostratus. According to some sources, mother of Iphigeneia by Theseus. She was abducted by Peirithous and Theseus when she was nine (or twelve) years old and was rescued by her brothers, the Dioscuri. Lover of Paris. Her abduction by Paris led to the ten-year-long Trojan War. After the death of Paris, she married Deiphobus. The most beautiful woman of her age, there are many versions of her death. The most probable was that she was hanged by the maids of Argive Polyxo, avenging the death at Troy of Tlepolemus.

HELEN, suitors of Her suitors were obliged to raise fleets and armies to fetch Helen from Troy. Some bought or tricked their way out of their obligation. The most celebrated suitors were: Agasthenes, Ajax, Lesser and Greater, Amphilochus, Ascalaphus, Amphimachus, Cinyras, Diomedes, Echepolus, Eurypylus, Ialmenus, Leitus, Machaon, Meges, Menestheus, Odysseus, Penelaus, Philoctetes, Podalirius, Polyxenus, Schedius, Sthenelus, Thalpius, Antilochus, Menelaus and Tlepolemus.

HELENOR A Lydian prince, who accompanied Aeneas to Italy. Killed by the Rutuli.

HELENUS King of Epirus. Son of Priam and Hecuba. Twin of Cassandra. (*See* Hecuba for brothers and sisters.) Married Andromache after both had been given to Pyrrhus as slaves. Father of Cestrinus.

The only son of Priam to survive the Trojan War, he predicted that Troy would not fall while the city contained the Palladium. Helenus founded Epirus.

HELEUS Son of Andromeda and Perseus. Brother of Alcaeus, Electryon, Gorgophone, Mestor, Perses and Sthenelus.

HELIADES Sons of Helios and Rhode, called Actis, Candalus, Cercaphus, Macar, Ochimus, Tenages and Triopas. Tenages, the cleverest, was killed by Actis, Candalus, Macar and Triopas who all went into exile. Brilliant at many things, particularly astrology, they were the first to divide the day into hours and the first to sacrifice to Athena without fire.

HELIADES Daughters of Helios. By Clymene, he fathered Aegiale, Aegle and Aetheria (though some call Apollo the father); by Neaera, Lampetie and Phaethusa; by Perseis, Circe and Pasiphae. After their death, the daughters of Clymene and Neaera were changed into poplar trees.

HELICAON Son of Antenor and Theano. Brother of Acamas, Agenor, Archelous, Glaucus, Coon, Crino, Lycaon, Laocoon, Polydamas, Demoleon, Iphidamas, Laodamas and Polybus. Half-brother of Pedaeus. Wounded in the Trojan War by the Greeks, he was rescued by Odysseus in repayment of a debt to Antenor.

HELICE Daughter of Selinus, king of Aegialus. Married Ion, king of Athens. Mother of Aegicores, Argades, Geleon and Hoples.

Eponym of the seaport on the Gulf of Corinth, in Achaea.

HELICE A nymph, the wife of Oenopion, and mother of Merope and several sons.

HELICON Brother of Cithaeron.

HELIOS (Helius, Sol) The sun-god. Son of the Titans, Hyperion and Theia. Brother of Eos and Selene. Married Perseis (Perse). Father of Aeetes, Circe, Pasiphae and Perses. Father of seven sons by Rhode and several daughters by Clymene and Neaera, who were called the Heliades (qv). Possibly father of the following: Aex, Augeias by Naupiadame, the Corybantes by Athena. When Zeus divided the world Helios was away (or forgotten) and received no portion, so to placate him Zeus gave him the island of Rhodes which may have just emerged from the sea. Worshipped in Rhodes, the Colossus at Rhodes was dedicated to him. He drove across the sky daily, in his four-horse chariot, Quadriga. The Romans knew him as Sol. Epithets: Acamas (untiring); Panderces (all-seeing); Terpimbrotos (he who makes mortals rejoice).

HELIOTROPE *See* Clytia.

HELLE Daughter of Athamas and Nephele. Sister of Phrixus. Escaping with her brother from Boeotia on the back of the ram with the golden fleece, she fell off its back and drowned in the sea-strait between Asia and Europe, which was then named the Hellespont after her. However, according to Hyginus, she did not drown but was rescued by Poseidon and was later named as the mother of his two children, Edonus and Paeon.

HELLEN King of Phthia. Son of Deucalion and Pyrrha or, according to some, of Zeus and Dorippe, or Prometheus and Clymene. Brother of Amphictyon, Pandora,

Thyia and Protogeneia. Married Ortheis (Orseis). Father of Aeolus, Dorus and Xuthus.

HELLESPONT The Sea of Helle, the narrow strait of water that separates Asia from Europe.

HEMERA (Day) Daughter of Erebus and Nyx, as were Aether, Charon, Cer, Dreams, Hypnos, Momus, Moros, Nemesis and Thanatos. Mother of Phaethon by Cephalus.

HEMITHEA Daughter of Cycnus and Procleia. Sister of Tenes.

HEPHAESTUS (Vulcan) God of fire. Son of Zeus and Hera, or of Hera alone. Brother of Ares, Arge, Discordia, Eleithyia and Hebe. Married either Aphrodite, Charis or Aglaea, one of the Graces (but note that Charis and Aglaea are closely connected with Aphrodite). Father of Eros by Aphrodite. Father of Camillus by Cabeiro. Fathered Erichthonius alone or some call Gaea or even Attis the mother. Father of Palaemon by the wife of Lernus. Father of Periphetes (alternatively Poseidon) by Anticleia. Father of Olenus and of Tullius, sixth king of Rome, by Ocrisia. Father of the two Palici volcanoes by Aetna. Father of Cercyon.

Deformed and lame, Hera abandoned him in disgust. He lived the first nine years of his life in the sea, cared for by Eurynome and Thetis. An expert metalsmith, he created in his smithy under Mount Aetna: 1. Arms for Achilles 2. Arms for Aeneas 3. A sceptre for Agamemnon 4. The necklace of Harmonia, fatal to all who wore it 5. The shield of Heracles. The Cyclopes were his workmen.

HEPTAPORUS River of Ida near Troy.

HERA (Juno) Queen of heaven. Daughter of Cronos and Rhea. Sister of Demeter, Hades, Hestia, Poseidon and Zeus. Married Zeus after he had disguised himself as a cuckoo and seduced her. Mother of Ares, Arge, Discordia, Eleithyia, Hebe and Hephaestus. Possibly mother of Typhon. Hera was also goddess of childbirth, marriage and women. Her epithet was Argeia (Argive Hera). Argos (her favourite city which she won from Poseidon), Euboea, Samos and Stymphalus were all claimed as her birthplace. She was universally worshipped. Her nurse was Euboea. A good friend to the Argonauts, she helped them many times. Her sacred bird was the peacock and her sacred fruits were the apple and pomegranate. The most jealous woman in mythology, she persecuted many of her husband's mistresses including Aegina, Alcmene, Io, Leto and Semele. There are many stories of fighting between Hera and Zeus on account of his affairs. Because of the judgement of Paris, she was hostile to the Trojans in the Trojan War.

HERACLES the Dactyl Son of Rhea and Anchiale. He had four brothers: Epimedes, Iasus, Idas and Paeonaeus, and five sisters. Leader of the Idaean Dactyls, he founded the Olympic Games.

HERACLES (Alcaeus, Hercules) The most popular of all Greek heroes, he was known to the Romans as Hercules. Son of Zeus and Alcmene. Twin of Iphicles, though they shared only a mother. Married Megara. Father of Creontidas, Deicoon and Therimachus.

He had many love affairs:

Heracles' Lovers	Children of the Union
Arge	two sons
Astydameia	(possibly) Ctesippus and Tlepolemus
Astyoche	Tlepolemus (cf above)
Auge	Telephus
Chalciope	Thessalus
Deianeira	Ctesippus and Tlepolemus (as alternative to above), Hyllus and Macaria
Omphale	Agelaos, Alcaeus and Lamus
Praxithea	Lycurgus
Pyrene	a serpent

He was the father of Antimachus by a daughter of Thespius; of Aventinus by a priestess of Rhea; and of Mentor and Phaestus. *See also* Heraclids. His epithets were Alcides, after Alcaeus (the name he was given at birth) and Menoeceus. His armour bearer was Abderus. His weapons were made by the gods: Apollo made his bow and arrows, Athena his robe, Hephaestus his golden breastplate, and Hermes his sword. Poseidon gave him horses but his club he made himself.

Heracles was renowned for eight deeds: beating Antaeus in a fight; rescuing Alcestis from the Underworld; travelling as an Argonaut; rescuing Hesione; acting as a servant to Omphale; stealing the sacred tripod of Delphi after Apollo refused him purification; the sacking of Troy; and his twelve labours.

His funeral pyre was lit by Philoctetes. Heracles was honoured after his death with the task of guarding the Gates of Olympia.

Heracles

HERACLES, the labours of Eurystheus set Heracles twelve labours in twelve years to prevent him attaining the kingdom of Mycenae. The weakly king had priority to the throne because he was prematurely born, due to Hera's jealous manoeuvres. Eurystheus set the labours, but he never dealt directly with Heracles, always through a herald, Copreus. Some stories say Heracles chose to undertake the labours to atone for the fact that he killed Megara, his wife, and at least some of his children, during a fit of madness (caused by Hera), and now sought purification. The labours were: 1. Killing the Nemean Lion. 2. Slaying the Lernean Hydra. 3. Capturing the Cerynean stag. 4. Capturing the Erymanthian boar. 5. Cleaning the Augeian stables. 6. Killing the Stymphalian birds. 7. Capturing the man-eating mares of Diomedes. 8. Capturing the Cretan bull. 9. Capturing the girdle of Hippolyte. 10. Fetching the cattle of Geryon. 11. Fetching three Golden Apples from the Garden of the Hesperides. 12. Snatching Cerberus from the Underworld.

There is a secondary list, not in any chronological order, of twelve lesser labours that Heracles carried out: 1. Killing Busiris. 2. Killing Cacus, the cattle thief. 3. Killing Antaeus. 4. Killing Eryx, the boxer. 5. Fighting Achelous for Deianeira. 6. Regaining his throne for Tyndareus. 7. Sailing with the Argonauts. 8. Killing the Lydian serpent for Queen Omphale. 9. Aiding the gods against the Giants. 10. Rescuing Hesione from a sea-monster. 11. Killing a lion on Mount Cithaeron. 12. Plundering Troy seventy-nine years before the Trojan War. Some add his fathering of fifty-one sons by forty-nine of Thespius' daughters, perhaps in one night, as another labour.

HERACLIDS (Heraclidae) Patronymic from Heracles for all his children. During one night Heracles fathered fifty-one sons by forty-nine of the fifty daughters of Thespius. These children included: by Astydameia, Ctesippus; by Astyoche, Tlepolemus; by Auge, Telephus; by Autonoe, Palaemon; by Chalciope, Thessalus; by Deianeira, Glycisonetes, Gyneus, Hyllus, Macaria and Odites; by Echidna, Agathyrsus, Gelon and Scylla; by Epicaste, Thestalus; by Megara, Deicoon and Therimachus; by Omphale, Agelaus and Lamon; and by Parthenope, Everes.

HERAEAN GAMES Women's athletic festivals held every four years throughout Greece. Possibly older than the Olympic Games. Those at Elis held in honour of Hera, and started by Hippodameia.

HERCULES Son of Jupiter. Roman equivalent of Heracles. (Heracles came to Italy in the course of his tenth labour.) Father of Pallas by Pallantia and possibly of Latinus (cf Faunus). Hercules abolished human sacrifice in Italy.

HERDS, god and protector of Greek: Apollo. Roman: Apollo.

HERMAON The husband of Thronia and father of Arabus.

HERMAPHRODITUS (Atlantiades, Atlantius) Son of Hermes and Aphrodite. A Naiad named Salmacis fell in love with him and their bodies fused into one, although both sets of sex organs were retained. Hermaphroditus was raised by Naiads on Mt Parnassus.

HERMES (Mercury) Messenger of the gods. Son of Zeus and Maia. Married Lara. Father of the two Lares. He had many love affairs:

Hermes

Hermes' Lovers	Children of the Union
Acacallis	Cydon (possibly)
Alcidamea	Bubus
Antianeira	Eurytus, Echion
Aphrodite	Hermaphroditus, Peitho
Carmenta	Evander
Chione	Autolycus
Chthonophyle	Polybus
Clytie	Myrtilus
Eupolemeia	Aethalides
Herse	Cephalus, Ceryx

Hermes' Lovers **Children of the**
Union
Penelope or
   Dryope   Pan
Phylodameia   Pharis

He was also the father of Abderus, Arabus, Chryses, Daphnis, Eurymedon, Harpalycus, Nephalion, Philocaus and possibly Silenus.

He had many epithets: 1. Argiphontes (slayer of Argus) 2. Cylleneius 3. Epimelios (guardian of flocks) 4. Hodios (patron of travellers and wayfarers) 5. Nomios 6. Oneiropompus (conductor of dreams) 7. Psychopompus (conductor of souls to the Underworld).

Hermes wore a broad-rimmed hat (petasus), winged sandals (talaria) and a herald's staff entwined with snakes (caduceus). He invented the lyre by stretching cow-gut across a tortoise shell, and gave it to Apollo. He was the first to make fire by rubbing together two sticks. On the very day that he was born, he stole the sheep of Apollo. Sided with the Greeks in the Trojan War. Patron of commerce, unexpected wealth and gaming.

HERMIONE   Only daughter of Menelaus and Helen; abandoned by her mother when nine years old. Sister of Pleisthenes, and possibly of Nicostratus. Married first to Neoptolemus (without issue) then, after his death, to Orestes. By this marriage, Hermione became the mother of Tisamenus.

HERMIONE (Harmonia)   Wife of Cadmus.

HERO   A beautiful priestess of Aphrodite who lived at Sestos. At the annual festival held there, Leander fell in love with her and nightly swam across the Hellespont to be with her. One night he drowned and she, overcome with grief, leapt into the sea and was herself drowned.

HERODOTUS   5th century BC Greek historian, the 'Father of History'.

HERON   *See* Ardea.

HEROPHILE   Daughter of Dardanus and Neso. Perhaps the Sibyl of Marpessa, though others had this name.

HEROPHILE   The name of several Sibyls. *See* Cumaean Sibyl.

HERSE (the dew)   Daughter of Cecrops or Acteus and Agraulos. Sister of Agraulos, Erysichthon and Pandrosos. Mother of Cephalus and Ceryx by Hermes. *See* Agraulos.

HERSILIA   A Sabine woman, abducted by the Romans. Daughter of Hersilius. The only married woman abducted, she acted as mediator between Sabines and Romans. Married first to Hostilius, by whom she bore Hostus Hostilius and, after Hostilius' death, to Romulus. After Romulus died, Hersilia too was deified, as Hora Quirini.

HERSILIUS   Father of Hersilia.

HESIONE   Daughter of Laomedon and Strymo. Sister of Astioche, Cilla, Clytius, Hicetaon, Lampus, Priam and Tithonus. Mother of Teucer by Telamon.

Hesione was rescued from the belly of a whale by Heracles, but when Laomedon refused to reward him with the horses he had received from Zeus, Heracles killed all her brothers except Priam, whom she ransomed. She was given to Telamon. As Priam resented his sister being given to a foreigner, this started the sequence that finally led to the Trojan War.

HESIONE (Asia, Axiothea)   Wife of Prometheus and possibly mother of Deucalion.

HESIONE   Possibly wife of Nauplius.

HESPERA (Eos, evening)   Daughter of Erebus and Nyx. Sister of Aether and Hemera. Originally a goddess of the dawn.

HESPERE (Hesperia)   Daughter of Atlas and Pleione. One of the Hesperides.

HESPERIDES Daughters of Atlas and Pleione. Sisters of Calypso, Hyas, the Hyades and Pleiades. They were named Aegle, Arethusa, Erythia and Hesperia, but some say there were seven, other suggested names being Hesperia, Hesperusa and Hestia. Apollodorus calls Vesta a Hesperide, and some writers question their parentage. Zeus and Themis, Atlas and Hesperis, Phorcys and Ceto, or even Nyx or Erebus are suggested parents. The Hesperides, together with Ladon, guarded the Golden Apples.

HESPERIS Daughter of Hesperus. Wife of Atlas. Possibly the mother of the Hesperides.

HESPERUS Son of Iapetos. Father of Hesperis.

HESPERUS (Vesper) Son of Astraeus and Eos, or Eos and Cephalus. He was carried away by the wind to become the evening star, and his name is often applied to the planet Venus.

HESTIA (Vesta) Goddess of the hearth. Eldest child of Cronos and Rhea. Sister of Demeter, Hades, Hera, Poseidon and Zeus. One of the twelve great Olympians, she remained a virgin all her life, refusing to marry Apollo or Poseidon. She was called Vesta by the Romans.

A guardian of homes, she was the first to build a house; her temple at Rome was tended by the vestal virgins.

HICETAON A Trojan elder. Son of Laomedon and Strymo. (Some say his mother was Leucippe or Placia.) Brother of Astyoche, Cilla, Clytius, Hesione, Lampus and Priam. Father of Melanippus.

He advised the Trojans to return Helen to Menelaus to avoid war. Either he was too old to fight in the Trojan War, or else he was killed by Heracles (*see* Hesione).

HIEROMNEME Daughter of the river god Simoeis. Sister of Astyoche. Married Assaracus. Mother of Capys.

HILAERA (Talaira) Daughter of Leucippus and Philodice. Sister of Arsinoe and Phoebe. Promised in marriage to Idas, but Polydeuces killed him and married her himself. She became the mother of Anogen by Castor.

HIMEROPA A Siren. Daughter of Achelous and Calliope, Melpomene, Terpsichore or Sterope. Sister of Thelxiepeia. *See* Sirens.

HIMERUS (Pothos) God of desire. Father of Gelon by Aetna. An attendant of Eros.

HINGES, Goddess of Carna.

HIPPALCIMUS (Hippalmus) An Argonaut. Son of Itonus. Father of Penelaus by Asterope.

HIPPASUS (1) Son of Ceyx and Alcyone. Possibly the father of Amphion and Asterius. Killed fighting Eurytus. (2) Son of Leucippe. His mother and aunts killed him while in a Dionysiac frenzy. (3) Father of Actor, the Argonaut. (4) Father of Charops and Socus. (5) Father of Apisaon. (6) Father of Hypsenor.

HIPPE Daughter of Cheiron. Lover of Aeolus, son of Hellen. Mother of Melanippe.

HIPPEA Daughter of Antiphus. Married Elatus. Mother of Caenis, Ischys and Polyphemus.

HIPPOCOON King of Sparta. Son of Oebalus and Gorgophone or Bateia. Brother or half-brother of Arene, Icarius, Peirene and Tyndareus. Father of twelve sons including Deiphobus. May have been present on the Calydonian Boar Hunt. Hippocoon had expelled Tyndareus to have the kingdom for himself. He and his sons were killed by Heracles after Hippocoon had refused to purify Heracles of his murder of Iphitus, and that Tyndareus might be restored.

HIPPOCOON (1) Accompanied Aeneas on his journey to Italy and excelled in the funeral games of Anchises. (2) An ally of the Trojans, who alerted Rhesus that Diomedes and Odysseus were stealing his horses.

HIPPOCRENE Fountain, a source of poetic inspiration, on Mt Helicon, sacred to the Muses. It was created by Pegasus striking his hoofs on the ground.

HIPPODAMAS King of Aetolia. Possibly the father of Perimele (cf Aeolus), but more likely the son of Achelous and Perimele. Brother of Orestes. Father of Euryte.

HIPPODAMEIA Daughter of Oenomaus and Evarete. Sister of Leucippus. Married Pelops. Mother of Alcathous, Astydameia, Atreus, Chrysippus, Copreus, Lysidice, Nicippe, Pittheus, Thyestes and Troezen, and perhaps others.

Her father held a chariot race for her twelve suitors, but she bribed Myrtilus to enable Pelops to win. Killed herself after murdering Chrysippus, who may have been a bastard son of Pelops.

HIPPODAMEIA (1) Daughter of Adrastus or Butes and Amphithea. Sister of Argeia, Aegialeia, Aegialeus, Cyanippus and Deipyle. Married Peirithous. Mother of Polypoetes. (2) Daughter of Anchises. Sister of Aeneas and Lyrus. Married Alcathous.

HIPPODAMUS Son of Agenor and Epicasta. Brother of Demonice and Porthaon, and possibly Thestius. Killed in the Trojan War by Odysseus.

HIPPOLOCHUS (1) Son of Antimachus. Brother of Hippomachus and Peisander. Murdered during the Trojan War. (2) Son of Bellerophon and Philonoe. Brother of Deidameia, Isander and Laodameia. Father of Glaucus.

HIPPOLYTE Queen of the Amazons. Daughter of Ares and Otrera. Sister of Antiope (Melanippe) and Penthesileia. Possibly the mother of Hippolytus by Theseus. Was either killed by Heracles or

died of a broken heart after Heracles took her girdle, given to her by Ares, as his ninth labour.

HIPPOLYTE Daughter of Cretheus. Sister of Amythaon, Pheres and Promachus. Possibly the wife of Acastus, she fell in love with Peleus who rejected her, but who later killed Acastus.

HIPPOLYTUS Son of Theseus and Hippolyte. After the death of Hippolyte, Theseus married Phaedra, daughter of Minos, but she fell in love with Hippolytus. He refused her and she lied to Theseus, claiming Hippolytus had made advances to her. Hippolytus fled from Theseus, who believed Phaedra; and Poseidon's sea-calves overturned his chariot, killing him. He was transported to the heavens to become the constellation Auriga, the charioteer but, through Artemis, he was deified as Virbius.

HIPPOLYTUS Son of Gaea and brother of the other giants: Agrius, Alcyoneus, Gration, Mimas, Polybotes, Porphyrion and Thoon. Hippolytus was killed in the war between the gods and Giants by Hermes, wearing his cap of invisibility.

HIPPOMACHUS Son of Antimachus. Brother of Hippolochus and Peisander. Killed by Leonteus.

HIPPOMEDON Probably son of Talaus and Lysimache or Lysianassa. Brother to Adrastus, Aristomachus, Astynome, Eriphyle, Mecisteus, Metidice, Parthenopaeus and Pronax. Father of Polydorus by Evanippe. One of the Seven against Thebes, he was killed by Hyperbius or Ismarus.

HIPPOMENES Son of Megareus (or possibly his father) and Iphinoe. Brother of Evacheme, Evippus and Timalcus. He or Melanion married Atalanta after beating her in a race. Possibly father of Parthenopaeus.

HIPPONA Roman goddess of horses.

HIPPONOME Daughter of Menoeceus. Sister of Creon and Jocasta. Married Alcaeus. Mother of Amphityron and Anaxo.

HIPPONOUS (1) The last Trojan killed by Achilles before his own death. (2) Another name for Bellerophon, son of Glaucus and Eurymede. (3) A son of Priam. (4) King of Olenus. Husband of Astynome. Father of Capaneus and Periboea.

HIPPOSTRATUS Son of Amarynceus. Brother of Diores. Raped Periboea, daughter of Hipponous.

HIPPOTADES Epithet of Aeolus, god of the winds.

HIPPOTAS Father of Aeolus, god of the winds.

HIPPOTES (1) Father of Egesta, wife of Crimisus. (2) Father of Aletes.

HIPPOTHOE (1) Daughter of Mestor and Lysidice. Mother of Taphius by Poseidon after he had abducted her to the Taphian islands. (2) Daughter of Pelias and Anaxibia or Phylomache. Sister of Acastus, Alcestis, Pelopia and Pisidice.

HIPPOTHOON King of Eleusis. Son of Poseidon and Alope.
Eponym of one of the ten tribes of Athens.

HIPPOTHOUS Bastard son of Priam.

HIPPOTHOUS Leader of the Pelasgians, allies of Troy in the Trojan War, he was killed by Greater Ajax as he tried to recover the body of Patroclus.

HIPPOTION An Ascanian. Father of Ascanius and Morys. Killed in the Trojan War by Meriones.

HISCILLA Wife of Triopas. Mother of Erysichthon, Iphimedeia, Messene and Phorbas.

HODEODOCUS Husband of Agrianome. Father of Oileus.

HODIOS (wayfarer) Epithet of Hermes, the god of travellers.

HOMER With a few unimportant exceptions, the Greeks believed Homer wrote both the *Iliad* and the *Odyssey*. They seem, however, to have known little of his private life.
There have been many suggestions as to the period at which he lived: some make him contemporary with the Trojan War; others place him in the middle of the seventh century BC. All that can be said with certainty is that he lived before 700 BC.
Ancient authorities dispute the place of his birth. The towns with the best supported claims are Chios and Smyrna. Very little credence can be given to other traditions relating to his life, except, perhaps, that he was blind, as were many bards.
There is great unity in style in both the *Iliad* and the *Odyssey*, suggesting that each is the work of a single author. Major stylistic differences between the two great works perhaps lend credence to the notion that they are not the work of one man.

HONESTY, Roman goddess of Fides.

HONOUR, Roman goddess of Maiestas.

HOOPOE *See* Tereus.

HOPE All that remained in Pandora's box after she lifted the lid.

HOPLADAMAS One of the giants who protected Rhea from her husband, Cronos.

HOPLES Son of Ion and Helice. Brother of Aegicores, Argades and Geleon.

HOPLEUS Son of Poseidon and Canace. Brother of Aloeus, Epopeus, Nireus and Triopas.

HORA QUIRINI Roman goddess of beauty. Deification of Hersilia, the wife of Romulus.

HORACE 1st century BC. Roman lyric poet.

HORAE (seasons) Daughters of Zeus and Themis. Three sisters called Dike (justice), Eirene (peace), and Eunomia (lawfulness). The Athenians worshipped only two Horae: Thallo and Carpo, spring and autumn. They were sisters of Astraea and the Moirae, guardians of the entrance to heaven and to Olympus, where they supervised the Olympic Games. With the Moirae, they also superintended all mortal actions.

HORATIUS, PUBLIUS Legendary Roman champion. The lone survivor of six combat fighters. Three Horatii from Rome met three Curiatii from Alba Longa. Killed his sister on returning to Rome, as she was still wearing the mantle of her lover, one of the Curiatii.

HORN OF PLENTY *See* Cornucopia.

HORSE *See* Evippe (Theia), Menalippe, Ocyrrhoe.

HORSES, Roman goddess of Hippona.

HORSES, protectress of Bubona (Epona).

HORUS *See* Nephthys and Set.

HOSTILIUS The husband of Hersilia and father of Hostus Hostilius. Killed fighting the Sabines.

HOSTUS HOSTILIUS Son of Hostilius and Hersilia.

HOURS Another name for the Horae or Seasons.

HUNDRED-HANDED Another name for the Hecatoncheroi or Centimani. Sons of Uranus and Gaea, they were three giants

called Briareus, Cottus and Gyges, each with fifty heads and a hundred arms. They were the brothers of Typhon and the Cyclopes.

HYANCINTHUS (Hyacinth) Son of Amyclas and Diomede, or of Pierus, son of Magnes, and the Muse, Cleio. Brother of Argalus, Cynortas and Leaneira. He was loved by Apollo, Thamyris or Zephyrus. Killed by Apollo's discus, he was changed into a lily. Hyacinthus was carried to heaven by Aphrodite, Artemis and Athena.

HYACINTH, daughters of (Hycanthides) Daughters of an Athenian immigrant from Sparta, who were sacrificed in an unsuccessful attempt to cure a plague ravaging Athens. One was called Antheis.

HYADES (Dodonides, Suculae) Daughters of Atlas and Pleione, Atlas and Aethra, or Oceanus and Tethys, five or seven in number. Among the names offered by various sources: Cleeia, Coronis, Eudora, Phaeo and Phaesyle. They were the sisters of Calypso, Hyas, the Hesperides and the Pleiades. They were nurses of Dionysus on Mt Nysa. After the death of Hyas, their grief was so great that Zeus placed them among the stars as a constellation.

HYAS Son of Atlas and Pleione. Brother of Calypso, the Hyades, Hesperides and Pleiades. Killed in Libya by a bull, lion, snake or wild boar. (*See also* Hyades, above.)

HYBRIS (Thymbris) Possibly the mother of Pan by Zeus (cf Hermes and Penelope). Hybris was the personification of arrogance, outrage and violence. Defendants stood on the stone of Hybris at the Areopagus.

HYDRA, Lernean A nine-headed monster, the offspring of Typhon and Echidna, as were Cerberus, Chimaera, the Sphinx, the Caucasian Eagle, the Crommyonian Sow, the Nemean Lion, the Vultures and Orthus. If one head was cut off, two grew

Hydra

in its place, though finally it was killed by Heracles, assisted by Iolaus, as his second labour.

Arrows dipped in the Hydra's venom killed Cheiron, Nessus and Philoctetes and the Hydra was the direct cause of Heracles' own death.

HYETTUS An Argive, the first person to commit murder because of adultery. The victim was called Molurus.

HYGIEIA (Salus) Goddess of health. Daughter of Asclepius and Epione. Sister of Acesis, Aegle, Iaso, Janiscus, Machaon, Panacea and Podalirius.

HYGINUS Roman mythographer who lived at the close of 1st century BC, famous for his *Fabulae* and *Poetica Astronomica*.

HYLAS An Argonaut. Son of Theiodamas and Menodice. Lover of Heracles and his squire, he was was drowned as a sacrifice by the nymph, Pegae, who fell in love with him.

HYLLUS Son of Heracles and Deianeira or Melite. Brother of Ctessipus, Macaria and Tlepolemus. Married Iole. Father of Cleodaeus. He may have killed Eurystheus and sent his head to Alcmene, his grandmother. Was himself killed by Echemus.

HYLONOME Daughter of Ixion and Nephele, she was the most beautiful of all the Centaurs. Fell in love with Cyllarus and committed suicide after his death at the hands of the Lapiths.

HYMARUS *See* Himerus.

HYMEN (Hymenaeus) God of marriage. Son of Dionysus and Aphrodite or of Apollo or Dionysus and Urania, a Muse. Personification of the wedding feast, he sang at the wedding of Dionysus and Ariadne and the Hymenaeus was named after him. Hymen is represented as a god, wearing a wreath or carrying a torch. Another tradition presents him as son of Magnes. Brother of Eioneus and Pierus. Lover of Apollo, though some say this is a different person.

HYPATE Delphic Muse, the high note of a lyre. Sister of Mese and Nete.

HYPEIROCHUS Father of Itymoneus. A Trojan killed in the War by Odysseus.

HYPERASIUS Possibly the father of Amphion and Asterius.

HYPERBIUS One of the fifty sons of Aegyptus, he helped Eteocles defend Thebes. Murdered by his wife on his wedding night.

HYPERBOREANS A fabulous race of people from a place north of the river Oceanus. These people lived to the age of a thousand in perpetual springtime. There were two harvests a year as the land was so fertile and the climate very mild. From here Heracles brought the olive tree to Olympus. Believed by some to be the North Pole, or even Britain.

HYPERENOR (1) Son of Panthous and Phrontis. Brother of Euphorbus and Polydamas. Killed by Menelaus. (2) Son of Poseidon and Alcyone. Brother of Anthas and Arethusa. (3) One of the Sparti, the people that sprang up when Cadmus sowed dragon's teeth. Brother of Echion, Chthonius, Pelorus and Udaeus.

HYPERES King of Althepia (Troezen). Possibly the son of Alcyone.

HYPERION (the one above) A sun-god. Son of Uranus and Gaea. Brother of the Titans. Married his sister, Theia. Father of Helios, Selene, Eos and possibly Aurora. Hyperion may have been nothing more than the personification of the sun itself.

HYPERIPPE Daughter of Arcas and Erato. Sister of Apheidas, Azan and Elatus. Half-sister of Autolaus.

HYPERIPPE Possibly the mother of Aetolus, Epeius, Eurycyda, Naxus and Paeon by Endymion.

HYPERMNESTRA Eldest of the fifty daughters of Danaus and the only Danaid not to murder her husband (Lynceus) on their wedding night. Mother of Abas. After their death, all three were buried in the same tomb at Argos.

HYPERMNESTRA Daughter of Thestius and Eurythemis. Sister of Althaea, Leda and Plexippus. Married Oicles. Mother of Amphiarus.

HYPNOS (Somnus) God of sleep. Son of Nyx and Erebus. Brother of Thanatos, Aether, Cer, Dreams, Hemera, Momus, Moros and Nemesis. Married Pasithea. Father of Morpheus and the Dreams.

HYPSENOR Son of Hippasus. Killed in the Trojan War by Deiphobus.

HYPSEUS King of the Lapiths. Son of Peneius and Creusa. Father of Astyagyia, Cyrene, Stilbe and Themisto.

HYPSIPYLE Queen of Lemnos. Daughter of Thoas and Myrina. Mother of Euneus (Evenus), Deipylus, Nebrophonus and Thoas by Jason, though several of these names may be doublets.

She saved her father from being killed by the women of his kingdom, and was banished to Lemnos. Rescued from pirates by Lycurgus or Lycus to be nurse to Opheltes.

HYRIEUS King of Hyria. Son of Poseidon or Lycus and Alcyone. Brother or half-brother of Anthas, Arethusa and Hyperenor. Probable father (of Chthonius) of Lycus and Nycteus by the nymph, Clonia; and possibly the father of Orion.

Eponym of a once-powerful city of Boeotia where Agamedes and Trophonius built Hyrieus a wonderful treasure house which they systematically robbed until caught.

HYRMINA Daughter of Epeius and Anaxiroe. Married Phorbas. Mother of Actor, Augeias and Tiphys.

HYRNETHO Daughter of Temenus. Sister of Ceisus, Agraeus, Cerynes and Phalces. Married Deiphontes. Mother of three sons and a daughter, she was accidentally killed by her husband and was buried in an olive grove.

HYRTACUS King of Arisbe in the Troad. Father of Asius by Arisbe (Bateia), daughter of Merops, and possibly of Nisus. Hyrtacus was an ally of the Trojans.

HYRTIUS Mysian son of Gyrtias. Killed in the Trojan War by Greater Ajax.

I

IACCHUS Epithet of Bacchus (Dionysus) at his Athenian festivals.

IACCHUS An obscure Eleusinian god, son of Demeter, Dionysus or Persephone. Possibly the husband of Demeter. Identified with Bacchus (cf above).

IAERA A Nereid. One of the fifty daughters of Nereus and Doris.

IALMENUS Co-ruler of Minyan Orchomenus. Son of Ares and Astyoche. Brother of Ascalaphus. An Argonaut. As a suitor of Helen, he took thirty ships to the Trojan War with his brother.

IALYSUS Son of Cercaphus and Cydippe. Brother of Cameirus and Lindus. Grandson of Helios and Rhode.
  Co-founded the city of Ialysus, later naming it Rhodes after his grandmother.

IAMBE Servant of Celeus and Metaneira who induced Doso (Demeter) to smile.

IAMUS Son of Apollo and Evadne, he had the gift of prophecy.

IANASSA A Nereid. One of the fifty daughters of Nereus and Doris.

IANEIRA A Nereid. One of the fifty daughters of Nereus and Doris.

IANISCUS King of Sicyon. A descendant of Attican Clytius. Succeeded Adrastus and was succeeded by Phaestus.

IANTHE A Cretan maid promised in marriage to Iphis, daughter of Ligdus and Telethusa, who was raised as a boy. (*See* Iphis.) Isis changed Iphis into a real boy at the last moment before the marriage.

IAPETOS A Titan. Son of Uranus and Gaea. Brother of Cronos, Pallas, Oceanus, the Titans, and others. Married Asia, Clymene or Themis. Father of Atlas, Epimetheus, Menoetius and Prometheus. Father of Hesperus. Father of mankind. Thrown into Tartarus by Zeus, and the isle of Inarine settled on top of him.

IAPETOS Father of Buphagus by Thornax. Perhaps identifiable with the above.

IAPIS A Trojan to whom Apollo gave the understanding and power of healing herbs.

IAPYX Son of Lycaon. Brother of Daunus and Peucetius.

IARBAS King of Gaetulia in North Africa. Son of Hammon or Zeus and a nymph. Sold the site of Carthage to Dido.

IARDANUS Father of Omphale. King of Lydia.

IASION Son of Zeus and Electra. Brother of Dardanus. Demeter fell in love with him and became the mother of Philomelus and Plutus by him. He perfected the Samothracian mysteries, and the Arcadians called him a god.

IASO (cure) Goddess of healing. Daughter of Asclepius and Epione. Sister of Aegle, Acesis, Hygeia, Janiscus, Machaon, Panacea and Podalirius.

IASUS One of the Dactyli. Son of Rhea and Anchiale. Brother of five sisters and Epimedes, Heracles, Idas and Paeonaeus.

IASUS Son of Lycurgus and Cleophyle or Eurynome. Brother of Amphidamas, Ancaeus and Epochus. Father of Atalanta by Clymene. He devised a foot-race, to protect the virginity of his daughter.

IASUS King of Argos. Son of Argus Panoptes, Ecbasus or Triopas and Ismene. Brother of Agenor and Pelasgus. Possibly the father of Io and Agenor.

IASUS Son of Sphelus. A Greek killed in the Trojan War by Aeneas.

ICARIUS Son of Perieres and Gorgophone or Oebalus and Bateia. Brother or half-brother of Arene, Borus, Peirene, Hippocoon and Tyndareus. Married Periboea or Polycaste. Father of Iphthime, Penelope, Perileus and four other sons.

ICARIUS An Athenian farmer. Father of Erigone, he taught Dionysus' culture of wine to his fellow farmers until, drunk, they beat him to death. An annual festival, the Agora, was created in honour of father and daughter, and the two became the constellation Bootes.

ICARUS Son of Daedalus. He and his father escaped from Crete and King Minos by fastening wax wings to their arms. Icarus unfortunately flew too close to the sun, the wax melted and he plunged to his death into the Icarian Sea, south of Samos. His body was washed up on the isle of Icaria.

ICELOS (Phobetar) One of the Oneiroi. One of the thousand sons of Somnus, and brother of Morpheus and Phantasos. Had the power to change his shape into that of an animal.

IDA Daughter of Melisseus. Sister of Adrasteia. Married Lycastus. Mother of Minos the lawgiver. Nursemaid of Zeus and nymph of Cretan Mt Ida.

Icarus

IDA, Mount (1) Cretan mountain. (2) Phrygian mountain of the Troad, where Paris judged the beauty contest between Aphrodite, Athena and Hera. Source of the rivers Aesepus, Granicus, Scamander, Heptaporus, Caresus, Rhodeius, Rhesus and Simois. Highest peak: Gargarus.

IDAEA (1) Second wife of Phineus. Mother of Thynius and Mariandynus who were imprisoned because of her lies but were rescued by the Argonauts. She was condemned to death by her father. (2) Daughter of Dardanus. The nymph of Mt Ida in Phrygia. Mother of Teucer by Scamander, and thus the ancestor of the Trojan kings. (3) Epithet of Rhea, who was worshipped on Mt Ida.

IDAEAN DACTYLS Priests of Rhea living on Mt Ida in Phrygia.

IDAEUS The Trojan herald who drove Priam's cart when the latter went to Achilles to recover the body of Hector, his son.

IDAMANTE Son of Idomeneus, the man who promised to sacrifice the first living thing he saw if the gods would return him safely to Crete from the Trojan War. This fate befell his son.

IDAS An Argonaut. Son of Aphareus of Messene or Poseidon and Arene. Brother of Lynceus and Peisus. Idas should have married his cousin, Phoebe, daughter of Leucippus, but she was abducted by Castor and Polydeuces. His next love, Marpessa, was abducted by Apollo and Idas gave chase, armed with his bow and arrows. Zeus asked Marpessa to choose between the two suitors and she chose and married Idas. Father of Cleopatra. Alcyone may have been another daughter, or simply an epithet of Cleopatra. Idas was present at the Calydonian Boar Hunt. He and his brother, Lynceus, had grown up with the Dioscuri, but he killed Castor and was, in turn, killed by Zeus.

IDAS (Acesidas) One of the Dactyli. Son of Rhea or Anchiale. Brother of Heracles, Epimedes, Iasius, Paeonaeus and five sisters.

IDMON (1) One of fifty sons of Aegyptus. Murdered by his wife on their wedding night. (2) The father of Arachne by Colophon. (3) Son of Abas or Apollo and Asteria or Cyrene. Became an Argonaut although he knew it meant his death to do so. He foretold their quest for the Golden Fleece. Killed by a boar.

IDOMENE Daughter of Pheres and Periclymene. Sister of Admetus, Lycurgus and Periopis. Married Amythaon. Mother of Aeolia, Bias, Melampus and Perimele.

IDOMENEUS King of Crete. Son of Deucalion. Brother of Crete. Married Meda. Father of Idamante. With the son of his half-brother, Meriones, he took eighty ships to the Trojan War. Was in the Wooden Horse. He sacrificed his son to Poseidon after his safe return home. His wife's lover, Leucus, banished him from his throne to Italy.

IDYIA (Eidyia) Daughter of Oceanus and Tethys. Married Aeetes. Mother of Absyrtus and Medea.

ILIA Daughter of Lausus. Epithet of Rhea Silvia, mother of Romulus and Remus.

ILIAD Homer's epic about the Trojan War. It covers a period of about seven weeks at the end of the ninth, or start of the tenth, year.

ILION (Ilios) The citadel of Troy.

ILIONE Eldest daughter of Priam and Hecuba. Sister of many. (*See* Hecuba.) Reared her brother Polydorus. Married Polymestor. Mother of Deipylus.

ILIONEUS Companion of Aeneas on his journey to Italy from Troy.

ILIONEUS One of the twelve children, six boys and six girls, of Amphion and Niobe.

ILISSUS Athenian river where Boreas abducted Oreithyia.

ILLYRIUS Son of Cadmus and Harmonia. Brother of Agave, Autonoe, Ino, Polydorus and Semele. Came from Illyria, which is now part of Albania.

ILUS Fourth king of Troy. Son of Tros and Callirrhoe. Brother of Assaracus, Cleopatra and Ganymede. Married Eurydice, daughter of Adrastus. Father of Laomedon and Themiste.

Ilus took part in the wrestling contest in the Phrygian Games. He won fifty youths, fifty maidens and one dappled cow. An oracle told him to found a city wherever the cow lay down, which it did on a hill sacred to Ate. The city was named Ilion; later he changed it to Troy. Ilus was given the Palladium by Zeus.

ILUS (1) Elder son of Dardanus and Bateia (Arisbe). Brother of Erichthonius. Died childless. (2) Also called Iulus and Ascanius, he was the son of Aeneas and Creusa. (3) Son of Mermerus. King of Thresprotian Ephyra. Ilus, a grandson of Medea, knew how to make poison, but would not reveal the secret to Odysseus.

IMBRIUS Son of Mentor. Married Medesicaste, daughter of Priam. Killed in the Trojan War by Teucer.

IMENARETE Possibly the wife of Chalcodon (cf Alcyone).

IMMARDUS Another name for Ismarus, son of Eumolpus.

IMPOSTORS, Roman goddess of Laverna.

INACHUS First king of Argos and river god. Son of Oceanus and Tethys. Married his sister, Melia. Father of Aegialeius, Io and Phoroneus. Possibly father of Argus. Panoptes. Father of Mycene, but the mother may not have been his wife. Reigned for sixty years. Said to have given his name to the river after jumping into it when pursued by a Fury sent by Zeus. He, Asterion and Cephisus were asked to award control of Argolis to either Poseidon or Hera. They chose Hera, so Poseidon caused all the rivers to dry up each summer.

INDIGETES Name given to deified mortal heroes, such as Aeneas, Heracles and Romulus.

INFATUATION, goddess of Ate; Eris; Discordia.

INO (Mater Matuta) Daughter of Cadmus and Harmonia. Sister of Agave, Autonoe, Illyrius, Polydorus and Semele. Married Athamas. Mother of Learchus and Melicertes. Step-mother of Helle and Phrixus.

As a child she reared Dionysus and suffered the divine madness of the Bacchants. She helped Agave kill Pentheus, and tried to kill her step-children; but they escaped on the ram with the Golden Fleece. Hera drove Ino and Athamas mad and they killed their own children, Ino jumping into the sea with Melicertes. She became the goddess Leucothea, and Melicertes, Palaemon.

IO Priestess of Hera at Argos. Daughter of Inachus or Iasus and Melia. Sister of Aegialeus and Phoroneus. To avoid Hera's revenge, Zeus changed her into a cow, but Hera was not deceived and set Argus to watch her. Tormented by a gadfly, Io wandered round Europe and Egypt, and was finally restored by Zeus by whom she bore a son, Epaphus. Later married Telegonus, king of Egypt; they were ancestors of Danaus. The Bosphorus was named after her.

IOBATES (Amphianax) King of Lycia. Father of Philonoe and Stheneboea.

Bellerophon wanted Stheneboea as a wife and Iobates sent him to fight the Chimaera. On his safe return Iobates allowed him to marry his other daughter, Philonoe.

IOLAUS Charioteer of Heracles. Son of Iphicles and Automedusa. May have married Megara, former wife of Heracles. Father of Leipephile. Founder of Iolaea in Sardinia.

Helped Heracles kill the Hydra and was restored to youthfulness by Hebe. Took part in the Calydonian Boar Hunt and was a chariot-race winner at the Olympic Games.

IOLCUS Thessalian town, now called Volos, at the head of the Gulf of Pagasae. The Argonauts sailed from there after Jason, the Dioscuri and Peleus had destroyed it and given it to the Haemones.

IOLCUS, kings of Cretheus was the first king, followed by Pelias, Jason, Thessalus and Acastus. Neleus was also a king of Iolcus.

IOLE Daughter of Eurytus and Antiope. Sister of Clytius and Iphitus. She witnessed Heracles' murder of her whole family and was then taken as his mistress. Married Hyllus after Heracles' death, as this was one of Heracles' death-bed wishes. Mother of Cleodaeus.

ION Son of Apollo and Creusa, wife of Xuthus. Brother of Janus. Married Helice, daughter of Selinus. Father of Aegicores, Argades, Geleon and Hoples.

Abandoned by his mother as a baby, he was rescued by Apollo and sent to Delphi. The Oracle at Delphi gave Ion to Xuthus as a ward since Xuthus' marriage had been childless. Mother and son were later reconciled. Ion, ancestor of the Ionians, was killed in the Trojan War.

IONIA The coastal regions of Asia Minor, plus the two islands, Chios and Samos. Its principal city: Lydia.

IOVIALIS (Genius) Father of Tages.

IOXUS Ancestor of the Ioxids. Son of Melanippus and grandson of Theseus and Perigune. The Ioxids held the asparagus to be sacred, a cult started by Perigune.

IPHEUS A Lycian killed in the Trojan War by Odysseus.

IPHIANASSA (1) Daughter of Agamemnon and Clytemnestra, usually called Iphigeneia. Sister of Electra, Orestes and Chrysothemis. (2) Daughter of Proetus and Stheneboea (Anteia). Sister of Iphinoe, Megapenthes and Lysippe. Second wife of Bias. Mother of Anaxibia. Melampus, brother of Bias, cured her of madness. (3) Possibly mother of Aetolus, Epeius, Eurycyda and Paeon by Endymion.

IPHICLES (Iphiclus) Son of Amphitryon and Alcmene. Born at the same time as his half-brother, Heracles. Married Automedusa. Father of Iolaus. Then married the youngest daughter of Creon, king of Corinth. Present on the Calydonian Boar Hunt. Killed either fighting Hippocoon of Sparta or Augeias of Elis.

IPHICLUS Son of Phylacus or Cephalus and Clymene. Brother of Alcimede. Father of Podarces and Protesilaus by Diomedeia, after Melampus cured his impotence. Was an Argonaut.

IPHIDAMAS Son of Antenor and Theano. Brother of Acamas, Agenor, Archelous, Coon, Crino, Demoleon, Glaucus, Helicaon, Laocoon, Laodamas, Lycaon, Polybus and Polydamas. Half-brother of Pedaeus. Killed in the Trojan War by Agamemnon.

IPHIGENEIA (Chrysothemis, Iphianassa) Eldest daughter of Agamemnon and Clytemnestra. Sister of Electra and Orestes. Her father tried to sacrifice her to Artemis but she was saved at the last minute when the goddess substituted a deer. Hera transported her to the land of the Taurians to be her priestess; or else she became the goddess, Hecate.

IPHIMEDEIA Daughter of Triopas and Hiscilla. Sister of Erysichthon, Messene and Phorbas. Married her uncle, Aloeus. Mother of Pancratis. Mother of Ephialtes and Otus, the Aloedae, by her lover, Poseidon although some call Aloeus their father. She and her daughter were kidnapped by Thracian pirates but were rescued by the Aloeidae.

IPHIMEDEIA Daughter of Theseus and Helen.

IPHINOE (1) Daughter of Alcathous and Evaechme. Sister of Automedusa, Callipolis, Ischepolis and Periboea. A virgin all her life, the brides of Megara use to place a lock of hair on her tomb before their wedding. (2) A Lemnian chieftain messenger of Hypsipyle, she welcomed the Argonauts to Lemnos. (3) Daughter of Nisus. Sister of Erymede and Scylla. Married Megareus. Mother of Evaecheme, Evippus, Hippomenes and Timalcus. (4) Daughter of Proetus and Stheneboea or Anteia. Sister of Iphianassa, Megapenthes and Lysippe. She was driven mad by Dionysus or Hera and Melampus failed to cure her.

IPHIS King of Argos. Son of Alector. Brother of Capaneus. Father of Eteoclus and Evadne.

It was he who told Polyneices to bribe Eriphyle with Harmonia's necklace. As Eteoclus died in the war against Thebes, rule of Argos passed to Sthenelus.

IPHIS Daughter of Ligdus and Telethusa. Her parents were poor and believed the child would be killed if known to be a girl, so for thirteen years they dressed her as a boy. Isis transformed her into an actual boy so that she could marry Ianthe.

IPHIS Cypriot youth who hanged himself after Anaxarete refused his love. Aphrodite punished the girl by turning her to stone.

IPHITEA Mother of Carya, Lyco and Orphe by Dion.

IPHITION Trojan son of Otrynteus and a Naiad. Killed in the Trojan War by Achilles.

IPHITUS (1) Son of Eurytus and Antiope. Brother of Clytius and Iole. Killed by Heracles in a fit of madness and flung from the walls of Tiryns after he had given Heracles a bow and arrows. (2) Son of Haemon or Praxonides. If the former, brother of Oxylus and Thermius. He was king of Elis and reinstituted the Olympic Games because the Delphic Oracle said this was the only way to halt a pestilence in the country. Helped the Heraclids against the people of Peloponnesus. (3) Son of Naubolus, king of Phocis. Father of Epistrophus, Schedius and Eurynome. An Argonaut, he entertained Jason at Delphi.

IPHTHIME Daughter of Icarius and Periboea or Polycaste. Sister of Penelope, Perileus and four others. Married Eumelus. Athena once disguised herself as Iphthime to console Penelope.

IRENE (Eirene, Pax) Goddess of Peace. Daughter of Zeus and Themis. One of the Horae. Sister of Dike and Eunomia.

IRIS Messenger of the gods. Daughter of Thaumas and Electra. Sister of the Harpies. Epithet: Beroe (adviser of the Trojans). Also goddess of rainbows – the literal meaning of her name. Swift of foot, she was pre-eminently Hera's servant.

IRUS Son of Actor and Aegina. Brother of Menoetius and Polymela. Married Demonassa. Father of Eurydamas and Eurytion. After the death of Eurytion, Peleus, his killer, offered Irus compensation in the form of a large flock of sheep. Irus refused.

IRUS (original name, Arnaeus) A beggar at the palace of Odysseus, serving

Penelope's suitors. On his return Odysseus killed him in a boxing match.

ISANDER Son of Bellerophon and Philinoe. Brother of Deidameia, Hippolochus and Laodameia. Killed fighting the Solymi.

ISCHEPOLIS Son of Alcathous and Evaechme. Brother of Automedusa, Callipolis, Iphinoe and Periboea. Killed on the Calydonian Boar Hunt.

ISCHYS Son of Elatus of Arcadia and Hippea. Brother of Caenis and Polyphemus. Lover of Coronis.

ISIS (the sky) Goddess of fertility. Wife and sister of Osiris. Sister also of Nephthys and Set. Mother of Horus. This Egyptian goddess was the equivalent of Demeter or Io. Was worshipped in Greece and Italy; her Roman festival was held on 29–31 October. In Greek mythology, daughter of Cronos and Rhea.

ISMARUS (1) Lydian companion of Aeneas on his journey from Troy to Italy. (2) Son of Astacus. Brother of Amphidocus, Leades and Melanippus. He defended Thebes against the Seven, killing Hippomedon. (3) Son of Eumolpus and a daughter of Benthesicyme. Brother of Ceryx. Married a daughter of Tegyrius of Thrace. Also known as Immaradus.

ISMENE (1) Daughter of Oedipus and Jocasta or Euryganeia. Sister of Antigone, Eteocles and Polyneices. (2) Daughter of Asopus and Metope. Sister of Antiope, Aegina, Cleone, Corcyra, Chalcis, Ismenus, Metope, Pelagon, Pelasgus, Plataea, Salamis, Thebe and ten others. Mother of Iasus by Argus Panoptes, Ecbasus or Triopas.

ISMENIUS Father of Linus.

ISMENOS Son of Amphion and Niobe. Eldest brother of six boys and six girls, including Amyclas, Chloris, Cleodoxa, Neaera, Phthia and Phylomache. All the sons (except, perhaps, one) were killed by Apollo, and Artemis killed all the girls but Chloris.

ISMENUS Son of the river god Asopus and Metope. Brother of Aegina, Antiope, Cleone, Corcyra, Chalcis, Ismene, Pelagon, Salamis, Pelasgus, Metope, Plataea, Thebe and ten others.

ISSEDONES A legendary race from Asia, living farther north than even the Hyperboreans.

ISTHMIAN GAMES One of the four great Panhellenic games. The others were the Pythian, the Olympic, and the Nemean. Started by Theseus, in honour of his father, by Poseidon, or by Sisyphus in honour of Poseidon and in memory of Melicertes in 776 BC.

ISUS Son of Priam and perhaps Hecuba. Had many brothers (*see* Priam). Achilles captured him on Mt Ida but he was ransomed by Priam. Killed in the Trojan War by Agamemnon.

ITALUS King of Sicily. Son of Telegonus and Penelope. Italy was named after him.

ITHACA An island in the Ionian Sea, west of Greece, legendary home of Odysseus and Laertes.

ITONUS Son of Boeotus. Father of Hippalcimus.

ITYLUS Son of Zethus and Aedon. Accidentally killed by his mother.

ITYMONEUS Eleian son of Hypeirochus. Killed in the Trojan War by Nestor.

ITYS Son of Tereus of Thrace and Procne. When six years old, his mother killed him and served him as food to his father whom she bitterly hated. Itys became a sandpiper.

IULUS (Ilus, Ascanius)   Son of Aeneas and Creusa. Founder of Alba Longa. Ancestor of the Julian family.

IUTURNA (Juturna)   Roman goddess of rivers and springs. Daughter of Daunus and Venilia. Sister of Turnus. Mother of Fontus by Janus. Jupiter seduced her, but in compensation deified her. Festival date: 11 January.

IXION   King of the Lapiths of Thessaly. Son of Antion and Perimele, though some sources give his father as Ares or Phlegyas. If so, brother of Coronis. Married Dia, daughter of Eionneus. Father of Peirithous, but Zeus may have been the father. Father of Amycus and the Centaurs by Nephele, a cloud, and of Agelaos. Zeus made an image of Hera from a cloud and embracing this, Ixion became father of the Centaurs. When he killed his father-in-law, he became the first murderer and was punished by Zeus who had promised to purify him. Instead, because he had also tried to seduce Hera, Zeus struck him with thunder and tied him to a perpetually rotating wheel in Hades, surrounded by snakes.

Ixion

J

JANA Wife of Janus.

JANICULUM A citadel at Rome. The highest hill of Rome (100 metres). The first bridge across the Tiber, connecting the Janiculum to the city, was called Pons Sublicius.

JANISCUS Son of Asclepius and Epione. Brother of Acesis, Aegle, Hygieia, Iaso, Machaon, Panacea and Podalirius.

JANUS Most ancient king of Italy. After death became Roman god of beginnings and endings. Son of Apollo and Creusa. Husband of Jana. Father of Tiberinus by Camasena, of Canens by Venilia and of Fontus by Juturna. This two- or four-faced god (Bifrons or Quadrifons) was second only to Jupiter and was possibly one of the Penates. He was also god of doors, presiding over bridges and passageways. His name was the first invoked in all religious ceremonies. Festival date: 9 January.

Janus

JASON King of Iolcus, leader of the Argonauts. Son of Aeson and Alcimede or Polymede. Brother of Promachus. He succeeded Pelias to the throne after Medea murdered him. Married for ten years to Medea. Father of Mermerus and Pheres, and of Alcimenes, Argus, Eriopis, Medeius, Thessalus and Tisandrus, possibly by Medea. Father of Euneus, Thoas and either Deipylus or Nebrophonus by Hypsipyle, queen of Lemnos.

An oracle told Pelias that his successor would come to him wearing one sandal. When Jason arrived so dressed, Pelias sent him in search of the Golden Fleece, hoping he would be killed. This led to the great, and successful, expedition of the Argonauts. When Jason divorced Medea, she killed his second wife Glauce (Creusa) on her wedding day by giving her, as a bridal gift, a gown that burst into flames when Glauce put it on. In his old age, while sitting in the Argo, Jason was killed by a falling beam from his ship. He had also taken part in the Calydonian Boar Hunt, and possibly killed Aeetes.

JEALOUS, the most in mythology Title given to Hera (Juno).

JOCASTA (Epicasta) Daughter of Menoeceus. Sister of Creon and Hipponome. Married Laius. Mother of Oedipus. Later married Oedipus. Mother of Antigone, Eteocles, Ismene and Polyneices. Killed herself when she discovered that her husband was her own son.

JOVE Alternative for Jupiter.

JUDGEMENT OF PARIS Beauty contest held on Mt Ida in Phrygia between Aphrodite, Athena and Hera. Was judged by Paris and he awarded the prize of one

133

Golden Apple to Aphrodite, because she had promised her help in his pursuit of Helen. This in turn led to the Trojan War after Paris abducted Helen.

JUNO (Hera) Goddess of marriage. Daughter of Saturn. Married Jupiter. Mother of Mars by Jupiter. Epithets: Juno Lucina, goddess of childbirth; Juno Moneta, goddess of finance; Saturnia, daughter of Saturn. Her sacred animal, a goat; sacred fruit, a fig. Her festival date: 7 July.

JUPITER (Zeus) Supreme Roman god. God of the skies, god of rain (as Pluvius), and god of weather. Husband of Juno. Epithets: Fulgurator (the sender of lightning) and Serenus (the bright). Also known as Jove. There was a temple to Jupiter Optimus Maximus (best and greatest) on the Capitoline. His sacred days were the Ides (13 or 15) of each month, full moon, and his festival date was 19 August.

JUSTICE Epithet of Themis. She and Dike, her daughter, were called goddesses of Justice.

JUSTICE, goddess of Greek: Dike, Praxidice, Themis. Roman: Astraea, Justitia.

JUSTITIA (Iustitia) Roman goddess of justice. Presided, with Jupiter, at a cult started by Augustus.

JUTURNA (Iuturna) Roman goddess of springs. Daughter of Daunus and Venilia. Sister of Turnus, king of Rutulia, and also his charioteer. Mother of Fontus by Janus. *See* Iuturna.

JUVENTAS (Hebe) Roman goddess of eternal youth. Mother of Alexiares and Anticetus by Hercules. Patron goddess of the youth of Rome.

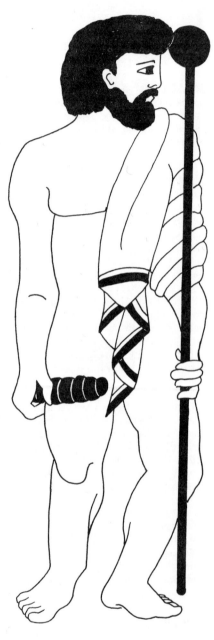

Jupiter

K

KALIA   Goddess of vice. Tried to distract Heracles from his studies with Cheiron.

KER (Cer)   Female death spirit. Daughter of Nyx. Sister of Moros (doom), Momus, Hypnos, Dreams, Aether, Nemesis, Charon and Thanatos. Often quoted in the plural: Keres. Their functions and appearance were similar to those of the Erinnyes.

KINGFISHER   *See* Alcyone, Ceyx.

KORE   Eleusinian epithet of Persephone.

KRATOS (power)   Son of Styx and the Titan, Pallas. Brother of Bia, Nike and Zelos.

KRONOS   *See* Cronos.

KTESIOS   Ancient spirit who guarded storerooms. Epithet of Zeus.

Keres

L

LABDACUS King of Thebes. Son of Polydorus and Nycteis. Father of Laius. Killed fighting Pandion of Athens.

LABOURS OF HERACLES 1. Nemean lion, 2. Hydra of Lerna, 3. Cerynean hind, 4. Erymanthian boar, 5. Cleaning the Augeian stables, 6. Stymphalian birds, 7. Cretan bull, 8. Mares of Diomedes, 9. Girdle of Hippolyte, 10. Cattle of Geryon, 11. Cerberus, 12. Golden Apples of the Hesperides. (*See also* Heracles.)

LABYRINTH Built at Cnossus by Daedalus for Minos, to house the Minotaur.

LACEDAEMON King of Sparta. Son of Zeus and Taygete, one of the Pleiades. Married Sparte. Father of Amyclas and Eurydice. A follower of the Graces. Founder of Sparta.

LACHESIS One of the Moirae. Daughter of Zeus and Themis. The 'caster of lots', she was the sister of Atropos and Clotho.

LACONIA Country of southern Greece, in the Peloponnesus. Main city: Sparta.

LACONIA, kings of Myles, Eurotas.

LACRITUS Possibly the father of Leitus by Cleobule.

LADDER *See* Capaneus.

LADON A dragon. Offspring of Phorcys and Ceto as, were the Gorgons, Echidna, Scylla and the Graiae. Some authorities name the parents as Typhon and Echidna. Ladon had a hundred heads and voices, and was killed by Heracles when he came to fetch the Golden Apples of the Hesperides (his twelfth labour), Ladon and the Hesperides being protectors of the garden. Ladon became the constellation Draco.

LADON (1) An Arcadian river and its god. Son of Oceanus and Tethys. Possibly father of Daphne and Metope. The prettiest river in Greece. (2) One of Actaeon's dogs. (3) Companion of Aeneas on his journey from Troy to Italy.

LAELAPS The storm wind personified as a dog. Given to Procris by Artemis or Minos, she later gave it to Cephalus. Laelaps was fated always to catch his prey until the Teumassian Vixen (also inevitably successful) evaded him; or perhaps, to solve the impasse, Zeus turned them both to stone, though some say this happened after the death of Procris.

LAERTES King of Ithaca. Son of Arceisius and Chalcomedusa. Married Anticleia. Father of Odysseus and Ctimene, although Anticleia may have been already pregnant by Sisyphus. Some say his parents were Cephalus and Procris.

Participant in the Calydonian Boar Hunt and an Argonaut, he killed Eupeithes, a suitor of Penelope.

LAESTRYGONES Cannibal giants who inhabited the city of Telepylus in Sicily, and were the island's most ancient inhabitants. Antiphates was their king; they badly damaged eleven of the twelve ships of Odysseus, and ate the crew.

LAIAS Son of Oxylus. Last king of Elis.

LAIUS King of Thebes. Son of Labdacus. Married Jocasta. Father of Oedipus.

Labdacus died when Laius was a child and Lycus ruled as regent for the boy. As king, Laius was dethroned by Amphion and Zethus and exiled to Pisa. He later regained the throne, returning to Thebes with Chrysippus, bastard son of Pelops, whom he had abducted. An oracle warned Laius that his son would one day kill him and later Oedipus did accidentally kill his father. Laius was buried by Damisistratus, king of Plataea, at the crossroads at the foot of Mt Parnassus, the place of his death.

LAMEDON King of Sicyon. Son of Coronus of Sicyon. Brother of Corax.

LAMIA (1) Daughter of Belus and possibly Libya. Had the face and breasts of a woman and the body of a snake. Lover of Zeus when still a normal human being, the jealous Hera deformed her and killed all but one of her children. Lamia went on to prey on other children. Lamia would then lure strange youths to her and eat them until she was killed, possibly by Eurybatus (cf below). (2) A Crissan monster that ravaged the countryside until the Delphic Oracle suggested humans be sacrificed to appease her. Alcyoneus was the first selected, but Eurybatus, son of Euphemus, killed her first. (3) A Cretan god worshipped at Eleusis. (4) Daughter of Poseidon. Mother of the Sibyl Herophile by Zeus.

LAMPETIE (Lampethusa) One of the Heliades. Daughter of Helios or Apollo and Neaera. Sister of the other Heliades and Phaethon. With Phaethusa, they used to guard the sacred cattle of Apollo on the island of Thrincia. Was changed into a poplar after the death of Phaethon.

LAMPUS A Trojan elder. Son of Laomedon and Leucippe, Placia or Strymo. Brother of Astyoche, Cilla, Clytius, Hicetaon, Hesione, Priam and Tithonus. Father of Dolops.

LAMUS (1) Son of Poseidon. Founder of Telepylus, he was the leader of the Laestrygonians. (2) Son of Heracles and Omphale. Brother of Agelaos and Alcaeus.

LANDMARKS, Roman god of Terminus.

LAOCOON Trojan priest of Apollo and Poseidon. Son of Priam and Hecuba. Had many brothers (*see* Priam). Warned the Trojans that there were soldiers within the Wooden Horse. He and his two sons were killed by a sea-serpent.

LAOCOON (1) Son of Antenor and Theano. Brother of Acamas, Agenor, Archelous, Coon, Crino, Demoleon, Glaucus, Helicaon, Iphidamas, Laodamas, Lycaon, Polybus and Polydamas. Half-brother of Pedaeus. (2) Son of Capys and Themiste. Brother of Anchises. Married Antiope. Father of Antiphas, Ethron, Melanthus and Thymbraeus. (3) Son of Oeneus and a servant. An Argonaut, he went on the Argo as guardian of his half-brother, Meleager.

LAODAMAS King of Thebes. Son of Eteocles. Creon ruled as regent while Laodamas was a child. Led the Thebans against the Epigoni, killing Aegialeus. Killed either by Alcmeon, or he fled to Illyria.

LAODAMAS Son of Antenor and Theano. Brother of Acamas, Agenor, Archelous, Coon, Crino, Demoleon, Glaucus, Helicaon, Iphidamas, Laocoon, Lycaon, Polybus and Polydamas. Half-brother of Pedaeus.

LAODAMEIA Daughter of Acastus and Astydameia. Sister of Sthenele, Sterope and unnamed brothers. Married Protesilaus though one authority says his wife was Polydora, daughter of Meleager. She was so disconsolate at her husband's death that he was allowed back to life for a short time. When he had to return again she accompanied him. Another tradition asserts that she kept a wooden statue of her husband. When her father ordered this burnt, she threw herself into the flames.

LAODAMEIA Daughter of Bellerophon and Philonoe. Sister of Deidameia, Hippolochus and Isander. Married Sarpedon who was either the son of Zeus and Europa, or her own son by Zeus. Mother of Evander. Killed by Artemis.

LAODICE (1) Daughter of Cinyras. Married Elatus. Mother of Stymphalus. (2) Also called Electra. Daughter of

Agamemnon and Clytemnestra. Sister of Chrysothemis, Iphigeneia and Orestes. (3) Fairest daughter of Priam and Hecuba. Married either Helicaon or Telephus. Mother of Grynus. Lover of Acamas or Demophon, and bore Munitus. Swallowed up by the earth after the fall of Troy.

LAODOCUS Son of Apollo and Phthia. Brother of Dorus and Polypoetes. Killed by Aetolus.

LAOGONUS (1) Son of Bias. Brother of Dardanus. Both brothers were killed in the Trojan War by Achilles. (2) Son of Onetor. Killed in the Trojan War by Meriones.

LAOGORE Daughter of Cinyras of Cyprus. Sister of Braesia, Mygdalion and Orsedice. Emigrated to Egypt after a love affair with a total stranger.

LAOMEDON King of Troy. Son of Ilus and Eurydice. Brother of Themiste. Married Rhoeo or Strymo. Father of Astyoche, Cilla, Clytius, Hesione, Hicetaon, Lampus, Priam and Tithonus. Father of Bucolion by the nymph, Calybe.

Laomedon persuaded Apollo and Poseidon to build the walls of Troy but when he refused to pay them, in revenge they sent a sea monster. He bribed Heracles to kill it, but then refused to pay him either. Heracles took eighteen ships to Troy and killed Laomedon and all his sons except Priam. They were buried in a tomb outside the Scaean gate. An Oracle decreed that Troy would not fall while the tomb remained intact.

LAONOME Daughter of Guneus. Possibly the mother of Amphitryon and Anaxo by Alcaeus.

LAOTHOE Daughter of Altes. Mother of Lycaon by Priam and possibly also mother of Polydorus.

LAPITHAE (Lapiths) Thessalians, descendants of Ixion (as were the Centaurs),

ruled by Peirithous. They continually fought the Centaurs, most violently at the wedding of Peirithous and Hippodameia. Under Leonteus and Polypoetes, they sent forty ships to the Trojan War.

LAPITHUS (Lapithes) King of Thessaly. Son of Apollo and Stilbe. Brother of Centaurus. Married Orsinome. Father of Periphas and Phorbas.

LARA Daughter of the river god Almon. Married Hermes. Mother of the Lares.

LARENTIA (Acca Larentia) Obscure Roman goddess who may have been two different women. *See* Acca Larentia.

LARES Roman gods of the home. Two fertility gods (singular: Lar) who also guarded people. Every home and each state

Lar

had its own Lares. Some say they were sons of Hermes and Lara.

LARES COMPITALES Guardians of crossroads. Festival date: 5 January.

LARISSA (1) A Thessalian city, home of Achilles. (2) Another Thessalian city, where Perseus killed Acrisius. (3) The acropolis at Argos. (4) Daughter of Pelasgus. Mother of Achaeus, Pelasgus II and Phthius by Poseidon.

LARK *See* Scylla.

LARVAE (Lemures) Roman equivalent of ghosts, especially frightening to children.

LASTHENES Helped Eteocles defend Thebes.

LATINUS King of Latium. Son of Circe and Odysseus or Telemachus, or of Heracles and a Hyperborean maiden, or, according to Virgil, of Faunus and Marica. Brother of Agrius, Ardea and Telegonus. Married Amata. Father of Lavinia.

There is conflict as to whether he fought with or against Aeneas, who became his son-in-law and successor to his throne. Was first to cultivate the laurel in Italy.

LATIUM Italian region, south of Rome, capital Laurentum.

LATIUM, kings of Saturn, followed by Picus, Faunus, Latinus and Aeneas, who ruled from Lavinium. Later kings ruled from Alba Longa, then Rome.

LATMOS (Latmus) Mountain of Asia Minor, home of the eternally sleeping Endymion, visited nightly by Artemis.

LATONA (Leto) Daughter of Coeus and Phoebe. Mother of Apollo and Artemis.

LAUGHTER, Roman god of Comus.

LAUREL Sacred tree of Apollo. *See* Daphne, Latinus.

LAUSUS 'Scorner of the gods'. Son of Mezentius. Ally of Turnus. Killed by Aeneas.

LAUSUS Son of Numitor. Brother of Ilia (Rhea Silvia). Killed by his uncle, Amulius.

LAVERNA Roman goddess of thieves and rogues.

LAVINIA Eponym of Lavinium. Daughter of Latinus and Amata. Second wife of Aeneas. Possibly mother of Ascanius, but more probably this was Creusa, Aeneas' first wife.

LAWFULNESS, Greek goddess of Eunomia.

LEADES Son of Astacus. Brother of Amphidocus, Ismarus and Melanippus. Defended Thebes against the Seven, possibly killing Eteoclus.

LEANDER The lover of Hero (qv). Lived in Abydos.

LEANEIRA Daughter of Amyclas and Diomede. Sister of Argalus, Hyacinthus and Cynortas.

LEARCHUS Son of Athamas and Ino. Brother of Melicertes. Accidentally killed by his father.

LECHES Son of Peirene. Brother of Cenchrias. The harbour of Corinth, Lechaion, was named after him.

LEDA Daughter of Thestius and Eurythemis. Sister of Althaea, Hypermnestra, Plexippus and others. Married Tyndareus. Mother of Castor, Clytemnestra, Philonoe, Phoebe and Timandra. Mother of Helen and Polydeuces, by Zeus.

LEIOCRITUS Son of Arisbas. Killed in the Trojan War by Aeneas.

LEIODES A suitor of Penelope, killed by Odysseus, and the only one who really loved her.

LEIPEPHILE Daughter of Iolaus and Megara.

LEIRIOPE Mother of Narcissus by the river god Cephisus.

LEIS Daughter of Orus, king of Oraea (Troezen). Married the next king, Althepus.

LEISURE, Sabine goddess of Vacuna.

LEITUS Boeotian leader and Argonaut. Son of Alector, Alectryon, Electryon or Lacritus and Cleobule.

As a suitor of Helen, he and Penelaus took fifty ships to the Trojan War. The only Boeotian leader to survive, though wounded by Hector. He brought home the bones of Arcesilaus.

LELEGIANS Early inhabitants of Greece, with the Carians and Pelasgians. Lived on the Aegean Islands until driven to the mainland of Asia Minor. Were allies of the Trojans.

LELEX King of Megara. Son of Poseidon and Libya. Brother of Agenor and Belus. Father of Cteson.

LELEX Son of Libya. Husband of Cleocharia. Father of Eurotas, Myles, Polycaon and Therapne.

LEMNOS Island of the Aegean Sea, the centre of the cult of the Cabeiri and sacred to Hephaestus.

The womenfolk of the island killed all the men, except Thoas. The Argonauts stopped there on their outward journey and repopulated the island. Dionysus took Ariadne there after their marriage. Philoctetes was stranded there by the Greeks.

LEMNOS, kings and queens of Hypsipyle, followed by Euneus (at the time of the Trojan War) and Thoas.

LEMURIA Roman festivals for the Lemures, spirits of the dead, held on 9, 11 and 13 May. Originally called Remuria after the ghost of Remus.

LENAEUS Epithet of Dionysus (he of the winepress).

LENEA Greek winter festival of Dionysus.

LEO Fifth sign of the zodiac, representing the Nemean lion.

LEOBOTAS King of Sparta. Son of Eunomus. His uncle, Lycurgus, was his guardian.

LEODOCUS An Argonaut. Son of Bias and Pero. Brother of Areius and Talaus, and possibly Alphesiboea, Aretus and Perialces.

LEONTEUS Son of Coronus. With Polypoetes, took forty ships to Troy, where he killed Hippomachus, son of Antimachus. After the war, retired to Colophon near Ephesus.

LEONTOPHONUS Son of Odysseus and the daughter of Thoas, king of Aetolia.

LERNA Town on the Gulf of Argolis, south of Argos. Home of the Hydra, and an area where one could enter the Underworld via the Alcyonian lake. The Danaids threw the heads of their murdered husbands into this lake.

LERNUS Possibly the father of Palaemon, the Argonaut (cf Aetolus, Hephaestus).

LESBOS A large island off the west coast of Asia Minor, in the Aegean Sea. Here, Aphrodite gave Phaon the magic ointment which made him beautiful. Home of many lyric poets.

LETHE River of forgetfulness. One of the five rivers of Hades. Others were Acheron, Cocytus, Phlegethon and Styx. The nymph of the river was a daughter of Eris.

LETHAE Wife of Olenus, turned to stone for boasting that her beauty was greater than that of goddesses.

LETO (Latona) Daughter of the Titans, Coeus and Phoebe. Sister of Asteria. Mother of Apollo and Artemis, by Zeus.

LEUCIPPE Daughter of Minyas. Sister of Alcithoe and Arsippe. When the three sisters refused to honour Dionysus, he drove them mad. Leucippe surrendered her son and they killed him, and were then changed to bats. Was also the sister of Clymene and Periclymene.

LEUCIPPE (1) Daughter of Thestor and Megara. Sister of Alcmaon, Calchas and Theonoe. (2) Possibly the mother of Clytius and Hicetaon.

LEUCIPPUS (1) Son of Oenomaus and Evarete. Brother of Hippodameia. He tried to befriend Daphne by dressing as a girl, but her friends killed him with Apollo's darts. (2) Son of Perieres and Gorgophone. Brother of Aphareus, Borus, Icarius and Tyndareus. Father of Arsinoe, Hilaera and Phoebe. Founder of Leuctra in Laconia.

LEUCON Son of Athamas and Themisto. Brother of Erythrius, Ptous and Schoeneus. Father of Evippe, the wife of Andreus, and Erythras.

LEUCONOE Daughter of Eosphorus. Sister of Ceyx.

LEUCOSIA One of the Sirens. Daughter of Achelous and Calliope. Sister of Ligeia and Parthenope.
The Sirens lured sailors to their doom

with their song; but drowned themselves when they failed to attract Odysseus and his crew, who had put wax in their ears and could not hear a note.

LEUCOTHEA (Mater Matuta) White goddess. Ino's name, after her drowning and deification. A sea-goddess, she helped sailors in distress and with her veil rescued Odysseus from drowning. (*See also* Ino.)

LEUCOTHOE Daughter of Orchamus, king of Persia, and Euryonome. Aphrodite caused her to fall in love with Helios, and her love affair with Apollo was reported to her father by Clytie. He buried her alive and she became a shrub bearing frankincense.

LEUCUS (1) Cretan usurper who seduced Meda, wife of Idomeneus, then killed her and her daughter, overthrew the king and made a kingdom of ten of his cities. (2) A companion of Odysseus in the Trojan War, killed by Antiphus, son of Priam.

LIBATION The wine poured on a sacrifice in honour of a god.

LIBER Ancient Roman god of fertility. Identified with Bacchus and often confused with Iacchus by the Greeks, Liber was worshipped with Ceres and Libera. Husband of Libera. Festival date: 17 March.

LIBERA Ancient Roman fertility goddess. Wife of Liber, worshipped with Ceres and Liber. Identified with Persephone.

LIBERTAS Roman goddess of liberty of all Roman people.

LIBITINA Roman goddess of death.

LIBRA The seventh sign of the zodiac, depicted by scales.

LIBS (Lips) The south-west wind. Born of Astraeus and Eos. (*See* Winds.)

LIBYA Daughter of Epaphus and Memphis. Sister of Lysianassa. Wife of Triton. Mother of Lelex. Mother of Agenor and Belus by Poseidon. Possibly mother of Lamia by Belus. Eponym of Libya which, to the ancients, was Egypt, her homeland.

LICHAS Herald of Heracles. It was he who took the poisoned robe to Heracles which killed him. Was turned to stone and became a rock in the sea, off the coast of Cape Cenaeum in north-west Euboea.

LICYMNIUS Son of Electryon and Midea. Half-brother of six sons, including Everes and Alcmene. Married Perimede, daughter of Amphitryon. Father of Argeius, Melas and Oeonus.

Foot-race winner at the Olympic Games. He was the only son of Electryon to survive the war with Taphos. Accidentally killed by Tlepolemus in a Heraclid attack on Argos.

LIES, mother of Eris (Discordia).

LIGDUS Husband of Telethusa. Father of Iphis. A poor Cretan.

LIGEIA One of the Sirens. Daughter of Achelous and Calliope. Sister of Leucosia and Parthenope, and perhaps others (*See* Sirens.)

LIGHT, Greek god of Aether.

LIGHTNING, Roman goddess of Fulgora.

LIGURIA Coastal area of north-west Italy stretching from Genoa to Marseilles in France. King: Cycnus.

LIGYRON Son of Peleus and Thetis. The first name given to Achilles.

LILY *See* Hyacinthus.

LIME TREE *See* Philyra.

LIMNADES Dangerous nymphs of lakes and swamps who lured the unwary to their death with false cries for help.

LIMNOREIA A Nereid. One of the fifty daughters of Nereus and Doris.

LIMONIADES Nymphs of flowers and meadows.

LINDEN *See* Baucis, Philemon.

LINDUS Grandson of Helios and Rhode, and son of Cercaphus and Cydippe. Brother of Ialysus and Cameirus. Co-founder of the city of Rhodes, named after his grandmother.

LINUS (1) Son of Apollo and Psamathe. Torn to pieces by Crotopus' dogs. (2) Son of Calliope and Oeagrus or Apollo. Brother of Orpheus. Died as a child. (3) Son of Ismenius. He taught Heracles, Orpheus and Thamyris to play the lyre. Heracles killed him with a lyre, in a fit of anger. (4) There are many variations of his parentage, but the favourite one was that Amphimarus, son of Poseidon, was the father and Urania, the Muse, his mother. A poet and musician.

Note that all are musicians. 'Linus' is the personification of a dirge or lamentation. All the above may be the same person.

LION *See* Atalanta, Battus, Chimaera, Hippomenes, Melanion, Pyramus, Thisbe.

LIPARUS Father of Cyane.

LIPS (Libs) The south-west wind. (*See* Winds.)

LIRIOPE (Leiriope) An Oceanid. Wife of Cephisus. Mother of Narcissus.

LITAE Daughters of Zeus. Sweet-tempered goddesses who invoked the help of Zeus after Ate had caused them distress.

LITERSES A poet who lost a poetry contest with Daphnis. One of his daughters,

Lyce, Nais, Nomia, Piplea (most likely) or Xenea, then married Daphnis.

LITYERSES Bastard son of Midas who decapitated guests of the king when they lost reaping contests.

LIZARD *See* Abas, son of Celeus; Ascalabus.

LOCRIANS People of Central Greece.

LOCRIS Two areas of Greece had this name: 1. On the north shore of the Gulf of Corinth 2. On the mainland side of the Euboean Sea. Capital, Opus; king, Oileus.

LOTIS Daughter of Poseidon. Pursued by Priapus, she was changed into a lotus tree.

LOTOPHAGI The Lotus eaters of North Africa, where it was 'always after-noon', visited by Odysseus on his return journey from Troy. Eating their food made people lose their desire to leave.

LOTUS-TREE *See* Dryope, Lotis.

LOVE, god of Greek: Eros. Roman: Amor, Cupid.

LOVE, goddess of Greek: Aphrodite. Roman: Flora, Venus.

LOXIAS Epithet of Apollo: he who could read the will of Zeus.

LUA Obscure Roman goddess presiding over lustrations. Identified with Rhea, therefore possibly the wife of Saturn.

LUCIFER (Eosphorus) Son of Eurybia. Father of Daedalion. The morning star. Possibly a son of Zeus and Eos.

LUCINA (Eleithyia) Roman goddess of childbirth. Goddess associated with Juno and, possibly, Diana.

LUCIUS Son of Tarquinius Superbus and Tanaquil. Brother of Aruns. Married Tullia, daughter of Servius Tullius. He was ambitious but his wife was gentle and meek. He killed her and married her sister.

LUCIUS TARQUINIUS COLLATI-NUS Husband of Lucretia.

LUCK, goddess of Greek: Tyche. Roman: Fortuna.

LUCRETIA Wife of Lucius Tarquinius Collatinus. Raped by Sextus Tarquinius, she stabbed herself to death after admitting it to her husband.

LUNA Goddess of the moon. Epithet of Artemis. Festival date: 31 March.

LUPERCA (Lupercus) Roman god and goddess of flocks and fertility.

LUPERCAL A sacred cave of Pan on Mt Aventine where the she-wolf raised Romulus and Remus.

LUPERCALIA Roman festivals in honour of Pan, held in a grotto on Mt Aventine on 15 February, when a dog and two sheep were sacrificed. A fertility cult, in which young men, having been smeared with the blood of sacrifices, beat women's wrists with leather thongs to make them fertile.

LYAEUS Epithet of Dionysus, the libera-tor.

LYCAETHUS Possibly father of Creon, king of Corinth.

LYCABETTUS A hill in Athens, 300 metres high, placed there by Athena.

LYCAEUS Arcadian mountain, birth-place of Zeus.

LYCAON (1) Son of Antenor and Theano. Brother of Acamas, Agenor, Archelous, Crino, Glaucus, Coon, Helicaon,

Laocoon, Demoleon, Iphidamas, Laodamas, Polydamas and Polybus. Half-brother of Pedaeus. Wounded in the Trojan War. (2) King of Arcadia. Son of Pelasgus and Meliboea or Cyllene, who was more likely his wife. Father of fifty sons, including Lycaon, Maenalus, Nyctimus and Pallas, most of whom were killed by a thunderbolt from Zeus. Also father of Callisto. (3) Another king of Arcadia who killed his son, cut him up and sacrificed him to Zeus. (4) Son of Priam and Laothoe. Killed in the Trojan War by Achilles who had earlier sold him to Euneus as a slave. (5) King of Zeleia. Husband of Zeleia. Father of Eurytion and Pandarus. (6) Father of Daunus, Iapyx and Peucetius.

LYCASTE Daughter of Priam. Married Polydamas, son of Antenor.

LYCASTUS Son of Minos and Pasiphae. Brother of Acacallis, Androgeus, Ariadne, Catreus, Deucalion, Euryale, Glaucus, Phaedra and Xenodice. Married Ida. Father of Minos II.

LYCE Daughter of Literses. Sister of Nais, Nomia, Piplea and Xenea. May have married Daphnis.

LYCIA Southern coastal region of Asia Minor to the east of Caria. Originally called Milyan, it was renamed by Lycus. Leto, fleeing from Hera, sought refuge there.

LYCIA, kings of Lycus, Glaucus, Iobates, Bellerophon.

LYCIDAS (1) A Centaur killed in the battle which broke out at the wedding of Peirithous. (2) A shepherd.

LYCIUS Epithet of Apollo, the wolf-god who rid Athens of wolves.

LYCO Daughter of Dion and Iphitea. Sister of Carya and Orphe. Had the power of prophecy.

LYCOMEDES King of Scyros. Son of Apollo and Parthenope. Father of Deida-

meia, the lover of Achilles. It was Lycomedes who dressed Achilles as a woman to keep him from the Trojan War, and who pushed Theseus over a cliff to his death.

LYCON Trojan leader killed in the War by Penelaus.

LYCOPHRON Son of Mastor. Squire of Ajax. Killed in the Trojan War by Hector.

LYCOTHERSES King of Illyria. The husband of Agave, murdered by her so that Cadmus could succeed to the throne.

LYCURGUS King of Arcadia. Eldest son of Aleus and Neaera. Brother of Amphidamas, Auge and Cepheus. Father of Amphidamas II, Iasus, Epochus and Anchaeus by Cleophyle or Eurynome.

LYCURGUS King of the Edonians of Thrace. Son of Dryas. Father of Dryas II and possibly Phyllis. Constant enemy of Dionysus and hated by the immortal gods. Blinded and driven mad by Zeus for refusing Dionysus refuge. Killed his son, tried to rape his mother and cut off his own legs. He then either killed himself or was thrown to panthers on Mt Rhodope, or man-eating mares on Mt Pangaeum.

LYCURGUS (Lycus) King of Nemea. Son of Pheres and Periclymene. Brother of Admetus, Idomene and Periopis. Married Amphithea or Eurydice. Father of Opheltes. Took part in war of Seven against Thebes. Raised from the dead by Asclepius.

LYCURGUS A mythical lawgiver of Sparta. Son of Eunomus. Friend of the gods and guardian of Leobotas, king of Sparta, his nephew. It was Lycurgus who abolished all social distinctions in Sparta. This tradition puts Lycurgus in the 9th century BC – another puts him in the 7th century BC. There may have been two lawgivers of this name in Sparta.

LYCURGUS (1) An Athenian orator at the time of Demosthenes. (2) A giant, killed in Thrace by Osiris. (3) Son of Heracles and Praxithea. (4) Son of Pronax. Brother of Amphithea.

LYCUS (1) King of the Mariandyni. Son of Dascylus. Father of Dascylus II. Succeeded his father to the throne. Aided Heracles in his fight with the Bebryces. (2) Son of Pandion and Pylia. Brother of Aegeus, Nisus and Pallas. Eponym of Lycia. One of the few mortals to utter oracles. (3) King of Thebes. Son of Chthonius or of Hyrieus and Clonia, or of Poseidon and Celaeno. Brother of Nycteus. Married Dirce. Father of Lycus II by his wife and Nycteis by Polyxo. Killed Epopeus, husband of his niece, Antiope. Then her children, Amphion and Zetes, killed him. (4) King of Thebes. Son of Lycus I and Dirce. Brother of Nycteis. Murdered Creon to gain the throne. Killed by Heracles for mistreating his family. (5) A companion of Aeneas on his journey from Troy to Italy. (6) Son of Aegyptus, one of fifty. See Danaids. Murdered by his wife on their wedding night. (7) A son of Ares. (8) A king of Boeotia. (9) A Centaur, son of Ixion and Nephele. (10) King of Libya, father of Callirrhoe. (11) A son of Priam. (12) Possibly the father of Hyrieus by Alcyone.

LYDE A maiden beloved of a satyr who, in turn, was loved by Echo.

LYDIA Region of Asia Minor between Caria and Mysia. Named after Lydus, the mythical son of Attis.

LYDIA, kings and queens of Candaules (the last); Croesus (the richest man in the world); Alyattes I and II; Omphale (a queen); Tmolus (her husband); Iardanus (her father); Gyges; and Pelops.

LYNCEUS An Argonaut. Son of Aphareus and Arene. Brother of Idas and Peisus. Married Hypermnestra.
A member of the Calydonian Boar Hunt. He could clearly see objects fifteen kilometres away and could gaze through tree trunks. He and his brother Idas were killed by Polydeuces for stealing sheep, and for killing Castor, Polydeuces' beloved half-brother.

LYNCEUS (1) Son of Aegyptus. Married Hypermnestra. The only one of fifty brothers not killed by his wife on their wedding night. Father of Abas who killed him. Some sources say he killed Danaus and his family to avenge the death of his brothers. See Danaids. (2) A companion of Aeneas on his journey to Italy from Troy. Killed by Turnus.

LYNX See Lyncus, Triptolemus.

LYRCUS Bastard son of Abas, king of Argos.

LYRE (harp) The musical instrument played by Apollo, invented by Hermes, and formed by stretching strings across a tortoise shell.

LYRE See Terpsichore.

LYRUS Son of Anchises and Aphrodite. Brother of Aeneas. Died childless.

LYSANDER Trojan ally, wounded in the Trojan War by Greater Ajax.

LYSIANASSA (1) Daughter of Epaphus and Memphis. Sister of Libya. Mother of Busiris by Poseidon. (2) Daughter of Polybus. Sister of Eurymachus. Married Talaus (cf Lysimache). Mother of Adrastus, Aristomachus, Astynome, Eriphyle, Hippomedon, Mecisteus, Parthenopaeus and Pronax.

LYSIDICE Daughter of Pelops and Hippodameia. Sister of Alcathous, Astydameia, Atreus, Chrysippus, Copreus, Nicippe, Pittheus, Thyestes and Troezen. Married Mestor. Mother of Hippothoe.

LYSIMACHE Daughter of Abas. Sister of Coeranus. Married Talaus. Mother of Adrastus, Aristomachus, Astynome, Eriphyle, Hippomedon, Mecisteus, Metidice, Parthenopaeus and Pronax.

LYSIPPE (1) Daughter of Proetus and Stheneboea or Anteia. Sister of Iphianassa, Megapenthes and Iphinoe. Married Melampus after he had cured her madness. Mother of Abas, Antiphates and Mantius. (2) One of the fifty daughters of Thespius.

M

MACAR One of the Heliades. Son of Helios and Rhode. Brother of Actis, Candalus, Cercaphus, Ochimus, Tenages and Triopas. A co-murderer of Tenages, he went into exile. Macar and his brothers were the first to sacrifice to Athena.

MACAREUS Son of Aeolus and Enarete. Brother of Athamas, Cretheus, Deion, Perieres, Salmoneus and Sisyphus; and of Alcyone, Arne, Calyce, Canace, Peisidice, Perimele and Tanagra. Committed suicide after having an incestuous relationship with Canace.

MACARIA Daughter of Heracles and Deianeira. Sister of Ctesippus, Hyllus, Tlepolemus and one other. When Eurystheus and the Peloponnesians were defeating the Athenians at Marathon, Macaria offered herself, in accordance with an oracle given to her father, as a sacrifice, in order to turn the tide of battle.

MACHAON Co-ruler of parts of Thessaly. Son of Asclepius and Epione. Brother of Acesis, Aegle, Hygieia, Iaso, Janiscus, Panacea and Podalirius. Married Anticleia. Father of Alexanor, Gorgasus and Nichomachus.
As a suitor of Helen, he and Podalirius took thirty ships to the Trojan War from Oechalia, Ithome and Tricca. He was wounded by Paris but saved by Nestor. He was in the Wooden Horse. A surgeon, he healed many Greeks, including Philoctetes. Was killed by Eurypylus or Penthesilia and was buried in Laconian Gerenia.

MACRIS (1) Daughter of Aristaeus and Autonoe. Sister of Actaeon. After Dionysus escaped from his mother's attempt to murder him, he hid in a cave near Mt Nysa and there invented wine. Macris brought the god honey for food. (2) A small island, initially called Drepane or Scherie, near Corcyra (Corfu). Renamed from Macris who lived in a small cave on the island. Jason and Medea married on this island.

MAEANDER A river god. Son of Oceanus and Tethys. Father of Cyanee and Samia. The River Maeander twisted and turned through 1000 km of land west from Miletus to the Aegean Sea.

MAEMALUS Father of Peisander.

MAENADS Female followers of Dionysus, together with the Satyrs. They indulged in orgies, and riotous festivals.

MAENALUS (1) Eldest son (of fifty) of Lycaon. Killed by a thunderbolt from Zeus after he served human flesh to the god. (2) An Arcadian mountain, sacred to Pan. (3) Father of Atalanta.

MAEON A Theban warrior. Son of Haemon. Lone survivor of an ambush that killed fifty companions.

Maenad

146

MAEONIDES   Epithet of the Muses.

MAERA   (1) Faithful dog of Icarius and his daughter Erigone. After Icarius was murdered, Maera led Erigone to his master's burial place, then killed himself. Became Sirius, the dog-star. (2) A Nereid. One of the fifty daughters of Nereus and Doris.

MAGNA MATER   Roman mother of the gods. Epithet of Rhea.

MAGNES   Son of Aeolus and Enarete. Father of Dictys and Polydectes by a Naiad, and father of Eioneus, Hymenaeus and Pierus. As his name suggests, was a human magnet and found it impossible to walk over a stone mine because of the nails in his shoes which caused his feet to become firmly fixed to the ground.

MAGNES   Son of Argus and Perimele. Father of Hymenaeus (cf above).

MAGNES   Son of Zeus and Thyia. Brother of Macedon.

MAGNET   *See* Celmus.

MAGPIE   *See* Pierides.

MAIA   One of the Pleiades. Eldest daughter of Atlas and Pleione. Sister of Alcyone, Celaeno, Electra, Merope, Sterope and Taygete. Maia, of the beautiful hair, was the mother of Hermes by Zeus. She reared Arcas after the death of Callisto, his mother.

MAIESTA   Also called Maia and identified with Bona Dea. Possibly the wife of Vulcan. (Cf. Maiestas.)

MAIESTAS   Roman goddess of honour and reverence. Daughter of Honor and Reverentia. Perhaps to be identified with the above.

MALIS   Southern part of Thessaly. Principal city: Trachus. Home of Philoctetes and Poeas.

MALLOPHORA   Surname under which Demeter had a temple at Megara, because she taught the inhabitants the utility of wool.

MALLUS   City founded by Amphilochus and Mopsus.

MAMURIUS   A blacksmith who forged eleven copies of the Ancile for Numa.

MANES (Keres)   Good Roman spirits of the dead worshipped with great solemnity. Inhabitants of the Underworld, who returned to earth between 18 and 21 February, a festival called Feralia, when the temples were closed.

MANES   Father of Cotys by Callirrhoe.

MANIA   Roman goddess of the dead. Mother of Lares and Manes, and the mother or grandmother of ghosts.

MANTINEUS   Father of Ocalea, wife of Abas.

MANTIUS   Son of Melampus and Lysippe. Brother of Abas and Antiphates. Father of Cleitus and Polypheides. Either he or Antiphates was the father of Oicles.

MANTO (Daphne)   Daughter of Teiresias. Married Rhacius. Mother of Mopsus, possibly by Apollo, to whom Manto was given by the Delphic Oracle. Mother of Amphilochus and Tisiphone by Alcmeon; of Ocnus, by the river god Tiber. The Argives made her a prisoner when they raided Thebes. Like Mopsus, she was a seer.

MARATHON   Son of Epopeus and Ephyraea. Father of Corinthus and Sicyon.

MARATHON   A plain, 29 km from Athens, where the Greeks fought and beat the Persians on the 28th September 490 BC. The fully-armed figure of Theseus is said to have led the Greeks, who were also helped by Pan. All the Greek heroes were buried in a single grave.

MARATHONIAN (Cretan) BULL A bull that ravaged the countryside of Marathon and was captured by Heracles as his seventh labour. It was later killed by Theseus.

MARBLE *See* Niobe.

MARE *See* Ocyrrhoe.

MARIANDYNUS Son of Phineus and Idaea. Brother of Thynius. Eponym of a tribe from the south coast of the Black Sea.

MARICA A water nymph. An ancient Latin goddess identified with Diana, Circe and Venus. Some say, the wife of Faunus and mother of Acis and Dryas. Was certainly mother of Latinus.

MARIS Son of Amisodaurus. Brother of Atymnius. Killed in the Trojan War by Thrasymedes.

MARMAX The first suitor of Hippodameia; killed by her father, Oenomaus.

MARON Priest of Apollo at Ismarus. Son of Evanthes, Dionysus or Oenopion. When Odysseus sacked Ismarus, Maron was the only one spared. He introduced viticulture to Thrace.

MARPESSA Daughter of Evenus and Alcippe. Sister of Epistrophus and Mynes. Married Idas. Mother of Cleopatra. Abducted by Apollo, she chose to return to Idas. Committed suicide after the death of her husband.

MARRIAGE, god of Hymen.

MARRIAGE, goddess of Greek: Hera. Roman: Juno.

MARS (Ares) Roman god of war and agriculture. Son of Jupiter and Juno, or of Juno alone. Married Nerio. Father of

Romulus and Remus by Rhea Silvia (Ilia). Father of Amor by Venus. Epithets: 1. Gradivus 2. Quirinus 3. Silvanus (an agricultural surname) 4. Ultor (avenger), the name of a temple dedicated by Octavian after Philippi.

His sacred shield, the Ancile, was guarded by the Salii. Picus, the woodpecker, was his attendant as a god of prophecy. His sacred bird was the vulture. Bellona was the sister, wife or just friend of Quirinus. Patron god of the city of Florence.

MARSYAS A Phrygian satyr. Son of Olympus. Lover of Cybele. Possibly the inventor of the flute. He was flayed alive by Apollo after losing a musical contest. His death is said to have been universally lamented.

MARTIUS, CAMPUS *See* Campus Martius.

MASTUSIUS A Thracian noble. When Demophon sacrificed one of his daughters to halt a plague, Mastusius murdered Demophon's other daughters.

MATER MATUTA Roman goddess of sea travel. Roman equivalent of Leucothea (Ino). Festival date: 11 June.

MATER TURRITA A Roman name for Cybele.

MATRONALIA Roman festivals of Mars and Juno, celebrated by married women, commemorating the rape of the Sabine women.

MECHANEUS Epithet of Zeus, meaning the contriver and manager.

MECHANITIS Epithet of Athena, goddess of undertakings.

MECIONICE Either she or Europa was the mother of Euphemus by Poseidon.

MECISTEUS (1) Son of Talaus and Lysimache or Lysianassa. Brother of

Adrastus, Aristomachus, Astynome, Eriphyle, Hippomedon, Metidice, Parthenopaeus and Pronax. Father of Euryalus, one of the Epigoni. One of the Seven against Thebes, he was killed by Melanippus. (2) Son of Echius. Killed in the Trojan War by Polydamas.

MEDA Wife of Idomeneus, king of Crete, she committed adultery with the usurper, Leucus, who later murdered her and her daughter and seized part of her husband's kingdom.

MEDE Another name for Periboea, wife of Icarius. Mother of Penelope.

MEDEA Priestess of Hecate. Daughter of Aeetes and Eidyia. Sister of Absyrtus and half-sister of Chalciope. Married Jason. Mother of Alcimedes, Argus, Eriopis, Medeius, Mermerus, Pheres, Thessalus and Tisandrus. Deserted by Jason, she married Aegeus, king of Athens. Mother of Medus.

Medea was a skilled magician with the gift of prophecy. She helped Jason to find the Golden Fleece and coincidentally her brother, Absyrtus. She murdered all her children by Jason except Thessalus and may have killed her father. She restored Aeson, Jason's father, to youth. After her death, was transported to Elysium and became the consort of Achilles.

MEDEIAS (Medeius, Medus) Son of Jason or Aegeus and Medea. May have been two different people. Brother or half-brother of many. (*See* Medea.)

When his mother failed to kill Theseus and give him the Athenian throne, was exiled from Athens to Colchis where he killed Perses and restored Aeetes, later renaming the territory, Medes.

MEDESICASTE Bastard daughter of Priam. Wife of Imbrius.

MEDICA Epithet of Minerva, patroness of physicians.

MEDICINE, Roman goddess of Meditrina. Her festival was Meditranalia.

MEDITRINA Roman goddess of medicine.

MEDON (1) Son of Codrus. Had many brothers and was lame. Last king of Athens. (2) A Centaur. Son of Ixion and Nephele. (3) Odysseus' herald, forced to serve the suitors of Penelope. He and the minstrel, Phemios, were spared by Odysseus on his return. (4) Bastard son of Oileus and Rhene, exiled from Locris after he killed Eriopis, a relative of Oileus' wife. Killed in the Trojan War by Aeneas. (5) Son of Pylades and Electra (Laodice). Brother of Strophius II. (6) Son of Ceisus.

MEDUS (Medeias, Medeius) Son of Jason or Aegeus and Medea. Eponym of Medes. *See* Medeias and Medea.

MEDUSA A Gorgon. Daughter of Phorcys and Ceto. Sister of Echiodna, Euryae, Stheno and Scylla, and of Ladon and the Graiae. Married Poseidon. From her blood came Chrysaor and Pegasus. Mother of Caca and Cacus by Vulcan.

Originally beautiful, her hair was turned to snakes by Athena because of her liaison with Poseidon. One glance at her turned people to stone. Perseus cut her head off and set it in the aegis of Athena, and it retained the ability to turn people to stone. Her blood fell on the sand of the Libyan desert and turned into snakes, one of which killed Mopsus. Medusa's body was buried in the marketplace of Argos.

MEDUSA Daughter of Sthenelus and Nicippe. Sister of Alcinoe and Eurystheus.

MEGAERA One of the Erinnyes. Daughter of Gaea. Sister of Alecto and Tisiphone. *See* Erinnyes.

MEGAMEDES Father of Pallas, and grandfather of Selene.

MEGAPENTHES (1) Bastard son of Menelaus and Pieris or Tereis. Brother of Nicostratus. Married the daughter of Alector. He and his brother drove Helen from Sparta after the death of Menelaus. (2) King of Tiryns. Son of Proetus and Stheneboea. Brother of Iphinoe and Lysippe. Father of Anaxagoras. Exchanged his throne for that of Perseus at Argos, and may later have killed Perseus. Was killed by Abas.

MEGARA (1) Daughter of Creon, king of Thebes, and Anioche or Eurydice. Sister of Enioche, Haemon, Menoeceus and Pyrrha. Married Heracles. Mother of Creontidas, Deicoon and Therimachus, amongst others. Heracles killed Lycus for attempting to ravish Megara, in his absence, and killed his children in a fit of madness; this led to his undertaking the twelve labours as atonement. Some versions say Megara also died at this time. If not, and if she lived, Megara then married Iolaus. Mother of Leipephile. (2) Wife of Thestor. Mother of Alcmaon, Calchas, Leucippe and Theonoe. (3) Principal city of Megaris, on the Isthmus of Corinth. Founded by Car.

MEGARA, kings of Car, son of Phoroneus, was the first and, after twelve generations, Lelex was followed by Cleson, Pylas, Pandion, Nisus, Megareus, Alcathous and Greater Ajax.

MEGAREUS King of part of Boeotia. Son of Onchestus or Poseidon and Oenope, of Aegeus, Hippomenes or even Apollo. Married Iphinoe, daughter of Nisus. Father of Evaecheme, Evippus, Hippomenes and Timalcus.

Megareus supported Nisus in his war against Minos. Nisus was killed together with the sons of Megareus. Megareus then ruled in Megara and was succeeded by Alcathous.

MEGAREUS An ally of Eteocles against the Seven.

MEGES King of Dulichium. Son of Phyleus and Timandra. As a suitor of Helen, he took forty ships to Troy. Drowned on the return voyage from Troy.

MEILICHOIS Epithet of Zeus, meaning he who is easily placated. Also an epithet of Dionysus.

MEION Possibly the father of Cybele by Dindyme.

MELAMPUS Greatest of all Greek prophets. Son of Amythaon and Idomene. Brother of Aeolia, Bias and Perimele. Married Lysippe after failing to cure her sister Iphinoe of bacchic madness. Father of Abas, Antiphates and Mantius. He, or another Melampus, was the father of Cisseus and Gyas. First mortal to receive the power of prophecy. Could talk to the animals and understand their speech.

MELAMPUS (1) One of the dogs of Actaeon. (2) Father of Cisseus and Gyas. May have been Melampus, son of Amythaon. (3) A son of Priam.

MELANEUS King of Messenia. Son of Apollo. Married Oechalia. Father of Eurytus. A skilful archer.

MELANION Son of Amphidamas. Brother of Antimache. Either he or Hippomenes, whom he beat in a footrace, married Atalanta. Possibly father of Parthenopaeus. He and Atalanta were changed into lions after they made love in a holy place.

MELANIPPE (Arne) Daughter of Aeolus and Hippe. Sister of many. Mother of Aeolus II and Boeotus by Poseidon. Her children were taken from her and exposed by Aeolus, but were saved and reared by a cowherd. Later they were adopted by Theano, wife of Metapontus, and raised with her two sons. But the four fought and when Aeolus II and Boeotus killed Theano's sons, Theano committed suicide. Melanippe, who was blinded by Aeolus, had her sight restored by Poseidon, then married Metapontus.

MELANIPPE (1) Another name for Antiope, daughter of Ares, an Amazon queen. Sister of Hippolyte and Penthesileia. (2) Daughter of Aeolus, god of the winds. Sister of Metapontus whom she married.

MELANIPPUS (1) Son of Astacus. Brother of Amphidocus, Ismarus and Leades. Descendant of the Sparti. An ally of Eteocles against the Seven, he killed Mecisteus and mortally wounded Tydeus before being killed by Amphiarus or Tydeus, who ate his brains. (2) A son of Ares. (3) Lover of Comaetho, priestess of Artemis. They slept together in Artemis' holy shrine and both were sacrificed to Artemis. (4) Son of Hicetaon. As he was also said to have fought the Seven, may be the same as above, or two people with some of their deeds credited to each. (5) A son of Priam. (6) Son of Theseus and Perigune. Half-brother of Hippolytus, Demophon and Acamas. Father of Ioxus. Ancestor of the Ioxids.

MELANTHO Daughter of Dolius. Sister of seven brothers including Melanthus. Maidservant of Penelope, she was the mistress of Eurymachus. She was hanged for siding with the suitors of Penelope.

MELANTHUS (1) Eleventh king of Athens and father of Codrus, the twelfth king. A descendant of Neleus, he was a Messenian immigrant and drove Thymoetes from the throne. (2) Son of Laocoon and Antiope. Brother of Ethron.

MELANTHUS Son of Dolius. Brother of Melantho. The head goatherd of Odysseus, he betrayed him to the suitors of Penelope, so Eumaeus and Philoetius mutilated his body, then hanged him.

MELAS (1) Son of Licymnius and Perimede. Brother of Argeius and Oeonus. An ally of Heracles, he died fighting with him against Eurytas. (2) Son of Phrixus and Chalciope. Brother of Argus, Cytissorus, Presbon and Phrontis. (3) Son of Porthaon and Euryte. Brother of Agrius, Alcathous, Sterope, Oeneus and Leucopeus. Father of eight sons, all killed by Tydeus for plotting to kill Oeneus.

MELEAGER An Argonaut. Son of Ares or Oeneus and Althaea. Brother or half-brother of Deianeira, Gorge and Toxeus. Married Cleopatra, daughter of Idas. Father of Polydora. Possibly father of Parthenopaeus by Atalanta.

It was Meleager who finally killed the Calydonian Boar. At his birth, the two Fates predicted a brave future for him, but Atropos predicted he would die when a stick, then burning in the fire, was consumed. Althaea hid the stick until he killed his uncles; she then burnt it in revenge. Meleager, who may have killed Aeetes, died agonizingly in the fighting which took place when the Curetes attacked the Calydonians. After his death, Artemis changed him into a guinea-fowl.

MELETE Boeotian Muse of Practice. Worshipped on Helicon. Daughter of Uranus and Gaea. Sister of Aoide (Aeode) and Mneme.

MELIA Daughter of Oceanus and Tethys. Married her brother, Inachus. Mother of Aegialeus, Io and Phoroneus. Possibly the mother of Mycene, a daughter of Inachus. Became mother of Ismenius by Apollo.

MELIAE Nymphs of manna ash trees. They sprang from the blood and semen of the castrated Uranus. Sisters of the Erinnyes and Giants.

MELIAN NYMPHS Nurses of the infant Zeus.

MELIBOEA (Chloris) Daughter of Amphion and Niobe. Sister to six boys and five girls including Amyclas, Cleodoxa, Ismenos, Neaera, Phthia and Phylomache. Was the sole survivor of the twelve when Apollo killed the boys and Artemis the girls, though some accounts say a brother too was saved.

MELIBOEA An Oceanid. Daughter of Oceanus and Tethys. Sister of Clymene, Doris, Eidyia, Electra, Metis, Perseis, Proteus, Pleione and others. Married Pelasgus, king of Arcadia. Mother of Lycaon.

MELICERTES (Portunus) God of harbours and ports. Son of Athamas and Ino. Brother of Learchus. When drowned by his mother, possibly in oil (though more probably in the sea), he became the god, Palaemon. Sisyphus started the Isthmian Games in his memory.

MELIE An ash-nymph. Mother of Amycus and Mygdon by Poseidon.

MELISSA Daughter of Melissus, king of Crete. Sister of Amalthea. The two sisters were nurses of the infant Zeus, feeding him goat's milk. Melissa learned how to collect honey, and was changed into a bee.

MELISSEUS Father of Adrasteia and Ida, nursemaids of Zeus.

MELISSUS King of Crete. Father of Amalthea and Melissa, nursemaids of Zeus.

MELITE A Nereid. One of the fifty daughters of Nereus and Doris. Possibly mother of Hyllus by Heracles.

MELOS The most south-westerly of the Cyclades. A volcanic island. Chief city: also Melos. The Venus de Milo was found here.

MELOS, kings of Acamas and Demophon, jointly; Menestheus, Polyanax.

MELPOMENE Muse of tragedy. Daughter of Zeus and Mnemosyne. One of the nine Muses. Possibly mother of Aglaopheme, Molpe, Pelsinoe and Telexiepeia, the Sirens by Achelous. Her symbols were a tragic mask and buskin (cothurnus), a thick-soled boot worn by ancient tragic actors. In one hand she held a dagger, in the other sceptre and crown. Melpomene sang in a clear voice songs of mourning for poets and men of action.

MELTAS Last of the ten generations of descendants of Ceisus, king of Argos. He was deposed.

Melpomene

MEMBLIARUS King of Thera (Calliste). Son of Poeciles. Brother of Europa. When his sister was kidnapped by Zeus, he and Cadmus went to Calliste from Tyre, to search for her. His descendants ruled for eight generations.

MEMNON King of Ethiopa. Son of Tithonus and Eos. Brother of Emathion and perhaps Phaethon. Ally of the Trojans (Priam was his uncle), he took a force of 10,000 to the War. Killed Antilochus and was himself killed by Achilles. Smoke from his funeral pyre formed into birds.

MEMORY Epithet of Mnemosyne, mother of the Muses.

MEMPHIS Daughter of the river god, Nile. Sister of Anchinoe. Married Epaphus, king of Egypt. Mother of Libya and Lysianassa.

MENA Roman goddess of menstruation, said to be same as Juno. Young puppies were sacrificed to her.

MENALIPPE Alternative spelling of Melanippe, sister of Hippolyte.

MENALIPPE Daughter of Cheiron and Chariclo. Sister of Theia and Endeis. Raped by Aeolus, she became the mare Ocyrrhoe. Mother of Phasis by Apollo. She could prophecy the future.

MENELAUS King of Sparta. One of the Atreidae. Son of Atreus and Aerope, or possibly of Pleisthenes and Cleolla. Brother of Agamemnon, and possibly Anixibia and Pleisthenes. Married Helen who was abducted by Paris. The Trojan War came about because the Greeks rallied to Menelaus' side to secure her return from Troy. Father of Hermione and Pleisthenes II, and possibly Nicostratus, though Nicostratus may have been his son by Tereis or Pieris, as was Megapenthes. Father of Xenodamus by Cnossia. Father of Antianeira.

Spent his youth in exile, but when Tyndareus helped Agamemnon and Menelaus expel Thyestes, Menelaus succeeded Tyndareus to the throne. He won Helen with the help of Odysseus' cunning. Was in the Wooden Horse. Did not die but went straight to the Elysian fields.

MENEPHRON A man who sexually assaulted his own mother.

MENESTHEUS Regent of Athens. Son of Peteus. As a suitor of Helen he took fifty ships to Troy. He had earlier kidnapped her but she was rescued by the Dioscuri, the finest of Greek strategists. Menestheus was the first demagogue and ruled Athens during the absence of Theseus. At Troy, was in the Wooden Horse. His herald was Thootes. After the war, went to Melos, succeeding Polyanax as king. He and Stichius recovered the body of Amphimachus.

MENESTHIUS Son of Spercheius and Polydora. Raised by Polydora and her husband, Borus.

MENESTRATUS A Thespian youth. The lover of Cleostratus, whom he saved from being eaten by a dragon which annually attacked Thespiae.

MENETES Possibly father of Antianeira. Grandfather of Echion and Eurytus.

MENIPPE One of the Coronides. Daughter of Orion. Sister of Metioche. Aphrodite gave her beauty, and she taught Athena to weave. She and her sister committed suicide to stop a plague in Orchomenus. They became comets.

MENODICE Daughter of Orion. Mother of Hylas by Theiodamas.

MENOECEUS (1) Son of Creon and Anioche or Eurydice. Brother of Enioche, Haemon, Megara and Pyrrha. Committed suicide, in accordance with an oracle, to save Thebes from the Seven. (2) Theban descendant of the Sparti. Father of Creon, Hipponome and Jocasta. Committed suicide by jumping from the walls of Thebes, to relieve the city of a plague or drought.

MENOETES Herdsman of Hades. Son of Ceuthonymus. Heracles killed him on earth and would have done so a second time in the Underworld, but Persephone saved him.

MENOETIUS (1) Son of Actor and Aegina. Brother of Irus and Polymela. Married Sthenele or, possibly, Periopis. Father of Patroclus. An Argonaut. (2) Son of Iapetos and Clymene or Asia. Brother of Atlas, Epimethius and Prometheus. When he fought the gods, a thunderbolt from Zeus blasted him into Tartarus.

MENSTRUATION, Roman goddess of Mena.

MENTES A Taphian king. Son of Anchialus.

MENTHA (Minthe) Daughter of Cocytus. Lover of Hades, they were discovered by Persephone and Mentha was changed into the herb, mint.

MENTOR (1) Son of Alcimus. Helped to rouse Telemachus to action to find his father, Odysseus. (2) A son of Heracles. (3) Father of Imbrius.

MERA (1) A priest of Aphrodite. (2) Faithful dog of Icarius. After helping Erigone find the burial place of her murdered father, he died and became Sirius, the dog-star, or Canis, the lesser dog-star. Cf Maera.

MERCHANTS, god of Greek: Hermes. Roman: Mercury.

MERCURY (Hermes) Roman messenger of the gods. Son of Jupiter and Maia. Possibly the father of Cupid by Venus. A patron of astronomy and the god of merchants. *See* Hermes.

MERIONES Son of Molus. Charioteer of Idomeneus and second-in-command of the Cretan force of eighty ships in the Trojan War. The second best archer (after Teucer), was the archery contest winner at the funeral games of Patroclus. Had a famous helmet which Autolycus had stolen from Amyntor and given to Odysseus. In the fighting, wounded Deiphobus and killed Acamas, son of Antenor, and many others. Helped Ajax to recover the body of Patroclus.

MERMAIDS (1) The Nereids and Oceanids. They had the bodies of women but the tails of fish. (2) *See* Eurynome.

MERMERUS (1) Son of Jason and Medea. Brother of Alcimenes, Argus, Eriopis, Medeias, Pheres, Thessalus and Tisandrus. Killed either by Medea or a lioness. (2) Son of Pheres. Father of Ilus. King of Threspotian Ephyra. An expert poison maker. (3) A Trojan ally killed in the War by Antilochus.

MEROPE (1) Daughter of Atlas and Pleione. One of the Pleiades. Sister of Alcyone, Celaeno, Electra, Maia, Sterope and Taygete. Married Sisyphus of Corinth, the only one of the sisters to marry a mortal. Mother of Glaucus, Halmus, Ornytion and Thersander. Because she married a mortal, she is the only one of the Pleiades not visible in the night sky. (2) Daughter of Pandareus and Harmothoe. Also called Clytie. Sister of Aedon and Cleothera (Cameiro). She and Cleothera were raised by Athena after their parents were killed by Zeus. They were later abducted by the Harpies and forced to serve the Erinnyes. (3) Daughter of Cypselus. Married Cresphontes. Mother of Aepytus and two others. (4) Daughter of Erechtheus. Possibly mother of Daedalus. (5) Daughter of Oenopion and Helice. When she refused Orion's love, he insulted her and as a result her father blinded him. (6) The wife of Polybus. Also called Periboea or Eriboea. Looked after Oedipus when he had been exposed on Mt Cithaeron.

MEROPS (1) The father of Epione, king of Percote. Perhaps same as (2). (2) King of Percote. Son of another Merops. Father of Arisbe, Adrastus, Amphius and Cleite. Present at the Trojan War. Taught Aesacus how to interpret dreams. (3) A companion of Aeneas on his journey from Troy to Italy. Killed by Turnus. (4) King of Cos. Married Clymene. Became the 'eagle' constellation. (5) Merops of Miletus, father of Pandareus.

MESE Delphic Muse, the middle string of the lyre. Sister of Hypate and Nete.

MESSENE Daughter of Triopas and Hiscilla. Sister of Erysichthon, Phorbas and Iphimedeia. Married Polycaon. Eponym of Messenia.

MESSENIA Region of south-west Peloponnesus, west of Laconia and south of

Arcadia and Elis. Named after Messene, wife of Polycaon.

MESSENIA, kings of First was Polycaon, followed by five generations, then Perieres, Aphareus and Leucippus, Neleus, Nestor, Thrasymedes and Peisistratus (jointly), Cresphontes, Polyphontes, Aepytus. Asclepius, Machaon and Podalirius ruled parts of Messenia; also, possibly, Melanthus.

MESTA (Mestos) River of Thrace. City of Abdera was at its mouth.

MESTOR Son of Andromeda and Perseus. Brother of Alcaeus, Electryon, Gorgophone, Heleus, Perses and Sthenelus. Father of Hippothoe by Lysidice.

MESTOR Bastard son of Priam.

MESTRA (Metra) Daughter of Erysichthon. Poseidon gave her the power to change shape. Was possibly married to Autolycus, who had the same powers. *See also* Metra.

METABUS Tyrant king of the Volsci. Husband of Casmilla. Father of Camilla. Was so cruel that his own people deposed him.

METALWORKING, god of Greek: Hephaestus. Roman: Vulcan.

METANEIRA Wife of Celeus, king of Eleusis. Mother of Abas, Demophon, Triptolemus and four girls.

METAPONTUS Possibly a son of Aeolus and brother of Melanippe. Married Theano who had two sons; she bore him two sons. He thought all four children were his own, and he showed preference for the first two until he discovered the truth, when he killed them and their mother. Then married Melanippe, adopting Aeolus II and Boeotus.

METHARME Daughter of Pygmalion. Possibly wife of Cinyras.

METHONE A nymph, mother of Oeagrus by Pierus.

METIADUSA Daughter of Eupalamus. Married Cecrops. Mother of Pandion and three daughters.

METIDICE *See* Adrastus.

METIOCHE One of the Coronides. Daughter of Orion. Sister of Menippe. Aphrodite gave her beauty. She taught Athena to weave. She and her sister killed themselves to stop a plague in Orchomenus.

METION Son of Erechtheus and Praxithea. Brother of Cecrops, Creusa, Cthonia, Eupalamus, Orneus, Oreithyia, Pandorus, Procris, Protogeneia and Thespius. Father of Daedalus, Perdix and Sicyon by Alcippe, though the father may have been Eupalamus.

METIS Personification of Prudence. Daughter of Oceanus and Tethys. Sister of Clymene, Doris, Eidyia, Electra, Meliboea, Perseis, Pleione, Proteus and the 3000 Oceanids.

The first wife of Zeus, she became pregnant with Athena whereupon Zeus swallowed her believing a second child, a son, would be greater than he. Athena was born from Zeus' head. It was also Metis who caused Cronos to vomit up the brothers and sisters of Zeus.

METIS Probably the same as Procne, wife of Tereus.

METOPE Daughter of one of the river gods, Ladon or Peneius. Sister of Daphne. Married the river god Asopus. Mother of three sons: Ismenus, Pelagon and Pelasgus; and twenty daughters, including Antiope, Corcyra, Aegina, Salamis, Thebe, Chalcis, Ismene, Metope, Cleone and Plataea. Possibly the mother of Hecuba by Sangarius.

METOPE Daughter of Asopus and Metope. Sister to many (cf above).

METRA (Mestra) Daughter of Erysichthon. Poseidon gave her the power to change her shape into the animal of her choice. Her putative husband, Autolycus, had the same power. Demeter inflicted the punishment of perpetual hunger on her father, and he sold her many times in order to buy food for himself.

METUS Son of Ares and one of his attendants.

MEZENTIUS Tyrant king of the Etruscans. The father of Lausus. A cruel man who delighted in slow and fatal tortures until his subjects expelled him, and he went to Italy. There he allied himself with Turnus against Aeneas. After killing Acron, Aeneas or, according to a lesser tradition, Ascanius killed him.

MIDAS King of Phrygia. Son of Gordius and Cybele. Father of a bastard son, Lityerses.
   Founder of the city of Ancyra (Ankara). He was the owner of fabulous rose gardens. In return for his hospitality, Silenus, a companion of Dionysus, gave Midas the 'golden touch', but he was cured when he bathed in the river Pactolus. Apollo gave him the ears of an ass. Midas was the discoverer of both black and white lead.

MIDEA A Phrygian servant, mother of Licymnius by Electryon. Eponym of the city in north-east Argolis.

MILANION (Melanion, Hippomenes) Husband of Atalanta. Father of Parthenopaeus. *See* Hippomenes.

MILETUS Son of Apollo and Acacallis, Areia or Deione. Brother of Amphithemis. Married Cyanee, daughter of Maeander. Father of twins, Byblis and Caunus. Lover of Sarpedon, son of Zeus, and possibly of Minos (alternatively Atymnius). Eponym of the city in Ionia.

MILETUS Chief city of Ionia, in Asia

Midas

Minor, near the mouth of the river Maeander.

MILTIADES Son of Cimon. Father of Cimon II, ruler of Athens.

MIMAS Son of Gaea. A Giant, killed in the war of gods and giants by Ares, Hephaestus, Heracles or Zeus, and buried under Mt Vesuvius.

MINERVA (Athena) Roman goddess of war. Daughter of Jupiter. Epithet: Medica, a patroness of physicians.
   Keeper of the city of Rome, she was the patron-goddess of craftsmen. Her Roman festivals were called Quinquatria and began on 19 March, except for flute players, who held a festival on 13 June in her honour.

MINERVALIA (Quinquatria) Roman festivals, held annually in honour of Minerva on 19 March and 13 June.

MINOIS Patronymic of Ariadne, daughter of Minos.

MINOS Kings of Crete. (1) Son of Zeus and Europa. Brother of Rhadamanthys and Sarpedon. Married Pasiphae. Father of Acacallis, Androgeus, Ariadne, Catreus, Deucalion, Euryale, Glaucus, Lycastus, Phaedra and Xenodice. Was either the father or possibly grandfather of Minos II. Minos, called a kindly man by some but a tyrant by others, had many love affairs, but the women who slept with him tended to die soon afterwards, until Procris cured him with a herb, Circe's root. Lover of Atymnius or Miletus. Minos commissioned Daedalus to build a labyrinth in the basement of his palace at Cnossus, to house the Minotaur. Not satisfied with victory over Megara, he ordered them to provide seven youths and seven maidens for the Minotaur. When Theseus killed the Minotaur, the son of Pasiphae, Minos imprisoned Daedalaus there, but he escaped. Minos was killed pursuing Daedalus. (2) Son of Lycastus and Ida or of Minos I. It could well be that both Minos I and Minos II were the same person. Minos II was called a judge of the dead with Rhadamanthys and Sarpedon. He was also a great Cretan law-giver.

MINOTAUR Monstrous offspring of Pasiphae, wife of Minos, and a bull. He had the body of a man and the head of a bull. Called Asterius, he fed on the human flesh of seven Athenian youths and seven maidens. Minos placed him in the labyrinth built by Daedalus. Was killed by Theseus.

MINT *See* Mentha.

MINYAS Son of Aeolus, Chryses or Poseidon. Father of Alcithoe, Arsippe, Clymene (wife of Cephalus), Leucippe and Periclymene. He may also have been the father (or even the son) of Orchomenus. Minyas was rich enough to build his own treasure house.

MISCHIEF, goddess of Ate, Discordia, Eris.

MISENUS (1) Son of Aeolus. Brother of Clytius and ten others. He was Hector's piper in the Trojan War and after Hector's death did the same job for Aeneas, even following him from Troy to Italy. Misenus challenged the gods to a musical contest and was drowned by a Triton. He was buried on the headland of Misenus, thus giving it its name. (2) A companion of Odysseus. (3) A headland near Cumae, about 15 km southwest of modern Naples. The city of Misenum built nearby took its name from (1) above.

MISTRESS Cult title of Despoina, daughter of Poseidon, Hippios and Demeter.

MNEME Boeotian Muse of Memory. Daughter of Uranus and Gaea. Sister of Aoide (Aeode) and Melete. Worshipped on Helicon.

MNEMOSYNE (Memory) A Titan. Daughter of Uranus and Gaea. Sister of the Titans and giants. Mother of the Muses by Zeus.

MNESILEUS Son of Polydeuces and Phoebe.

MNESIMACHE Daughter of Dexamenus. Sister of Eurypylus, Theraephone and Theronice. Heracles saved her from a forced marriage with the Centaur, Eurytion.

MNESTHEUS A companion of Aeneas on his journey from Troy to Italy. A competitor in both archery and sailing contests at the funeral games of Anchises.

MNESUS A Trojan killed in the Trojan War by Achilles.

MOIRA Personification of fate. Decided the outcome of battles and the fates of the combatants. Her decisions were irrevocable, even by Jupiter.

MOIRAE (Fates) Daughters of Zeus and Themis. They were called Atropos (the unbending), Clotho (the spinner), and Lachesis (the caster of lots). Sisters of the Horae, they supervised with them the actions of all mortals, having greater power than even Zeus.

MOIRAGETES Epithets of Apollo and Zeus at Delphi, guides of the Moirae.

MOLION Squire of Hector. Killed in the Trojan War by Odysseus.

MOLIONE Wife of Actor, son of Phorbas. Mother of Eurytus and Cteatus, though possibly by Poseidon.

MOLIONIDAE Twin sons (possibly physically joined) of Actor and Molione. Called Cteatus and Eurytus. Sided with their uncle, Augeias, in a fight against Heracles.

MOLORCHUS An old Nemean shepherd who planted the grove in which the Nemean Games were held, and who was killed by the same lion that Heracles killed as his first labour.

MOLOSSUS King of Epirus. Son of Neoptolemus and Andromache. Brother of Pergamus and Pielus. Married Hermione, daughter of Menelaus and Helen; they had no children. Thus ended the line of Aeacus. Founder of Molossia. Molossus was an epithet of Zeus, in Epirus.

MOLPE One of the Sirens. Daughter of Achelous and Calliope, Melpomone, Sterope or Terpsichore. Sister of Aglaopheme (Peisinoe) and Thelexiepeia, and perhaps of Leucasia, Ligeia, Peisinoe and Parthenope. *See* Sirens.

MOLURUS Son of Arisbas. Murdered for his adultery with the wife of Hyettus. The first recorded case of either infidelity or murder for adultery.

MOLUS (1) Son of Ares and Demonice or Alcippe. Brother of Evenus, Pylus, Oeneus and Thestus. (2) Bastard son of Deucalion. Half-brother of Idomenus. Father of Meriones.

MOLY The magic herb that prevented Odysseus being enchanted by Circe.

MOMUS Fault finder of Olympus. Son of Nyx and Erebus. Brother of Aether, Cer, Dreams, Hemera, Hypnos, Moros, Nemesis, Thanatos and Charon. A god of fault-finding and adverse criticism, was banished from Olympus for mocking the other gods.

MONKEY *See* Cercopes.

MONOECUS Epithet of Heracles, used at the Ligurian port of Monoecus (Monaco).

MOON, goddess of Greek: Usually Artemis, but also Delia, Hecate. and Selene. Roman: Cynthia, Diana and Luna. Arcadian: Auge.

MOPSUS (1) Son of Ampycus and Chloris. A Thessalian. Ally of the Lapiths against the Centaurs. Present on the Calydonian Boar Hunt. An Argonaut. Killed in Libya, by a snake. (2) Son of Rhacius or Apollo and Manto. With his half-brother, Amphilochus, founded Mallus in Cilicia. These two later quarrelled with each other, possibly killing each other; or they parted company, and Mopsus, a great seer, won a contest of prophecies against Calchas, the latter dying of embarrassment.

MOROS Daughter of Nyx and Erebus. Sister of Aether, Cer, Dreams, Hemera, Hypnos, Momus, Charon, Nemesis and Thanatos.

MORPHEUS Roman god of dreams and sleep. Brother of Icelos and Phantasos and 997 others. Son of Somnus, he was one of the Oneiroi. In dreams, he appeared in human form.

MORS (Thanatos) God of death.

MORTA Epithet of Parca, one of the Fates.

MORYS Son of Hippotion. Brother of Ascanius. Killed in the Trojan War by Meriones.

MOUNTAINS, Greek goddess of Leucothea. Roman, Mater Matuta.

MULBERRY *See* Pyramus and Thisbe.

MULCIBER Epithet of Vulcan.

MULIUS An Epaean killed in the Trojan War by Achilles or Nestor. Husband of Agamede.

MUNITUS Son of Laodice and Acamas, her lover; or (less likely) by Demophoon, his brother.

MURDERS, mother of Eris (Discordia).

MUSAGETES Epithet of Apollo, patron of the Muses.

MUSAEUS Son of Antiphemus, Eumolpus or Orpheus. Married Deiope, priestess of Demeter at Eleusis. Father of another Eumolpus. A poet and musician, pupil of Orpheus, helped to found the Eleusinian Mysteries.

MUSES (Camenae) Daughters of Mnemosyne and Zeus, nine in number: Calliope, of epic poetry; Cleio, of history; Erato, of love lyrics and bridal songs; Euterpe, of lyric poems; Melpomene, of tragedy; Polyhymnia, of song, rhetoric and geometry; Thalia, of comedy; Terpsichore, of the dance; Urania, of astronomy and astrology.

MUSES (Boeotian) Worshipped at Helicon. Three daughters of Uranus and Gaea. Older than the nine. Aoide (Aeode), of song; Melete, of practice; Mneme, of memory.

MUSES (Delphic) Hypate, Mese and Nete, the high, middle and low strings of a lyre.

MUSIC, god of Greek: Apollo. Roman: Apollo.

MUTA Roman goddess of silence.

MUTTO Possibly father of Anna, Dido and Pygmalion. Alternatives: Agenor or Belus.

MYAGRO An Arcadian fly-catcher, honoured in the town of Alipherus.

MYCENAE City in north-east Argolis in the Peloponnesus. Founded by Perseus. Destroyed by the people of Argos in 468 BC. Named after Mycene, daughter of Inachus.

MYCENAE, kings of Aegisthus, Agamemnon, Aletes, Atreus, Eurystheus, Orestes, Perseus (the founder), Sthenelus and Thyestes.

MYCENE Daughter of Inachus and Melia. Sister of Aegialeius, Io and Phoroneus. Married Arestor. Eponym of Mycenae.

MYDON A Trojan killed in the War by Achilles.

MYGDALION Son of Cinyras. Brother of Braesia, Laogore and Orsedice. Commanded the last of the fifty ships that his father sent to the Trojan War. The other forty-nine were made of clay.

MYGDON King of Phrygia. Son of Poseidon and the ash-nymph, Melie. Brother of Amycus. Father of Coroebus. Was killed by Heracles during the war between the Mygdonians and the Mariandynians.

MYLES King of Laconia. Son of Lelex and Cleocharia. Brother or father of Eurotas. Brother of Polycaon and Therapne. Inventor of the mill.

MYNES Son of Evenus and Alcippe. Brother of Epistrophus and Marpessa.

MYRINA Wife of Thoas, king of Lemnos. Mother of Hypsipyle.

MYRMIDON Husband of Peisidice. Father of Actor, Antiphus and Eupolemeia.

MYRMIDONS Allies of Achilles in the Trojan War. An old Thessalian race that started when Zeus changed ants into people.

MYRRHA (Smyrna) Daughter of Cinyras or Theias and Cenchreis. Sister of Adonis, though some call her his mother, because, according to one story, Myrrha committed incest with her father and was changed into a myrrh tree to avoid her father's murderous advances. After nine months, the tree split open and Adonis emerged.

MYRTILUS Charioteer of Oenomaus.

Son of Hermes and Clytie. Pelops and Hippodameia bribed him to pre-arrange the result of the race of her suitors, in order that Pelops should win. Oenomaus was killed; as was Myrtilus by Pelops when he claimed his reward. Some state he became the constellation Auriga, the charioteer.

MYRTLE *See* Aphrodite.

MYRTO An Euboean woman, eponym of the Myrtoan Sea.

MYSIA Part of Asia Minor, north of Lydia and west of Phrygia. Troy was one of its divisions.

N

NAENIA Roman goddess of funerals. Her temple was outside the city gate.

NAIADS Minor female deities of fountains and lakes.

NAIS (1) Possibly mother of Glaucus by Poseidon. (2) Daughter of Literses. Sister of Lyce, Nomia, Piplea and Xenea. May have married Daphnis.

NANA Daughter of the river god, Sangarius. Mother of Attis.

NAPAEAE Ancient divinities of hills and woods.

NARCAEUS Son of Dionysus and Physcoa.

NARCISSUS Son of Cephisus and Leiriope. Teiresias prophesied that this beautiful youth would live to a great age, 'provided he did not know himself'–the meaning of which was not understood. A very vain person, many fell in love with him including Echo; but all found their love unrequited. Nemesis punished him for his vanity by causing him to fall in love with his own reflection, seen in a pool of water. He gazed at this sight of himself until he wasted away, becoming a flower of the same name, and thus the prophecy was fulfilled.

NASAMON Son of Amphithemis and Tritonis. Brother of Caphaurus.

NATURE, god of Greek: Pan. Roman: Faunus.

NATURE, goddess of Roman: Bona Dea, Bona Mater, Fauna.

NAUBOLUS Son of Phocus and Endeis. Brother of Crisus and Panopeus.

NAUBOLUS King of Phocis. Son of Ornytus. Father of Iphitus.

NAUPIADAME Possibly mother of Augeias by Helios.

NAUPLIUS An Argonaut. Son of Clytoneus.

NAUPLIUS (Perhaps same as above.) Married Clymene, daughter of Catreus, or Hesione or Philyra. Father of Nausimedon, Oeax and Palamedes.

A notorious wrecker of both marriages and ships, Nauplius was nevertheless an expert on astronomy and sailing. He caused many ships to be shipwrecked on their return journey from the Trojan War because the Greeks had not avenged the death of Palamedes in the War. Nauplius caused Aegialeia, wife of Diomedes, to have an affair with Cometes; Clytemnestra, wife of Agamemnon, with Aegisthus; and Meda, wife of Idomenus, with Leucus.

NAUPLIUS Son of Poseidon and Amymone. An Argive sailor and navigator, he was an ancestor of Nauplius, son of Clytoneus. A pirate and slave-trader, founded the city of Nauplia.

NAUSICAA Daughter of Alcinous and Arete. Had five brothers. Married Telemachus. Mother of Perseptolis or Poliporthus. Resembled Artemis and befriended the shipwrecked Odysseus.

NAUSIMEDON Son of Nauplius and Clymene. Brother of Oeax and Palamedes.

NAUSINOUS Son of Odysseus and Calypso. Brother of Nausithous.

NAUSITHOUS King of the Phaecians. Son of Poseidon and Periboea. Father of Alcinous and Rhexenor. Purified Heracles after he had murdered his children. Nausithous took his people to Drepane because the Cyclopes, their neighbours, were harassing them.

NAUSITHOUS Son of Odysseus and Calypso. Brother of Nausinous.

NAUTES A companion of Aeneas on his journey from Troy to Italy. A soothsayer.

NAXOS Largest and most fertile island of the Cyclades, midway between Greece and Asia Minor, in the Aegean Sea. Originally called Strongyle, then Dia. Named after Naxos, king of the Carians. Here Dionysus married Ariadne, who had been deserted by Theseus. Famous for its wine.

NEAERA (1) Mother of Aegle and Epeius by Panopeus. (2) Daughter of Amphion and Niobe. One of twelve children, six boys and six girls. (3) Wife of Autolycus. Possibly mother of Polymede. (4) Mother of Lampetie and Phaethusa by Helios or Apollo. A nymph. (5) Daughter of Pereus. Married Aleus. Mother of Auge, Cepheus, Amphidamas and Lycurgus. (6) Wife of Strymon. Mother of Evadne, wife of Argus.

NEBROPHONUS Possibly a son of Jason and Hypsipyle, and thus brother of Euneus, Deipylus and Thoas. But the name may be a doublet for Deipylus.

NECESSITAS Goddess of the destiny of mankind. Mother of the three Fates.

NECTAR The drink of the gods, just as ambrosia was their food. Drinking it gave the drinker perpetual youth, hence immortality. The cupbearers were Hebe and Ganymede.

NEDA A nurse of the infant Zeus.

NEKYIA The 'Book of the Dead' – Book XI of the *Odyssey*.

NELEUS King of Pylos. Son of Poseidon and Tyro. Twin of Pelias. Married Chloris, daughter of Amphion. Father of Pero and twelve sons, including Chromius, Nestor and Periclymenus. All but Nestor were killed by Heracles, after Neleus refused to purify him for the murder of Iphitus.

Abandoned at birth by Tyro, he was reared by horse-herders. After his death, was buried in a secret grave known only to Sisyphus.

NEMEA A very fertile valley of Argolis in the Peloponnesus, where there was also a town. It contained a sacred grove of Zeus, site of the Nemean Games. Home of the Nemean Lion.

NEMEAN GAMES One of the four Panhellenic festivals. Established by Adrastus and the Seven against Thebes to commemorate the death of Opheltes, son of Lycurgus. In 573 BC the Games became a Panhellenic festival.

NEMEAN LION Son of Typhon and Echidna. Brother of Cerberus, Chimaera, possibly Orthus, the Hydra, Sphinx, Crommyonian Sow, Caucasian Eagle and Vultures. It roamed the streets and was killed by Heracles as his first labour.

NEMERTES A Nereid. One of the fifty daughters of Nereus and Doris.

NEMESIS Goddess of retribution. Daughter of Erebus and Nyx. Sister of Cer, Aether, Dreams, Hemera, Hypnos, Momus, Moros, Thanatos and Charon. A personification of resentment or conscience.

Zeus pursued her, and she tried to avoid him by changing into a goose, but failed when he became a swan. Her egg was hatched by Leda, who called the child, Helen, her own.

NEOPTOLEMUS (Pyrrhus) Son of Achilles and Deidameia. Father of Pergamus, Pielus and Molossus by Andromache, his concubine after the Trojan War.

Went to Troy after the death of his father, and was the first Greek to enter the Wooden Horse. The killer of Antenor, Astyanax, Coroebus, Eurypylus and Priam, he

Nemesis

NEREIDS Fifty sea-nymphs (mermaids), daughters of Nereus and Doris and attendants of Poseidon. Included: Actaee, Agave, Amatheia, Amphinome, Amphithoe, Amphitrite, Apseudes, Callianassa, Callianeira, Clymene, Creusa, Cymodoce, Cymothoe, Dexamene, Doris, Doto, Dynamene, Erato, Eudora, Galatea, Glauce, Halie, Iaera, Ianassa, Ianeira, Limnoreia, Maera, Melite, Nemertes, Nesaea, Oreithyia, Panope, Pasithea, Pherusa, Proto, Psamanthe, Speio, Thalia, Thetis and Thoe.

NEREUS Old man of the sea. Son of Oceanus and Gaea. Brother of Ceto, Crius, Eurybia, Phorcys and Thaumas. Father of the Nereids by Doris.
  An ancient sea-god, he had the power to change shape and the gift of prophecy. Heracles captured him and forced him to reveal the location of the Garden of the Hesperides.

NERIO A minor Roman goddess, wife of Mars.

NESAEA A Nereid. One of the fifty daughters of Nereus and Doris.

executed Polyxena. After Troy, married Hermione. Was killed by Orestes at Delphi.

NEPENTHE A magic potion, used by Helen and Telemachus, that alleviated all unhappiness.

NEPHALION Co-ruler of Paros. Son of Hermes. Brother of Chryses, Eurymedon and Philocaus.

NEPHELE A cloud fashioned by Zeus to look like Hera. By Ixion, Nephele became the mother of Amycus and the Centaurs. Married Athamas. Mother of Helle and Phrixus.

NEPTUNE (Poseidon) Roman god of the waters. Originally a minor Italian god until associated with Poseidon, as late as the 4th century BC. Possibly borrowed from the Etruscan god, Nethunus. Husband of Salacia. Festival date: 23 July.

NESO A nymph, mother of Herophile, Sibyl of Marpessa, by Dardanus.

NESSUS A Centaur. Son of Ixion and Nephele. When he attempted to rape Deianeira, Heracles, her husband, killed him. In the Underworld, he became ferryman of the River Evenus. A mixture of his blood and semen containing Hydra poison killed Heracles.

NESTOR King of Pylos. Son of Neleus and Chloris. Brother of Pero and eleven boys, including Chromius and Periclymenus, all killed by Heracles. Married Eurydice, daughter of Clymenus. Father of seven sons: Antilochus, Aretus, Echephron, Perseus, Peisistratus, Stratius and Thrasymedes (but some add Paeon), and two daughters: Polycaste and Peisidice. Some claim his wife as Anaxibia.

He took ninety ships to the Trojan War and returned safely. Took part in all the Greek war councils. Noted for his wisdom, bravery and justice. Ruled for three generations.

NETE Delphic Muse, the low note of a lyre. Sister of Hypate and Mese.

NICHOMACHUS Son of Machaon and Anticleia. Brother of Alexanor and Gorgassus. A physician and forefather of Aristotle.

NICIPPE (Amphibia) Daughter of Pelops and Hippodameia. Sister of Alcathous, Astydameia, Atreus, Chrysippus, Copreus, Lysidice, Pittheus, Troezen and Thyestes, and perhaps others. Married Sthenelus. Mother of Alcino, Eurystheus and Medusa.

NICOSTRATA (Carmenta) Mother of Evander, whom she accompanied to Italy, by Hermes. A prophetess, she chose the site of Pallanteum on the Tiber.

NICOSTRATUS Bastard son of Menelaus and a slave called Pieris or Tereis, though some call Helen his mother. Brother of Megapenthes. The pair of them drove Helen from Sparta after the death of Menelaus. Half-brother of Hermione and Pleisthenes.

NIGHT, goddess of Nyx, Nox.

NIGHT ENTERTAINMENT, Roman god of Comus.

NIGHTINGALE *See* Aedon, Philomela.

NIKE (Victoria) Goddess of victory. Daughter of Pallas and Styx. Sister of Bia, Kratos and Zelos. A constant companion of Zeus.

NILE A river god. Father of Anchinoe and Memphis. Son of Oceanus and Tethys.

NIMROD Builder of the tower used by the Giants in their attack on the gods of Olympus.

NINUS King of ancient Babylon. Son of Belus. Brother of Babylon. Was known as Assyrian Zeus and Chaldaean Heracles.

NIOBE Daughter of Tantalus and Dione. Sister of Broteas and Pelops. Married Amphion. Mother of six sons and six daughters. Different sources give different names, the most common being: Alphenor, Amyclas, Callirrhoe, Chloris (Meliboea), Cleodoxa, Damasichthon, Iloneus, Ismenos, Neaera, Phaedimus, Phthia, Sipylus and Tantalus.

When she boasted that her children were more beautiful than Leto's, Apollo and Artemis, Leto's son and daughter, killed eleven of her children. Most authorities say that Chloris was the sole survivor, but some claim that Amyclas, too, was spared. In sorrow, Niobe turned to marble, and her body lies on Mt Sipylus, in Lydia.

NIOBE Daughter of Phoroneus and Cerdo, Peitho or Teledicè. Sister of Apis and Car. Mother of Argus, Osiris, Pelasgus and Typhon by Zeus. First mortal woman to be loved by a god.

NIOBIDS Generic name of the children of Niobe.

NIREUS Son of Poseidon and Canace. Brother of Aloeus, Epopeus, Hopleus and Triopas.

NISUS King of Megara. Son of Pandion and Pylia. Brother of Aegeus, Lycus and Pallas. Father of Eurymede (Eurynome), Iphinoe and Scylla.

He had red hair or, some say, a lock of shining purple hair; it was foretold that if it were cut off he would die. Minos had besieged his kingdom, and captured the city only after Scylla, who loved him, had cut off the lock. Nisus then became an osprey (sea eagle).

NISUS Possibly son of Hyrtacus. A Trojan prince, was a companion of Aeneas on his journey from Troy to Italy. At the funeral games of Anchises, he helped his friend, Euryalus, win the foot-race event. Both were later killed raiding a Latin camp.

NOEMON (Noman) Name adopted by Odysseus to confuse Polyphemus.

NOMIA Daughter of Literses. Sister of Lyce, Nais, Piplea and Xenea. Possibly married Daphnis.

NOMIOS (Nomius) Epithet of Apollo as herdsman of Admetus.

NOMIOS Epithet of Hermes, god of pastures.

NONA (ninth month) One of the three Fates (Parcae). Companion of Decima and Parca.

NORTH WIND Greek: Boreas. Roman: Aquilo.

NOTUS (Auster) Son of Astraeus and Eos. Brother of the Winds (qv). Usually referred to as the south wind, which blows mainly in the autumn.

NUMANUS Brother-in-law of Turnus, killed by Ascanius.

NUMA POMPILIUS Second king of Rome. Son of Pompon. Married Tatia, daughter of Titus Tatius. Elected king after death of Romulus. Was born on the day Romulus founded Rome. After Tatia died, married Egeria, a nymph.
He reigned thirty-nine years (some say forty-three). Builder of the temples of Janus and Vesta, he was first to appoint four Vestal virgins. A wise and happy king, he brought law and order to the city. He left behind him one daughter, Pompilia.

NUMINA Invisible spirits working with force in a particular department of human life and its environment.

'Numina' belong to the period of animism in the history of Roman religion. The original conception of a 'numen' was of a spirit inhabiting a spot. Each man made his own and began to propitiate them. Slowly, as these spirits became more clearcut in men's minds, their functions became more definite. Examples of 'numina' are Silvanus, the wild spirit that makes the woods dangerous, Pales, Pomona, Terminus and Vertumnus.

NUMITOR King of Alba Longa. Son of Procas. Brother of Amulius. Father of Ilia and Lausus. Amulius usurped the throne and killed the sons of Numitor. Romulus and Remus, sons of Rhea Silvia, killed Amulius and returned the throne to Numitor.

NYCTEIS Daughter of Nycteus and Polyxo. Mother of Labdacus.

NYCTEUS Regent of Thebes. Son of Chthonius or Hyrieus and Clonia, or of Poseidon and Celaeno. Married Polyxo. Father of Nycteis. Father of Nyctimene, and possibly Antiope and Callisto (cf Celeus or Lycaon). Brother of Lycus. Unknowingly committed incest with Nyctimene. Incited his brother to kill his enemy, Epopeus. Committed suicide after learning that Antiope was pregnant by Zeus.

NYCTIMENE Daughter of Epopeus, king of Lesbos or of Nycteus. Possibly sister of Antiope and Callisto. Was raped by her father, and was changed into an owl by Athena.

NYCTIMUS King of Arcadia. Youngest son of Lycaon. Brother of Callisto, Pallas and forty-seven others. Killed in the Deluge or by a thunderbolt of Zeus.

NYMPHS Minor female deities. Oceanids (nymphs of the great Ocean), Nereids (sea-nymphs), Dryads and Hamadryads (nymphs of oak trees), Meliae (nymphs of ash trees), Oreads (mountain nymphs), Epipotamides (river nymphs), Naiads (nymphs of brooks, lakes and springs), Crenids (nymphs of springs), Limnades (nymphs of lakes, marshes and swamps), Nyseides (Bacchant nymphs), Potameides (nymphs of fountains, lakes, rivers and springs), Limoniades (nymphs of meadows of flowers), Napaeae (nymphs of glens).

NYSA A mountain, possibly in Thrace, where nymphs reared Dionysus.

NYSEIDES (Nysiades) Bacchant nymphs on Mt Nysa. Zeus placed them among the stars as the Hyades.

NYX (Nox) Goddess of night. Daughter of Chaos. Sister of Erebus, Eros, Gaea, Tartarus and others. Married Erebus. Mother of Aether, Hemera, Charon, Cer, Dreams, Hypnos, Moros, Nemesis, Momus and Thanatos. Possibly mother of the Hesperides and Old Age. Mother of Fraus, by Orcus.

O

OAK *See* Baucis, Philemon.

OATHS, Roman goddess of Fides.

OAXUS Cretan city, ruled by Etearchus.

OBLIGATION, Roman goddess of Pietas. (Obligation to gods, parents and country.)

OBOL Small coin placed in the mouth of a dead person to pay the ferryman for taking the body across the River Styx.

OBRIAREUS *See* Briareus.

OCALEIA Wife of Abas. Mother of twin sons Acrisius and Proetus, and of Chalcodon.

OCEANIDS Daughters of Oceanus and Tethys, 3000 in number. They had the power to change shape; only some of them lived in the sea. Included Amphitrite, Asia, Aethra, Calypso, Clymene, Doris, Europa, Metis, Pluto and Urania.

OCEANUS Eldest son of Uranus and Gaea. Married his sister, a fellow Titan, Tethys. Father of the Oceanids, rivers and fountains; Doris, Eidyia, Electra, Callirrhoe, Perseis, Proteus, Pleione, Styx, Inachus, Melia, Meliboea, Arethusa, Fortuna. (*See* River Gods, Oceanids.) Father of Acmon and Passalus, by Theia. Possibly father of Amphitrite. Father of Ceto, Crius, Eurybia, Nereus, Phorcys and Thaumas, by Gaea. Possibly father of Chariclo.

OCEANUS The great sea that surrounds the world. Originally, it was a river that encircled the world but later it became associated with the Atlantic Ocean.

OCHIMUS One of the Heliades. Son of Helios and Rhode. Brother of Actis, Candalus, Cercaphus, Macar, Tenages and Triopas. Married Hegetoria. Father of Cydippe. Perhaps first to sacrifice to Athena.

OCNUS Son of Tiber and Manto and the husband of an extravagant wife. One of the condemned in Hades, he plaited ropes which a she-ass continually ate.

OCRISIA A Roman slave. Mother of Tullius, sixth king of Rome, by Hephaestus.

OCTYUS Father of Guneus, king of Cyphus.

OCYPETE One of the Harpies. Daughter of Thaumas and Electra. Sister of Aello and Podarge (Celaeno).

OCYRRHOE (Menalippe) Daughter of Cheiron and Chariclo. Sister of Endeis and Theia. Mother of Phasis by Apollo. Changed into a horse by the gods because she could prophesy the future.

ODIUS A Greek herald at Troy who went with Eurybates to appease Achilles.

ODYSSEUS (Ulysses) King of Ithaca. Son of Laertes and Anticleia, though some call his father Sisyphus. Married Penelope. Father of Telemachus and Arcesilaus (Ptoliporthes). Married Circe. Father of Ardea, Agrius and Telegonus. Married Callidice, queen of Thresprotia. Father of Polypoetes. Father of Nausinous and Nausithous, and possibly Teledamas (Telegonus), by Calypso. Possibly father of Latinus by Circe. Possibly father of Leontophonus by the daughter of Thoas. Father of Auson.

As a suitor of Helen, he took twelve ships to the Trojan War where he killed Dolon. Successfully fought Ajax for the armour of Achilles. A leader of the Greeks and recognised as the wiliest strategist. Some say he was the inventor of the Wooden Horse. His twenty-year return journey was called the Odyssey.

His childhood nurses were Eurycleia and Peisenor. Was a foot-race winner at the funeral games of Patroclus. Was accompanied into Hades by Perimedes. Odysseus disguised himself and approached Penelope, reassuring her that he was still alive, as Eurybates (a fictitious person) had seen him. Was killed by a spear thrown by Telegonus.

ODYSSEY Homer's story of the twenty-year return journey of Odysseus from Troy. 1. First they raided the Ciconians. 2. Visited the Lotus eaters. 3. Visit to the Cyclopes. 4. Visit to Aeolus, king of the winds. 5. Visit to Telepylus and the Laestrygones. 6. Visit to Circe and the isle of Aeaea. 7. Visit to the land of the Cimmerians. 8. Visit to the Underworld. 9. Return to Aeaea. 10. The Sirens. 11. Scylla and Charybdis. 12. Thrinacia, herds of Helios. 13. Eight-year visit to Calypso and the isle of Ogygia. 14. Scheria and Nausicaa. 15. Return to Ithaca. 16. The contest against the suitors which comprised the shooting of arrows through twelve axe-heads.

OEAGRUS (Oeager) King of Thrace. Son of Pierus and Methone. Possibly father of Orpheus, by one of the Muses, and of Linus (cf Apollo).

OEAX Son of Nauplius and Clymene, Hesione or Philyra. Brother of Nausimedon and Palamedes. Told Clytemnestra of Agamemnon's return from the Trojan War with a concubine, Cassandra, which led to the murder plot against him.

OEBALUS King of Sparta. Son of Cynortas. Brother of Perieres. Married Gorgophone, his brother's widow. Father of Arene.

OECHALIA Wife of Melaneus and mother of Eurytus.

OEDIPUS King of Thebes. Only child of Laius and Jocasta. Exposed at birth with his feet pierced, was found on Mt Citheron and raised by Polybus. An oracle had warned Laius that his own son would kill him and, after this came true through an accident, Oedipus married his own mother,

neither one knowing their kinship. Father of Antigone, Eteocles, Ismene and Polyneices. When he learned the truth, blinded himself and ran away with Antigone, the earth finally swallowing him up. Solved the riddle of the Sphinx.

OENEUS King of Calydon. Son of Porthaon and Euryte. Brother of Alcathous, Agrius, Melas, Sterope and Leucopeus. Married first to Althaea. Father of Deianeira, Gorge and Toxeus, and possibly Meleager. After Althaea's suicide, he married Periboea. Father of Olenias, Perimede and Tydeus. Father of Laocoon by a serving woman. His cup-bearer was called Eunomus.

After he forgot to pay proper homage to Athena, she sent the Calydonian Boar to ravage the land. Killed Toxeus for jumping over a ditch, and was himself killed, possibly by the sons of Agrius.

OENEUS Son of Ares and Demonice or Alcippe. Brother of Evenus, Molus, Pylus and Thestius.

OENOE A water nymph. Mother of Sicinus by Thoas. Eponym of one of the Cyclades.

OENOMAUS King of Pisa. Son of Alxion or Ares and Harpina or perhaps Asterope. Married Evarete, daughter of Acrisius. Father of Hippodameia and Leucippus. Killed all the suitors of his daughter, until his eventual son-in-law, Pelops, killed him in a chariot race.

OENONE Daughter of Cebren, a river god. Married Paris. Mother of Corythus and Daphnis. Nymph of Phrygian Mt Ida. Prophesied her husband's abduction of Helen. When he returned from Sparta, injured, she refused to heal him, committing suicide instead.

OENONE (Oenopia) The original name of the island of Aegina.

OENOPE Possibly the mother of Megareus by Poseidon or Onchestus.

OENOPION King of Chios. Son of Dionysus or Theseus and Ariadne. Brother of Ceramus, Peparethus, Phanus, Staphylus and Thoas. Married Helice. Father of several sons and Merope. Possibly father of Maron. Dionysus taught him vine cultivation. He blinded Orion for raping Merope, but was forced to hide when Orion, his sight restored, returned.

OENOTRIA (Lucania) The ancient name for all southern Italy except the heel.

OELYCUS (sheep-wolf) Son of Theras. Refused to accompany his father from Sparta to Thera.

OEONUS Son of Licymnius and Perimede. Brother of Argeius and Melas. Killed by the sons of Hippocoon for throwing stones at their dog.

OETA Thessalian mountain where Heracles was cremated.

OGYGES King of Athens. Son of Poseidon and Gaea. Brother of Antaeus and Charybdis. Married Thebe, daughter of Zeus. King at the time of a deluge (c1765 BC).

OGYGIA The island where Odysseus stayed eight years with Calypso.

OGYGUS King of Eleusis. Father of Alalcomenia, Aulus and Thelxinoea in Boeotian tradition, and of Eleusis in Attic tradition. A Boeotian aboriginal king.

OICLES King of Arcadia. Son of Mantius or Antiphates. Married Hypermnestra, daughter of Thestius. Father of Amphiarus. He was possibly killed in the Trojan War by Laomedon.

OILEUS King of Locris. Son of Hodeodocus and Agrianome. Married Eriopis. Father of Lesser Ajax though the mother may have been Rhene. Father of Medon by Rhene. Lover of Apollo. An Argonaut.

OINO (wine) Devotee of Dionysus. Daughter of Anius. Sister of Elais and Spermo. Could produce wine from the earth just by touching the ground.

OLD MAN OF THE SEA Name applied to Nereus, Phorcys and Proteus.

OLENIAS Son of Oenus and Periboea. Brother of Perimede and Tydeus.

OLENUS Son of Hephaestus and Ocrisia. Brother of Tullius. Married Lethae. She claimed to be more beautiful than the goddesses, and both were turned to stone.

OLENUS A city of Achaea on the gulf of Patrae.

OLENUS, kings of Dexamenus, Hipponous.

OLIVE The sacred tree of Athena.

OLYMPIC GAMES Founded by Heracles the Dactyl, son of Zeus. Fell into disuse. Named after the town of Olympia in Elis and re-established on a permanent basis on 21 or 22 July, 776 BC. The victor's reward was a crown of olive, and the games were held every four years.

OLYMPUS The highest mountain of Greece rising to 2980 metres, between Thessaly and Macedonia. The home of the gods and goddesses of the Greeks.

OLYMPUS A Phrygian who taught the flute to Marsyas and the syrinx to Pan. Father of Marsyas.

OMPHALE Queen of Lydia. Daughter of Iardanus. Married Tmolus. A queen of Maeonia in Asia Minor. Heracles was forced to serve her as a slave for three years, after he had killed Iphitus. She became his mistress and bore Agelaos, Alceus and Lamus by him. She forced Heracles to dress as a woman.

OMPHALUS The sacred stone that

Cronos swallowed instead of Zeus. After regurgitation, it was placed in the temple of the Delphic Oracle.

ONCA (Onga) A Phoenician goddess. Identified with Athena, a goddess worshipped in Greece at Thebes, by Cadmus.

ONCHESTUS (1) Son of Agrius. Brother of Thersites and others. He survived when Diomedes killed some of the sons of Agrius. (2) Eponym of a city on the south shore of Lake Copais in Boeotia. Possibly the father of Megareus by Oenope.

ONCIUS (Oncus) King of Thelpusa in Arcadia. Son of Apollo. Owner of the horse Arion, which he gave to Heracles.

ONEIROPOMPUS Epithet of Hermes, the conductor of dreams.

ONEIROI (Dreams) The children of Hypnos or Nyx. Named Icelos (Phobetor), Morpheus and Phantasos. They lived near an entrance to the Underworld.

ONETOR Priest of Idaean Zeus. Father of Laogonus.

OPHELESTES A Trojan killed in the Trojan War by Achilles.

OPHELTES Son of Lycurgus and Amphithea or Eurydice. He was nursed by Hypsipyle. After being killed by a snake, he was buried under the name of Archemorus (start of doom) by the Seven against Thebes. The Nemean Games were founded in his honour.

OPHELTIUS A Greek killed in the Trojan War by Hector.

OPHION A Titan. An ancient god who, together with his wife, Eurynome, ruled Olympus until deposed and thrown into Oceanus or Tartarus by Cronos and Rhea.

OPIS (Upis) An attendant of Artemis,

though some call Opis an epithet of Artemis herself.

OPITES A Greek killed in the Trojan War by Hector.

OPS (Rhea) Roman harvest goddess of plenty. The wife of Saturn. Worshipped with Consus. Mother of Eurypylus by Evaemon. Festival dates: 25 August (Opiconsivia); 19 December (Opalia). Sacrificial date: 23 August (Volcanalia).

OPS Father of Eurycleia.

OPUS Son of Zeus and Protogeneia. Brother of Aethlius.

ORACLE AT DELPHI The most famous oracle of Apollo, it foretold the future. The Omphalus was here.

ORACLES Ancient places where gods and goddesses answered questions and foretold the future. There were twenty-five in Boeotia and another twenty-five in the Peloponnessus. The most famous Greek Oracle was at Delphi. Other Oracles of Apollo were at Delos and Tenedos and Abae in Phocis, Ptoon (destroyed by Alexander the Great), and at Ismenus, south of Thebes. The most famous oracle of Zeus was at Dodona and he had another at Olympia. Amphiarus and Trophonius had secondary oracles as deified seers, and there were also written oracles.

ORCHAMUS King of Persia. A descendant of Belus. Married Eurynome. Father of Leucothoe, whom he buried alive after her love affair with Helios.

ORCHARDS, Roman god of Vertumnus.

ORCHARDS, Roman goddess of Feronia.

ORCHOMENUS (1) Ancient city of

Boeotia, capital of the kingdom of the Minyans. Originally called Andreis. (2) Eponym of the Boeotian city. Father or son of Minyas. (3) Ancient city of Arcadia, north of Mantinea. (4) Eponym of the Arcadian city. Son of Lycaon. (5) Father of Elara.

ORCHOMENUS, kings of Boeotian Athamas (1st), followed by Andreus, Eteocles, Halmus, Phlegyas, Chryses, Minyas and Orchomenus. Later, Clymenus was followed by Ascalaphus and Ialmenus, kings at the time of the Trojan War, to which the region sent thirty ships.

ORCUS (Pluto, Hades) Also called Dis Pater, was the father of Fraus.

ORDER, Greek goddess of Eunomia.

OREADS Mountain nymphs. Attendants of Artemis on her hunts.

OREITHYIA A Nereid. One of the fifty daughters of Nereus and Doris.

OREITHYIA Daughter of Erechtheus and Praxithea. Sister of Cecrops, Creusa, Cthonia, Eupalamus, Orneus, Protogeneia, Metion, Thespius, Pandorus and Procris. Carried off and raped by Boreas. Mother of Calais, Chione, Cleopatra, Haemus and Zetes.

ORESTES King of Argos, Arcadia, Mycenae and Sparta. Son of Agamemnon and Clytemnestra. Brother of Chrysothemis, Electra and Iphigeneia. Father of Tisamenus by Hermione.

Raised as a child by an old servant and taught by his uncle, Strophius, he supposedly grew to a height of three metres and lived until he was ninety. He and Pylades killed his mother and her lover after these two had murdered his father. Orestes was saved from the same fate because Electra sent him to the court of

Strophius, father of Pylades. His matricide drove him mad but he was later cured after being purged of his guilt on the Areopagus. Recovered his father's kingdom by slaying Neoptolemus and marrying Hermione, daughter of Menelaus. Then lived in peace and security until his death. The last major Greek mythological character.

ORESTES Son of Achelous and Perimele. Brother of Hippodamas.

ORGIA Bacchant festivals or orgies.

ORION The hunter. Son of Poseidon or Hyrieus and Euryale. Married Side. Father of the Coronides, Menippe and Metioche. Father of Menodice. Side died young, and Orion attempted to rape Merope, daughter of Oenopion, who blinded him. Hephaestus gave him a servant, Cedalion, as a guide and his eyesight was restored when Cedalion carried him from Lemnos to the sun and Orion turned his face towards its light. With his eyesight returned, Orion hunted with Artemis and had an affair with her maid, Uris. When Eos fell in love with Orion and carried him off to Ortygia, Artemis may have killed him in a jealous rage, though some say that he was killed by a scorpion. The Pleiades were turned to stars to avoid Orion and after his death he became the brightest constellation in the sky, accompanied by his faithful dog, Sirius.

ORMENUS (1) Possibly the father of Amyntor, (alternatively Zeus). (2) The father of Ctesius. King of the island of Syria. (3) One of the Lapithes. Killed by Polypoetes.

ORNEUS Son of Erechtheus, king of Athens and Praxithea. Brother of Cecrops, Chthonia, Creusa, Eupalamus, Metion, Pandorus, Oreithyia, Procris, Protogeneia and Thespius. Father of Peteus and grandfather of Menestheus.

ORNYTION Son of Sisyphus and

Merope. Brother of Halmus, Glaucus and Thersander. Father of Phocus and Thoas.

ORNYTUS King of Phocis. Father of Naubolus.

ORPHE Daughter of Dion and Iphitea. Sister of Carya and Lyco. She had the power of prophecy.

ORPHEUS Son of Apollo and Calliope, or of Oeagrus and Cleio or Polyhymnia. Some call Aphrodite his mother. Married Eurydice.

This Thracian minstrel played so sweetly on a lyre given him by Apollo that everything and everyone stopped to listen to him. An Argonaut, he saved his companions many times by his musical talents. When his wife died of a snake bite, he even persuaded Hades and Persephone to allow him to return from the Underworld with his wife. They made it a condition that he should not glance back at her while doing so, but he forgot ¬nd his wife was lost to him for ever. He was killed either by a thunderbolt from Zeus or by the Bacchantes tearing him limb from limb. The Muses buried his remains at the foot of Mt Olympus.

ORPHNE Possibly the wife of Acheron, if so, mother of Ascalaphus.

ORSEDICE Daughter of Cinyras. Sister of Braesia, Laogore and Mygdalion. After a love affair, she emigrated from Cyprus to Egypt.

ORSEIS (Ortheis) A nymph. Wife of Hellen. Mother ·of Aeolus, Dorus and Xuthus.

ORSILOCHUS Son of the river god Alpheius.

ORSINOME Daughter of Eurynomus. Married Lapithus. Mother of Periphas and Phorbas.

ORTHEIS *See* Orseis.

ORTHUS (Orthrus) The two-headed dog of Eurytion, and offspring of Typhon and Echidna. Brother of Cerberus, Chimaera, the Crommyonian Sow, Caucasian Eagle, Hydra, Vultures, the Nemean lion and the Sphinx. He guarded the cattle of Geryon which Heracles captured as his tenth labour, killing Orthus in the process.

ORUS First king of Oraea (Troezen). Father of Leis, the wife of Althepus, his successor to the throne.

ORUS A Greek killed in the Trojan War by Hector.

ORTYGIA Original name of the island of Delos.

Orpheus

OSIRIS   Egyptian god of the Underworld. In Greek mythology, son of Zeus and Niobe. Brother of Argus, Pelasgus and Typhon. Married Isis. Father of Horus. Murdered by Typhon. Epithet: Serapis.

OSPREY   *See* Nisus.

OSSA   Mountain of eastern Thessaly, 1920 metres high, near Mt Pelion, separated from Mt Olympus by the vale of Tempe. Ephialtes and Otus piled both mountains on top of Olympus to try and reach the gods.

OTHRYADES   Sole Spartan survivor of a battle between three hundred Argives and three hundred Spartans. Alcenor and Chromius were the two surviving Argives.

OTHRYONEUS of Cabesus   A Trojan killed by Idomeneus after he had paid for the hand of Cassandra.

OTHRYS   (1) Thessalian mountain stronghold of the Titans and Centaurs. Possibly the same as Ossa. (2) Father of Panthous, a Trojan elder.

OTRERA   An Amazon queen. The mother of Antiope (Melanippe), Hippolyte and Penthesileia by her husband, Ares.

OTREUS   King of Phrygia. Ally of Priam in his fight with the Amazons.

OTRYNTEUS   Father of Iphition by a Naiad. A pillager of towns.

OTUS   Twin son of Poseidon or Aloeus and Iphimedeia. Brother of Ephialtes, the twins being called the Aloeidae (qv). He and his brother tried to attack the gods by piling Mts Ossa and Pelion on Mt Olympus. He was the first to worship the three Muses at the foot of Mt Helicon. Was killed either by his brother or by Apollo. He was punished in Hades by being tied to a pole with snakes and a screech-owl sitting on top of the pole.

OWL   *See* Ascalaphus, Harpalyce, Nyctimene.

OXEN, protector of   Bubona (Epona).

OXYLUS   King of Elis. Son of Andraemon or Haemon. Possibly brother of Thermius and Iphitus. Father of Laias.

   He won his kingdom from Dius when his Aetolian slinger, Pyraechmes, defeated Dius' champion, Degmenus, an Eleian archer, in single combat.

OXYLUS   Son of Ares and Protogeneia.

P

PACTOLUS Lydian river rising on Mt Tmolus and flowing into the Hermus. Never more than three metres wide, or thirty centimetres deep. The sands of this river contained gold after Midas bathed in the water, and much of Croesus' wealth came from this gold.

PAEAN The healing god. Epithet of other gods: Apollo, Asclepius and Thanatos.

PAEON (1) Another name for Asclepius, son of Apollo. (2) Son of Endymion and a Naiad, or his mother may have been Hyperippe, Iphianassa or Selene. Brother of Aetolus, Epeius and Eurycyda. When his father held a foot-race to determine his successor as king of Elis, Epeius won and Paeon was exiled to Macedonia. (3) Son of Nestor and Eurydice. Brother of Antilochus, Peisistratus, Polycaste, Thrasymedes, Aretus, Echephron, Perseus and Stratius. (4) Possibly a son of Poseidon and Helle. Brother of Edonus. (5) Father of Agastrophus.

PAEONAEUS One of the Dactyli. Son of Anchiale or Rhea. Brother of Epimedes, Heracles, Iasus, Idas and five sisters.

PAGASAE Thessalian seaport where the *Argo* was built.

PALAECHTHON Son of Gaea. Father of Pelasgus, king of Argos.

PALAEMON An Argonaut. Lame son of Hephaestus and the wife of Lernus, but he claimed his father was either Aetolus or Lernus.

PALAEMON (Portunus) Son of Athamas and Ino. Brother of Learchus. Born Melicertes, but deified after his death. The Isthmian Games were founded in his honour.

PALAMEDES Son of Nauplius and Clymene or Philyra. Brother of Nausimedon and Oeax.

Inventor of certain coinage, numbers, alphabet letters and dice. Was sent to fetch Odysseus, who was pretending to be mad in order to avoid going to the Trojan War. Palamedes saw through his ruse, and thus began an enmity that led ultimately to his death, by stoning, after Odysseus hid stolen Trojan gold in Palamedes' tent.

PALATINE The central and highest of the seven hills of Rome, on which Romulus built the original city.

PALES Roman god or goddess of cattle, flocks, pastures and shepherds. Festival date: 21 April (Parilia).

PALICI Sicilian gods, twin sons of Zeus and Thalia, born out of the bowels of the earth. Some call their parents Hephaestus and Aetna. Their shrine was a sanctuary for slaves.

PALINURUS Helmsman of the flagship of Aeneas. Either he drowned off the coast of Italy, after falling asleep and tumbling off his ship; or he survived by swimming for four days to the Italian shore, where he was murdered by the natives. Was refused access to the Underworld because he had not been given a proper burial, but Aeneas later rectified this.

PALLADIUM An ancient wooden image of Athena (Pallas) which fell from heaven and was preserved at Troy as a sacred object that protected the city. Others say it was made of metal, so it may have been a meteorite. Odysseus and Diomedes stole it to secure the fall of Troy, but Aeneas rescued it and took it to Italy to the temple of Vesta.

PALLANTIA Daughter of Evander and Deidameia. Sister of Pallas, Roma and Sarpedon II. Mother of another Pallas by

Heracles (Hercules). Eponym of the Palatine hill.

PALLANTIDS The fifty sons of Pallas, son of Pandion. They were all killed by Theseus.

PALLAS (1) Epithet of Athena. She received the name after she had killed a giant of the same name, or because of the way she brandishes her spear. (2) Son of Crius and Eurybia. Titan brother of Astraeus and Perses. Married Styx, daughter of Oceanus and Tethys. Father of Bia, Kratos, Nike and Zelos. (3) Son of Evander and Deidameia. Brother of Pallantia, Roma and Sarpedon. Founder of Pallanteum in Italy. Ally of Aeneas. Killed by Turnus. (4) Son of Heracles and Pallantia. Eponym of Palatine hill (cf his mother). (5) Son of Lycaon and Cyllene. Brother of Nyctimus and Callisto. Father of Chryse. Founder of Pallanteum in Arcadia. (6) Son of Megamedes. Possibly father of Selene, Helios and Eos. (7) Youngest son of Pandion and Pylia. Also called Achaea. Brother of Nisus, Aegeus and Lycus. Claimant to the throne of Athens. Father of fifty sons, all of whom were killed by Theseus. (8) Daughter of Triton. Accidentally killed by her friend, Athena. (9) Son of Uranus and Gaea. A giant, he was flayed alive by Athena in the war of the gods and Giants. His skin was used in an aegis.

PALLAS ATHENA *See* Pallas (1).

PALLENE A peninsula of the Aegean Sea. Home of Alcyoneus and sometime home of Proteus.

PALLOR (Terror) Son and attendant of Ares and Aphrodite. Brother of Anteros, Deimos, Enyo, Eros, Harmonia and Phobos.

PAMMON Bastard son of Priam.

PAMPHYLUS Son of Aegimius. Brother of Dymas. Killed by the Dorians in their invasion of the Peloponnesus.

PAN (Faunus) An Arcadian shepherd-god. Son of Hermes and Dryope or Penelope, or of Zeus and Hybris (Thymbris). Other sources cite other parents. A lecher, with goat's legs and horns, he pursued many nymphs, including Echo, Pithys and Syrinx – though not always successfully. He was born on Mt Cyllene in Arcadia and was raised by nymphs after his mother abandoned him. Hermes took him into Olympus where all the gods were pleased with him. Father of Acis and Crotus by Eupheme. Possibly father of Aex and possibly father or brother of Silenus.

A patron of beekeepers, fishermen, hunters and shepherds, and a god of flocks, forests and wild life. Invented the syrinx, a seven-reeded flute, and used it to defeat Apollo in a musical contest. The fir tree was sacred to him, and he had temples in Athens, Sicyon and Troezen, as well as in many places throughout Arcadia. A favourite pastime of his was to frighten unwary travellers.

PANACEA (all-healing) Goddess of health. Daughter of Asclepius and Epione. Sister of Acesis, Aegle, Hygieia, Iaso, Janiscus, Machaon and Podalirius.

PANATHENAEA The most famous Attican festival, held in honour of Athena. Some writers claim that the Lesser Panathenaea were held annually and the Greater Panathenaea were held four-yearly.

PANCRATIS Daughter of Aloeus and Iphimedeia. Abducted with her mother by Thracian pirates, she was rescued by her half-brothers, the Aloedae. Married Agassamenus.

PANDAREUS King of Miletus in Crete. Son of Merops and an Oread nymph. Married Harmothoe. Father of Aedon, Cleothera (Cameiro) and Merope (Clytie). After he stole a golden dog, made by Hephaestus, from a shrine of Zeus, both he and his wife were killed by Zeus and buried under Mt Sipylus.

PANDARUS Son of Lycaon of Zeleia. Brother of Eurytion. Leader of the Zeleian forces at Troy. The second-best Trojan archer after Paris, Apollo having taught him. Killed by Diomedes.

PANDIA Daughter of Zeus and Selene.

PANDION King of Athens. Son of Erichthonius and Praxithea. Possibly brother of Parthenius (cf next entry). Married Zeuxippe, his mother's sister. Father of Philomela, Procne and twin sons, Butes and Erechtheus. His ally in his boundary war with Labdacus was Tereus. Having reigned for forty years, he died of sorrow after his daughters became birds.

PANDION King of Megara and Athens. Son of Cecrops and Metiadusa. Had three sisters. Great-grandson of the other Pandion. Married Pylia, daughter of Pylas, king of Megara, whom he succeeded to the throne. Was exiled from Athens by the sons of Metion after a brief rule. Father of Aegeus, Cecrops, Lycus, Nisus and Pallas, though some authors call Aegeus his adopted son. Either he or his namesake was the brother of Parthenius.

PANDION Son of Phineus and Cleopatra. Brother of Plexippus, and half-brother of Mariandynus and Thynius.

PANDOCUS Trojan ally wounded in the Trojan War by Greater Ajax.

PANDORA The first mortal woman, fashioned from clay by Hephaestus, who intended that by her charms she should bring misery on the human race. Aphrodite gave her beauty and the art of healing; Apollo, the ability to sing; Athena, rich ornaments and skills in woman's work; the Graces, captivating charm; Hermes, eloquence; and Zeus gave her a beautiful box which he forbade her to open. Pandora was offered as a wife to Prometheus, as his punishment for stealing the fire of Ares, but he refused her. She married his brother Epimetheus instead and was the mother of Pyrrha. When she opened the box given by Zeus, the plagues of mankind escaped and all that remained in the box was Elpis (hope).

PANDORA Daughter of Deucalion and Pyrrha. Sister of Amphictyon, Hellen, Protogeneia and Thyia. Mother of Graecus by Zeus.

PANDORUS Son of Erechtheus and Praxithea. Brother of Cecrops, Creusa, Cthonia, Metion, Oreithyia, Procris, Protogeneia and Thespius.

PANDROSOS (the bedewed) Daughter of Acteus or of Cecrops and Agraulos. Sister of Agraulos, Erysichthon and Herse. *See* Agraulos.

PANHELLENIC GAMES *See* Isthmian, Olympic, Nemean and Pythian Games.

PANHELLENIUS Epithet of Zeus, god of all Greeks.

PANIC Son of Ares. Brother of Eros, Deimos, Pallor and Phobos.

PANOPAEUS Son of Phocus. Brother of Naubolus and twin brother of Crisus, whom he hated all his life and fought even in the womb. Married Neaera. Father of Epeius and Aegle, wife of Theseus. Present on the Calydonian Boar Hunt.

PANOPE A Nereid. Daughter of Nereus and Doris. Greatest of the fifty daughters (called Nereids), she was invoked by sailors during storms.

PANTHEON Circular Roman temple of the gods, built by Agrippa in 27 BC. Later converted into a Christian church.

PANTHIA (Panthea) Mother of Eumaeus by Ctesius.

PANTHOUS Priest of Apollo at Troy. Son of Othrys. Married Phrontis. Father of Euphorbus, Hyperenor and Polydamas.

Counsellor of Priam. Killed in the Trojan War

PAPHIA Epithet of Aphrodite, derived from her temple at Paphos.

PAPHOS (1) Daughter of Pygmalion, king of Cyprus, and Galatea. (2) City on the western side of Cyprus, near which (1 km away) Aphrodite arose from the foam of the sea.

PAPHUS Possibly the father of Cinyras.

PARAEBUS The loyal vassal of Phineus who, when cursed by a Hamadryad, grew steadily poorer, the harder he worked.

PARCA (Morta) Roman goddess of childbirth. Companion of Nona and Decima. Also called Morta, in case mother and baby die during childbirth. One of the Parcae (Fates).

PARCAE *See* Fates.

PARIAS Son of Philomelus. Founder of Parion in Mysia.

PARIS (Alexander) Second son of Priam and Hecuba. Brother of Aesacus, Cassandra, Creusa, Deiphobus, Hector, Helenus, Polyxena and Troilus. Married Oenone. Father of Corythus and Daphnis.

Aesacus prophesied that Paris would cause the downfall of Troy, and Priam forced Agelaus, his chief herdsman, to expose him on Mt Ida immediately after birth. A she-bear suckled him for five days, then Agelaus rescued him, raising him as his own son and a shepherd.

At the Judgement of Paris, he awarded the Golden Apple to Aphrodite, as the most beautiful of the three contesting goddesses, and claimed his prize by abducting Helen to Troy. When he refused to return her, the Greeks marched against Troy, so beginning the Trojan War.

Paris, the slayer of Achilles, offered to fight Menelaus in single combat for Helen but took flight by a stratagem, was wounded

by a poisoned arrow from Philoctetes and returned to his wife (whom he had deserted for Helen) to be cured. When she refused to heal him, he returned to Troy to die.

PARNASSUS Son of Poseidon and Cleodora. Eponym of the mountain.

PARNASSUS, Mount Mountain of Phocis, the highest peak being almost 2500 metres above sea level. On its southern slope was Delphi, seat of the most renowned of Apollo's oracles. The famous fountain of Castalia was also there. The mountain was sacred to the Muses and to Apollo and Dionysus, though the latter claimed only the peaks. The ark of Deucalion came to rest on the slopes when the Flood finally subsided.

PARTHAON Same as Porthaon, king of Calydon.

PARTHENIA Epithet of Athena, Artemis and Hestia – the virgin goddesses.

PARTHENIUS Son of Erichthonius and Praxithea. Brother of Pandion. Blinded by Phineus.

PARTHENIUS (1) Artemis' favourite river, where she often bathed. (2) The mountain where Atalanta was exposed. Mountain of eastern Arcadia, where many tortoises lived. Auge and Telephus were born there and Parthenopaeus and Telephus were exposed on its slopes.

PARTHENON Doric temple of Athena on the Acropolis at Athens. Built by Ictinus and Callicrates under the supervision of Phidias.

PARTHENOPAEUS (1) Son of Ares, Hippomenes, Melanion or Meleager, and Atalanta. Fostered by Corythus. Father of Promachus and Tlesimenes by Clymene. One of the Seven against Thebes, was killed by Amphidocus, Asphodocus or Periclymenus. (2) *See* Adrastus.

PARTHENOPE One of the Sirens.

Daughter of Achelous and Calliope, Melpomene or Terpsichore. Sister of Leucosia and Ligeia, and perhaps others. Drowned herself after failing to lure Odysseus to his death.

PARTHENOPE (1) Daughter of Ancaeus and Samia. Had four brothers. (2) Daughter of Stymphalus. Sister of Agamedes and Gortys. Mother of Lycomedes by Apollo.

PARTHENOS Epithet of Athena as senior of the three Virgin Goddesses. The other two were Artemis and Hestia.

PARTRIDGE *See* Perdix (Talus).

PASIPHAE Daughter of Helios and Perseis (Perse). Sister of Aeetes, Circe and Perses. Married Minos. Mother of Acacallis, Androgeus, Ariadne, Catreus, Deucalion, Euryale, Glaucus, Lycastus, Phaedra and Xenodice.

Daedalus built a cow body for her and in this disguise she mated with a bull to mother the Minotaur. She bewitched Minos so that all his lovers died after sleeping with him.

PASITHEA (1) One of the Charites (Graces). Daughter of Zeus and Eurynome. Sister of Aglaea, Euphrosyne and Thalia, but possibly eponym for Aegle (Aeglaia). Married Hypnos. Mother of Morpheus. (2) Daughter of Nereus and Doris. One of fifty sisters, called the Nereids. (3) Also called Praxithea (qv). Daughter of Phrasimus and Diogeneia. Sister of Zeuxippe.

PASSALUS One of the Cercopes. Son of Oceanus and Theia. Brother of Acmon. A two-tailed thievish gnome. Both were turned to stone or into apes by Zeus.

PASSION, Greek god of Anteros.

PAST, Roman goddess of the Postverta, but at times she shared this function with Antevorta.

PASTURES, Roman god or goddess of Pales.

PATRAE Fortified seaport town on the eastern coast of the Gulf of Patrae, in Achaea. Named after Patreus, the city of Aroe was one of its early constituent settlements. Eumolus was the first king.

PATREUS Spartan son of Preugenes. Founder of Patrae. Ally of Tisamenus in his invasion of Ionia.

PATROCLUS Son of Menoetius and Periopis or Sthenele. Killed Clisonymus in a quarrel over a game of dice. Later became a close friend of Achilles, and the two fought together as leaders of the Myrmidons in the Trojan War. The slayer of Sarpedon, was killed by Hector after being wounded by Euphorbus, who was aided by Apollo. Twelve nobles were sacrificed on his funeral pyre, and later his bones were mixed with those of Achilles, both heroes becoming immortalised and living on White Island.

PATROCLUS, funeral games of First event: a chariot race. The prizes: first, a slave woman and a 12.5-litre tripod; second, a pregnant mare; third, a two-litre cauldron; fourth, two talents of gold; fifth, a two-handled pan. The contestants: Diomedes (the winner), Antilochus (second), Menelaus (third), Meriones (fourth), and Eumelus who did not finish. The fifth prize was awarded to Nestor.

Second event: boxing. Epeius defeated Euryalus, the winner receiving a mule and the loser a two-handled mug.

Third event: wrestling. Greater Ajax fought Odysseus, the event finishing in stalemate, and the two prizes, a three-legged cauldron worth twelve oxen and a domestic slave worth four oxen, being shared.

Fourth event: a foot race. The prizes: first, a 3.5-litre silver mixing bowl of chased silver; second, a well-fattened ox; third, a half-talent of gold. The contestants: Odysseus (the winner), Lesser Ajax (second) and Antilochus (third), his prize being doubled by Achilles.

Fifth event: fighting. Diomedes defeated Greater Ajax for the arms of Patroclus.

Sixth event: discus throwing. The prize was a quoit of pig-iron and the contestants were Polypoetes (winner), Greater Ajax (second), Leonteus (third) and Epeius (fourth).

Seventh event: archery. The prizes were ten double-headed axes and ten single-headed axes. Meriones defeated Teucer.

Eighth event: javelin. The prizes: first, an unused floral-patterned cauldron worth one ox; second, a far-shadowing spear. The contestants were Agamemnon and Meriones, but the first prize was awarded to Agamemnon without a contest.

PAVOR (Phobos) Son and attendant of Mars.

PAX (Irene) Roman goddess of peace. Festival date: 3 January.

PEACE, goddesses of Greek: Irene (Eirene). Roman: Concordia, Pax, Salus.

PEACOCK The sacred bird of Hera. The hundred eyes of Argus Panoptes were set in its tail.

PEDAEUS Son of Antenor. Half-brother of Acamas, Agenor, Archelous, Coon, Crino, Demoleon, Glaucus, Helicaon, Iphidamas, Laocoon, Laodamas, Lycaon, Polydamas and Polybus. Raised by his step-mother, Theano.

PEDIAS Spartan wife of Cranaus and mother of Attis and Cranae.

PEGAE A nymph who fell in love with Hylas and later drowned him.

PEGASUS Winged horse, offspring of Poseidon and Medusa. He rose from his mother's blood after Perseus cut off her head. Brother of Chrysaor.

Pegasus

179

The divine horse of Bellerophon, in his fight with the Chimaera, carried Zeus' thunderbolts, and when he struck the slopes of Mt Helicon with his hoof, the fountain Hippocrene burst forth. The divine horse of the Muses.

PEIRAS Son of Argus and Evadne. Brother of Criasus, Ecbasus and Epidaurus.

PEIRAS Possibly the father of Echidna by Styx.

PEIRENE (1) Daughter of the river god, Achelous. Nymph of the spring of the same name which sprang forth either when Pegasus struck his hoof on the ground at Corinth, or from the tears of Peirene grieving for her son. The fountain was sacred to the nine Muses. Sister of Callirrhoe and Castalia. Mother of Cenchrias and Leches. (2) Daughter of Oebalus and Gorgophone. Sister or half-sister of Arene, Hippocoon, Icarius, Leucippus, Aphareus and Tyndareus.

PEIRITHOUS King of the Lapiths. Son of Ixion or Zeus and Dia. Half-brother of the Centaurs. Married Hippodameia. Father of Polypoetes. Friend of Theseus. At his wedding, a terrible battle between Centaurs and Lapiths broke out.
Took part in the Calydonian Boar Hunt. Became a perpetual prisoner of Hades for trying to abduct Persephone.

PEISANDER (1) Son of Antimachus. Brother of Hippolochus and Hippomachus. Murdered by the Greeks in the Trojan War. (2) Son of Maemalus. One of the lieutenants of Achilles.

PEISENOR (1) Ancestor of Eurycleia, nurse of Odysseus. (2) Father of Cleitus.

PEISIDICE Daughter of Aeolus and Enarete. Had seven brothers: Athamas, Cretheus, Deion, Macareus, Perieres, Salmoneus and Sisyphus; and six sisters: Alcyone, Arne, Calyce, Canace, Perimele and Tanagra. Married Myrmidon. Mother of Actor, Antiphus and Eupolemeia.

PEISIDICE Daughter of Nestor and Anaxibia or Eurydice. Sister of Antilochus, Aretus, Echephron, Peisistratus, Perseus, Polycaste, Stratius and Thrasymedes.

PEISINOE One of the Sirens. Daughter of Achelous and Calliope, Melpomene, Sterope or Terpsichore. Sister of Aglaopheme, Molpe and Thelexiepeia, and perhaps of others. *See* Sirens.

PEISISTRATUS Son of Nestor and Eurydice or Anaxibia. Brother of Antilochus, Paeon, Polycaste, Aretus, Echephron, Perseus, Thrasymedes and Peisidice. Accompanied Telemachus to Sparta.

PEISUS Son of Aphareus and Arene. Brother of Idas and Lynceus.

PEITHO Greek goddess of persuasion. Daughter of Hermes and Aphrodite. Sister of Hermaphroditus. Possibly married to Phoroneus though this may be a different Peitho. If so, the mother of Car and Niobe. An attendant of Eros. Known to the Romans as Suada.

PELAGIA Epithet of Aphrodite.

PELAGON Son of the river god, Asopus, and Metope. Brother of Aegina, Antiope, Cleone, Chalcis, Ismene, Pelasgus, Plataea, Corcyra, Ismenus, Metope, Salamis, Thebe and ten others.

PELASGUS First king of Arcadia. Son of Zeus and Niobe or Gaea. Brother of Argus, Isis, Osiris and Typhon. Married Meliboea, an Oceanid. Later married Cyllene. Father of Lycaon. Inventor of huts and sheepskin coats. Lycaon succeeded him to the throne.

PELASGUS (1) Son of Larissa and Poseidon. Brother of Achaeus and Phthius. Eponym of Pelasgiotis in Thessaly. (2) Son of Triopas and Sois. Brother of Agenor, Iasus and Xanthus. Father of Larissa. He built a temple of Demeter at Argos, then fortified the city and renamed it Larissa.

(3) Son of Asopus and Metope. Brother of Aegina, Antiope, Cleone, Chalcis, Corcyra, Ismene, Ismenus, Metope, Pelagon, Plataea, Salamis, Thebe and ten others. (4) Son of Palaechthon. (5) Father of Temenus.

PELEGON A Trojan killed in the War by Achilles.

PELEUS King of the Myrmidons and an Argonaut. Son of Aeacus and Endeis. Brother of Telamon, half-brother of Phocus in whose murder he took part, but Actor purified him of this murder. May have married Polymela, daughter of Actor, king of Phthia, though most say he married Antigone, daughter of Actor. Became by her father of Polydora or Polymela. After her death he married Thetis, daughter of Nereus and Doris, the only mortal–goddess marriage. Father of Achilles (Ligyron).

Present on the Calydonian Boar Hunt, he accidentally killed his nephew, Eurytion, son of Irus. Astydameia, wife of Acastus, fell in love with him, to no avail. She then made false accusations against him to Polymela who hanged herself, and to Acastus who exposed Peleus on Mt Pelion. He owned a sword given to him by Hephaestus. Eris rolled the Golden Apple at his marriage to Thetis. Possibly the murderer of Acastus. Peleus outlived both Achilles and Achilles' son, Neoptolemus.

PELIADES The daughters of Pelias.

PELIAS King of Iolcus. Twin son of Poseidon and Tyro. Brother of Neleus. Raised by a horse-keeper after their mother exposed the twins at birth, he bore a mark on his face where a horse had kicked him. Married Anaxibia. Father of Acastus, Alcestis, Hippothoe, Pelopia and Pisidice, though some claim their mother to be Phylomache. Possibly father to several others. Seized the throne from Neleus, preventing Aeson from gaining the throne by natural succession. Sending Jason in search of the Golden Fleece, he murdered Aeson and Promachus, then Sidero, step-mother of Tyro, for mistreating their mother. His four daughters unwittingly murdered him, following Medea's instructions. Acastus succeeded to the throne.

PELIDES Epithet of Achilles, son of Peleus.

PELION, Mount Wooded mountain range of Central Magnesia in Thessaly. Highest peak 1630 metres. Wood from it was used the build the *Argo*. Ephialtes and Otus piled the mountain between Olympus and Ossa in order to try to reach the gods. Cheiron lived in a cave there.

PELOPIA (1) Daughter of Pelias and Anaxibia or Phylomache. Sister of Acastus, Alcestis, Hippothoe and Pisidice. Possibly mother of Cycnus by Ares. (2) Daughter of Thyestes and a Naiad. Mother of Aegisthus by her father. Some say she married Atreus.

PELOPONNESUS Peninsula of southern Greece, south of the Isthmus of Corinth, now called Morea. Sparta and Argos were here.

PELOPS King of Lydia and Pisa in Elis. Son of Tantalus and Dione. Brother of Broteas and Niobe. Father of Chrysippus by Astyoche or Axioche. With the aid of Myrtilus, he became the fourteenth (but first successful) suitor of Hippodameia, whom he married. Father of Alcathous, Astydameia, Atreus, Chrysippus (a bastard), Copreus, Lysidice, Nicippe, Pittheus, Thyestes, Troezen and others. According to the Eleians, father of Epidaurus. He was killed as a child by his father and served as a meal to the gods, who perceived this disgusting act immediately and only Demeter ate part of one of his shoulders. Clotho, one of the Moirae, brought him back to life after Zeus or Hermes had fetched him from the Underworld. His mutilated shoulder was replaced with one of ivory, and Poseidon gave him a golden chariot, driven by immortal winged horses. His charioteer was called Sphaerus. Some say he instituted the Olympic Games, being much honoured in Olympia.

PELOPS (1) One of the twelve children, six boys and six girls, of Amphion and Niobe. (2) Son of Agamemnon and Cassandra. Brother of Teledamus. (3) Possibly father of Sceiron.

PELORUS One of the sown-men (Sparti). Brother of Chthonius, Echion, Hyperenor and Udaeus.

PENATES (Lares) Roman household gods. Every home had penates, which were honoured by families at mealtimes as gods of storerooms. The state also had penates.

PENEIUS (Peneus) Thessalian river god. Son of Oceanus and Tethys. Father of Hypseus by Creusa. Possibly father of Daphne and perhaps Metope and the nymphs of Thessaly (more likely to have been their great-grandfather). Father of Stilbe and Andreus. Before temples were built, images of Peneius were placed on river bridges.

PENELAUS After Thersander's death in the Trojan War, Penelaus served, until his own death, as regent for the infant Tisamenus.

PENELAUS An Argonaut. Son of Hippalcimus and Asterope. As a suitor of Helen, he took fifty ships from Boeotia to the Trojan War, together with Leitus. Killed by Eurypylus.

PENELOPE Daughter of Icarius and Periboea (Eriboea), though some name her mother as either Asterodia, Dorodoche or Mede. Sister of Iphthime, Perileus and four others. Married Odysseus. Mother of Telemachus, and of a second child, Ptoliporthes (Arcesilaus) after her husband's return from his twenty-year absence. According to one tradition, she was the mother of Pan by Hermes. Circe made her immortal. Mother of Italus by Telegonus.

PENELOPE, suitors of During Odysseus' twenty-year absence, Penelope had many suitors for her hand. She avoided making a decision in favour of any, saying she first had to finish making a shroud. But each night she unravelled the work she had completed that day. There were 108, or even 112, suitors including Agelaus, Amphinomus, Antinous. Amphimedon, Ctesippus, Elatus, Eupeithes, Eurydamas, Leiodes and Polybus. Phemius the bard was forced to serve the suitors; Medon was their herald and Arnaeus (Irus) their errand boy. Most of the suitors were killed by Odysseus on his return.

PENEUS (Peneius) Thessalian river god. *See* Peneius.

PENTHESILEIA An Amazon queen. Daughter of Ares and Otrera. Sister of Antiope (Melanippe) and Hippolyte. Possibly mother of Caistrus by Achilles. After she accidentally killed an ally or perhaps Hippolyte, Priam purified her and she became an ally of the Trojans in the War. Killed by Achilles.

PENTHEUS King of Thebes. Son of Echion and Agave. Succeeded his grandfather, Cadmus, to the throne. After he and Agave mocked Dionysus, Dionysus forced Agave and her sisters to tear Pentheus to pieces.

PENTHILUS Bastard son of Orestes and Erigone. Possibly brother of Tisamenus. Father of Damasias and Echelas.

PEPARETHUS Son of Dionysus and Ariadne. Brother of Ceramus, Phanus, Oenopion, Staphylus and Thoas.

PEPHREDO One of the Graiae. Daughter of Phorcys and Ceto. Sister of Deino and Enyo.

PEPLOPS Father of Corinthus.

PERDIX (Calus, Talus) An Athenian inventor. Son of Perdix, the sister of

Daedalus. Inventor of the saw and, possibly, the compass and potter's wheel. When Daedalus killed him through jealousy, Athena changed him into a partridge.

PERDIX Daughter of Eupalamus or Metion and Alcippe or Merope. Sister of Daedalus and Sicyon. Mother of Perdix the inventor.

PEREUS Son of Elatus and Laodice. Father of Neaera, wife of Aleus.

PERGAMUM (Pergamon) City of ancient Mysia, now called Bergama. Named after Pergamus. Originally called Teuthrania.

PERGAMUM Citadel of Troy.

PERGAMUS Youngest son of Neoptolemus and Andromache. Brother of Molossus and Pielus. A friend and ally of Grynus, he emigrated to Mysia, capturing the city of Teuthrania, renaming it Pergamon and killing the king, Areius.

PERIALCES Possibly a son of Bias and Pero.

PERIANDER Tyrant of Corinth 625–585 BC. One of the seven wise men of Greece. Others were Bias, Chilon, Cleobulus, Pittacus, Solon and Thales. He murdered the richest and wisest men of Corinth. He committed incest with his mother; murdered his wife, and exiled his son.

PERIBOEA (1) Daughter of Alcathous and Evaechme. Sister of Automedusa, Callipolis, Iphinoe and Ischepolis. Second wife of Telamon. Mother of Ajax. Went to Crete with Theseus as a sacrifice for the Minotaur. Minos fell in love with her, but she rejected him and returned to Greece. (2) The wife of Icarius. Mother of Iphthime, Penelope, Perileus and four other sons. Also called Asterodia, Dorodoche and Mede. (3) Also called Merope. The wife of Polybus. Foster-mother of Oedipus. (4)

Daughter of Hipponous. Second wife of Oenus. Mother of Olenias, Perimede and Tydeus. Seduced by Hippostratus, although she claimed it was Ares, and was exiled by her father. (5) Mother of Nausithous by Poseidon. (6) Eldest daughter of Acessamenus. Mother of Pelagon by Axius.

PERICLYMENE Daughter of Minyas. Sister of Alcithoe, Arsippe, Clymene and Leucippe. Married Pheres. Mother of Admetus, Lycurgus, Idomene and Periopis.

PERICLYMENUS (1) Son of Neleus and Chloris. Brother of Pero, Chromius, Nestor and nine others. He had the ability to change shape, and Heracles shot him after he had taken the shape of an eagle. One of the Argonauts. (2) Son of Poseidon and Chloris, daughter of Teiresias. A champion of Thebes against the Seven, he killed Parthenopaeus.

PERIERES King of Messenia. Son of Aeolus and Enarete. Brother of six boys: Athamas, Cretheus, Deion, Macareus, Salmoneus and Sisyphus; and seven sisters: Alcyone, Arne, Calyce, Canace, Peisidice, Perimele and Tanagra. Married Gorgophone, daughter of Perseus. Father of Aphareus, Borus, Halirrhothius, Icarius, Leucippus, Pisus and Tyndareus.

PERIERES Son of Cynortas. Brother of Oebalus.

PERIGUNE (Perigone) Daughter of Sinis. Mother of Melanippus by Theseus. Started the Asparagus cult.

PERILEUS (Perilaus) Son of Icarius and Periboea. Brother of Iphthime, Penelope, and four others.

PERIMEDE Sister of Amphitryon. Married Licymnius. Mother of Argeius, Melas and Oeonus.

PERIMEDE Daughter of Oeneus and Periboea. Sister of Olenias and Tydeus.

Married Phoenix. Mother of Astypalea and Europa.

PERIMEDES (1) A companion of Odysseus on his trip into the Underworld. (2) A Phocian chief. Father of Schedius.

PERIMELA (Perimele) Daughter of Amythaon. Married Antion. Mother of Ixion, though the father may have been Ares or Phlegyas.

PERIMELE (Perimede) Daughter of Aeolus and Enarete. Sister of seven boys: Athamas, Cretheus, Deion, Macareus, Perieres, Salmoneus and Sisyphus; and six girls: Alcyone, Arne, Calyce, Canace, Peisidice and Tanagra. Seduced by Achelous and gave birth to Hippodamas and Orestes as a result, so Aeolus threw her into the sea, where Poseidon changed her into an island.

PERIMELE Daughter of Admetus and Alcestis. Sister of Eumelus. Possibly mother of Magnes by Argus.

PERIOPIS Daughter of Pheres and Periclymene. Sister of Admetus, Idomene and Lycurgus. Either she or Sthenele was the mother of Patroclus by Menoetius.

PERIPHAS King of Thessaly. Son of Lapithus and Orsinome. Brother of Phorbas. Married Astyagyia. Father of eight sons including Antion.

PERIPHETES (1) Son of Copreus. Killed in the Trojan War by Hector or Teucer. (2) Son of Hephaestus or Poseidon or even Daedalus, and Anticleia. A lame Epidaurian outlaw, he carried a bronze or iron club which he used to kill travellers. Also called Corynetes. Killed by Theseus.

PERMESSUS A river god. Son of Oceanus and Tethys. Father of Aganippe.

PERO (Perone) Daughter of Neleus and Chloris. Sister of twelve boys, including Chromius, Nestor and Periclymenus. Had many suitors, and married Bias. Mother of Areius, Leodocus and Talaus, and possibly Perialces and Alphesiboea. Celebrated for her beauty.

PERSEIS (Perse) An Oceanid. Daughter of Oceanus and Tethys. Sister of Clymene, Eidyia, Electra, Doris, Meliboea, Metis, Pleione, Proteus, and many more, the rivers and the fountains. Married Helios. Mother of Aeetes, Circe, Pasiphae and Perses.

PERSEON Father of Agrianome, wife of Hodeodocus.

PERSEPHONE (Proserpine) Goddess of the Underworld. Daughter of Zeus and Demeter or Styx. Possibly mother of Iacchus.

Persephone

Abducted to the Underworld by Hades and forced to become his wife. Peirithous and Theseus tried to recover her, so great was Demeter's grief. Hades permitted her to return only if she had eaten nothing in the Underworld, but she had tasted pomegranate seeds, so was allowed to remain above ground only for four months (though some say six) of each year, her return marking the beginning of spring. Peirithous, however, found himself trapped in the Underworld.

Persephone was also known as Cora (Core, Kore), queen of Hades; Pherephatta, the grower of corn; and the Romans called her Proserpine or Libera. May have been the personification of spring. Sacred birds: pigeon and cock.

PERSEPTOLIS (Persepolis) Son of Telemachus and Polycaste or Nausicaa.

PERSES (1) Eldest son of Perseus and Andromeda. Brother of Alcaeus, Electryon, Gorgophone, Heleus, Mestor and Sthenelus. King of Ethiopia. Ancestor of the kings of Persia. (2) Titan son of Crius and Eurybia. Brother of Astraeus and Pallas. Married Asteria. Father of Hecate. (3) Son of Helios and Perseis (Perse). Brother of Aeetes, Circe and Pasiphae. Usurped the throne of Aeetes, king of Colchis, but was himself deposed by Aeetes' children. (4) Possibly father of Chariclo.

PERSEUS King of Mycenae and Tiryns. Son of Zeus (who took the form of a shower of gold) and Danae. Reared by Dictys the fisherman. After rescuing Andromeda from a rock to which she was chained, he married her and remained faithful to her. Father of Alcaeus, Electryon, Gorgophone, Heleus, Mestor, Perses and Sthenelus.

As an infant, was placed in a wooden chest and thrown in the sea by Acrisius, Danae's father, who feared the baby would grow up and cause his death, as prophesied. Rescued by Dictys. Later, he did accidentally kill Acrisius with a discus at the funeral games of the father of Tentamides of Larissa. Perseus killed Medusa, cutting off her head and placing it in the aegis of Athena. Turned Atlas to stone, and also Polydectes after rescuing Danae from him. Was probably killed by Megapenthes.

PERSEUS Son of Nestor and Eurydice or Anaxibia. Brother of Aretus, Antilochus, Echephron, Peisidice, Peisistratus, Polycaste, Stratius and Thrasymedes.

PERSUASION, goddess of Greek: Peitho. Roman: Suada.

PETASUS The winged cap of Hermes.

PETEUS Son of Orneus. Father of Menestheus. A half-human monster.

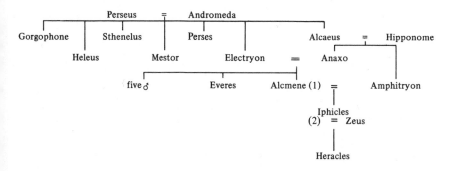

PETREL *See* Scylla.

PEUCETIUS Son of Lycaon. Brother of Daunus and Iapyx.

PHAEA Daughter of Echidna and Typhon. She was either the Crommyonian Sow or its owner. If the former, then possibly the mother of the Calydonian Boar.

PHAEACIA (Corcyra) An Ionian island where the men were ship-builders and expert seamen, and the women skilled weavers. Also called Scherie or Drepane, now called Corfu. Among its kings were Alcinous and Nausithous. It was Alcinous and his daughter, Nausicaa, who cared for Odysseus after his shipwreck on the island.

PHAEDIMUS One of the twelve children, six boys and six girls, of Amphion and Niobe.

PHAEAX Son of Poseidon and Corcyra. Ancestor of the Phaeacians.

PHAEDRA Daughter of Minos and Pasiphae. Sister of Acacallis, Androgeus, Ariadne, Catreus, Deucalion, Euryale, Glaucus, Lycastus and Xenodice. Second wife of Theseus. Mother of Acamas and Demophon. Her stepson, Hippolytus, rejected her advances; she calumniated him to Theseus, his father, and after his death killed herself.

PHAENON A beautiful youth created by Prometheus and given immortality by Zeus. Placed among the stars as the planet Phaenon (either Jupiter or Saturn).

PHAENOPS Father of Phorcys.

PHAEO One of the Hyades. Daughter of Atlas and Pleione. (*See* Hyades.)

PHAESTUS King of Sicyon. Son of Heracles. Succeeded Ianiscus to the throne and was succeeded by Zeuxippus after an oracle had advised him to emigrate to Crete.

PHAESTUS Son of Talus or Zeus and Europa. According to Cretan tradition, he was the father of Rhadamanthys.

PHAESYLE One of the Hyades. Daughter of Atlas and Pleione. (*See* Hyades.)

PHAETHON Son of Helios or Apollo and Clymene, although the name was also an epithet of Helios himself. Brother of the Heliades.

Phaethon took his father's chariot and rode off across the sky. When he almost crashed it into the earth, Zeus killed him with a thunderbolt and he fell into the Eridanus, or Po, becoming a swan. Some state that Phaethon was set among the constellations as Auriga, the charioteer. His sisters mourned for him until they were changed into poplars.

PHAETHON Son of Cephalus or Tithonus and Eos. Brother of Emathion and Memnon. Father of Astynous. Abducted by Aphrodite to be the guardian of her shrine.

PHAETHON Another name for Absyrtus, son of Aeetes and Eidyia. A grandson of Helios and the nephew of Phaethon, son of Clymene and Helios.

PHAETHUSA One of the Heliades. Daughter of Helios or Apollo and Neaera. Sister of Lampetie (Lampethusa), and half-sister of Phaethon. After Phaethon's death she mourned for him until she was changed into a poplar tree, and her tears turned to amber.

PHALCES Co-ruler of Sicyon. Son of Temenus. Brother of Agraeus, Ceisus, Cerynes and Hyrnetho. Father of Rhegnidas. Ruled with Lacestades.

PHALCES Trojan killed in the War by Antilochus.

PHALERUS An Argonaut. Son of Alcon. Eponym of the port of Phalerum.

PHANTASOS God of dreams when he appeared in dreams. Son of Somnus. Brother of Morpheus, Phobetor, Icelos and 996 others. Had the power to change into earth, rocks, water, trees and other attributes of nature.

PHANUS An Argonaut. Son of Dionysus and, possibly, Ariadne. Brother of Ceramus, Oenopion, Peparethus, Staphylus and Thoas.

PHAON A very old and ugly boatman of Mytilene in Lesbos to whom Aphrodite gave a small flask of ointment which made him very beautiful. Sappho fell in love with him but killed herself after he rejected her.

PHAROS A small island in the bay at Alexandria where stood the lighthouse, one of the Seven Wonders of the World (qv).

PHASIS (1) Son of Apollo and Ocyrrhoe (Menalippe). (2) River of Colchis, now called Rion or Faz, rising in the Caucasus and flowing to the Black Sea. The Argonauts sailed along it.

PHEGEUS (Phlegius) (1) King of Phegia. Father of Agenor, Arsinoe (Alphesiboea) and Pronous. Possibly father of Axion and Temenus. The priest of Dionysus who purified Alcmeon of his mother's murder. Killed (with his wife?) by Acarnan and perhaps his brothers, after killing his sons. (2) A companion of Aeneas on his journey to Italy from Troy. Killed by Turnus.

PHEME (Fama) Greek goddess of rumour or report.

PHEMIUS Son of Terpes. A trusted servant of Odysseus and his minstrel, was forced to serve Penelope's suitors. He and Medon were spared by Odysseus on his return.

PHEREPHATTA Epithet of Persephone, the grower of corn.

PHERES (1) Father of Antigone, wife of Cometes. (2) Son of Jason and Medea. Brother of Mermerus, Alcimenes, Argus, Eriopis, Medeias, Thessalus and Tisandrus. Either Medea killed him as a child, or he was stoned to death by the Corinthians. (3) Son of Cretheus and Tyro. Brother of Aeson, Amythaon and Promachus. Married Periclymene. Father of Admetus, Idomene, Lycurgus and Periopis. The first king of Pherae in Thessaly, he was succeeded by Admetus. (4) Father of Mermerus, the poison-maker.

PHERUSA A Nereid. One of the fifty daughters of Nereus and Doris.

PHICIUM A mountain, south-east of Lake Copais, the home of the sphinx.

PHIDIAS c 500–432 BC. Greatest of the ancient Greek sculptors. Son of Charmides. Pericles commissioned him to build the giant statue of Zeus at Olympia, one of the Seven Wonders of the World (qv).

PHIDIPPIDES The famous Athenian runner who ran the 243 km from Athens to Sparta in two days, to summon help after the Persians had landed at Marathon. The Athenians raised a temple to him.

PHILAEUS Son of Greater Ajax.

PHILAMMON Son of Apollo and Chione. Twin of Autolycus, though Autolycus' father was Hermes. Father of Thamyris by the nymph, Argiope. An outstanding poet and musician, was killed in battle, defending the temple of Apollo at Delphi against Phlegyas.

PHILEMON Philemon and Baucis were a devoted married couple from Bithynia who offered refuge to Zeus and Hermes, not knowing them to be gods. Zeus made them guardians of his temple until they died, both at the same time. He then became an oak and she was changed into a linden tree.

PHILETOR   Father of Demuchus.

PHILINOE   Daughter of Iobates. Married Bellerophon. Mother of Deidameia, Hippolochus, Isander and Laodameia.

PHILLO   Daughter of Alcimedon. Raped by Heracles.

PHILOCAUS   Son of Hermes. Brother of Chryses, Eurymedon and Nephalion. Co-ruler of the Island of Pharos.

PHILOCTETES   An Argonaut. Son of Poeas and Demonassa. As a suitor of Helen, led seven ships from Malia to the Trojan War. However, he was bitten by a snake and when the wound became malodorous, was abandoned on the island of Tenedos (Lemnos).

Nine years later, Odysseus and Diomedes rescued him after an oracle of Heracles told the Greeks that Troy could not fall without his arrows and marksmanship. Podalirius healed his wound. He lit the funeral pyre of Heracles, and killed Paris. After the war, settled in Italy, founding the cities of Crimissa and Petelia.

PHILODICE   Wife of Leucippus. Mother of Arsinoe, Hilaera and Phoebe.

PHILOETIUS   Odysseus' cowherd who remained loyal to his master and fought beside him on his return.

PHILOMELA (Philomena)   Daughter of Pandion and Zeuxippe. Sister of Butes, Erechtheus and Procne. After Tereus raped her, he cut out her tongue to prevent her telling Procne, his wife. She wove a tapestry depicting the rape, which was found by Procne and in revenge the two sisters killed Procne's young son, Itylus, serving him as a meal to Tereus. Philomela became a swallow which, without a tongue, cannot sing.

PHILOMELUS   Son of Iasion and Demeter. Brother of Plutus. Father of Parias. Inventor of the wagon.

PHILONIS   Epithet of Chione.

PHILONOE   (1) Daughter of Tyndareus and Leda. Sister of the Dioscuri, Phoebe, Timandra and Clytemnestra, and half-sister of Helen. (2) Daughter of Iobates. Sister of Stheneboea. Wife of Bellerophon.

PHILONOME   Daughter of Craugasus. Second wife of Cycnus, she fell in love with her stepson, Tenes. When he rejected her she accused him of rape, and her husband buried her alive for lying.

PHILYRA   Daughter of Oceanus and Tethys. Sister of many (*see* Oceanus). Possibly wife of Nauplius. Mother of Cheiron by Cronos, both having changed into horses to mate. She may have changed into a lime tree. Possibly the mother of Nausimedon, Oeax and Palamedes by Nauplius.

PHINEUS   King of Thrace. Son of Agenor and Telephassa or Argiope. Brother of Cadmus, Cilix, Demodoce, Electra, Europa, Phoenix, Thasus, and possibly Argus, though some claim that Phoenix and Cassiopeia were his parents. Married first to Cleopatra, daughter of Boreas. Later married Idaea, by whom he became father of Mariandynus and Thynius. It was possible that Pandion and Plexippus were also his children by Cleopatra. Was exposed to the Harpies for cruelty to the sons of his first marriage. A soothsayer, he blinded his own children and was punished by the gods who blinded him. His sight was restored after he guided the Argonauts past the Clashing Rocks.

PHINEUS   Possibly a son of Belus and Anchinoe. Brother of Cepheus, Aegyptus, Danaus and Thronia. Turned to stone by Perseus after he refused to rescue his niece, Andromeda, from a sea-monster.

PHLEGETHON   River of fire of Hades. A tributary of the Acheron and one of the five rivers of the Underworld. The others: Cocytus, Lethe, Styx and the Acheron.

PHLEGIUS (Phegeus) (1) Father of Agenor, Arsinoe and Pronous, and possibly Axion and Temenus. King of Phegia and a priest of Dionysus. He and his sons were killed by the sons of Alcmeon after he had purified the latter of his mother's murder. (2) A companion of Aeneas on his journey from Troy to Italy. Killed by Turnus.

PHLEGRA The area of Macedonia where the Giants attacked the gods, though others place it near Naples.

PHLEGYAS King of Orchomenus. Son of Ares and Chryse or Dotis. Father of Coronis and possibly Ixion.

When Apollo raped his daughter Phlegyas, who had renamed his people Phlegyans, burned Apollo's temple at Delphi. Apollo then killed him, sent him to Hades, and hung a large stone over his head. Others say that Phlegyas was killed by Lycus and Nycteus. Was succeeded by Chryses.

PHLIAS An Argonaut. Son of Dionysus or Ceisus and Araethyrea. Married Chthonophyle. Father of Androdamas.

PHLIUS A totally land-enclosed country of Sicyon, founded by Aras. The capital was Phliasa. Its kings were Aras, Phlias, Androdamas and Rhegnides.

PHLOGIOS (flame) One of the four horses of Ares. Others: Aithon, Conabos and Phobos.

PHLOGIUS Son of Deimachus. Brother of Autolycus and Deileon.

PHOBETOR God of Dreams. A son of Somnus. This was the name mortals gave to Icelos, who was able to take on the form of beast, bird or serpent in dreams.

PHOBOS (terror) One of the four horses of Ares. Others: Aithon, Conabos and Phlogios.

PHOBOS (panic) God of fear and terror.

Son of Ares and Aphrodite. Brother of Anteros, Enyo, Eros, Harmonia, Pallor and Deimos. The brothers accompanied their father into battle.

PHOCIS Country or province of Greece, on the north of the Gulf of Corinth and west of Boeotia. Mt Parnassus, site of the oracle of Delphi, was here.

PHOCIS, kings of Ornytus, Naubolus and Strophius.

PHOCUS Son of Ornytion or Poseidon. Brother of Thoas. Married Antiope after curing her madness. Eponym of Phocis.

PHOCUS Son of Aeacus and Psamathe. Married Endeis. Father of Crisus, Naubolus and Panopaeus. Emigrated to Phocis and extended the colony. Killed by Peleus and Telamon, children of his father and his own wife.

PHOCUS An Argonaut. Son of Caeneus. Brother of Priasus.

PHOEBAS Priestess of Apollo at Delphi.

PHOEBE (1) Epithet of Artemis, the moon-goddess. (2) Daughter of Leucippus and Philodice. Sister of Arsinoe and Hilaera. Betrothed to Lynceus, she was abducted by Polydeuces. Married Castor, although she was the mother of Mnesileus by Polydeuces. (3) Daughter of Tyndareus and Leda. Sister of Clytemnestra, Philonoe, Timandra and the Dioscuri, and half-sister of Helen. She and Timandra may have been the same. (4) Titan daughter of Uranus and Gaea. Married her brother, Coeus. Mother of Asteria and Leto. Grandmother of Apollo and Artemis. She wore a wreath of gold.

PHOEBUS (sun god) Roman epithet and name of Apollo as god of the sun. The son of Jupiter and Latona and brother of Diana. Apollo became identified with Helios.

PHOENIX King of Phoenicia. Son of Agenor and Telephassa or Argiope. Brother of Cadmus, Cilix, Demodoce, Electra, Europa, Phineus, Thasus and possibly Argus. Married Perimede. Father of Astypalea and Europa. Possibly father of Adonis by Alphesiboea. Possibly father of a Belus. Some call him the father, not brother, of Phineus by Cassiopeia. When Europa was kidnapped, the brothers were sent either to find her or face exile.

PHOENIX King of the Dolopians. Son of Amyntor and Cleobule. Brother of Crantor and Deidameia. After he had seduced his father's concubine, possibly called Phthia, his father blinded him in revenge. At the request of Peleus of Phthia, Cheiron restored his sight. Present on the Calydonian Boar Hunt.

PHOENIX (1) Possibly the father of Adonis by Alphesiboea, may be same as Phoenix, son of Agenor. (2) The mythical Egyptian bird that lived for 500 years. After building its own funeral pyre and fanning the flames with its wings, it was reincarnated. Others say that its life cycle was between 250 and 7000 years. (3) One of the five lieutenants of Achilles.

PHOLUS A centaur. Son of Ixion or Silenus and Nephele. After accidentally killing himself with one of the poison arrows of Heracles, he was buried under Mt Pholoe in Elis.

PHORBAS (1) Son of Lapithus and Orsinome, or of Triopas and Hiscilla. Brother of Erysichthon, Iphimedeia and Messene if son of Triopas. Brother of Periphas if son of Lapithus. Married Hyrmina. Father of Actor, Augeias and Tiphys. King of Thessaly. Emigrated to Elis and fought Pelops, king of Pisa. (2) Son of Argus. Father of Triopas. King of Argolis. (3) A famous boxer killed by Apollo. (4) A leader of the Phrygians against the Greeks in the Trojan War. A great cattle-owner, lover of Hermes.

PHORBUS Father of Pronoe, the wife of Aetolus.

PHORCYS (the haughty) An ancient sea-god. Son of Oceanus and Gaea. Brother of Ceto, Crius, Eurybia, Nereus and Thaumas. Married Ceto. Father of the Gorgons, Graiae and Ladon. Possibly father of Echidna. Possibly father of Scylla by Crataeis, Ceto or Hecate. Father of Thoosa. Called the Old Man of the Sea (qv).

PHORCYS (1) Son of Phaenops. A Trojan killed by Greater Ajax, at Troy. (2) Father of seven sons who aided Turnus in his fight with Aeneas.

PHORONEUS First king of Argos. Son of Inachus and Melia. Brother of Aegialeius and Io. Married either Cerdo, Peitho or Laodice. Father of Apis, Car and Niobe. The first to erect an altar to Hera, in Argolis, the Argolians claimed that he, not Prometheus, was the first to bring fire to mortals.

PHOSPHORUS The morning star. Son of Astraeus or Cephalus and Eos. Brother of the stars. Phosphorus was the name given to the planet Venus, when seen before sunrise.

PHRASIMUS Husband of Diogeneia and father of Praxithea and Zeuxippe.

PHRIXUS Son of Athamas and Nephele. Brother of Helle. Married Chalciope, daughter of Aeetes. Father of Argus, Cytissorus, Melas, Phrontis and Presbon. Escaping from Ino, their step-mother, Phrixus and Helle rode the ram with the Golden Fleece from Thebes to Colchis but only Phrixus arrived safely. Aeetes killed Phrixus after misunderstanding an oracle.

PHRONIME Daughter of Etearchus. Concubine of Polymnestus. Mother of Battus (Aristoteles). Rescued from drowning by Themison after her father threw her in the sea.

PHRONTIS The pilot of Menelaus' ship.

PHRONTIS (1) Son of Phrixus and Chalciope. Brother of Argus, Cytissorus, Melas and Presbon. (2) Wife of Panthous. Mother of Euphorbus, Hyperenor and Polydamas.

PHRYGIA A large area of Asia Minor, comprising a large part of the peninsula between the Aegean and Black Seas. Cybele was the major goddess. The river Maeander rose in its hills; main cities were Ancyra (Ankara), Gorgium and Pessinus.

PHRYGIA, kings of The names Midas and Gordius alternated for many generations. Others were Mygdon, Otreus, Teucer and Teuthras.

PHTHIA (1) Daughter of Amphion and Niobe, one of the twelve children, six boys and six girls, killed by Artemis. (2) Mother of Dorus, Laodocus and Polypoetes by Apollo. (3) The mistress of Amyntor. (4) A mistress of Zeus when he became a pigeon. (5) The principal city of Achaea in Thessaly, also called Phthiotis. Birthplace of Achilles, and adopted home of Peleus.

PHTHIA, kings of Hellen, followed by Aeolus (who renamed it Aeolia), Actor and Eurytion.

PHTHIOTIS Same as Phthia, city of Achaea.

PHTHIUS Son of Larissa and Poseidon. Brother of Achaeus and Pelasgus. Eponym of Phthia in Achaea.

PHYLACE City of Thessaly, west of the Gulf of Pagasae. Its kings were Phylacus, followed by Iphiclus and Protesilaus.

PHYLACUS King of Phylace. Son of Deion and Diomede. Brother of Actor, Aenetus, Asteropeia and Cephalus. Married Clymene, daughter of Minyas. Father of Alcimede and Iphiclus. He or Iphiclus owned cattle which Melampus tried to steal

for his brother, Bias. Succeeded to the throne by Iphiclus.
Eponym of Phylace in Italy.

PHYLAS King of Ephyra in Thresprotia. Father of Astyoche. Killed by Heracles in the war with the Calydonians.

PHYLAS Father of Polymele, wife of Echecles. May be the same as above.

PHYLEUS King of Dulichium. Eldest son of Augeias or Phorbas and Hyrmina. Brother of Augeias, Actor, Tiphys and Agasthenes (if Phorbas was his father). Married Timandra. Father of Meges. Present on the Calydonian Boar Hunt.

PHYLEUS King of Thrace. Either he or Lycurgus was the father of Phyllis.

PHYLEUS A Greek captain in the Trojan War.

PHYLIUS Son of Apollo by Thyria. A brother of Cycnus.

PHYLLIS (1) Daughter of Lycurgus or Phyleus or Sithon, all kings of Thrace. Sister of Dryas. Married Demophoon and loved by his brother Acamas, by whom she conceived Munitus. If Demophoon was her husband, he deserted her and went to Athens. A month later she committed suicide and became an almond tree. Another version of this story states that Phyllis went eight times to an appointed spot to search for a sign of her husband's return after the fall of Troy, and that on the ninth visit Athena was so overcome by Phyllis' grief she turned the girl into an almond tree. The very next day her husband returned to find, not his wife, but a tree. (2) Daughter of a Bisaltian king and the wife of Acamas who hanged herself after he deserted her. The two may have been the same person.

PHYLOMACHE Daughter of Amphion and Niobe. One of twelve children, six boys and six girls. Either she or Anaxibia was the wife of Pelias, hence mother of his children, Alcestis, Acastus, Hippothoe, Pelopia and Pisidice.

PHYLONOE *See* Philonoe.

PHYSCOA Mother of Narcaeus by Dionysus.

PHYXIOS God of escape. An epithet of Zeus.

PICUS Roman woodland demigod. Son of Saturn and Venilia or of Sterculus. Brother of Juno. Lover of Pomona and Canens. Father of Faunus. Circe fell in love with him, but he rejected her for Canens. Circe then changed him into a woodpecker. Famed as a soothsayer.

PIELUS Son of Neoptelemus and Andromache. Brother of Molossus and Pergamus.

PIERIA (1) An area of Macedonia, north of Olympus, birthplace of the Muses or Pierides. (2) A spring on the slopes of Mt Olympus.

PIERIDES A name given to the Muses.

PIERIDES The nine daughters of Pierus and Evippe, whom Pierus named after the Muses. All nine challenged the Muses to a musical contest. When they lost, they were changed into magpies, so that they still had the power to imitate speech.

PIERIS A slave woman; either she or Tereis was the mother of Megapenthes and Nicostratus by Menelaus.

PIEROUS A Thracian leader, who killed Diores in the Trojan War.

PIERUS King of Pella in Macedonia. Son of Magnes. Brother of Eioneus and Hymenaeus. Married Euippe. Father of the Pierides. Father of Hyacinth by the Muse, Cleio.

PIERUS Father of Oeagrus by the nymph, Methone.

PIETAS Roman goddess of respect. A virtue, she was also goddess of affection, duty, piety and obligation to gods, parents and country.

PIETY, Roman goddess of Pietas.

PIG *See* Elpenor, Eurylochus.

PILLARS OF HERACLES (Hercules) The promontories of Gibraltar and Jebel Musa in Morocco, separated by the Straits of Gibraltar. Originally called Calpe and Abyla.

PILUMNUS An ancient Roman agricultural god. Father of Daunus by Danae. Grandfather of Turnus and Iuturna. Inventor of the pestle.

PINE *See* Attis.

PINE-BENDER Nickname of Sinis (Pityocamptes).

PIPLEA Daughter of Literses. Sister of Lyce, Nais, Nomia and Xenea. Possibly lover of Daphnis.

PIRENE (Peirene) Daughter of Achelous or Asopus. After she grieved for her son, killed by Artemis, she was changed into a fountain.

PISA A city between Elis and the Arcadian border, founded by Pisus, son of Perieres. It was destroyed by invaders from Elis after a fight over the Olympic Games. Its inhabitants accompanied Nestor to the Trojan War.

PISA, kings of Pisus, Oenomaus and Pelops.

PISANDER (1) A captain of the Myrmidons who accompanied Patroclus when the latter fought in the armour of Achilles. (2) A Trojan soldier killed by Agamemnon. (3) A Trojan soldier killed by Menelaus.

PISCES (fishes) A constellation. Twelfth sign of the zodiac.

PISIDICE Daughter of Pelias and Anaxibia or Phylomache. Sister of Acastus, Alcestis, Hippothoe and Pelopia.

PISUS Son of Perieres. Eponym and founder of Pisa.

PITANE A Laconian nymph and mother of Evadne by Poseidon.

PITHYS (Pitys) A nymph loved by both Boreas and Pan. Fleeing from Boreas, she fell against a rock and was changed into a pine tree.

PITTACUS One of the Seven Wise Men of Greece (qv). Others: Bias, Chilon, Cleobulus, Periander, Solon and Thales.

PITTHEUS King of Troezen. Son of Pelops and Hippodameia. Brother of Troezen, Alcathous, Astydameia, Atreus, Copreus, Lysidice, Nicippe and Thyestes. Father of Aethra. Grandfather of Theseus.

PLACIA Possibly the mother of Clytius and Hicetaon.

PLATAEA Daughter of Asopus and Metope. Sister of Aegina, Antiope, Chalcis, Cleone, Corcyra, Ismene, Ismenus, Pelagon, Pelasgus, Salamis, Thebe and ten others. Married Cithaeron. Eponym of a city between Attica and Boeotia.

PLEASURE (Delight, Voluptas) Daughter of Eros and Psyche born in Olympus.

PLEASURE, goddess of Voluptas (sensual); Charis.

PLEIADES The seven daughters of Atlas and Pleione. Sisters of Calypso, Hyas, the Hyades and the Hesperides. Born in Arcadia on Mt Cyllene. All except Merope had love affairs with gods, she marrying a mortal. Alcyone was the mother of Hyrieus by Lycus; Celaeno, of Lycus by Poseidon; Electra, of Dardanus and Iasion by Zeus; Maia, of Hermes by Zeus; Sterope, of Oenomaus by Ares; and Taygete of Lacedaemon, also by Zeus. In the star constellation of the Pleiades, only six are visible. The missing one is Merope (through shame) or Electra, mourning over death of Dardanus, though a few call Sterope the invisible one. The Pleiades were companions of Artemis and when they were pursued by Orion, the gods saved them by changing them into stars.

PLEIONE (Aethra) Daughter of Oceanus and Tethys. Sister of Clymene, Doris, Eidyia, Electra, Meliboea, Metis, Perseis and Proteus. Married Atlas. Mother of Calypso, Hyas, the Hyades, Hesperides and Pleiades.

PLEISTHENES King of Argos and Mycenae. Several versions of his parentage exist, or there may be more than one Pleisthenes. Could have been the son of Atreus and Aerope, reared by his uncle, Thyestes. Alternatively, he may have been the son of Pelops and Hippodameia, which would make him brother to Atreus and Thyestes. If the former, he married Cleolla, daughter of Dias and was father of Anaxibia and possibly of Agamemnon and Menelaus. If the latter, he married Aerope and was father of Agamemnon and Menelaus. A third alternative is that Pleisthenes was the bastard son of Thyestes and Aerope, hence the brother of Tantalus.

PLEISTHENES Son of Helen and Menelaus. Brother of Hermione and possibly Nicostratus. Taken to Troy with his mother by Paris.

PLENTY, Roman god and goddess of Porus, Copia.

PLENTY, goddess of Greek: Rhea. Roman: Ops, Copia.

PLEURON Son of Aetolus and Pronoe. Brother of Calydon. Married Xanthippe, daughter of Dorus. Father of Agenor.

PLEXIPPUS (1) Son of Phineus and Cleopatra. Brother of Pandion, and half-brother of Mariandynus and Thynius. (2) Son of Thestius and Eurythemis. Brother of Althaea, Hypermnestra, Leda and others. He and his brother were present on the Calydonian Boar Hunt and were both killed by Meleager.

PLUTO (1) Epithet of Hades, god of the Underworld. Known to the Romans as Dis and Orcus. (2) An Oceanid. Daughter of Oceanus and Tethys. (3) A daughter of Cronos. Mother of Tantalus by Zeus.

PLUTON (the giver of wealth) Epithet of Hades.

PLUTUS Greek god of riches and wealth (agricultural). Son of Iasion and Demeter. Brother of Philomelus. The first plutocrat, he was revered in the Eleusinian Mysteries with Demeter and Kore. Blinded by Zeus so that he might favour both righteous and irreverent men indiscriminately.

PLUVIUS Roman god of rain. Epithet of Jupiter.

PODALIRIUS Co-ruler of Ithone, Oechalia and Tricca. Son of Asclepius and Epione. Brother of Acesis, Aegle, Hygieia, Iaso, Janiscus, Machaon and Panacea. Married Syrna, daughter of Bybassus. As a suitor of Helen, he took thirty ships to the Trojan War with Machaon. There, he cured Philoctetes of his wounds, and was concealed in the Wooden Horse. He founded the cities of Bybassus and Syrnus.

PODARCES (1) Younger son of Iphiclus and Diomedeia. Brother of Protesilaus. After the death of his brother, he took command of his forty ships and sailed them

from Phylace to the Trojan War. (2) Original name of Priam until he was ransomed from Telamon by Hesione.

PODARGE (Celaeno) One of the Harpies. Daughter of Thaumas and Electra. Sister of Aello and Ocypete. Mother of Balius and Xanthus, the immortal horses of Achilles, by Boreas.

PODES Trojan son of Eetion. Killed in the Trojan War by Menelaus.

POEAS A Malian king and Argonaut. Son of Thaumacus. Married Demonassa. Father of Philoctetes. Destroyer of Talus, either he or his son fired the funeral pyre of Heracles.

POECILES Father of Europa and Membliarus.

POENA Roman goddess of punishment. In Greek mythology, an attendant of Nemesis.

POENAE Epithet of the Furies.

POLIPORTHES (Ptoliporthes) Son of Odysseus and Penelope. Brother of Telemachus.

POLIPORTHUS Possibly son of Telemachus and Nausicaa.

POLITES (1) Son of Priam and Hecuba. Father of another Polites. Last of the fifty sons of Priam to die in the Trojan War, he was killed by Neoptolemus. Helenus was the sole survivor. (2) Son of Polites. Friend of Ascanius. (3) Boatman of Odysseus, changed into a pig and then back to human form by Circe.

POLLUX Roman name of Polydeuces.

POLYBOTES Giant son of Gaea. Buried under the southern tip of the island of Cos, now Nisyros, by Poseidon.

POLYBUS (1) Son of Hermes and

Chthonophyle. Married Periboea. Father of Eurymachus and Lysianassa. King of Sicyon, he was succeeded by Adrastus. (2) Son of Helios. Married Merope (Periboea). King of Corinth. Foster-parent of Oedipus. (3) Husband of Alcandre. King of Egyptian Thebes during the Trojan War, he offered refuge to Menelaus and Helen after the war. (4) A suitor of Penelope. (5) Son of Antenor and Theano. Brother of Acamas, Agenor, Archelous, Coon, Crino, Demoleon, Glaucus, Helicaon, Iphidamas, Laocoon, Laodamas, Lycaon and Polydamas. Half-brother of Pedaeus.

POLYCAON (1) Younger son of Lelex and Cleocharia. Brother of Myles and Therapne. Brother or uncle of Eurotas. Married Messene. First king of Messenia. (2) Son of Butes.

POLYCASTE (1) Daughter of Nestor and Eurydice or Anaxibia. Youngest sister of Antilochus, Aretus, Echephron, Paeon, Peisidice, Peisistratus, Perseus, Stratius and Thrasymedes. Possibly mother of Perseptolis by Telemachus. (2) Possibly the wife of Icarius.

POLYCLEITUS A sculptor whose work was surpassed only by Phidias.

POLYCRATES Tyrant of Samos, c 536–522 BC. Son of Aeacus. Famous for his riches and good luck. Crucified by Oroetes, a jealous Persian governor.

POLYDAMAS Trojan son of Antenor and Theano. Brother of Acamas, Agenor, Archelous, Polybus, Iphidamas, Coon, Crino, Demoleon, Glaucus, Helicaon, Laocoon, Lycaon and Laodamas. Half-brother of Pedaeus. Married Lycaste, daughter of Priam. Like his father, he was accused of being a traitor to the Trojan cause in the War.

POLYDAMAS Trojan son of Panthous and Phrontis. Brother of Euphorbus and Hyperenor. A close friend of Hector (and born the same night), he had knowledge of the future and could interpret the flight of birds. A brave fighter in the Trojan War, he was killed either by Achilles or Ajax. His squire was called Cleitus.

POLYDAMNA (**Polydama**) Wife of Thon (Thonis) who was king of Egypt and warden of the mouth of the river Nile. He taught Helen how to use healing herbs.

POLYDECTES King of Seriphus. Son of Magnes and a Naiad. Brother of Dictys. Given the task of looking after Danae and her son, Perseus, he tried to rape Danae, but was prevented by Dictys. Later, Perseus turned him to stone by showing him the head of Medusa.

POLYDEUCES One of the Dioscuri. Son of Leda and Zeus. Brother of Helen. Married Hilaera, but was the father of Mnesileus by Phoebe, the wife of his inseparable friend, Castor. Polydeuces killed Lynceus and Idas. The latter had previously been a close friend, to whom his wife had once been pledged.

POLYDORA (1) Daughter of Meleager and Cleopatra. According to some, married to Protesilaus. (2) Daughter of Peleus and Antigone or Polymela. Half-sister of Achilles. Married Borus. Mother of Menesthius by the river god, Spercheius.

POLYDORE One of the fifty daughters of Danaus. Married Dryops. Mother of Dryope. Murdered her husband on their wedding night.

POLYDORUS (1) Son of Cadmus and Harmonia. Brother of Agave, Autonoe, Illyrius, Ino and Semele. Married Nycteis. Father of Labdacus. King of Thebes. Died while Labdacus was still a child. (2) Son of Hippomedon and Evanippe. One of the Epigoni. (3) Youngest son of Priam and Laothoe or, possibly, Hecuba. Brother of Lycaon, and half-brother to many. He was too young to fight in the Trojan War, so was sent with a great deal of treasure to Polymnestor for protection. But the latter murdered him and stole the treasure. His ghost warned Aeneas against founding the city of Avenus in Thrace.

POLYEIDUS Seer of Corinth. Son of Coeranus. Grandfather of Euchenor. Restored to life Glaucus, son of Minos. Advised Bellerophon to capture Pegasus.

POLYGONUS Son of Proteus. Brother of Telegonus. Killed with his brother by Heracles in a wrestling match.

POLYHYMNIA (Polymnia) Muse of song and oratory. Daughter of Zeus and Mnemosyne. One of the nine Muses. Her symbol was a veil. Possibly mother of Orpheus by Oeagrus.

POLYMEDE Daughter of Autolycus and, possibly, Neaera. Often confused with Alcimede, wife of Aeson. Mother of Jason.

POLYMELA Daughter of Actor and Aegina. Sister of Irus and Menoetius. According to some, first wife of Peleus. Mother of Polymela. Hanged herself after thinking Peleus had deserted her for another woman.

POLYMELA Daughter of Polymela and Peleus.

POLYMELE (Polymela) Daughter of Phylas. Married Echecles. Mother of Eudorus by her lover, Hermes.

POLYMELUS A Lycian leader at the Trojan War. Son of Argeas. Brother of Euippus. Killed in the War by Patroclus.

POLYMESTOR (Polymnestor) King of Thrace. Husband of Ilione. Father of Deipylus. After he killed Polydorus, Hecuba avenged her son by blinding Polymestor and killing his son.

POLYMNESTUS A nobleman of Thera, father of Battus (Aristoteles) by his concubine, Phronime.

POLYNEICES Son of Oedipus and Jocasta or Euryganeia. Brother of Antigone, Eteocles and Ismene. Married Argeia. Father of Adrastus II, Thersander and Timeas.

He and Eteocles agreed to hold the throne of Thebes in alternate years, but when Eteocles refused to give up the throne, the two brothers fought and killed each other. This in turn led to Adrastus leading the Seven against Thebes.

POLYPEMON (Damastes) Another name for Procrustes, the 'stretcher'. Father of Sinis by Sylea. Killed by Theseus.

POLYPHEIDES A seer. Son of Mantius. Brother of Cleitus. Father of Theoclymenus, who could also foretell the future.

POLYPHEMUS A Cyclops from Sicily. Son of Poseidon and Thoosa. Killed Acis, the lover of Galatea, after she had rejected his own advances. Captured Odysseus and his crew and ate two of them each day. After Odysseus blinded his one eye, they escaped from Polyphemus by tying themselves to the undersides of goats and sheep.

POLYPHEMUS An Argonaut and Lapith. Son of Elatus and Hippea. Brother of Caenis and Ischys. Fought against the Centaurs. Founder of Cius in Mysia and its first king. Abandoned by the Argonauts because of old age.

POLYPHONTES (1) Son of Autophonus. A Theban, he helped Eteocles defend Thebes against the Seven. Killed by Aepytus leading an ambush on Tydeus. (2) The killer of Cresphontes, Heraclid king of Messenia, and his two eldest sons, he usurped the throne and forced Merope to marry him, and she bore three children by him. Aepytus, youngest son of Cresphontes, escaped and killed Polyphontes after he grew up.

POLYPOETES (1) Son of Apollo and Phthia. Brother of Dorus and Laodocus. Killed by Aetolus. (2) Son of Odysseus and Callidice. Succeeded his mother to the throne of Thresprotia. (3) Son of Peirithous and Hippodameia. Born on the day the Lapiths fought the Centaurs, he had golden hair. He and Leonteus took forty ships to the Trojan War. He was in the Wooden Horse. Winner of the iron-ball throwing contest at the funeral games of Patroclus.

POLYPORTHES (Ptoliporthes) Son of Odysseus and Penelope, born after the hero's twenty-year absence. Also called Arcesilaus. Brother of Telemachus.

POLYXEINUS King of Elis. Looked after the sheep of Electryon which had been stolen by Taphian pirates. He then ransomed them to Amphitryon.

POLYXEINUS Son of Agasthenes. Leader of the Eleian forces at the Trojan War.

POLYXENA Daughter of Priam and Hecuba. Sister of Aesacus, Cassandra, Creusa, Deiphobus, Hector, Helenus, Paris and Troilus. She accompanied her father to Achilles to claim the body of Hector, and was later sacrificed on the tomb of the Greek hero after he had himself been killed by Paris.

POLYXO An Argive woman. The wife of Tlepolemus, king of Rhodes. Mother of Deipylus. After he was killed at Troy, she tried to gain her revenge by killing Helen, but only succeeded in killing a servant disguised as her.

POLYXO (1) Wife of Nycteus and possibly mother of Antiope. (2) Priestess of Apollo at Lemnos and nurse of Hypsipyle. Told the women of Lemnos to kill their husbands, and later advised the queen to welcome the Argonauts to Lemnos, in order to repopulate the country.

POMEGRANATE SEEDS *See* Persephone.

POMONA Roman goddess of gardens and fruit trees. One of the Numina, she was courted by Pan, Picus, Priapus and Silenus; but Vertumnus finally won her as a wife by disguising himself, after she had earlier spurned his advances. Sacred month: September.

POMPON Father of Numa Pompilius.

PONTIA Epithet of Aphrodite, she who has risen from the foam.

PONTUS (Oceanus) Son of Gaea. By his mother, father of Ceto, Crius, Eurybia, Nereus, Phorcys and Thaumas. Father of many more. He may have been little more than the personification of the deep barren sea. Possibly father of Telchines and Halia by Thalassa.

PONTUS An ancient country in the north-east of Asia Minor, bordering the Black Sea. The Romans called the Black Sea Pontus (the Greeks, Euxine).

POPLAR *See* Dryope, Heliades.

PORPHYRION Son of Uranus and Gaea. Leader of the Giants, his brothers. Killed by Heracles.

PORTHAON First king of Calydon. Son of Agenor and Epicaste. Brother of Hippodamus, Demonice and Thestius. Married Euryte, daughter of Hippodamas. Father of Alcathous, Agrius, Melas, Oeneus and Sterope. Father of Laocoon by a servant. Succeeded to the throne by Oeneus.

PORTS, god of Greek: Melicertes. Roman: Portunus.

PORTUNUS Roman god of ports and harbours. Latin name for Palaemon. Known to the Greeks as Melicertes. Festival date: 17 August.

PORUS Roman god of plenty.

POSEIDON Greek god of the sea. Son of Cronos and Rhea. Brother of Demeter,

Hades, Hera, Hestia and Zeus. One of the twelve great Olympians. Swallowed by his father but rescued by Metis. Married Amphitrite. Father of Albion, Benthesicyme, Charybdis, Rhode and Triton. He had many love affairs.

Poseidon's Lovers	Children of the Union
Aethra	Theseus
Alcyone	Anthus, Arethusa, Hyperenor, possibly Hyrieus
Alope	Hippothous
Amymone	Nauplius
Anticleia	Periphetes
Arene	Idas (possibly)
Arne (Melanippe)	Aeolus II and Boeotus
Astypalea	Ancaeus and Eurypylus
Calyce	Cycnus
Canace	Aloeus, Epopeus, Hopleus, Nireus and Triopas
Chione	Eumolpus
Chloris	Periclymenus
Chrysogeneia	Chryses
Cleodora	Parnassus
Corcyra	Phaex
Demeter	Arion and Despoina
Ergea	Celaeno
Europa or Mecionice	Euphemus
Euryale	Orion (possibly)
Eurycyda	Eleius
Eurynome	Asopus and Bellerophon
Euryte	Halirrhothius
Gaea	Antaeus, Charybdis (possibly) and Ogyges
Helle	Edonus and Paeon
Hippothoe	Taphius
Iphimedeia	Ephialtes and Otus
Larissa	Achaeus, Pelasgus II and Phthius
Leis	Althepus
Libya	Agenor, Belus and Lelex
Lysianassa	Busiris
Medusa	Chrysaor and Pegasus

Poseidon

Poseidon's Lovers	Children of the Union
Melie	Amycus and Mygdon
Molione	the Moliones (possibly)
Oenope	Megareus (possibly)
Periboea	Nausithous
Pitane	Evadne
Thalassa	Halia and Telchines (possibly)
Theophane	ram with the golden fleece
Thoosa	Polyphemus (possibly)
Tyro	Neleus and Pelias
Zeuxippe	Butes (possibly)

He was also the father of Cercyon, Eryx, Sceiron, Actor, Lamus, Lamia, Amphimarus, Lotis, Sarpedon and a number of horses. Possibly the father of Augeias, Phocus and Erginus. Helped Apollo build the walls of Troy. Bore an implacable hatred of Troy after Laomedon refused to pay him. His epithets: 1. Enosichthon (the earth-shaker); 2. Gaieochus (the earthguarder); 3. Hippios or Consus (the horse-god). Ally of the Greeks in the Trojan War. Defeated in various quarrels by Apollo, Athena and Hera. His symbol of power was the trident which he used to create earthquakes. Known to the Romans as Neptune.

POSTVERTA or POSTVORTA (Carmenta) Roman goddess of the past. She was also a goddess of prophecy, of women's ailments and of childbirth. Sister of Antevorta (future). Linked with Carmenta as mother of Evander.

POTAMEIDES Nymphs of fountains, springs, lakes and rivers.

POTHOS Epithet of Himeros, attendant of Ares.

POTINA Roman goddess of children's potions.

POTIONS, Roman goddess of Potina.

PRAXIDICE (Roman: Poena) Greek goddess of enterprises, evil deeds and their punishment, and of justice and retribution.

PRAXITELES 4th century BC. A famous Greek sculptor.

PRAXITHEA (Pasithea) (1) Daughter of Phrasimus and Diogeneia. Sister of Zeuxippe. Married Erechtheus, king of Athens. Mother of Cecrops, Creusa, Cthonia, Eupalamus, Orneus, Metion, Oreithyia, Pandorus, Procris and Thespius. (2) Daughter of Thespius. One of fifty. Mother of Lycurgus by Heracles. (3) Wife of Erichthonius and mother of Pandion.

PRAXONIDES Either he or Haemon was the father of Iphitus, king of Elis.

PRESBON Son of Phrixus and Chalciope. Brother of Argus, Cytissorus, Melas and Phrontis. Father of Clymenus (Boeotian Orchomenus).

PREUGENES Spartan father of Patreus.

PRIAM Last king of Troy. Son of Laomedon and Strymo or Placia. Originally called Podarces, the name Priam means 'ransomed', as Hesione ransomed him from Heracles. Brother of Astyoche, Cilla, Clytius, Hicetaon, Lampus, Hesione and Tithonus. Married first to Arisbe, whom he gave away in order to marry Hecuba. According to Homer, this marriage produced nineteen sons and a number of daughters. In all, Priam had fifty sons and twelve daughters, though some say he had fifty daughters as well. Father of Aesacus (alternative mother, Arisbe), Antiphus, Cassandra, Creusa, Deiphobus, Hector, Helenus, Isus, Laodice, Paris, Polites, Polyxena Ilione and Troilus, all by Hecuba. Father of Lycaon and Polydorus, by Laothoe. Father of Aesacus, by Alexiroe. Also the father of Agathon, Agavus, Aretus, Antiphonus, Axion, Cebriones, Doryclus, Dius, Dryops, Hipponous, Leucas, Lycus, Lycaste, Medesicaste, Mestor, Hippothous, Pammon, Melampus and Melanippe.

He was king at the time of the Trojan War, but was too old to fight and was slain by Pyrrhus (Neoptolemus).

PRIAPUS Fertility god. Son of Dionysus and Aphrodite, but some call Hermes his father. Born at Lampsacus on the Hellespont, he was ugly and deformed. God of fruitfulness, especially of gardens, flocks of sheep and goats, bees and vines. His sacrificial animal was the donkey. Priapus pursued Lotis until she changed into a lotus tree. Statues of the god were usually found in gardens, made of red-painted wood and with unusually large sexual organs.

PRIASUS An Argonaut. Son of Caeneus. Brother of Phocus.

PROCAS King of Alba Longa. Father of Amulius and Numitor. Ruled twelve generations after Aeneas.

PROCLEIA Daughter of Laomedon. Mother of Tenes and Hemithea by her husband, Cycnus, though some call Apollo the father of Tenes.

PROCLES Heraclid son of Aristodemus and Argeia. Twin of Eurysthenes. Raised by his uncle, Theras, after his father's death, he later founded a kingdom in Sparta.

PROCNE Daughter of Pandion and Zeuxippe. Sister of Butes, Erechtheus and Philomela. Married Tereus. Mother of Itys, whom she killed. She became a swallow. Possibly also called Metis.

PROCRIS Daughter of Erechtheus and Praxithea. Sister of Cecrops, Creusa, Eupalamus, Orneus, Oreithyia, Cthonia, Metion, Protogeneia, Thespius and Pandorus. Married Arceisus, son of Cephalus or Zeus. Possibly the mother of Laertes. Cured Minos of his golden death-giving disease. Accidentally killed by her husband.

PROCRUSTES His real name was Damastes or Polypemon, and his nickname, meant 'the stretcher'. Father of Sinis by

Sylea. This Attican robber of Erineus invited strangers to his house. If they did not fit the bed, he either stretched them or cut off their legs, in order to make them the right size. Theseus, invited to the house, finally gave him the same treatment.

PROETUS King of Tiryns. Son of Abas, king of Argos and Ocaleia. Twin of Acrisius (the two brothers even fought in the womb) and brother of Chalcodon. Married Sthenboea, daughter of Iobates or Anteia. Father of Iphianassa, Iphinoe, Lysippe and Megapenthes, although some call one of his daughters Philonoe, Cassandra or Anticleia. Father of Euryale, possibly by Eurydice. Proetus fought for and lost the kingdom of Argos to his twin. Melampus gained half the kingdom of Tiryns after he had cured the daughters of Proetus of their madness. He was succeeded to the throne of Tiryns by Megapenthes after Perseus accidentally changed him to stone.

PROMACHORMA Epithet of Athena, guardian and protectress.

PROMACHUS (1) Son of Aeson and Alcimede or Polymede. Brother of Jason. Killed by Pelias. (2) Fourth son of Cretheus and Tyro. Brother of Aeson, Amythaon and Pheres. (3) Son of Parthenopaeus by Clymene. Brother of Tlesimenes. One of the Epigoni. Killed at Thebes.

PROMENAEA Priestess at Dodona where a Theban dove gave oracles.

PROMETHEUS (Forethought) The father of mankind. Son of Iapetos and Clymene (Asia). Brother of Atlas, Epimetheus and Menoetius. Married Hesione. Father of Deucalion by Pronoea, or his wife.

Prometheus ridiculed the gods by having Zeus choose a bag of bones rather than that containing the sacrificial victim and stealing fire from heaven. Zeus retaliated by causing Hephaestus to mould Pandora as a wife for Prometheus, but he rejected her, giving her to Epimetheus. Prometheus was then chained to a rock on Mt Caucasus by

Prometheus

Hermes or Bia; and each day for thirty years a vulture or eagle daily fed on his liver, which regenerated. Heracles finally released him.

According to Aeschylus, he was an immortal god and friend of the human race, and was the inventor of architecture, astronomy, figures, medicine, navigation, the mystery of prophecy, the art of metalwork and writing.

PRONAX Son of Talaus and Lysimache or Lysianassa. Brother of Adrastus, Aristomachus, Astynome, Eriphyle, Hippomedon, Mecisteus, Metidice and Parthenopaeus. Father of Amphithea and Lycurgus.

PRONOE Daughter of Phorbus. Married Aetolus. Mother of Calydon and Pleuron.

PRONOEA Possibly mother of Deucalion by Prometheus.

PRONOUS Son of Phegeus. Brother of Agenor and Arsinoe.

PROPHECY, god of Greek: Apollo. Roman: Apollo.

PROPHECY, Roman goddess of Postverta (Carmenta).

PROSERPINA Roman name of Persephone, daughter of Demeter. *See* Persephone.

PROTESILAUS King of Thessaly. Son of Iphiclus and Diomedeia. Brother of Podarces. Married Laodameia or possibly Polydora. As a suitor of Helen, he took forty ships from Phylace to the Trojan War where he was the first Greek to set foot on Trojan soil and also the first Greek to be killed, by either Achates or Hector.

PROTEUS Old Man of the Sea. Son of Oceanus and Tethys. Brother of Clymene, Doris, Eidyia, Electra, Meliboea, Metis, Perseis and Pleione. Father of Eidotheia.

Sealherder of Poseidon, he ·lived on Pharos and had the gift of prophecy and the ability to change shape.

PROTEUS King of Egypt. Husband of Psamathe. Father of Cabeiro, Eidothea (Theonoe) and Theoclymenus. Succeeded Pharos to the throne. It has been said that during the Trojan War he looked after the real Helen while a substitute one went with Paris to Troy. It is possible that this Proteus and the Old Man of the Sea were in fact the same man.

PROTEUS Father of Polygonus and Telegonus – likely to have been the same as above.

PROTHOENOR Trojan son of Areilycus. Killed in the War by Polydamas.

PROTHOON A Greek killed in the Trojan War by Teucer.

PROTO A Nereid. One of the fifty daughters of Nereus and Doris.

PROTOGENEIA (1) Daughter of Deucalion and Pyrrha. Sister of Amphictyon, Hellen, Pandora and Thyia. Possibly the mother of Aethlius, the father of Endymion, although some say, mother of Endymion by Zeus or Aeolus. Mother of Opus by Zeus. (2) Daughter of Erechtheus and Praxithea. Sister of Cecrops, Creusa, Cthonia, Eupalamus, Metion, Oreithyia, Orneus, Pandorus, Procris and Thespius. (3) Daughter of Aeolia and Calydon. Sister of Epicasta. (4) Mother of Oxylus by Ares.

PSAMATHE A Nereid. Daughter of Nereus and Doris. Sister of the other Nereids amongst whom were Amphitrite and Thetis. Loved by Aeacus, she changed into a seal in order to try and escape him. Failing, she bore Phocus by him. After his death, she married Proteus. Mother of Cabeiro, Eidothea (Theonoe) and Theoclymenus.

PSAMATHE Daughter of Crotopus, king of Argos. Possibly the mother of Linus by Apollo.

PSYCHE A beautiful maiden, whose beauty caused such jealousy in Venus that the goddess said she would love the ugliest of men. Personification of the soul, she was made immortal by Zeus. Youngest of three daughters of a king. Eros was so smitten with her that he caused her to come to his palace and she married him. Eros remained invisible until one night she shone a light on him, after her sisters had convinced her that he was a monster. Mother of Delight (Voluptas).

PSYCHOPOMPUS Epithet of Hermes, the conductor of souls to the Underworld.

PTAH The chief god of Memphis in Egypt.

PTERELAUS King of the Taphians.

Son of Taphius. Father of six sons and Comaetho. He had a single golden hair which, until his daughter cut it off, made him immortal.

PTOLIPORTHES (Arcesilaus, Polyporthes) Son of Odysseus and Penelope, born after the hero's twenty-year absence. Brother of Telemachus.

PTOUS Son of Athamas and Themisto. Brother of Erythrius, Leucon and Schoeneus.

PUNISHMENT, goddess of Greek: Praxidice. Roman: Poena.

PURIFICATION, Roman god of Februus, whose festivities were called Februa.

PYGMALION (1) Brother of Dido, first queen of Carthage, and Anna. They were the children of Agenor or Belus or Mutto. The murderer of Sichaeus, husband of Dido. (2) A king of Cyprus. Possibly father of Cinyras or his wife, Metharme. Pygmalion was a woman-hater but after he built a statue of ivory, fell in love with it. Aphrodite answered his prayer and gave life to the statue, Galatea, and he married her. Their son was Paphos.

PYGMIES A central African race of dwarfs whom Heracles sent to Eurystheus in a lion skin.

PYLADES Son of Strophius and Anaxibia. Boyhood friend of Orestes, he married his sister, Electra. Father of Medon and Strophius II.

PYLAEMENES Father of Harpalion.

PYLARTES A Trojan ally wounded in the War by Greater Ajax.

PYLAS King of Megara and Pylos. Son of Cteson. Father of Pylia and Sceiron. Exiled from Megara for killing Bias.

PYLIA Daughter of Pylas. Sister of

Sceiron. Married Pandion. Mother of Aegeus, Pallas, Lycus and Nisus.

PYLON One of the Lapiths. Killed by Polypoetes.

PYLOS A coastal region of Messenia, given to Neleus by Aphareus after Pelias drove Neleus out of Iolcus.

PYLOS, kings of First, Neleus, followed by Nestor. Also, Pylas.

PYLUS Son of Ares and Demonice or Alcippe. Brother of Evenus, Molus, Oeneus and Thestius.

PYRAECHMES A successful Aetolian slinger who defeated Degmenus in single combat. As a result, Oxylus replaced Dius as king of Elis.

PYRAMUS A youth who fell in love with his neighbour, Thisbe, but their families forbade their union. Hearing (wrongly) that she had been killed by a lion, he killed himself. This prompted her to commit suicide also, and their blood turned the white mulberry tree purple.

PYRASUS Trojan ally wounded in the Trojan War by Greater Ajax.

PYRENE Possibly mother of Cycnus by Ares.

PYRENE A woman who gave birth to a snake after being raped by Heracles.

PYRGO The nurse of Priam's children and a follower of Aeneas to Italy from Troy.

PYRIPHLEGETHON The river of fire in the Underworld. Also called Phlegethon.

PYRIS A Lycian killed in the Trojan War by Patroclus.

PYRRHA (1) Daughter of Epimetheus and Pandora. Married her cousin, Deucalion. Mother of Hellen, Amphictyon, Pandora II, Protogeneia and Thyia. The first mortal woman born and, with Deucalion, a survivor of the Deluge. (2) Daughter of Creon and Anioche or Eurydice. Sister of Enioche, Haemon, Megara and Menoeceus. (3) The name assumed by Achilles when he lived as a woman at the court of Lycomedes.

PYRRHUS Another name for Neoptolemus.

PYTHAGORUS *See* Aethalides.

PYTHEUS Epithet of Apollo, killer of Python.

PYTHIA The priestess of Apollo at Delphi, who spoke his oracles. The position was gained at the age of fifty.

PYTHIAN GAMES One of the four great Panhellenic Games, established in honour of Apollo. Held near his temple at Delphi every four years, and originally were singing contests only. Later athletics, poetry and art were added. Prizes were a laurel wreath and a palm branch. The games survived to the end of the 4th century AD.

PYTHIAS *See* Damon.

PYTHON A large snake (or dragon) that lived near Delphi until killed by Apollo.

PYTTHIUS Father of Amarynceus. Emigrated from Thessaly to Elis.

Q

QUADRIGA The four-horse chariot of Helios which he drove daily across the sky.

QUAIL *See* Asteria.

QUINQUATRIA The Roman festivals of Minerva.

QUIRINAL One of the seven hills of Rome.

QUIRINALIA Roman festivals of Romulus held on 17 February.

QUIRINUS Epithet of Mars. Quirinus was sometimes said to be the husband, son, or just friend of Bellona.

QUIRINUS Name applied to Romulus when he was referred to as a god.

R

RAIN, Roman god of Pluvius.

RAINBOWS, Greek goddess of Iris.

RAVEN The sacred white bird of Apollo which he turned black after it brought him bad news.

REED *See* Syrinx.

REMUS Son of Mars and Rhea Silvia. Twin of Romulus. Exposed at birth by Amulius, and raised by a she-wolf. Killed by Romulus.

REPOSE, Sabine goddess of Vacuna.

RESPECT, Roman goddess of Pietas.

RETRIBUTION, goddess of Nemesis, Praxidice.

REVELRY, Roman god of Comus.

REVERENCE, Roman goddess of Maiestas.

RHACIUS Husband of Manto and possibly father of Mopsus.

RHADAMANTHYS Son of Zeus and Europa, but a son of Phaestus in the Cretan tradition. Brother of Minos and Sarpedon. Married Alcmene. Father of Erythus and Gortys. Ruler of Crete before Minos, and one of the three judges of the Underworld with Aeacus and Minos.

RHAMNUSIA Epithet of Nemesis.

RHAMPSINITUS The king of Egypt who succeeded Proteus to the throne.

RHEA Mother of the gods. Daughter of Uranus and Gaea. Sister of the Titans. Married her brother, Cronos. Mother of Demeter, Hades, Hera, Hestia, Poseidon and Zeus. Possibly mother of the Dactyli. Possibly mother of the Corybantes by Cronos.

Epithets or otherwise known as: Idaea (born on Mt Ida), Bona Dea, Magna Mater, Ops, Opis, Tellus and Terra (all Roman); Cybele (Phrygian); Titaea.

RHEA SILVIA Daughter of Numitor or Tyrrheus. Sister of Lausus. A vestal virgin seduced by Mars. Mother of Remus and Romulus. Also called Ilia.

RHEGNIDAS Son of Phalces. Captured Phlius for the Dorians and made himself king.

RHENE Mother of Medon by Oileus, and possibly of Ajax.

RHESUS King of Thrace. Son of Strymon or Eioneus and Calliope or Euterpe. Reared by water nymphs. Married Arganthoe.

An ally of the Trojans, he owned two white horses and a golden chariot. An oracle decreed that Troy would not fall if the horses drank the waters of the river Scamander, or Xanthus. Diomedes and Odysseus captured the horses and killed Rhesus.

RHESUS River of Ida in Phrygia.

RHEXENOR Son of Nausithous. Brother of Alcinous. Father of Arete. Apollo killed him with a silver bow.

RHODE Daughter of Poseidon and Amphitrite. Sister of Albion, Benthesicyme, Charybdis and Triton. Mother of seven sons, the Heliades, by Helios. Eponym of Rhodes. *See also* Rhodus.

RHODE Daughter of Halia. Had six brothers.

RHODE (Rhodus) Daughter of Poseidon and Amphitrite. Mother of the

Heliades, Actis, Candalus, Cercaphus, Macar, Ochimus, Tenages and Triopas, by Helios.

RHODEIUS River of Ida in Phrygia.

RHODES Large island in the Aegean Sea, twenty kilometres off the south-west coast of Asia Minor. Sacred to Helios and named after his wife, Rhode. There were three cities: Cameirus, Ialysus and Lindus. The Colossus of Rhodes, a statue of Helios 36 metres high, and one of the seven wonders of the world, stood at the entrance to one of the ports. Helen may have been murdered there by the widow of Tlepolemus.

RHODOPE (1) A nymph, wife of Haemus, changed into a mountain by the gods, after the two had assumed the names of Zeus and Hera. (2) An attendant of Artemis changed into a mountain because of her vanity. Possibly the same as (1). (3) Ancient mountain chain of the Balkans, between Macedonia and Thrace, 2500 m high.

RHODUS *See* Rhode.

RHOECUS (1) A young man who saved the life of a Dryad but, after he insulted her, she blinded him. (2) A Centaur killed by Theseus at the wedding of Peirithous and Hippodameia. (3) A Giant killed by Dionysus in the war of the gods and Giants.

RHOEO (1) Daughter of Scamander. Sister of Callirrhoe, Strymo and Teucer. Either she or Strymo was the wife of Laomedon. Mother of Astyoche, Cilla, Clytius, Hesione, Hicetaon, Lampus, Podarces (Priam) and Tithonus. (2) Mother of Anius by Apollo (cf above).

RHOETUS Same as Rhoecus, a giant killed by Dionysus.

RHYGMUS Son of Peiros. An ally of Troy, he and his squire, Areithous, were killed in the Trojan War by Achilles.

RICHES, Greek god of Plutus.

RICHEST MAN IN MYTHOLOGY Croesus, king of Lydia.

RIPHEUS (1) A Centaur taller than the trees, killed by Theseus at the wedding of Peirithous and Hippodameia. (2) A Trojan ally of Aeneas, killed by the Greeks.

RIVERS Sacred children of Oceanus and Tethys. Their gods included Achelous, Alpheus, Asopus, Asterion, Axius, Caecinus, Cephissus, Cebren, Cocytus, Crimisus, Eridanus, Halys, Inachus, Ladon, Maeander, Nile, Peneius, Simois, Scamander, Spercheius, Strymon and Tiberinus.

RIVERS, Roman goddess of Iuturna.

ROBBERS, Roman goddess of Furina.

ROBIGO Roman goddess of corn and other grains.

ROBIGUS Roman god of corn and other grains. Festival date: 25 April. Invoked with Flora. (Cf Robigo.)

ROCK *See* Calydon, Prometheus.

ROMA Daughter of Evander and Deidameia. Sister of Pallantia, Pallas and Sarpedon. Eponym of Rome.

ROME Centre of Roman power and empire. Built on seven hills on the banks of the Tiber, some 25 kilometres from the sea. Romulus is said to have founded the city on 21 April 753 BC. National pride led the Romans to link their past with Greek mythology; thus, in the time of Aeneas, Zeus promised great power for Rome. Traditionally there previously existed the colony of Lanuvium founded by Aeneas and Alba Longa founded by Ascanius. In its original state Rome was a small stronghold on the summit of the Palatine. Romulus established an 'asylum' for murderers, criminals, etc, in order to establish Rome's nationhood. The kingdom grew, following many successful wars against her neighbours, and kings reigned for 244 years until the seventh, Tarquinius Superbus, became too oppressive. His son raped Lucretia, and this led directly to the expulsion of the Tarquins and the establishment of the Republic by L. Junius Brutus.

ROME, seven kings of Romulus, 38 years (later with Titus Tatius); Numa Pompilius, 43 years; Tullus Hostilius, 32 years; Ancus Martius, 24 years; Tarquinius Priscus, 38 years; Servius Tullius, 44 years; Tarquinius Superbus, 25 years (last king before republic). The monarchy ruled from 753 BC to 510 BC.

ROMULA The fig tree where a shepherd found Romulus and Remus.

ROMULUS First king of Rome. Son of Mars and Rhea Silvia. Twin of Remus. Married Hersilia. After being exposed by Amulius at birth, was suckled by a she-wolf and later reared by Faustulus and Larentia. United the Romans and Sabines into the kingdom of Rome and became her first king. Slayer of Remus, and of King Acron after the rape of the Sabine women. After a reign of about forty years, latterly with Titus Tatius, was carried up to heaven in a whirlwind, alternatively was murdered by his senators. Worshipped as the god Quirinus.

ROOSTER *See* Alectryon.

ROPES OF STRAW *See* Ocnus.

ROSE *See* Aphrodite.

ROSALIA Roman festival, held 21 and 23 May, when the tombs of the dead were wreathed in roses.

RUMINA Roman goddess of suckling infants, both animal and human.

RUMOR Last daughter of Gaea. Swift of foot, and a spreader of gossip and rumour.

RUMOURS, goddess of Greek: Pheme. Roman: Fama.

RUTULI A tribe of Italy, ruled by Turnus. Was Aeneas' rival for the hand of Lavinia. The tribe waged war against Aeneas and his companions when they landed in Italy after their flight from Troy.

S

SABAZIUS Thracian epithet of Dionysus.

SABBE The Sibyl of Babylon, Egypt or Palestine.

SABINES A people of ancient Italy, living in the Apennines, and neighbours of the Etruscans, Latins, Samnites and Umbrians. One tribe lived on the Quirinal hill. A garrison of men on the Palatine hill abducted and raped the Sabine women as there was a shortage of their own women, and war ensued. Later the two were united under one king, the Sabine Titus Tatius sharing the throne for a time with Romulus.

SACES A friend who urged Turnus not to fight Aeneas.

SAGITTARIUS The archer. Ninth sign of the zodiac. Represents Crotus.

SALACIA Roman goddess of springs. Wife of Neptune. Known to the Greeks as Amphitrite.

SALAMIS (1) Daughter of Asopus and Metope. Sister of Ismenus, Pelagon, Cleone, Chalcis, Ismene, Pelasgus, Plataea, Aegina, Antiope, Corcyra, Thebe and ten others. Abducted by Poseidon to an Aegean island of the same name. (2) Mountainous island of Greece in the Aegean Sea, off the coast of Attica. Now called Koluri. Eventually incorporated into Megara.

SALAMIS, kings of Cynchreus (first), Eurysaces, Telamon.

SALII Roman priests of Mars. Priests appointed by Numa to guard the Ancile, the sacred shield of Mars.

SALIUS A contestant in the funeral games of Anchises, he was tripped when lying second in the running event so that Euryalus could win.

SALMACIS (1) A fountain in Caria near Halicarnassus which made men effeminate when they drank from it. (2) Nymph of the fountain. When Hermaphroditus drank from the fountain, his body fused with that of the nymph.

SALMONEUS King of Elis. Son of Aeolus and Enarete. Brother of six boys: Athamas, Cretheus, Deion, Macareus, Perieres and Sisyphus; and of seven sisters: Alcyone, Arne, Calyce, Canace, Peisidice, Perimele and Tanagra. Married Alcidice. She died in childbirth, producing Tyro. He then married Sidero. Expelled from Thessaly by Sisyphus, and killed by Zeus for imitating thunder and lightning, and sent to the Underworld.

SALUS (Hygieia) Roman goddess of health. Known to the Greeks as Hygeia, her festival date was 30 March.

SAMIA Daughter of Maeander. Sister of Cyanee. Married Ancaeus. Mother of Parthenope and four sons.

SANDORCUS Probably the father of Cinyras.

SANDPIPER *See* Itys.

SANGARIUS Phrygian river god. Son of Oceanus and Tethys. Father of Nana and possibly father of Hecuba by Metope. Father of a daughter who became pregnant by eating an almond, then a tree sprang up by the riverside.

SARON King of Althepia (Troezen). Succeeded Althepus to the throne and was drowned while pursuing a hind, falling into the Gulf of Althepia, which was later renamed the Saronic.

SARPEDON Son of Europa and Zeus. Brother of Minos and Rhadamanthys. Reared by Asterius. Lover of Miletus. Married Laodameia. Father of Evander (Evandrus).

 Went into exile when Minos became king of Crete. Became an ally of Priam in the Trojan War, commanding the Lycian forces with Glaucus. Killed by Patroclus.

SARPEDON (1) Son of Evander and Deidameia. Brother of Pallantia, Pallas and Roma. Some say that it was he, rather than his grandfather, who commanded the Lycian troops. (2) Possibly a son of Poseidon who was killed by Heracles for torturing visitors to his home.

SATINUS Trojan son of Enops and a nymph. Killed in the Trojan War by Greater Ajax.

SATURN Roman god of agriculture. Associated by the Greeks with Cronos, but rather resembles Demeter; the early Italians associated him with Lua. Husband of Ops and father of Jupiter, who deposed him as ruler of the world. Father of Juno and Picus by Venilia, and possibly of Sterculus. His festivals began on 17 December.

SATURNALIA Ancient Roman harvest festivals of Saturn. Date: 17 December, but later extended to 17–19 December or even 15–19 December. The holiday was made into a carnival and distinctions of rank between master and servant were reversed.

SATURNIA Epithet of Juno, daughter of Saturn.

SATYR *See* Antiope, Zeus.

SATYRS (Fauns) Half-human woodland spirits, with the legs and feet of goats. Followers of Dionysus, and some of Pan. They had hairy bodies and short horns on their foreheads. Older Satyrs were called Sileni. They were descendants of Hecaterus and Apis, Car or Niobe, the three daughters of Phoroneus.

Satyr

SCAEAN GATE The north-west gate of Troy, only opened in times of war. The Wooden Horse entered the city through this gate.

SCAMANDER (Xanthus) A river god. Son of Oceanus and Tethys. Father of Teucer, king of Troy, by Idaea and of Callirrhoe, Rhoeo, and Strymo. By flooding his river, aided the Trojans against the Greeks in the War. The river rises on Mt Ida and, after being joined by the Simois, flows into the Hellespont. Xanthus means yellow, the name applied by the Greeks because it could dye all hair that colour. Now called Mendereh.

SCAMANDRIUS Another name for Astyanax.

SCEIRON (Sciron) (1) The north-west wind, son of Astraeus and Eos. (2) Son of Pelops or Poseidon. Father of Endeis. An

209

outlaw. Killed by Theseus. (3) Son of Pylas. Brother of Pylia. Warlord of Megara.

SCHEDIUS Son of Iphitus. Brother of Epistrophus. With his brother, took forty ships to Troy from Phocis. Killed by Hector.

SCHEDIUS Son of Perimedes.

SCHERIE Another name for Corcyra or Drepane, now called Corfu.

SCHOENEUS King of part of Boeotia. Son of Athamas and Themisto. Brother of Erythrius, Leucon and Ptous.

SCORPIO (the scorpion) Eighth sign of the zodiac. Represents the scorpion that killed Orion.

SCORPION *See* Orion.

SCYLACEUS A friend of Glaucus and Sarpedon in the Trojan War. Wounded by Lesser Ajax, he returned home to Lycia where he told the womenfolk which men had fallen. For this, they stoned him to death but at Apollo's command he was later worshipped as a god.

SCYLLA Daughter of Nisus, king of Megara. Sister of Eurymede and Iphinoe.
Her father had a purple lock of hair which made him invulnerable. She cut off the lock to enable Minos to conquer the city of Megara. Refusing then to marry her in return, he killed her. She became a lark or petrel.

SCYLLA According to various traditions, daughter of Phorcys, Trienus, Triton or Typhon and Crataeis, Echidna, Hecate or Lamia. Sister of Echidna, the Graiae and Gorgons. She was a beautiful virgin but when Glaucus showed preference for her over Circe, Circe transformed her into a monster with her upper part human and her lower trunk encircled with the necks and heads of six barking dogs. She lived on the Italian side of a strait opposite Charybdis,

her sister. Lived on a cliff where a large fig tree grew. Snatched six sailors from Odysseus' ship. Killed by Heracles, but returned to life as she was immortal.

SCYRIUS Said to be the real father of Aegeus, which meant that Pandion was only his guardian.

SEA-EAGLE *See* Nisus.

SEA-GULL *See* Ceyx.

SEA-SNAKE *See* Antiphas, Laocoon, Thymbraeus.

SEAL *See* Proteus, Psamathe.

SEASONS, goddesses of Spring: Thallo. Autumn: Carpo. They are the Athenian Horae.

SEASONS (Horae) Daughters of Zeus and Themis. Called Dike, Eirene and Eunomia. Companions of Aphrodite.

SELEMNUS Lover of the nymph, Argyra, he died of grief after she tired of him, and Aphrodite changed him into a river.

SELENE (Luna) Greek goddess of the moon. Daughter of Hyperion or Pallas and Euryphaessa or Theia. Sister of Eos and Helios if daughter of Hyperion and Thea. Mother of Pandia by Zeus, and of fifty daughters by Endymion. Identified with Artemis (Diana), she drove a chariot with two white horses across the sky. Epithet: Phoebe.

SELENE (1) Possibly daughter of Pallas, son of Megamedes. (2) Possibly mother of Aetolus, Epeius, Eurycyda and Paeon by Endymion.

SELINUS King of Aegialus. The father of Helice, wife of Ion, king of Athens.

SELLI An ancient race from Dodona, whose priests Perseus consulted when searching for Medusa.

SEMELE Daughter of Cadmus and Harmonia. Sister of Agave, Autonoe, Illyrius, Ino and Polydorus. Her nurse was Beroe. Possibly mother of Dionysus by Zeus. Died when Zeus appeared before her in his full glory as a result of Hera's jealousy.

SEMONES Collective name for the gods of Rome, including Faunus, Janus, Pan, Priapus, Silenus and Vertumnus. Also applied to the Satyrs and all deified mortal heroes after their death.

SENSUAL PLEASURE, Roman goddess of Voluptas.

SERAPIS Epithet of Osiris, Egyptian god of the Underworld.

SERESTUS *See* Sergestus.

SERGESTUS Mnestheus, Serestus and Sergestus were three Trojans who accompanied Aeneas to Italy from Troy. Sergestus finished last in the boat race in the funeral games of Anchises. Founder of the Sergian family of Rome.

SERIPHUS, kings of Polydectes, followed by Dictys.

SERVIUS TULLIUS Sixth king of Rome. Son of Ocrisia, a slave of Tanaquil, or he may have been an Etruscan. Married a daughter of Tarquinius. Father of two daughters both called Tullia.
During his forty-four-year reign, enlarged the city, taking in the Esquiline, Quirinal and Viminal hills. Placed great emphasis on religious practices. Built temples to the goddess of fortune, Fortuna, and also to Diana. His son-in-law, Lucius killed him and usurped his throne.

SESTOS Thracian town on the shores of the Hellespont, opposite Abydos. Respective homes of Hero and Leander. The people allied to the Trojans in the War.

SEVEN AGAINST THEBES Adrastus (alternatively Eteocles, son of Iphis); Amphiarus; Capaneus; Hippomedon; Parthenopaeus; Polyneices (alternatively Mecisteus, brother of Adrastus); and Tydeus.
Eteocles expelled his brother, Polyneices, from Thebes. The latter went to Argos, where he married Argeia, daughter of Adrastus. Polyneices and six other leaders tried to conquer the seven-gated city of Thebes and all but Adrastus were killed. Ten years later the sons of the Seven (Epigoni) successfully avenged their fathers.

SEVEN HILLS OF ROME Aventine, Caelian, Capitoline, Esquiline, Palatine, Quirinal and Viminal.

SEVEN KINGS OF ROME 1. Romulus. 2. Numa Pompilius. 3. Tullus Hostilius. 4. Ancus Martius. 5. Tarquinius Priscus. 6. Servius Tullius. 7. Tarquinius Superbus.

SEVEN WISE MEN OF GREECE 1. Bias of Priene, 6th century BC. 2. Chilon of Sparta, 6th century BC. 3. Cleobulus of Rhodes, 6th century BC. 4. Periander of Corinth, 7th–6th century BC. 5. Pittacus of Mytilene, 7th century BC. 6. Solon of Athens, 7th century BC. 7. Thales of Miletus, 7th century BC.

SEVEN WONDERS OF THE WORLD 1. The Pyramids of Egypt. 2. The Pharos Lighthouse at Alexandria. 3. The Hanging Gardens of Babylon. 4. The Temple of Diana at Ephesis. 5. The Statue of Zeus at Olympia. 6. The Mausoleum at Halicarnassus. 7. The Colossus of Helios at Rhodes.

SEXTUS TARQUINIUS Rapist of Lucretia.

SEXUAL LOVE, Greek goddess of Aphrodite.

SHEEP, Greek god of Priapus.

SHEPHERDS, Roman god of Pales. (May have been a female deity.)

SHIELD OF MARS Called the Ancile, it was guarded by the Salii.

SHOWER OF GOLD *See* Danae, Zeus.

SIBYL Name given to one or more prophetesses in ancient mythology. Pausanias mentions four, Egyptian, Erythraean, Samian and Sardian; Aristophanes and Plato mention just one; Varro enumerates ten, and says that they resided at Cimmeria, Cumae (the most famous), Delphi, Erythrae, Libya, Marpessa, Persia, Phrygia, Samos and Tibur. The Persian Sibyl was also called the Trojan or the Hellespontine. They interceded with the gods on behalf of mortals. The original Sibyl was called Sibylla, according to some, a daughter of Dardanus and Neso. The Libyan Sibyl was a daughter of Zeus and Lamia. The Egyptian was called Sabbe. The Marpessan was called Herophile and was a daughter of Dardanus and Neso. The Erythraean was identified with Herophile. The Cumaean Sibyl was called Amalthea, Deiphobe, Demo, Demophile, Herophile or Phemonoe. Aristotle associates her with the Erythraean.

SICHAEUS (Acerbas) Priest of Heracles at Phoenicia. Husband of Dido. Murdered by her brother, Pygmalion, for his money. Also called Acherbas, Adherbas or Sicherbas.

SICILY The largest island of the Mediterranean, three kilometres off the southwest coast of Italy and separated from the mainland by the Straits of Messina. Mt Aetna, the home of Hephaestus, was here. Italus was one of its kings.

SICINUS Son of Thoas and Oenoe.

SICYON (1) An ancient city in the Peloponnesus, about 3 km south of the Gulf of Corinth and 11 km north-west of Corinth. Earlier was called Aegialeia. Close to the river Asopus. (2) Possibly a son of Metion or Eupalamus and Alcippe. Married Zeuxippe. Sister of Daedalus and Perdix.

Father of Chthonophyle. (3) Son of Pelops or Marathon, or a son or grandson of Erechtheus. Brother of Corinthus.

SICYON, kings of Apis was the first, followed by nine generations of kings of the same name. Next came Corax, brother of Laomedon, Epopeus, Lamedon, Sicyon, Polybus, Adrastus, Janiscus, Phaestus, Zeuxippus, Hippolytus and, finally and jointly, Lacestades and Phalces. After that, Sicyon became a province of Argos.

SIDE First wife of Orion, sent to the Underworld by Hera for boasting that she was more beautiful than the goddess.

SIDERO The 'iron one'. Second wife of Salmoneus and stepmother of Tyro. She was killed by Neleus and Pelias for trying to persuade Salmoneus to kill Tyro.

SIDON Possibly father of Europa by Argiope.

SILENCE, Roman goddess of Muta.

SILENI Elderly companions of Dionysus. They were satyr-like.

SILENUS (plural Sileni) Primitive woodland gods of Asia Minor, followers of Dionysus and Pan. Silenus was the son of Hermes, Gaea or Pan and the teacher of Dionysus. Killer of Enceladus. He resembled a satyr, with which the Sileni are associated, and they were often drunk. Silenus was king of Nysa and was possibly the father of Pholus the centaur by an ash nymph. An expert musician.

SILLUS Son of Thrasymedes.

SILVANUS Roman agricultural god. One of the Numina. Half man, half goat, he is often associated with Mars. Presided over boundaries.

SILVIA Daughter of Tyrrheus. Mother of Romulus and Remus. *See* Rhea Silvia.

212

SILVIUS (Aeneas Silvius) The last son of Aeneas and Lavinia, born when the couple were old. Ancestor of the kings of Alba Longa.

SIMOEIS A river god. Son of Oceanus and Tethys. Father of Astyoche and Hieromneme. His river, now called the Dombrek, rose on Mt Ida and flowed into the Scamander near Troy.

SINIS Son of Polypemon (also called Damastes or Procrustes) and Sylea. Father of Perigune. This Corinthian outlaw was nicknamed Pitocamptes (pinebender) because of his habit of tying his victims to pine trees and catapulting them in the air. Theseus killed him in the same way.

SINON Son of Sisyphus and related to Odysseus. This Greek spy in the Trojan camp persuaded the Trojans to bring the Wooden Horse inside the walls of Troy and to consecrate it to Athena.

SINOPE Daughter of Asopus. Loved by Apollo, Zeus and Halys, she resisted all of them to remain a virgin, though some call her mother of Syrus by Apollo.

SIPYLUS Son of Amphion and Niobe. Brother of Alphenor, Damasichthon, Ilenus, Ismenos, Phaedimus and Tantalus, and of six sisters, Callirrhoe, Chloris, Cleodoxa, Phylomache, Neaera and Phthia. Killed by Apollo.

SIRENS (Acheloides) Sea nymphs of Greek mythology who sat on the shore of an island called Anthemoessa, located between those of Circe and Scylla. Daughters of Achelous and Calliope, Melpomene,

Sirens

Terpsichore or Sterope, the daughter of Porthaon. According to Homer, there were two, but other writers name three: Leucosia, Ligeia and Parthenope, or Aglaopheme, Molpe and Thelxiepeia (Telexiepeia). Others named Himeropa and Peisinoe as Sirens. Bird-like, they lured sailors to Anthemoessa with their song where the sailors died, enchanted, of hunger. They failed with Odysseus and his crew and with the Argonauts, then drowned themselves. Orpheus rivalled them in song.

SIRIUS The dog star. The brightest star in the sky, representing Maera, faithful dog of Orion.

SISYPHUS King of Corinth. Son of Aeolus and Enarete. Brother of six boys: Athamas, Cretheus, Deion, Macareus, Perieres and Salmoneus; and of seven sisters: Alcyone, Arne, Calyce, Canace, Peisidice, Perimele and Tanagra. Married Merope, one of the Pleiades. Father of Glaucus, Halmus, Ornytion and Thersander. Lover of Anticleia. Possibly the father of Odysseus and Sinon. Father of two sons by Tyro, who murdered both. Possibly father of Creon. A clever, cunning man, he owned cattle that were regularly stolen until he caught the culprit. Established the Isthmian Games in memory of his nephew, Melicertes. Various sources give different reasons for the harsh punishment he received in the Underworld where he was punished by constantly having to push up a hill a large stone that, just as constantly, rolled back down again before it reached the top. The principal explanations are: (1) Zeus punished him in this way after death because of his cruel and unscrupulous behaviour on earth. (2) He accused Zeus of abducting Aegina (as he did). (3) For the above reason, Zeus sent Death to avenge him, Hades released Aegina and gave Sisyphus this punishment. (4) He complained that his wife neglected him after his death. Having been allowed to remonstrate with her, he received his punishment when he refused to leave the upper world.

SKY, Roman god of the Dius Fidius.

SLEEP, god of Greek: Hypnos. Roman: Somnus.

SMILAX A shepherdess and lover of Crocus. She became a yew tree or crocus.

SMINTHEUS Epithet of Apollo, the mouse-god.

SMYRNA (Myrrha) Daughter of Cinyras with whom she had incestuous relations.

SNAKE *See* Cadmus, Chimaera, Harmonia, Opheltes, Philoctetes, Zagreus.

SOCUS Son of Hippasus. Brother of Charops. Killed in the Trojan War by Odysseus.

Sisyphus

SOIS Mother of Pelasgus by Triopas.

SOL Roman sun god. Sacrificial dates 9 August, 11 December. Greek equivalents: Apollo, Helios, Hyperion.

SOLON One of the Seven Wise Men of Greece (qv). Others were: Bias, Chilon, Cleobulus, Periander, Pittacus and Thales.

SOLYMI Race of mighty Lycian warriors who fought an unsuccessful war with Bellerophon.

SOMNOS (Hypnos) Roman god of sleep. Father of a thousand sons, including Icelos, Phantasos and Morpheus. *See* Phobetor.

SOTEIRA Epithet of Athena, Artemis and Persephone.

SOTER (1) An epithet of Zeus, the saviour. (2) Name given by the Greeks to gods of deliverance from danger. (3) Roman god of deliverance from danger.

SOTERIA Sacrificial thanksgiving days for deliverance from danger.

SOUTH WIND Auster or Notus.

SOWN-MEN *See* Sparti.

SPARROW *See* Aphrodite.

SPARTA Also called Lacedaemon, principal city of Laconia, the most famous city of the Peloponnesus, 32 km from the sea. A race of strict-discipline fighters.

SPARTA, kings of Lelex was the first king, followed by Eurotas, Lacedaemon, Amyclas, Oebalus, Tyndareus, Hippocoon, Tyndareus again, Menelaus, Orestes and Tisamenus. Other kings were Argalus, followed by Cynortas and Perieres; Leobotas; and Eurysthenes and Procles jointly, with Theras acting as regent for them.

SPARTE Daughter of Eurotas. Sister of Tiasa. Married Lacedaemon. Mother of Amyclas and Eurydice. Eponym of Sparta.

SPARTI (Spartae, sown-men) Theban men born when Cadmus threw dragon's teeth on the ground (Gaea). The sown-men started to fight at birth, and only five survived: Chthonius, Echion, Hyperenor, Pelorus and Udaeus. Jason sowed a second crop from the second dragon, but they all killed each other. Pentheus, son of Echion, succeeded Cadmus to the throne of Thebes.

SPEIO A Nereid. One of the fifty daughters of Nereus and Doris.

SPERCHEIUS A river god. Son of Oceanus and Tethys. Father of Menesthius by Polydora. God of a river of the same name in southern Thessaly.

SPERMO (seed) Devotee of Dionysus. Daughter of Anius. Sister of Elais and Oino. She could produce corn from the ground merely by touch.

SPES (hope) A goddess linked with Fortuna and invoked by all those who wished for success.

SPHAERUS Charioteer of Pelops. Called Cillas by the gods, he was buried on the sacred island of Hiera (Sphaeria), birthplace of Theseus.

SPHELUS Son of Bucolus. Father of Iasus.

SPHINX Daughter of Typhon and Echnidna, or possibly Orthus and Chimaera. Sister of Cerberus, Chimaera, Orthus, the Hydra, Crommyonian Sow, Caucasian Eagle, Nemean Lion and vultures. A monster, her upper part was woman, her lower part dog with the tail of a snake, wings of a bird, paws of a lion and a human voice. She ate all Thebans who could not answer her riddle, but killed herself after Oedipus solved it. The Sphinx was sent to Thebes by Hera to punish Laius.

SPHINX, riddle of the 'What is it that walks on four legs in the morning, two

Sphinx

legs at noon and three legs in the evening?'
Answer: Man.

SPIDER   *See* Arachne.

SPRINGS, Roman god of   Fontus.

SPRINGS, Roman goddess of   Juturna,
Salacia.

SPURIUS TARPEIUS   Father of
Tarpeia.

STAG   *See* Actaeon, Arge, Iphigeneia.

STAPHYLUS   (1) A goatherd of Oeneus
who found a wild vine and gave the grapes
to his master. Dionysus showed Oeneus
how to make wine from the grapes. (2) Son
of Dionysus or Theseus and Ariadne.
Brother of Ceramus, Oenopion, Phanus,
Peparethus and Thoas. Married Chrysothemis. An Argonaut and king of one of the
Aegean islands.

STENTOR   A Greek in the Trojan War
with a voice fifty times more powerful than
normal. Died after losing a shouting match
with Hermes.

STERCULUS   King of Latium. Son of
Faunus. Possibly father of Picus. Often
identified with Saturn. First to use manure,
and the inventor of agricultural tools.

STEROPE (Asterope)   (1) Daughter of
Acastus and Astydameia or possibly Hippolyte. Sister of Laodameia and Sthenele.
(2) Daughter of Atlas and Pleione. One of
the Pleiades. Sister of Alcyone, Celaeno,
Electra, Maia, Merope and Taygete. She
either married Oenomaus, or was his mother
by Ares or Alxion. (3) Daughter of
Cepheus. Sister of Aerope and perhaps
Echemus. (4) Daughter of Porthaon and
Euryte. Sister of Agrius, Alcathous, Melas,
Oeneus and Leucopeus. Possibly mother of
the Sirens (qv) by Achelous.

STEROPES (lightning)   One of the
Cyclopes. Son of Uranus and Gaea. Brother
of Arges and Brontes.

STHENEBOEA   Daughter of Iobates.
Sister of Philonoe. Wife of Proetus. Mother
of Iphinoe, Iphianassa, Lysippe and
Megapenthes. Committed suicide after failing to seduce Bellerophon. Bellerophon
married her sister.

STHENELE   Daughter of Acastus and
Astydameia. Sister of Laodameia and
Sterope. Married Menoetius. Mother of
Patroclus.

STHENELUS   (1) Son of Actor. Killed
while fighting the Amazons, with Heracles.
His ghost appeared to the Argonauts.
(2) Son of Androgeus. Brother of Alcaeus.
King of Thasos on the isle of Paros. Given
to Heracles as a hostage during his ninth
labour. (3) Son of Capaneus and Evadne.
Father of Cometes and Cylarbes. As a
suitor of Helen, he went to the Trojan
War to be the charioteer for his friend,
Diomedes. He was in the Wooden Horse.

One of the Epigoni. (4) Son of Perseus and Andromeda. Brother of Alcaeus, Gorgophone, Heleus, Mestor, Perses and Electryon. Married Antibia or Nicippe (Amphibia). Father of Alcyone, Eurystheus and Medusa. King of Mycenae, he seized the throne from Amphitryon. (5) Father of Cycnus.

STHENO A gorgan. Daughter of Phorcys and Ceto. Sister of Euryae, Medusa, Ladon and the Graiae.

STICHIUS An Athenian captain. During the Trojan War, he and Menestheus recovered the body of Amphimachus. Killed by Hector.

STILBE (1) Daughter of Hypseus. Sister of Astyagyia, Cyrene and Themisto. (2) Daughter of Peneius and Creusa. Mother of Centaurus and Lapithus by Apollo.

STONE *See* Anaxerete, Battus, Cleodoxa, Echo, Lethae, Lichas, Niobe, Passalus, Phineus, Polydectes, Proetus, Scylla.

STOREROOMS, Roman gods of Penates.

STOREROOMS, guardian of Ktesios, epithet of Zeus.

STORK *See* Antigone.

STORMS, Roman goddess of Tempestas.

STRATIUS Son of Nestor and Eurydice or Anaxibia. Brother of Antilochus, Aretus, Echephron, Paeon, Peisidice, Peisistratus, Perseus, Polycaste and Thrasymedes.

STRENUA Roman goddess of vigour. She gave energy to the weak and indolent.

STRIFE, goddess of Discordia, Eris.

STRIFE Son of Eris (Roman, Discordia).

STRIGES Descendants of the Harpies, they were vampires that attacked the young. Cardea was the goddess invoked to keep them at bay.

STROPHIUS I King of Phocis. Son of Crisus. Brother of Astyoche and possibly Anaxibia. Father of Pylades by Anaxibia, sister of Agamemnon. Disowned his son after he and Orestes murdered Aegisthus and Clytemnestra.

STROPHIUS II Son of Pylades and Electra (Laodice). Brother of Medon. Father of Pylades II.

STRYMO Daughter of Scamander. Sister of Callirrhoe, Rhoeo and Teucer. Married Laomedon. Mother of Astyoche, Cilla, Clytius, Hesione, Hicetaon, Lampus, Priam (Podarces) and Tithonus.

STRYMON Thracian river god. Son of Oceanus and Tethys. Father of Rhesus by Calliope or Euterpe. Father of Evadne by Neaera.

STYMPHALIAN BIRDS Long-legged man-eating birds that inhabited Lake Stymphalus in north-east Arcadia. Heracles killed them as his sixth labour.

STYMPHALUS King of Arcadia. Son of Elatus and Laodice. Father of Agamedes, Gortys and Parthenope. Killed by Pelops.

STYX An Oceanid. Eldest daughter of Oceanus and Tethys. Sister of many including Asia, Callirrhoe, Clymene, Clytia, Electra, Europa, Perseis, Pleione, the river gods and many more. Mother of Bia, Nike, Kratos and Zelos by the Titan, Pallas. Mother of Echidna by Peiras. Possibly mother of Persephone by Zeus, but it is more likely that her mother was Demeter. She was the first to aid Zeus when the Titans attacked. Ruled over the river Styx in the Underworld.

STYX One of the five rivers of Hades.

Others: Acheron, Cocytus, Lethe and Phlegethon.

SUADA (Suadela) Roman goddess of persuasion. Known to the Greeks as Peitho.

SUCKLING INFANTS, Roman goddess of Rumina.

SUCULAE Roman name for the Hyades.

SUMMANUS Roman Epithet, probably of Hades, referring to his power over the night sky.

SUNFLOWER *See* Clytia.

SUN-GOD Greek: Apollo, Helios, Hyperion. Roman: Sol.

SWALLOW *See* Aphrodite, Procne.

SWAN *See* Apollo, Cycnus, Helen, Leda, Phaethon, Polydeuces.

SYCHAEUS (Sichaeus) Husband of Dido and uncle of Pygmalion and Dido. Pygmalion murdered him for his money.

SYLEA Daughter of Corinthus. Mother of Sinis by Damastes.

SYLEUS A Lydian outlaw, native of Aulis and father of Xenodice. Killed by Heracles with the same hoe with which he forced people to till the ground for him.

SYLLIS A nymph. Mother of Zeuxippus by Apollo.

SYLVANI Woodland deities, followers of Pan.

SYRINX An Arcadian Hamadryad. A virgin huntress beloved by Pan. To escape him, she became a reed bed out of which Pan made his flute (pipes) called a syrinx.

SYRNA Daughter of Bybassus, a goatherd. Married Podalirius.

SYRUS Son of Apollo, possibly by Sinope. Eponym of Syria.

T

TAENARUM   Laconian promontory, the most southerly point of Europe and back entrance to the Underworld.

TAGES   Son of Genius (Roman, Iovialis). Grandson of Zeus (Jupiter). Taught the Etruscans the art of prophecy.

TAGUS   A Rutulian killed by Nisus.

TALAIRA (Hilaira, Hilara)   Sister of Phoebe. Abducted by Castor and Polydeuces. *See also* Hilaira.

TALARIA   The winged sandals of Hermes.

TALASSIUS   A Roman who abducted the most beautiful of the Sabine women.

TALAUS   An Argonaut. Son of Bias and Pero. Brother of Areius and Leodocus, and possibly Alphesiboea, Aretus and Perialces. Married either Lysianassa, daughter of Polybus, or Lysimache, or possibly Eurynome, daughter of Iphitus. Father of Adrastus, Aristomachus, Astynome, Eriphyle, Hippomedan, Mecisteus, Metidice, Parthenopaeus and Pronax.

TALTHYBIOS (Talthybius)   Agamemnon's chief herald at the Trojan War, he performed all the unpleasant missions. After his master's death, became herald to Orestes, sharing the job with Eurybates.

TALUS (Talos)   (1) Son of Cres. Possibly father of Phaestus by Europa. Guardian of Crete (cf (3)). (2) Son of Perdix. Brother of Daedalus. An inventor, also called Perdix, he was the creator of the compass and saw. Killed by his brother, he changed into a partridge. (3) A man of brass created by Hephaestus. A giant and possibly a robot. A guardian of Crete. Given to Minos or Europa, he was killed by the Argonaut, Poeas.

TANAGRA   Daughter of Aeolus and Enarete. Sister of seven boys: Athamas, Cretheus, Deion, Macareus, Perieres, Salmoneus and Sisyphus; and of six girls: Alcyone, Arne, Calyce, Canace, Peisidice and Perimele.

TANAQUIL   Etruscan wife of Lucius Tarquinius Priscus, fifth king of Rome.

TANTALUS   King of Sipylus. Son of Zeus and Pluto. Married Dione. Father of Broteas, Niobe and Pelops. Possessed great wealth, which corrupted him. Killed Pelops, cooked the body and served it as food for the gods. Zeus buried him under Mt Sipylus. Another story about him is that he stole a gold dog from Zeus, and also ambrosia and nectar for mortals. For these deeds Zeus consigned him to everlasting torture in the Underworld. He stands in a lake up to his chin, but the water recedes when he tries to drink. Above his head just out of reach, are clusters of fruit, and a huge rock is in constant danger of falling and crushing him. Some say his punishment was for divulging the divine counsels of Zeus.

TANTALUS   (1) One of the twelve children, six boys and six girls, of Amphion and Niobe. (2) Son of Broteas or Thyestes. Married Clytemnestra. Killed by Agamemnon. It was possibly he who killed Pelops, (see above entry). (3) Bastard son of Thyestes and Aerope. Twin of Aglaus and half-brother of Pleisthenes. He and his twin were killed by Atreus. Father of Broteas, Niobe and Pelops by Dione.

NB (2) and (3) are two versions of the life of one Tantalus.

TAPHIUS   King of Taphos. Son of Poseidon and Hippothoe. Father of Pterelaus, his successor.

TARAXHIPPOS (horse-scarer)   The ghost of Glaucus of Corinth, murdered by Pelops, was called Myrtilus. Pelops erected a monument to him, called Taraxhippos, at the Olympic or Isthmian stadium.

TARCHON King of Etruria. An ally of Aeneas in Italy. Some call him the ploughman who unearthed Tages.

TARPEIA A vestal virgin. Daughter of Spurius Tarpeius. She was attracted by the gold and ornament of the bracelets the Sabines wore on their left arms. She was tempted by this to open a gate of Rome for them to enter. As a reward for her treachery, they buried her under their armour shields which were also carried on the left.

TARQUINIUS PRISCUS, Lucius (Lucumo) Son of the exiled Corinthian, Demaratus. Married Tanaquil, an Etruscan. Father of Aruns and Lucius. The fifth king of Rome, he ruled thirty-eight years from 616–578 BC. He defeated the Sabines and annexed all the ancient Latin towns. Murdered by two sons of his predecessor, Ancus Martius.

TARQUINIUS SEXTUS Son of Lucius Tarquinius Superbus, who was the last king of Rome and ruled from 534–510 BC. His rape of Lucretia led to the rebellion against his father that heralded the end of the Roman monarchy. He, in turn, was murdered by the people of Gabii, whom he had earlier betrayed.

TARQUINIUS SUPERBUS, Lucius Seventh and last king of Rome. Husband of Tullia, daughter of Servius Tullius. Father of Tarquinius Sextus. He ruled from 534–510 BC. Built the Cloaca Maxima, the great sewer of Rome, and the temple of Jupiter on the Capitoline hill. After his son raped Lucretia, he was driven from his throne by Lucius Junius Brutus and others.

TARTARUS The lowest region of the Underworld. Here were sent the most wicked offenders of humanity and the greatest enemies of Zeus, such as the Titans.

TARTARUS Born out of Chaos, as were Eros and Gaea. Father of Echidna and Typhoeus by Gaea.

TATIA Daughter of Tatius, king of the Sabines. Married Numa Pompilius.

TATIUS, Titus King of the Sabines. Father of Tatia, wife of Numa Pompilius. After the rape of the Sabine women, he avenged his people, and later shared the throne of Rome with Romulus. Killed in a quarrel with the Laurentians.

TAURUS (1) An arrogant noble, captain of the navy of Minos of Crete. Defeated in competition by Theseus, to the delight of Minos who hated him. (2) Second sign of the zodiac, representing Zeus as a bull.

TAYGETE One of the Pleiades. Daughter of Atlas and Pleione. Sister of Alcyone, Celaeno, Electra, Maia, Merope and Sterope. Mother of Lacedaemon by Zeus.

TECMASSA (Tecmessa) Daughter of Teleutas. Wife or concubine of Greater Ajax. Mother of Eurysaces.

TECTAMUS King of Crete. Son of Dorus by a daughter of Cretheus. Brother of Aegimius. Father of Asterius by another daughter of Cretheus.

TEGEA The principal city of south-east Arcadia, which was later incorporated into Arcadia. Modern Piali is on the same site.

TEGEA, kings of Aleus, followed by Aphidamas, Cepheus and Lycurgus jointly, Echemus and Agapenor. Apheidas was also at one time king.

TEGEATES Possibly the father of Cydon by Acacallis, the alternative being Hermes.

TEIRESIAS (Tiresias) Seer of Thebes and the greatest of the prophets of mythology. Son of Everes and Chariclo and father of Chloris and Manto.

He was struck blind in his youth by Athena, either for observing her bathing or for siding with Zeus in a dispute between the god and goddess. Zeus gave him his powers. After killing a female snake he was transformed into a woman until, eight years later, he killed a male snake and was transformed back into a man.

TELAMON King of Salamis. Son of Aeacus and Creusa or Endeis. Brother of Peleus and half-brother of Phocus whom he later killed, aided by Peleus. Married Glauce, daughter of Cynchreus, king of Salamis. After her death, married Periboea, daughter of Alcathous. Father of Ajax though some call Eeriboea the mother. Finally married Hesione, daughter of Laomedon. Father of Teucer, though some call him a bastard. Present on the Calydonian Boar Hunt and an Argonaut.

TELAMUS A Cyclops. It was he who prophesied that Odysseus would blind Polyphemus.

TELCHIN With Thelxion, usurped the throne of Apis until deposed by Argus Panoptes.

TELCHINES Rhodian sorcerers. Sons of Pontus, Poseidon and Thalassa, or they may have been born from the blood of Uranus. They were named Antaeus, Lycus, Megalesius, Ormenos and five others. Brothers of Halia. They had webbed fingers and toes and had powers to bring rain. Inventors of many useful arts. Drowned by Zeus.

TELEDAMAS Twin son of Agamemnon and Cassandra. He and his brother, Pelops, were murdered in infancy by Aegisthus.

TELEDICE (the spreader of laws) Possibly the wife of Phoroneus, hence mother of Apis, Car and Niobe.

TELEGONUS (1) Son of Circe by Odysseus. Brother of Ardea and Agrius; brother or half-brother of Latinus. Married Penelope, his father's wife. Father of Italus. Accidentally killed his father, not knowing who he was. Founded the city of Prinistos.

He went to the Blessed Isles with Penelope. (2) The husband of Io King of Egypt. Ancestor of Danaus, Heracles and Perseus. (3) Son of Proteus. Brother of Polygonus. Killed, wrestling with Heracles.

TELEMACHUS Son of Odysseus and Penelope. Brother of Ptoliporthes (Acusilaus). Married Circe. Possibly the father of Latinus. Or married Nausicaa and was the father of Perseptolis. Or married Polycaste and was the father of Perseptolis. Some even say that his wife was Cassiphone, daughter of Circe.

After meeting his father in Eumaeus' hut after Odysseus' twenty-year absence, he helped him kill the suitors. Telemachus also killed Circe and fled to Italy. During the absence of Odysseus at Troy, Telemachus was taught by Athena and later went in search of his father.

TELEON Father of Eribotes (Eurybates). Either he or Poseidon was the father of Butes by Zeuxippe.

TELEPHASSA (Argiope) Wife of Agenor, king of Tyre or Sidon. Mother of Cadmus, Cilix, Demodoce, Europa, Phineus, Phoenix, Thasus and possibly Argus. Accompanied her sons in their search for the abducted Europa. Telephassa and Argiope may have been two different people.

TELEPHUS King of Mysia. Son of Heracles and Auge. Fostered by Corythus. After being exposed on Mt Parthenius, was rescued and reared by King Teuthras as his own son. Married Argiope, daughter of Teuthras. Father of Eurypylus, possibly by Astyoche, or by Laodice, daughter of Priam of Troy. An oracle said that Troy would not fall without his help; he guided the Greeks to Troy, but took no part in the fighting.

TELESPHORUS God of convalesence. An attendant of Aesculapius, god of medicine.

221

TELETE One of the Pierides. One of the nine sisters of Pierus (qv) and Evippe.

TELETHUSA Wife of Ligdus and mother of Iphis.

TELEUTAS Father of Tecmassa, Ajax's concubine.

TELEXIEPEIA A Siren. Daughter of Achelous and Calliope, Melpomene or Terpsichore, all Muses, or of Sterope, daughter of Porthaon. Sister of Aglaopheme, Molpe and Peisinoe and perhaps others. *See* Sirens.

TELLUS (Terra) Roman earth-goddess. Known to the Greeks as Gaea, is associated with Pluto. Her feast date was 15 April (Fordicidia) and her sacrificial date 13 December. The dead return to her.

TELPHUSA (Tilphussa) A prophetess. Daughter of the river-god Ladon, she was the nymph of a spring in Arcadia or Boeotia, the site of an oracle of Apollo. Tieresias died after drinking from this stream.

TEMENUS (1) Son of Aristomachus. Brother of Aristodemus and Cresphontes. Father of Ceisus, Hyrnetho and Phalces. A Heraclid king of Argos, was killed by his sons for making Deiphontes, husband of Hyrnetho, his adviser. (2) Son of Pelasgus. After rearing Hera, built three shrines for her at Stymphalus, those of a child, a bride and a widow. (3) Possibly a son of Phegeus and brother of Agenor, Arsinoe and Pronous and possibly Axion.

TEMPESTAS Roman goddess of winds and storms.

TENAGES One of the Heliades. Son of Helios and Rhode. Brother of Actis, Candalus, Cercaphus, Macar, Ochimus and Triopas. The cleverest brother. First to sacrifice to Athena. Murdered by Actis, Candalus, Macar and Triopas.

TENEDOS Small Aegean island twenty kilometres south of the Dardanelles, sacred to Apollo. It was behind the island, off the coast of Troy, that the Greek forces hid after leaving the Wooden Horse outside the walls of Troy.

TENES (Tennes) Eponym of Tenedos. Son of Cycnus, king of Colonae, or of Apollo and Procleia, daughter of Laomedon. Brother of Hemithea. Philonome, second wife of Cycnus, tried to seduce him. Killed by Achilles.

TEREIS A slave woman. Either she or Pieris was the mother of Megapenthes and Nicostratus by Menelaus.

TEREUS King of Thrace. Son of Ares. Husband of Procne. Father of Itys. After raping his sister-in-law, Philomela, he tried to prevent her telling anyone by cutting out her tongue. She conveyed a message to her sister by weaving the story into a tapestry. The two sisters served Itys as a meal to Tereus. He later changed into a hoopoe bird.

TERMILAE The name the Cretans gave themselves.

TERMINALIA Annual Roman festivals of Terminus, held on 23 February.

TERMINALIS Epithet of Zeus, guardian of land boundaries.

TERMINUS Roman god of boundaries. Festival date: 23 February. Originally an epithet of Jupiter,

TERPES Father of Phemius.

TERPSICHORE One of the Muses. Muse of the dance. Daughter of Zeus and Mnemosyne, one of nine sisters. She also educated the young. Possibly mother of the Sirens (Aglaopheme, Peisinoe, Molpe and Telexiepeia) by Achelous. She wore a crown of laurel and carried a lyre.

TERRA (Tellus) Roman goddess of the

earth. Greek equivalent of Gaea. Epithet: Titaea. *See* Tellus.

TERRA MATER Epithet of Rhea, mother of gods and goddesses.

TERROR (Pallor) Son and attendant of Ares and Bellona. Brother of Deimos, Eris and Phobos, and others.

TERROR, god of Phobos.

TETHYS A Titaness. Daughter of Uranus and Gaea. Married her brother, Oceanus. Mother of Asia, Callirrhoe, Clymene, Clytia, Doris, Europa, Eidyia, Electra, Inachus, Meliboea, Perseis, Pleione, Proteus, Styx, the rivers, fountains and Oceanides.

TEUCER (1) Son of Cretan Scamander and Idaea. Father of Bateia (Arisbe). Because of famine in Crete, he and one third of his subjects emigrated to Troy where he became the first king. A king of Phrygia, he introduced his subjects to the worship of Rhea. He was succeeded to the throne of Troy by Dardanus. (2) Son of Telamon and Hesione. Half-brother of Ajax. As a suitor of Helen he went to the Trojan War, where he was in the Wooden Horse. The best Greek archer at Troy, his father never forgave him for failing to avenge the death of Ajax. After the War, he went to Cyprus and married a daughter of Cinyras. Founded the city of Salamis.

TEUTAMIAS King of Larissa. Possibly the father of Danae (cf Acrisius, his friend).

TEUTHRAS (1) King of Phrygia. Also called Teleutas. Father of Tecmessa. After he was killed by Ajax, his daughter became concubine to Ajax. (2) King of Teuthrania in Mysia. Husband of Auge and father of Argiope. He fostered Telephus, son of Auge by Heracles. Telephus succeeded him to the throne.

THALASSA (Dione) Greek personification of the sea and, according to some,

mother of Aphrodite by Zeus. Wife of Pontus. Mother of the nine Telchines and Halia, though their father may have been Uranus or Poseidon.

THALES 7th century BC. One of the Seven Wise Men of Ancient Greece (qv). Others were: Bias, Chilon, Cleobulus, Periander, Pittacus and Solon. Founder of the Ionic school of philosophy. A native of Miletus.

THALIA (1) Daughter of Zeus and Eurynome. Also called 'rejoicing', she was one of the Charites (Graces). Sister of Aglaea, Pasithea and Euphrosyne. Mother of the Palici by Zeus. (2) Daughter of Zeus and Mnemosyne. One of the nine Muses. Muse of comedy, she carried a mask used by comedy actors and a shepherd's staff. (3) One of the Nereids.

THALLO (spring) One of the Seasons. Daughter of Zeus and Themis. Sister of Carpo (autumn).

THALPIUS Son of Eurytas and Theraephone. As a suitor of Helen, he and his cousin Amphimachus led the Eleian forces in the Trojan War.

THAMYRIS Minstrel of Thrace. Son of Philammon and Argiope. Possibly the lover of Hyacinthus. Inventor of the Dorian harmony, he lost a musical contest with the Muses who then took away his sight and his voice, and destroyed his lyre.

THANATOS (death) Son of Nyx and Erebus. Twin of Hypnos. Brother of Aether, Cer, Dreams, Hemera, Charon, Momus, Moros and Nemesis. Also called Paean, the healing god, this inhabitant of Tartarus was known to the Romans as Mors.

THARGELIA Early summer festival of Apollo.

THASUS Son of Agenor and Telephassa or Argiope. Brother of Cadmus, Cilix, Demodoce, Electra, Europa, Phineus,

Phoenix and possibly Argus. Eponym of the largest island of the North Aegean Sea, opposite Abdera.

THAUMACUS   Father of Poeas.

THAUMAS   A sea-god. Son of Oceanus or Pontus and Gaea. Brother of Ceto, Crius, Eurybia, Nereus and Phorcys. Married Electra, daughter of Oceanus and Tethys. Father of Iris, the Harpies and the gusts of winds.

THEA   Epithet of Tethys, daughter of Uranus and Gaea. Married her brother, Hyperion, another Titan. Mother of Eos, Helios and Selene.

THEANO   Priestess of Athena at Troy. Daughter of Cisseus, king of Thrace. Married Antenor. Mother of Acamas, Agenor, Archelous, Coon, Crino, Demoleon, Iphidamas, Laodamas, Polybus, Glaucus, Helicaon, Laocoon, Lycaon and Polydamas. Nurse to Pedaeus, bastard son of Antenor. Mother of two children by Metapontus. Gave the Palladium to Diomedes and Odysseus. After the fall of Troy, went to Italy and founded Padua.

THEBE   (1) Daughter of the river god, Asopus, and Metope. Sister of Aegina (twin), Antiope, Cleone, Corcyra, Ismenus, Pelagon, Chalcis, Ismene, Plataea, Pelasgus, Salamis and ten others. Abducted by Zeus. (2) Daughter of Zeus. Wife of Ogyges.

THEBES   The seven-gated principal city of southern Boeotia. On the slopes of Mt Teumessus, seventy kilometres northwest of Athens, Cadmus founded the citadel of Cadmeia, renamed Thebes by Amphion and Zethus. Birthplace of Dionysus, Heracles, Amphion and Teiresias. Scene of the tragedy of Oedipus, the war of the Seven against Thebes, and the vengeance of the Epigoni. There was a famous Egyptian city of the same name.

THEBES, kings of   Cadmus was the first king, followed by Pentheus, Polydorus,

Labdacus (Nycteus was his regent), Laius (Nycteus was also his regent), Amphion and Zethus jointly, Creon, Eteocles, Laodamas (Creon was his regent), Thersander, Tisamenus, Autesion and Damasichthon. Lycus succeeded Nycteus as regent for Labdacus and Laius. Penelaus was regent for Tisamenus; Eetion was a sometime king. Euboean Lycus usurped the throne of Laodamas and ruled briefly until deposed by Thersander. Xanthus, grandson of Damasichthon, changed the rule of Thebes from monarchy to oligarchy.

THEIA (Euryphaessa, Thia)   A Titan. Daughter of Uranus and Gaea. Married her brother Hyperion. Mother of Eos, Helios and Selene. Possibly mother of the Cercopes (alternatively Theia, daughter of Memnon).

THEIA   (1) Daughter of Memnon. Possibly the mother of the Cercopes by Oceanus. (2) Daughter of Cheiron and Chariclo. Sister of Endeis and Ocyrrhoe. (3) Daughter of Cheiron and a companion of Artemis. Raped by Aeolus, Poseidon changed her into a mare called Evippe, and she gave birth to a foal, Melanippe, which changed into a girl.

THEIAS   Possibly father of Myrrha by Cenchreis.

THEIODAMAS   King of the Dryopes. Father of Hylas by Menodice, daughter of Orion. Killed by Heracles.

THELXIEPEIA   A Siren. Daughter of Achelous by Calliope, Melpomene or Terpsichore, all Muses, or of Sterope. Sister of Himeropa. *See* Sirens.

THELXION   He and Telchin deposed Apis from his throne but were themselves deposed by Argus Panoptes.

THEMIS   A Titan. Daughter of Uranus and Gaea. Sister of the Titans and Giants. Married Zeus after Metis was swallowed. Mother of the Moirae, Horae,

Astraea and, possibly, Prometheus (but more probably this was Clymene). The personification of order and justice, like her daughter, Dike, she had the epithet Justice. The first to make prophecies, she started the oracle at Delphi which she gave Apollo as a birthday present. Advised Deucalion on how to repopulate the earth. Inventor of the hexameter, the meter in which oracles were given. Shared the temple of Rhamnus in Attica with Nemesis. Represented in art as carrying a cornucopia and a pair of scales.

THEMISON A Theraean leader who rescued Phronime after her father, Etearchus, threw her in the sea, believing her to be unchaste.

THEMISTE (Themis) Daughter of Ilus and Eurydice. Sister of Laomedon. Married Capys, son of Assaracus. Mother of Anchises and Laocoon.

THEMISTO Daughter of Hypseus. Sister of Astyagyia, Cyrene and Stilbe. Third wife of Athamas. Mother of Erythrius, Leucon, Ptous and Schoeneus. Committed suicide after killing her last two sons as she mistook them for the sons of Athamas and Ino.

THEOCLYMENUS (1) Son of Polypheides. A seer who foretold the return of Odysseus from Troy and that the suitors would be killed. (2) Son of Proteus and Psamathe. Brother of Eidothea (Theonoe) and Cabeiro, king of Egypt, he fell in love with Helen and almost killed his sister after she failed to warn him of the arrival in Egypt of Menelaus.

THEONOE (1) Daughter of Proteus and Psamathe. Also called Eidothea. Sister of Theoclymenus and Cabeiro. Almost killed by her brother (*see above*). (2) Daughter of Thestor and Megara. Sister of Alcmaon, Calchas and Leucippe. Abducted by pirates and sold as a slave to Icarus, king of Caria, but was later returned to her father. (3) A maiden who fell in love with the pilot of a

Trojan ship of Aeneas. Likely to have been the same person as (1).

THEOPHANE The beautiful daughter of Bisaltes who was abducted by Poseidon. She bore him a ram with a golden fleece, which could fly and speak and which was the quest of the Argonauts.

THERA The volcanic island north of Crete, originally called Calliste, that disappeared after a terrible earthquake. Possibly the mythical Atlantis.

THERAEPHONE Daughter of Dexamenus. Twin sister of Theronice and sister of Eurypylus and Mnesimache. Married Eurytas. Mother of Thalpius.

THERAPNE Daughter of Lelex and Cleocharia. Sister of Myles and Polycaon, and sister or aunt of Eurotas.

THERAS Regent of Sparta. Son of Autesion. Brother of Argeia. Fostering Argeia's children after the death of Aristodemus, he ruled as regent of Sparta until the two, Eurysthenes and Procles, were old enough to take over the throne. Then he took three ships and left Sparta for the Isle of Calliste, leaving behind his son, Oeolycus. Renamed the island Thera and became its king.

THERIMACHUS Son of Heracles and Megara. Brother of Creontidas. Killed by Heracles.

THERMIUS Son of Haemon. Brother of Oxylus.

THERMODON River of Cappadocia that flowed to the Black Sea. On the banks of the river stood the city of Termeh (Themiscyra), home of the Amazons.

THERONICE Daughter of Dexamenus. Twin of Theraephone and sister of Eurypylus and Mnesimache. Married Cteatus. Mother of Amphimachus.

THERSANDER (1) Son of Polyneices and Argeia. Brother of Adrastus II and Timeas. Married Demonassa. Father of Tisamenus. One of the Epigoni, he became king of Thebes. Gave Harmonia's robe to Eriphyle, mother of Alcmaeon, so that she would bribe her husband, Amphiarus, to fight in the Trojan War. Thersander took forty ships to Troy, and was either killed, before arriving, by Telephus on the Isle of Mysia, or else survived, and was in the Wooden Horse. (2) Son of Sisyphus and Merope. Brother of Halmus, Glaucus and Ornytion. Father of Coronus and Haliartus, the two being adopted by their uncle, Athamas.

THERSILOCHUS A Trojan killed by Achilles, and seen by Aeneas on his trip to the Underworld.

THERSITES Son of Agrius. Brother of Onchestus and others. The ugliest man in the Trojan War. Accused Agamemnon of extending the war for his own ends. Odysseus beat him for this, and Achilles later killed him.

THESEUS King of Athens. Son of Aegeus or Poseidon and Aethra. The major Attic hero. Married first to Hippolyte. Father of Hippolytus. After her death, married Phaedra. Father of Acamas and Demophon. Later married Ariadne, though some claim she preceded Phaedra. Father of Oenopion and Staphylus. Possibly married at some time to Aegle. Father of Melanippus by Perigune and, some say, of Iphigeneia by Helen.

On his way from Troezen to Athens he fought and beat Cercyon, Periphetes, Phaea,

Theseus with Minotaur, Ariadne

Procrustes, Sceiron, Sinis and the Crommyonian Sow. Medea, then residing with Aegeus, tried to poison him but his father recognised him in time. It was after he killed the fifty Pallantids who opposed his father's rule that he dealt with the Bull of Marathon. A member of the Calydonian Boar Hunt and an Argonaut, he killed the Marathonian Bull and the Minotaur. Promising his father that if he returned safely from this enterprise he would change the colour of his sail, he did return eventually but, forgetting this instruction, caused his father's death. He helped the Lapiths against the Centaurs and recovered the corpses of the Seven against Thebes.

His father hid a sword and some sandals under a stone after his birth, and only Theseus, helped by Aethra, could lift the stone to recover them. His father would only recognise him after he had done this. After Ariadne helped him kill the Minotaur, he married her, but deserted her for Aegle, and she either committed suicide or married Dionysus. After he married Phaedra, she lied to Theseus, telling him that Hippolytus, ruling as viceroy in Athens, had raped her. Hearing this Theseus prayed to Poseidon to kill his son, only learning the truth too late. Phaedra then committed suicide. He abducted Helen but the Dioscuri restored her, after causing great commotion in Athens. He helped his friend, Peirithous, to abduct Persephone, but only he, aided by Heracles, managed to escape from the Underworld.

After his return to Athens from Troezen, his people no longer wanted him as king and he went into exile to Scyros, cursing Athens. In Scyros, he demanded his father's land from King Lycomedes. One night, walking along the cliffs, he either fell to his death or was pushed by Lycomedes. His ghost marched at the front of the Athenians at Marathon.

THESPIUS King of Thespiae. Son of Erechtheus and Praxithea. Brother of Cecrops, Creusa, Cthonia, Eupalamus, Orneus, Metion, Oreithyia, Pandorus and Procris. Father of fifty daughters, including Arge, Euboea, Eurybia, Lysippe and Praxithea II. Forty-nine of them slept with Heracles in one night and mothered fifty-one children, but the fiftieth remained a virgin in the temple of Heracles all her life. Thespius purified Heracles of the murder of Megara and their children.

THESSALUS (1) King of Thessaly. Son of Heracles and Chalciope. His two sons, Antiphus and Pheidippus, took a fleet of thirty ships to the Trojan War. (2) Son of Jason and Medea. Twin of Alcimenes. Brother of Argus, Eriopis, Medeias, Mermerus, Pheres and Tisandrus. Succeeded Acastus to the throne.

THESSALY A province of northern Greece and the largest in the country. Originally called Iolcus, renamed by Thessalus. A vast plain shut in on all four sides by mountains: to the north, the Cambunian mountains separated it from Macedonia; to the west was Mt Pindus; to the south Mt Oeta; and to the east, Mts Ossa and Pelion. Mt Olympus was situated here, and Thessaly was the site of the Deluge.

THESSALY, kings of Acastus, Aeson, Ixion, Lapithus, Periphas, Phorbas, Protesilaus, Triopas and two kings named Thessalus.

THESTIUS (1) Son of Ares and Demonice or Alcippe, or of Agenor and Epicaste. Brother of Evenus, Molus, Oeneus and Pylus, if father Ares; or brother of Demonice, Hippodamus and Porthaon, if father Agenor. Father of Leda, Hypermnestra, Althaea, Plexippus and others by Eurythemis. Killed by Meleager. (2) A king of Thespia. (3) Father of Calydon.

THESTOR Son of Apollo or Idmon. Married Megara. Father of Calchas, Alcmaon, Leucippe and Theonoe.

THETIS of the silver feet Daughter of Nereus and Doris. Sister of the Nereids, including Amphitrite and Eurynome. Reared by Hera. Married Peleus after the gods had forced her into marriage. Originally, both Zeus and Poseidon courted her until an oracle stated that her son would be greater than his father. At her wedding, Eris rolled the Golden Apple. Mother of Achilles (Ligyron), she dipped her son in the waters of the Styx to make him invulnerable. Only his heel which she held out of the water remained vulnerable. Thetis and Eurynome looked after Hephaestus after his eviction from Olympus. Like Proteus, she lived in the deep sea and had the power to change shape.

THIA *See* Theia.

THIEVES, Roman goddess of Furina Laverna.

THISBE The Assyrian lover of Pyramus who killed herself after his suicide.

THOAS Kings of Lemnos and Tauris. (1) Son of Dionysus or Theseus and Ariadne. Brother of Ceramus, Oenopion, possibly Peparethus, Phanus and Staphylus. Married Myrina. Father of Hypsipyle. He was the sole survivor when the Lemnian women murdered their menfolk. (2) Son of Jason and Hypsipyle. Brother of Deipylus, Euneus and Nebrophonus. Father of a son by Oenoe called Sicinus. He would have sacrificed Orestes and Pylades to Artemis, but they were rescued by Iphigeneia. He was the brother of Evenus and was also known as Deipylus.

THOAS King of Aetolia. Son of Andraemon and Gorge. Father of Haemon and an unnamed daughter who was the mother of Leontophonus by Odysseus. As a suitor of Helen, he took forty ships to Troy and was in the Wooden Horse.

THOAS (1) Trojan leader killed in the War by Menelaus. (2) Son of Uranus and Gaea. Brother of Agrius. A Giant, killed by the Fates. (3) A companion of Aeneas, killed by the Rutuli of Italy. (4) Son of Ornytion. Brother of Phocus.

THOE A Nereid. One of the fifty daughters of Nereus and Doris.

THON (Thonis) King of Egypt. Husband of Polydamna and warden of the mouth of the river Nile.

THOON (1) Giant son of Gaea. Defeated in battle and killed by the Moirae at Phlegra. (2) Three Trojan soldiers, killed in the war by Antilochus, Diomedes and Odysseus respectively.

THOOSA Possibly daughter of Phorcys. Mother of Polyphemus by Poseidon.

THOOTES Herald of Menestheus.

THORNAX Mother of Buphagus by Iapetos.

THRACE A large European country placed to the south-west of the Black Sea and to the north of the Aegean Sea. Today, part of Turkey or Bulgaria.

THRACE, kings of Cisseus, Cotys, Eumolpus, Harpalycus, Lycurgus, Oeagrus, Phineus, Phylleus, Polymnestor, Rhesus, Tereus and Tegyrius.

THRASIUS A Trojan killed in the War by Achilles.

THRASYMEDES Son of Nestor and Anaxibia or Eurydice. Brother of Antilochus, Aretus, Echephron, Paeon, Peisidice, Peisistratus, Perseus, Polycaste and Stratius. Father of Sillus. A shepherd of the sentinels, he accompanied his father to the Trojan War.

THRESHOLDS, goddess of Cardea.

THRIAE Three prophetic nymphs of Mt Parnassus.

THRONIA Daughter of Belus and Anchinoe. Sister of Aegyptus, and possibly Cepheus and Phineus. Married Hermaon. Mother of Arabus.

THUNDER AND LIGHTNING, Roman god of Jupiter Elicius.

THUNDERSTORMS, Roman god of Summanus (qv).

THYESTES King of Mycenae. Son of Pelops and Hippodameia. Brother of Alcathous, Astydameia, Atreus, Copreus, Chrysippus, Troezen, Lysidice, Nicippe and Pittheus. Married a Naiad. Father of Pelopia. Possibly father of Pleisthenes by Aerope.

On the orders of an oracle, was father of Aegisthus by his incestuous relationship with Pelopia. He raped Aerope, wife of Atreus, and she had twin sons called Aglaus and Tantalus. In revenge, Atreus served Thyestes a meal of the two children. Dethroned by Agamemnon and Menelaus, sons of Atreus.

THYIA (1) Daughter of Castalius or Cephisus. Possibly mother of Delphus by Apollo. (2) Daughter of Deucalion and Pyrrha. Sister of Amphictyon, Hellen, Pandora and Protogeneia. Mother of Macedon and Magnes by Zeus, although some name as parents of Magnes, Aeolus and Enarete.

THYIAD Follower of Dionysus on Mt Parnassus. Also called a Bacchant or Maenad, the revels of Thyiads were instituted by Thyia.

THYMBRAEUS (1) Son of Laocoon and Antiope. Brother of Antiphas. He, his father and his brother were all killed by a sea-snake. (2) Epithet of Apollo.

THYMBRIS (Hybris) Possibly the mother of Pan by Zeus.

THYNIUS Son of Phineus and Idaea. Brother of Mariandynus, half-brother of Pandion and Plexippus.

THYONE Mother of Dionysus. Also the name given to the deified Semele.

THYRIA Mother of Cycnus and Phylius by Apollo.

THYRSUS The pine-cone-tipped spear carried by Dionysus and his followers.

TIASA Daughter of Eurotas and sister of Sparte.

TIBER The chief river of central Italy and the river of Rome. Originally called Albula. The father of Ocnus by Manto and son of Oceanus and Tethys. This river god had a feast of dedication on 8 December.

TIBERINUS King of Italy. Son of Janus and Camasena. Drowned in the river Albula which was renamed Tiber.

TILPHUSA *See* Telphusa.

TIMALCUS Son of Megareus and Iphinoe. Brother of Evaecheme, Evippus and Hippomenes.

TIMANDRA Daughter of Tyndareus and Leda. Sister of Phoebe, Philonoe and Clytemnestra and half-sister of Polydeuces, Castor and Helen. Married Echemus, whom she deserted for Phyleus. Mother of Agasthenes and Meges by Phyleus. It was because Tyndareus refused to pay homage to Aphrodite that the goddess made all three of his daughters adultresses. Timandra and Phoebe may have been the same.

TIMEAS Son of Polyneices and Argeia. Brother of Adrastus and Thersander.

TIMOLUS *See* Tmolus.

TIPHYS Son of Hagnias or Phorbas and Hyrmina. Brother of Actor, Augeias, Agasthenes and possibly Phyleus. Pilot of the *Argo* until his death. Succeeded by Ancaeus.

TIRESIAS *See* Teiresias.

TIRYNS Ancient city of Argolis in the

Peloponnesus, just south-east of Argos. It was founded either by Tirynx, son of Argus, or by Proetus, brother of Acrisius. Heracles spent his early life there.

TIRYNS, kings of Proetus, followed by Megapenthes, Perseus and Eurystheus. It was later ruled by neighbouring Mycenae in the person of a grandson of Pelops.

TIRYNX (Tiryns) Son of Argus. Eponym of Tiryns and its possible founder.

TISAMENUS (1) Son of Orestes and Erigone or Hermione. Brother of Penthilus. King of Argos and Lacedaemon after succeeding his father to both thrones. He was either killed in battle with the Heraclids, or was exiled to Achaea and later killed in battle. (2) Son of Thersander and Demonassa. Father of Autesion. A king of Thebes, Penelaus acted as his regent after his father's death at the Trojan War. Through his grandsons, Eurysthenes and Procles, he was ancestor of the Spartan royal family. Succeeded to the throne by Autesion. (3) A native of Elis, and the only non-Spartan ever awarded citizenship of Sparta. The winner of four Olympic contests, and fought with the Spartans in Persia.

TISANDRUS Son of Jason and Medea. Brother of Alcimenes, Argus, Eriopis, Medeias, Mermerus, Pheres and Thessalus.

TISIPHONE (1) Daughter of Alcmeon and Manto. Sister of Amphilochus. Reared by Creon until she was sold as a slave by the jealous wife of Creon to Alcmeon who did not recognise his daughter. (2) One of the Erinnyes (qv). Daughter of Gaea. Sister of Alecto and Megaera.

TITAEA Epithet of Gaea (Terra, Tella) and Rhea.

TITANS The children of Uranus and Gaea. Many of them married each other, their attributes relating. These included: Crius and Eurybia; Coeus and Phoebe (the

moon); Cronos and Rhea (harvests); Hyperion and Thyia (the sun); Iapetos and Themis (justice and the planets); Oceanus and Tethys (the sea). Mnemosyne (memory) was also a Titaness. The Titans were brothers and sisters of the Cyclops and Hecatoncheiroi.

TITARON Possibly father of Ampycus.

TITHONUS (1) Son of Laomedon and Leucippe, Placia or Strymo. Brother of Astyoche, Cilla, Clytius, Hesione, Hicetaon, Lampus and Priam. The lover of Eos and by her the father of Emathion, and possibly of Phaethon, later king of Ethiopia, of Memnon, later king of Arabia. Eos asked Zeus to immortalise Tithonus, but forgot to ask for his eternal youth, so she changed him into a grasshopper when he grew aged. (2) Possibly the son of Cephalus and Eos. (Possibly same as above.)

TITUS TATIUS King of the Sabines. *See* Tatius.

TITYUS Son of Gaea or of Zeus and Elara. Father of Europa. A Euboeoan giant killed either by Zeus or by Apollo and Artemis after he insulted Leto, according to different traditions. Sent to Tartarus where his regenerating liver was daily eaten by vultures.

TLEPOLEMUS King of Rhodes. Son of Heracles and Astyoche or Astydameia. Brother of Ctesippus, Hyllus and Macaria. Married Polyxo. Father of Deipylus.

Originally from Argus, he accidentally killed his uncle, Licymnus, and was exiled to Rhodes with several shiploads of followers. As a suitor of Helen, he took nine ships to the Trojan War where he was killed by Sarpedon.

TLEPOLEMUS Son of Damastor. A Lycian, killed in the Trojan War by Patroclus.

TLESIMENES Son of Parthenopaeus and Clymene, a Mysian nymph. Brother of Promachus. One of the Epigoni.

TMOLUS (Timolus) King of Lydia. Husband of Omphale. Judge of a musical contest between Apollo and Pan. Killed by Artemis for raping one of her attendants.

TORTOISE *See* Chelone, Mt Parthenius.

TOXEUS Son of Oeneus and Althaea. Brother of Gorge. Half-brother of Deianeira and Meleager. Killed by Oeneus for jumping a ditch dug for the protection of Calydon.

TRACHIS, king of Ceyx.

TRAGASUS Either he or Craugasus was the father of Philonome.

TREACHERY, Roman goddess of Fraus.

TREMBLING Son of Ares. Brother of Deimos, Eris, Fear, Panic, Phobos and Terror.

TRIDENT The three-pronged spear and symbol of Poseidon (Neptune), god of the sea.

TRIENUS Possibly the father of Scylla.

TRIODITIS Epithet of Hecate.

TRIOPAS (Triops) King of Thessaly. Son of Poseidon and Canace. Brother of Aloeus, Epopeus, Hopleus and Nireus. Married Hiscilla, daughter of Myrmidon. Father of Erysichthon, Iphimedeia and Phorbas.

TRIOPAS Father of Pelasgus by Sois. Possibly father of Agenor and Iasus.

TRIOPAS One of the Heliades. Son of Helios and Rhode. Brother of Actis, Candalus, Cercaphus, Macar, Ochimus and Tenages. A king of Rhodes, he went into exile after being co-murderer of Tenages. Perhaps first to sacrifice to Athena.

TRIOPAS Son of Phorbas. Father of Erysichthon, Messene, Iphimedeia and Phorbas II by Hiscilla.

TRIPTOLEMUS An Eleusinian prince. Son of Eleusis and Cothonea or of Metaneira and Celeus. Brother of Demophon and four sisters, and possibly Abas.

A favourite of Demeter, he established the Eleusinian Mysteries and festivals in her honour. Some say that Demeter put him into fire each night to make him immortal. When Metaneira saw this, Triptolemus was consumed by flames. Others say that when Eleusis saw this she dropped down dead. He invented the wheel and taught mankind grain culture and the use of the plough. King Lyncus of Scythia tried to kill him, but was changed into a lynx. After his death, Triptolemus became a god; and some say he became the fourth judge of the Underworld.

TRITON Son of Poseidon and Amphitrite. Brother of Albion, Charybdis, Benthesicyme and Rhode. Father of Pallas.

Sometimes spoken of in the plural, this merman had a human upper half (possibly with a horse's forefeet), and a dolphin's tail, green hair, blue eyes and scales. He lived with his parents at the bottom of the sea and was the attendant, messenger and trumpeter of his father. His horn blowing signalled the end of the Deluge.

TRITONIA Epithet of Athena.

TRITONIS Wife of Amphithemis and mother of Caphaurus and Nasamon.

TRIVIA Epithet of Diana as protector of the crossways of three roads. Also of Hecate.

TROAS (Troad) The region of Asia Minor that had Troy as its capital.

TROEZEN (1) Son of Pelops and Hippodameia. Brother of Alcathous, Astydameia, Atreus, Chrysippus, Copreus, Lysidice,

Triptolemus

Nicippe, Pittheus and Thyestes. Co-ruler with Pittheus of Troezen. (2) An ancient city of south-east Argolis, 65 km from Athens. Originally called Oraea, then Althepia. Pittheus renamed it after the death of his brother. After the death of Pittheus, Troezen was annexed by Argos.

TROEZEN, kings of Orus was the first, followed by Althepus, Saron, Hyperes, Anthas, Aetius and, finally, Pittheus and Troezen who ruled jointly.

TROILUS Youngest son of Priam and Hecuba, although some call Apollo his father. Brother of Aesacus, Cassandra, Creusa, Deiphobus, Helenus, Hector, Paris and Polyxena. Lover of Cressida, daughter of Calchas.

An oracle stated that Troy would never fall if Troilus reached the age of twenty. He was killed by Achilles in the Trojan War, before he reached that age.

TROJAN WAR 1194–1184 BC. The origins of the War can be traced back to Eris rolling the Golden Apple, and to the Judgement of Paris. The Greeks declared war on Troy after Paris, son of Priam, abducted Helen and refused to return her. Her suitors were obliged to embark on a ten-year war in order to recover her. The Greek fleet sailed from Aulis in Boeotia and may have landed accidentally in Mysia. They returned to Greece and sailed to Troy eight years later under the guidance of Telephus. Troy remained invincible whilst the Palladium protected the city, but it was stolen by Diomedes and Odysseus. The Wooden Horse was the means by which the Greeks finally entered the walled city. The story of the Trojan War is told by Homer in the *Iliad*, although the poem only covers the short period at the end of the campaign. The forces and allies of the two sides were as follows:

The Greeks (or Achaeans, as Homer called them)

Origin of the forces	The leaders of the forces	Number of ships
The Boeotians	Penelaus, Leitus, Archesilaus, Prothoenor, Clonius	50
Minyan Orchomenus and Aspledon	Ascalaphus, Ialmenus	30
Phocis	Schedius, Epistrophus, Iphitus	40
Locris	Oileus, Lesser Ajax	40
Euboea	Elephenor, Acamas, Demophon	40
Athens	Mnestheus	50
Salamis	Greater Ajax	12
Argos and Tiryns	Diomedes, Sthenelus, Euryalus	80
Mycenae and Corinth	Agamemnon	100
Lacedaemon and Sparta	Menelaus	60
Pylos and Arene	Nestor	90
Arcadia, Orchomenus, Pheneus, Tegea	Agapenor	60
Buprasion, part of Elis	Amphimachus, Thalpius, Diores, Polyxeinus	40
Dulchium, Echinean Isles	Meges	40
Ithaca, Samos	Odysseus	12
Aetolia, Calydon	Thoas	40
Crete	Idomenus, Meriones	80
Rhodes	Tlepolemus	9
Syme	Nireus	3
Nisyrus, Cos	Pheidippus, Antiphus	30
Pelasgian Argos, Alus, Alope, Trachis, Phthia	Achilles, Automedon	50
Phylace	Protesilaus, Podarces	40
Pherae, Iolcus	Eumelus	11
Methone, Meliboea	Philoctetes, Medon	7
Tricce, Oechalia	Podalirius, Machaon, Peirithous	30
Ormenion, Asterion	Eurypylus	40
Argissa	Polypoetes, Leonteus	40
Cyphus	Guneus	22
Magnete	Prothous	40
Cyprus	Mygdalion	1
Thebes	Thersander	40

The gods who supported the Greeks were: Athena, Hephaestus, Hera, Hermes and Poseidon. Admetus had the best horses, which Eumelus drove. Greater Ajax was the best fighter. Agamemnon was the commander-in-chief. Protesilaus was the first to die. Philoctetes was abandoned because of an evil-smelling injury, but was later retrieved because of an oracle. Other allies of the Greeks: Antilochus, Calchas, Patroclus, Phoenix, Talthybius, Teucer, Thersites and Palamedes. The soldiers in the Wooden Horse are listed under that heading.

Allies of the Trojans

Origin of the forces	Leaders of the forces
Dardania (Troy)	Aeneas, Archelous, Acamas
Zeleia	Pandarus
Adrasteia, Apaesus, Tereia	Adrastus, Amphius
Percote, Practius, Sestos, Abydos and Arisbe	Asius
Pelasgus	Hippothous, Pylaeus
Thrace	Acamas, Peirous, Rhesus
Cicones	Euphemus
Paeonia	Pyraechmes
Cytorus, Cromna, Aegialus	Pylaemenes
Alybe	Odius and Epistrophus
Mysia	Chromis, Ennomus
Phrygia	Phorcys, Ascanius
Maeonia	Mesthles, Antiphus
Caria, Miletus	Nastes, Amphimachus
Lycia	Sarpedon, Glaucus

Leader of the Trojans was Hector, son of Priam the king; and Amazon Penthesileia and Memnon of Ethiopia were allies. Gods on the side of the Trojans were Aphrodite, Apollo, Ares and Artemis. Of all the leaders, only Aeneas and Antenor escaped.

TROPHONIUS (1) Son of Apollo or Erginus. Brother of Agamedes, whom he later killed. He was an architect, and built the temple of Apollo at Delphi. With his brother, built a treasury for Hyrieus. He regularly robbed it through a secret way until Agamedes was trapped by the king. It was then that Trophonius cut off his brother's head in order that he would not expose himself as a robber. The earth then opened to swallow him. (2) A son of Apollo who was swallowed by the earth, and was deified as an earth god. He gave oracles at Lebadeia, in Boeotia. (cf above.)

TROS (1) Eponym of Troy. Son of

Erichthonius and Astyoche. Married Callirrhoe. Father of Assaracus, Cleopatra, Ganymede and Ilus. After Ganymede was abducted to Olympus, Zeus gave him two immortal horses and Hephaestus gave him a golden vine as compensation. (2) Trojan son of Alastor, killed in the Trojan War by Achilles.

TROY An ancient Phrygian city, near the southern entrance of the Hellespont. Originally called Ilium, it was always considered to be mythical because the legend of Troy is common to many nations. However, between 1870 and 1873, Heinrich Schliemann discovered the site of Troy, using the directions of the ancient writers, particularly Homer. The excavations showed that the city had been destroyed by fire.

Dardanus founded Dardania on the slopes of Mt Ida and, after the death of his father-in-law, Teucer, he became king of the entire area. Dardanus was succeeded by his son, Erichthonius who in turn was succeeded by his son, Tros. Tros had three sons, one of whom, Ilus, rebuilt or embellished Dardania, calling it Ilium, later Troy. Zeus gave him the Palladium, a wooden image of Athena, which was kept in the citadel (Pergamum) and which protected the city from invaders. Laomedon, successor to Ilus, built the outer walls of the city. Priam, his successor, rebuilt the walls and the city after they had been destroyed by Heracles. Priam was the last king of Troy, during the Trojan War.

TROY, kings of Among the kings of Troy were Teucer, Dardanus, Laomedon and Priam (Podarces).

TRUTH, goddess of Greek: Alethia. Roman: Veritas.

TULLIA (1) Daughter of Servius Tullius. Married Aruns, son of Tarquinius. She drove her chariot over her father's murdered body. After murdering her husband, she married Lucius Tarquinius Superbus. (2) Another daughter of Servius Tullius. Married Lucius Tarquinius Superbus, son of Tarquinius. Murdered by her husband so that he might have (1) above.

TULLIUS Sixth king of Rome. Son of Hephaestus and Ocrisia. Brother of Olenus.

TULLUS HOSTILIUS Third king of Rome. Son of Numa Pompilius. Father of Ancus Martius. Reigned thirty-two years from 671–639 BC. A warlike king, he conquered and destroyed Alba Longa, and successfully fought the Sabines.

TURNUS King of the Rutuli. Son of Daunus and Venilia. Brother of Juturna. A fearless warrior, he was promised in marriage to Lavinia, but she later married Aeneas. Inspired by Alecto, he fought Aeneas after his flight from Troy to Italy. Killed many Trojans, but lost in single combat to Aeneas and was sent to the Underworld.

TURTLE *See* Aphrodite.

TYCHE (Fortuna) Goddess of fortune and luck. Daughter of Oceanus or Zeus and Tethys. One of the Fates, she holds the cornucopia.

TYDEUS Son of Oeneus and Gorge or Periboea. Brother of Olenias and Perimede. Married Deipyle, daughter of Adrastus. Father of Diomedes.
One of the Seven against Thebes. Accidentally killing Alcathous, Olenias or one of the eight sons of Melas, he fled to the court of Adrastus at Argos. At Thebes, though mortally wounded, he killed his slayer, Melanippus, and ate his brains. For this deed, Athena refused to heal and immortalise him.

TYDIDES Epithet of Diomedes as the son of Tydeus.

TYNDAREUS King of Lacedaemon (Sparta). Son of Oebalus or Perieres and Bateia or Gorgophone. Brother or half-brother of Aphareus, Arene, Hippocoon, Leucippus, Icarius and Peirene. Married Leda. Father of Castor, Clytemnestra, Phoebe, Philonoe and Timandra. Foster-father of Helen and Polydeuces. Expelled from Sparta by Hippocoon, but restored to his throne by Heracles who later killed him.

TYNDARIDAE Epithet of the Dioscuri.

TYNDARIS Epithet of one of the daughters of Tyndareus. Normally used to refer to Helen.

TYPHOEUS Son of Tartarus and Gaea. Brother of Echidna. According to Hesiod, father of Typhon.

TYPHON Son of Typhoeus or the youngest son of Gaea. Consorted with Echidna. Their offspring were: Cerberus, Chimaera, Orthus, the Lernean Hydra, the Nemean lion, the Sphinx, the Caucasian Eagle, the Crommyonian Sow and Vultures. Possibly father of Scylla.
A powerful and destructive whirlwind which had one hundred dragon-heads and a body covered in serpents. He attacked Zeus and cut the sinews from his hands and feet. He imprisoned Zeus in a cave until Hermes and Pan rescued him. Typhon was killed by a thunderbolt from Zeus and buried under Mt Aetna.

TYPHON Son of Zeus and Niobe. Brother of Argus, Osiris and Pelasgus.

TYRO Daughter of Salmoneus and Alcidice. Married her uncle and stepfather, Cretheus. Mother of Aeson, Amythaon, Pheres and Promachus. Mother of Neleus and Pelias by Poseidon. When her step-mother, Sidero, imprisoned her, she was rescued by Neleus and Pelias.

TYRRHEUS Father of Silvia (Rhea Silvia), and master of the royal goatherds of Latinus.

U

UCALEGON One of the elders of Troy whose house was burnt at the destruction of the city.

UDAEUS One of the Sparti. A dragon-man born when Cadmus sowed the teeth of Ares' dragon. There were five survivors of the crop; the others: Chthonius, Echion, Hyperenor and Pelorus.

ULYSSES Roman equivalent of Odysseus (qv).

UNDERTAKINGS, goddess of Mechanitis (Athena).

UNDERWORLD The abode of the dead, ruled by Hades and Persephone. There were several access points, among them Lerna, the cave of Trophonius in Lebadeia, and Thesprotia. The five rivers of the Underworld were: Acheron, Cocytus, Lethe, Phlegethon and Styx. The ferryman was Charon and the guide of souls Hermes. The three judges were Aeacus, Minos and Rhadamanthys. Some nominate Triptolemus as fourth judge. The Asphodel Fields were in the Underworld.

UNDERWORLD, god of Greek: Hades (also called Ades, Aides, Aidoneus, Pluto, Pluton). Roman: Orcus, Dis.

UNDERWORLD, goddess of Greek: Hecate, Persephone. Roman: Proserpina.

UNITY, Roman goddesses of Concordia, Pax, Salus.

URANIA One of the Muses. Daughter of Zeus and Mnemosyne. One of nine sisters. Possibly the mother of Linus by Amphiarus or Apollo. Mother of Hymenaeus by Dionysus. Muse of astronomy and astrology, her symbols were a globe and a pair of compasses.

URANIA A daughter of Oceanus and Tethys.

URANUS God of the sky. The most ancient of gods. Known to the Romans as Coelus. Son and later husband of Gaea, Aether being sometimes called his father. Father of the Titans, Cyclopes, Hecatoncheiroi, Giants and Pallas. Imprisoned almost all his children but Cronos castrated him at the instigation of Gaea, and flung his genitals into the sea. Aphrodite arose from the place where they landed. His blood and semen fathered the Erinnyes, Giants and Meliae. He may have been father of the Telchines and Halia by Thalassa.

URIS An attendant of Artemis. Possibly the lover of Orion.

URSA MAJOR (great bear) Callisto was changed into this constellation.

URSA MINOR (little bear) Arcas, son of Callisto and Zeus, was changed into this constellation.

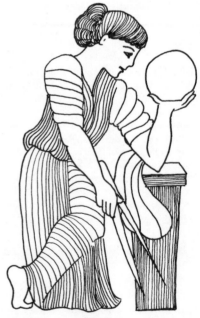

Urania

V

VACUNA Sabine goddess of leisure and repose associated with Bellona, Venus and Victoria. A goddess of agriculture.

VAMPIRE *See* Lamia.

VEIOVIS Epithet of Jupiter.

VENGEANCE, goddess of Nemesis.

VENILIA A Roman nymph, sister of Amata. Married Daunus. Mother of Juturna and Turnus. Mother of Picus by Saturn. Mother of Canens by Janus.

VENULUS A Rutulian elder sent by Turnus to seek Diomedes' help against Aeneas. Diomedes refused to send aid.

VENUS Roman goddess of love. Mother of Amor by Mars. Identified with Aphrodite. Festival dates 1 April (Veneralia) and 19 August.

VERGIL (Virgil) Roman poet 70–19 BC. Full name, Publius Vergilius Maro. His major work was *The Aeneid*, written in the later years of his life.

VERITAS (truth) Daughter of Saturn. Mother of Virtue.

VERPLACA Roman goddess of family harmony.

VERTUMNUS Roman god of change, gardens and orchards. He had the power to change shape, and used this power to woo and win Pomona.

VESPER Venus as the evening star. Known to the Greeks as Hesperus.

VESTA Roman goddess of the hearth. The rites of Vesta (Vestalia) were carried out by the Vestal virgins and her festival date was 9 June. Associated with Hestia.

Her temple at Rome, one of the earliest, was round. The eternal fire, burning there and tended by the Vestal virgins, was her living symbol.

VESTALES (Vestal Virgins) Originally four young girls, later six, priestesses of Vesta. They were guardians of a flame that was renewed each 1 March and burned continuously. Girls joined the cult at six to ten years old; the training took ten years and they remained priestesses at least thirty years. Aeneas started the cult. During the thousand-year history of Vestal Virgins, only eighteen violated their vows of celibacy.

VESTALIA Roman festivals of Vesta on 9 June each year.

VICE, goddess of Kakia.

VICTOR Roman epithet of certain gods, including Hercules, Jupiter and Mars.

VICTORIA Roman goddess of victory. Daughter of Pallas and Styx. Sister of Strength and Valour. An attendant of Zeus. Known to the Greeks as Nike.

VICTORY, goddess of Greek: Athena Nike. Roman: Victoria.

VIGOUR, Roman goddess of Strenua.

VIMINAL One of the seven hills of Rome.

VIRBIUS Consort of Diana. Roman god seen as the deification of Hippolytus, who according to some had established the worship of Diana.

VIRGINIA Daughter of Virginius. Killed by her father.

VIRGO (the virgin) Sixth sign of the zodiac. Erigone became this constellation.

VIRTUE, goddess of Arete.

VIRTUS   The Romans made gods of all the major virtues. 'Virtus' was the personification of manly courage.

VOLSCENS   A commander of the Rutuli cavalry, he killed Euryalus, and he and Nisus mortally wounded each other.

VOLSCI   Italian allies of Turnus in his fight against Aeneas. Ruled by their queen, Camilla.

VOLTURNUS   Roman god of the river Tiber, identified with Tiberinus, the two fusing into one. He came from Etrúria and his festival date was 27 August. Also applied to the Greek south-east wind, Eurus.

VOLUPTAS (Delight)   Daughter of Cupid and Psyche. Roman goddess of sensual pleasure and delight.

VORTUMNUS   The chief god of the Etruscan Volsini.

VULCANALIA   Roman festivals of Vulcan held on 23 August.

VULCAN(US)   Roman god of fire. Possibly the husband of Maiestas (Maia). Identified with the Greek Hephaestus, he was also the god of metal working. Had a forge on Mt Aetna and was possibly the father of Caeculus. Father of Caca and Cacus by Medusa. His festival date was 23 August. Epithet: Mulciber, the smelter.

VULTURE   The sacred bird of Mars (Ares). *See also* Prometheus and Titans.

VULTURES   Offspring of Typhon and Echidna, as were Cerberus, Chimaera, Orthus, the Hydra, Caucasian Eagle, Crommyonian Sow, Nemean Lion and Sphinx.

W

WAR, god of Greek: Ares (Enyalius). Roman: Mars (Gradivus).

WAR, goddess of Greek: Athena, Enyo. Roman: Bellona, Minerva.

WALNUT See Carya.

WEALTH, Greek god of Plutus. Roman goddess of Copia.

WEASEL See Galanthis.

WEST WIND Caurus, Favonius or Zephyrus.

WHIRLPOOL See Charybdis.

WHITE BULL See Europa, Zeus.

WHITE GODDESS The name given by the Nereids to Leucothoe.

WHITE ISLAND Island of the Black Sea at the mouth of the river Danube, although some connect it with the Elysian fields and hence it would perhaps be one of the Canaries. One of the Islands of the Blessed, several dead Greek heroes of the Trojan War live here. See also Elysium.

WIDOW, first to remarry Gorgophone.

WINDS Sons of Astraeus and Eos. North wind: Aquilo, Boreas, Thrascias. East wind: Argestes, Eurus. South wind: Auster, Notus. West wind: Caurus, Favonius, Zephyrus. North-east wind: Caicas. North-west wind: Corus, Sceiron. South-east wind: Apeliotes, Auster, Lips. South-west

wind: Afer, Africus. Destructive wind: Typhon.

WINDS, god of the Aeolus (Hippotades).

WINDS, Roman goddess of Tempestas.

WINE, god of Greek: Bacchus, Dionysus. Roman: Liber.

WISDOM, Boeotian goddess of Alalcomenean Athena.

WOLF See Lycaon, Romulus and Remus.

WOLF-GOD Lycius, epithet of Apollo.

WOMEN, goddess of Greek: Hera. Roman: Juno.

WOODEN HORSE The means by which the Greeks managed to gain entry into Troy at the end of the Trojan War. Antenor suggested it, Odysseus invented it and Calchas recommended it. It was designed and built by Epeius. The Greek spy, Sinon, persuaded the Trojans to accept it. Warriors in the horse included Acamas, Lesser Ajax, Amphilochus, Demophon, Diomedes, Echion, Epeius, Euryalus, Eurypylus, Idomenus, Leonteus, Machaon, Menelaus, Meriones, Menestheus, Neoptolemus, Nestor, Odysseus, Philoctetes, Podalirius, Polypoetes, Sthenelus, Teucer and Thoas.

WOODPECKER Sacred bird of Mars. See also Picus.

WOODS, Roman god of Silvanus.

WOODS, Roman goddess of Feronia.

X

XANTHIPPE Daughter of Dorus. Married Pleuron. Mother of Agenor and three others.

XANTHUS (1) Immortal horse of Achilles. Son of Boreas or Zephyrus and Podarge. Brother of Balius. Hera gave him the power of speech and he forewarned Achilles of his imminent death. He wept at the killing of Patroclus by Hector, in the Trojan War. (2) The name the gods gave to Scamander. (3) A Trojan killed in the Trojan War by Diomedes.

XENEA Daughter of Literses. Sister of Lyce, Nais, Nomia and Piplea. Possibly lover of Daphnis.

XENODAMUS Son of Menelaus and Cnossia.

XENODICE (1) Daughter of Minos and Pasiphae. Sister of Acacallis, Androgeus, Ariadne, Catreus, Deucalion, Euryale, Glaucus, Lycastus and Phaedra. (2) Daughter of Syleus.

XUTHUS Possibly king of Athens. Son of Hellen and Ortheis. Brother of Aeolus and Dorus. Married Creusa, daughter of Erechtheus. Father of Achaeus, Diomede and Dorus, according to some. Ion was the son of the union between his wife and Apollo. He went to Athens after his brother banished him from Thessaly.

Y

YEW *See* Crocus, Smilax.

YOUTH, goddess of   Greek: Ganymeda, Hebe. Roman: Juventas.

Z

ZAGREUS Son of Zeus (as a snake) and Persephone. Identified with Dionysus.

ZALMOXIS (Salmoxis) A Thracian god. Possibly an epithet of Dionysus, he was also known as Gebelzeizis. His followers went to him at their death to ask for immortality.

ZELEIA Wife of Lycaon. Mother of Eurytion and Pandarus.

ZELOS (zeal) Son of Pallas and Styx. Brother of Bia, Kratos and Nike. A companion of Zeus.

ZEMELO Thracian and Phrygian name of Semele, mother of Diounsis (Dionysus).

ZEPHYRUS (Caurus, Favonius) Son of Astraeus and Eos. The west wind. Married Chloris (Flora). Father of Balius and Xanthus, immortal horses of Achilles, by Podarge. Lived in a cave in Thrace.

ZETES Winged son of Boreas and Oreithyia. Twin of Calais and brother of Chione, Haemus and Cleopatra. An Argonaut, he and his twin freed Phineus from the Harpies. The pair were killed by Heracles on the Isle of Tenos.

ZETHUS Co-ruler of Thebes. Son of Zeus and Antiope. Twin of Amphion. Married Thebe or Aedon. Father of Itylus whom Aedon accidentally killed. He grew up in a shepherd's camp and learnt agriculture and cattle breeding. Killed Dirce and Lycus to avenge the death of Epopeus, husband of Antiope.

ZEUS (Jupiter) Father of gods and mortals. Son of Cronos and Rhea. Brother of Hades, Hera, Hestia, and Poseidon. Displaced his father on Olympus. He was married to Hera, whom he seduced after assuming the disguise of a cuckoo, and also had numerous love affairs.

Wives and major mistresses	Children
1. Metis	Athena
2. Themis	Astraea, Horae, Moirae, possibly Prometheus
3. Eurynome or Aphrodite	Graces (Charites)
4. Demeter	Persephone, Dionysus (though some call Semele his mother)
5. Mnemosyne	The Muses
6. Leto	Apollo and Artemis
7. Hera	Ares, Arge, Eleithyia, Hebe, Discordia, Hephaestus

Zeus' Lover	Offspring
Aegina (as a ball of fire)	Aeacus
Aex or Boetis	Aegipan
Alcmene	Heracles
Antiope (as a Satyr)	Amphion and Zethus
Calliope	the Cabeiri of Samothrace, possibly the Corybantes
Callisto	Arcas
Calyce	Endymion (possibly)
Carme	Britomartis
Cassiopeia	Atymnius
Danae (as shower of gold)	Perseus
Dia	Peirithous (possibly)
Dindyme	Cybele (possibly)
Dione	Aphrodite (possibly)
Elara	Tityus
Electra	Dardanus, Iasion
Eos	Lucifer (possibly)
Eris	Ate
Europa (as a white bull)	Minos, Rhadamanthys and Sarpedon
Europa	Phaestus (possibly)
Hesione	none
Hybris (Thymbris)	Pan (alternatively, Hermes and Penelope)

Zeus' Lover	Offspring
Io	Epaphus
Lamia	Herophile
Laodameia	Sarpedon
Leda (as a swan)	Helen and Polydeuces
Maia	Hermes
Mera	none
Neaera	none
Niobe	Argus, Osiris, Pelasgus and Typhon
Pandora	Graecus
Persephone	Zagreus
Pluto	Tantalus
Procris	Arceisius (alternative father, Cephalus)
Protogeneia	Aethlius (alternatively, Aeolus) and Opus
Rhea or Anichale	the Dactyli
Selene	Pandia
Semele	Dionysus
Styx	Persephone (possibly)
Taygete	Lacedaemon
Tethys	Tyche (possibly) (Fortuna)
Thalassa	Aphrodite (possibly)
Thalia	the Palici
Themis	Astraea, the Moirae and Carpo
Thebe	Thebe II (possibly)
Thyla	Macedon and Magnes
Thymbris	Pan (possibly)

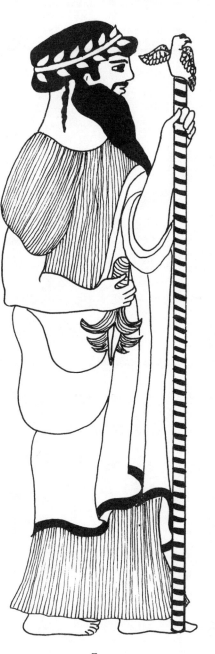

Zeus

Zeus was also the father of Alethia and the Litae. Possibly father of Amyntor and Iorbas.

His sacred bird was the eagle and his childhood nurses were Adamanthaea, Adrasteia, Agno, Amalthea, Cynosura, Ida, Neda and the Melian nymphs. His gold was guarded by the Griffins. His thunderbolts were forged by Hephaestus. He lived on Mt Olympus.

Epithets: 1. Basileus, the king. 2. Mechaneus, a manager and contriver. 3. Moiragete, guide of the Moirae. 4. Meilichios. 5. Panhellenius, god of all Greeks. 6. Soter, the saviour. 7. Terminalis, protector of boundaries.

His main places of worship were Arcadia, Crete, Dodona and Rhodes and he frequented Mt Ida in the Troad. The Olympic Games were held every four years on Mt Olympus, in his honour.

ZEUXIPPE Naiad daughter of Phrasimus and Diogeneia. Sister of Praxithea. Married her nephew, Pandion. Mother of Butes, Erechtheus, Philomela and Procne.

A Zeuxippe was also the mother of a Butes by Poseidon or Teleon; and a Zeuxippe was the wife of Sicyon and mother of Chthonophyle.

ZEUXIPPUS King of Sicyon. Son of Apollo and Syllis. He succeeded Phaestus to the throne and was followed by Hippolytus.

APPENDIX

A Select Roman Calendar

January	9	Agonium
	11	Carmentalia (Juturna)
	13	Ides of Jupiter (repeated each month). In March, July, October, May, the Ides are on the fifteenth day
February	15	Lupercalia
	17	Fornax, Quirinalia
	18–21	Feralia
	23	Terminalia
Late February/ early March		Diasia
March	17	Liber
	19	Quinquatrus
	30	Salus
	31	Luna
April	1	Veneralia (Venus)
	4	Cybele
	15	Fordicidia (Tellus)
	19	Ceralia (Ceres)
	21	Parilia, Venus and Rome, Roma Condita
	25	Robigalia (Robigus)
	28–30	Floralia (Flora)
May	1	Floralia (Flora)
	9, 11, 13	Lemuria
	21, 23	Rosalia (This festival was movable. There are instances of it occurring 24–26 May and 1 June)
June	3	Bellona
	9	Vestalia
	11	Matralia, Mater, Matuta
	13	Minerva
	24	Fortuna
July	7	Juno
August	9	Sol
	13	Diana
	17	Portunalia (Portunus)
	19	Venus
	21	Consualia (Tellus)
	23	Volcanalia (Vulcan)
	25	Opiconsivia (Ops)
	27	Volturnus

October	13	Fontalia (Fontus)
	19	Armilustrium
	29–31	Isis
December	8	Tiber
	11	Sol
	13	Consualia (Tellus)
	17	Saturnalia
	19	Opalia (Ops)
	21	Angerona
	23	Acca Laurentia